DATE DUE

WHITE PLAGUE, BLACK LABOR

COMPARATIVE STUDIES OF
HEALTH SYSTEMS AND MEDICAL CARE

For a list of titles in this series, see back of book.

WHITE PLAGUE, BLACK LABOR

*Tuberculosis and the Political
Economy of Health and Disease
in South Africa*

Randall M. Packard

UNIVERSITY OF CALIFORNIA PRESS
Berkeley • Los Angeles

University of California Press
Berkeley and Los Angeles, California

Copyright © 1989 by The Regents of the University of California

Library of Congress Cataloging-in-Publication Data

Packard, Randall M., 1945—
    White plague, black labor : tuberculosis and the political economy
of health and disease in South Africa / Randall M. Packard.
        p.   cm.—(Comparative studies of health systems and medical
care ; 23)
    Bibliography: p.
    Includes index.
    ISBN 0-520-06574-3 (alk. paper).—ISBN 0-520-06575-1 (pbk. :
alk. paper)
    1. Tuberculosis—South Africa—History. I. Title. II. Series.
RA644.T7P28 1989
614.5′42′0968—dc19   89-4802
                                                            CIP

Printed in the United States of America

1 2 3 4 5 6 7 8 9

For Carolyn, Kendra, and Matthew

Contents

List of Tables and Graphs

TABLES

GRAPHS

Abbreviations

AVS	Assisted Voluntary System
BCG	Bacillus Calmette Guerin (antituberculosis vaccine)
BSA	British South Africa
GNLB	Government Native Labour Bureau
INH	Isoniazid
JAH	*Journal of African History*
JCEA	Joint Committee of Europeans and Africans
JSAS	*Journal of Southern African Studies*
MOH	Medical Officer of Health
NAD	Native Affairs Department
NEC	Native Economic Commission
NRC	Native Recruiting Corporation
OFS	Orange Free State
PDL	Poverty Datum Line
PTMMOA	*Proceedings of the Transvaal Mine Medical Officers Association*
SAIMR	South African Institute for Medical Research

SAIRR	South African Institute of Race Relations
SALC	South African Labour Contingent
SAMJ	*South African Medical Journal*
SAMR	*South African Medical Record*
SANTA	South African National Tuberculosis Association
TBRC	Tuberculosis Research Committee (Chamber of Mines)
TBRI	Tuberculosis Research Institute (branch of S.A. Medical Research Council)
TEBA	The Employment Bureau of Africa (successor to NRC)
WNLA	Witwatersrand Native Labour Association

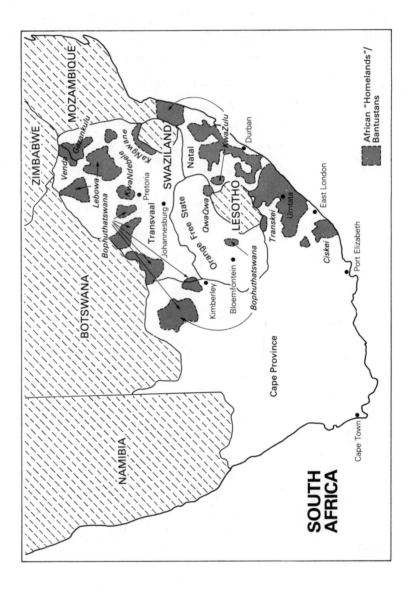

SOUTH
AFRICA

African "Homelands"/
Bantustans

NAMIBIA

BOTSWANA

ZIMBABWE

MOZAMBIQUE

Venda

Gazankulu

Lebowa

KwaNdebele

KaNgwane

Bophuthatswana

Transvaal

Pretoria

Johannesburg

SWAZILAND

Natal

KwaZulu

Durban

Orange Free State

QwaQwa

LESOTHO

Kimberley

Bloemfontein

Bophuthatswana

Transkei

Umtata

Ciskei

East London

Port Elizabeth

Cape Province

Cape Town

Preface

In a paper presented to the First Symposium of the South African Medical Research Council's Tuberculosis Research Institute, in August of 1985, Doctors P. B. Fourie, G. S. Townshend, and H. Kleeberg posed the following problem.

> Since the disease [TB] is totally curable and available control measures are sufficient to combat the disease effectively, the natural course of the epidemic can be altered to a rapid decline. Why then does the problem remain such a serious one?[1]

The question reveals the frustration of medical authorities in South Africa over the failure of control measures to effectively eradicate tuberculosis, a disease that attacks the lungs and other organs of the body, debilitating its victims and, if not properly treated, causing their death. The South Africa government currently spends nearly 70 million rand a year on TB control efforts, and yet the disease still produces between 50,000 to 60,000 official new cases annually. Over 25,000 people have died of this curable disease in the last ten years. Nearly all these cases and deaths have occurred among Africans, coloreds, and Asians. White cases make up only 1 percent of the total number of new cases each year. Unofficially, the total annual production of new cases is closer to 150,000. Africans living in the impoverished rural bantustans, which the South African government euphemistically refers to as "homelands" or "national states"—such as Ciskei, Transkei, Bophuthatswana, and Venda—as well as those living on white farms, have only limited access to medical services that would report their cases. Moreover, although prevalence surveys conducted in the "national states" suggest the presence of extemely high rates of active tuberculosis, residents of these areas fall outside the official statistical boundaries that currently define the Republic of South Africa. Their cases of TB therefore are conveniently omitted from official statistics.

In trying to understand the persistence of tuberculosis in South Africa the Tuberculosis Research Institute (TBRI) has conducted extensive research on the epidemiology of the disease and evaluated existing treatment and control programs. Although this research is important, it has failed to either explain or halt the continued onslaught of TB. This is because neither TBRI officials nor the state that employs them appear willing to address the foundations of black poverty, malnutrition, and disease upon which the current epidemic of TB is based. This is not to say that these officials are unaware of these problems and their impact on black health. They have rather chosen to place their faith in the ability of medical science to solve health problems in the face of adverse social and economic conditions.[2] This reliance on medical technology has deflected efforts to address the underlying causes of ill health in South Africa and ultimately undermined attempts to control tuberculosis.

To suggest that the current epidemic of TB in South Africa is a product of social and economic conditions is hardly original. Many critics of the South African government's policies of separate development, "apartheid," have identified these policies and the poverty they generate among blacks as the primary cause of black health problems.[3] Yet it is not enough to invoke apartheid, racial discrimination, and black poverty, for they are themselves symptoms of more fundamental political and economic transformations that have been associated with the rise of industrial capitalism in South Africa. Ultimately the answer to why TB remains such a serious problem in South Africa lies in understanding the history of these transformations.

White Plague, Black Labor traces the history of tuberculosis against this background of changing political and economic forces that have shaped South African society from the end of the nineteenth century to the present. It shows how these forces have generated a growing backlog of disease among black workers and their families and prevented the development of effective public health measures for controlling it. By doing so, this study hopefully contributes to a richer understanding of both the causes of ill health in South Africa and the forces that perpetuate their existence.

For many readers tuberculosis may be an unfamiliar disease. After all, in Europe and North America where it was once the leading cause of death, tuberculosis has become all but nonexistent in the experience of many people. Similarly, although TB is a major health problem in South Africa, it seldom touches the lives of the country's white population. There would appear, therefore, to be little reason to know about the disease, or its relationship to the political and economic conditions that prevail in South Africa.

TB is not, however, a disease about which one can afford to be ignorant or complacent. Worldwide, 5 million people a year died of tuberculosis during the early 1980s. Even in the United States TB continues to attack the poorest segments of society, and its range of victims is in fact expanding in a number of major urban centers. Official statistics reveal a disturbing increase in reported TB cases nationwide after years of steady decline. Much of this increase is attributed to the concurrent epidemic of AIDS that, by undermining the immune systems of thousands of men and women, disrupts the tenuous balance between TB infection and resistance which keeps most people from ever getting TB. Yet, some of the recent rise in TB has resulted from an increase in poverty among women, blacks, and hispanics and a rise in the number of homeless people over the last five years. In New York, for example, where TB notifications increased by 17 percent between June of 1987 and June of 1988, health authorities have noted that the disease is concentrated among the homeless.[4] The rise in TB cases among the nation's growing urban underclass during a period of unprecedented economic expansion, reveals the tragic association that exists between this disease and patterns of social and economic stratification associated with the growth of capitalist economies. It underscores, moreover, the need to understand the complex social etiology of this disease in order to prevent its further expansion.

For whites in South Africa the need to understand tuberculosis is even greater. Although the disease is presently concentrated among blacks, it is nonetheless on the rise among whites, fueled by the current recession and growing white unemployment. TB notifications among whites have increased by 40 percent over the last two years.[5] Although the number of white cases is still very small in comparison to black cases, infection levels among whites are very high. The disease therefore represents a potential threat to the health of a growing number of white workers and their families who face an uncertain economic future.

For blacks in South Africa, as well as for people in many parts of the developing world, the misery and suffering of TB is all too familiar. Yet knowledge of its causes and epidemiology may be equally incomplete. Such knowledge, after all, is of little value where political and economic conditions prevent one from acting on it. For Africans living in Cross-roads or KwaMashu, or coloreds in the western Cape, understanding the dangers of overcrowded quarters, much less the complex pattern of political and economic interests which produces them, may seem no more useful than knowing that the protein in steak is superior to that of mealie (indian corn) meal. In both cases the knowledge cannot be easily acted upon.

Yet, one must look ahead to a time when political conditions in South Africa will permit the translation of such knowledge into effective action. It will then be critically important for blacks to understand both the epidemiology of TB and the linkages that exist between it and the political economy of South Africa.

This study then has two intended audiences: first, those readers who have had the good fortune to be ignorant of TB, but who can ill afford to remain so, and second, those whose fortunes have been all too closely tied to the history of this disease and who will ultimately be faced with the task of breaking this bond.

THE ETIOLOGY OF TUBERCULOSIS

To appreciate the history of tuberculosis in South Africa it is neces-sary that the reader have a basic understanding of the etiology of the disease as it is currently known. Although some readers from medical backgrounds may possess this knowledge, many lay readers will not.

Tuberculosis is an infectious disease contracted primarily through the inhalation of airborne droplets containing tubercle bacilli that are emitted by persons with active TB. In some parts of the world today, and in many parts of Europe and America earlier in this century, people, especially young children, were also infected through the injestion of milk from cattle with bovine tuberculosis. Although tuberculosis ranks low among communicable diseases in infectiousness per unit of time exposure, long or frequent exposure, often associated with overcrowd-ing, may lead to a 30-percent risk of becoming infected among case contacts.

Infection with TB bacilli may or may not lead to the development of active disease. In most cases the infection will produce a primary lesion, usually situated within the lungs, within four to twelve weeks after infection. This lesion may heal or, more frequently, become calcified or ossified in a primary complex that contains the active bacilli. This process prevents the dissemination of the bacilli within the body. At this point the host may experience no symptoms but will normally test positive with tuberculin. Unless treated with modern antimicrobial therapy that destroy the bacilli, such an infected person will retain a latent infection that may reactivate in later life or be triggered if the immune system is compromised by other immunosuppressant diseases, malnutrition, or stress.

In other cases, the primary lesion is not contained and the infection spreads within the lungs and/or to other organs in the body through the blood or lymph systems. This progression usually occurs within the first six to twelve months after infection, though in some cases it may occur much more rapidly. Disease progression usually leads to extensive damage of these organs, resulting in serious debilitation and, if left untreated, death. The rate of disease progression, like the probability of reactivation, is determined by the state of the infected person's immune system. In general, young children under three and young adults seem the most susceptible to disease progression. Miliary TB and TB meningitis are a more frequent occurrence among these age groups. Women during childbearing years likewise appear to be more vulnerable due to their general lowered resistance during this period. Certain subpopulations suffering from malnutrition or the presence of other immunosuppressant infections, including measles, malaria, and most recently AIDS, are also particularly susceptible to disease progression. There is also evidence that other forms of physical stress, exhaustion, and alcoholism contribute to the progression of TB.

The association of TB transmission with overcrowding and of TB morbidity and mortality with malnutrition, immunosuppressant infections, and physical stresses, all often associated with poverty, has made TB a classic social disease, and its incidence is thus linked to changing social and economic conditions within society.

Finally, a number of studies have suggested the existence of a genetically linked susceptibility to TB in certain individuals. Although this phenomenon is not well understood, it may explain the particular susceptibility of newly exposed populations to TB. In these groups, most dramatically among certain island populations in the Pacific, initial exposure to the TB bacillus has been followed by extremely high morbidity and mortality rates. As in the history of other infectious diseases, this die-off reduced the proportion of susceptibles leaving a more resistant population (a process more generally known as "seasoning"). Unfortunately for those trying to understand the role of various cofactors in the epidemiology of TB, the initial exposure of populations to TB has often coincided with the introduction of adverse social and economic conditions that may have lowered resistance levels. This makes it difficult to know for certain whether environment or heredity plays a greater role in the susceptibility of newly exposed populations. In addition, the group resistance acquired through exposure to TB infection may be overwhelmed by exposure to adverse environmental conditions.

ACKNOWLEDGMENTS

Preparation of this study involved not only the collection of research materials but also exposure to new fields of knowledge and the acquisition of new methodological skills. I am indebted to a great number of people for assisting me in both endeavors.

Prior to beginning this study my understanding of health problems, other than my own, had been limited to the knowledge I acquired during a two-year stint as a public health worker in the Peace Corps in Uganda in the late 1960s. As informative as this experience was, the present study required a broader background in public health. Accordingly, I began this project as a Research Fellow at the Harvard School of Public Health in 1981. This work was supported by a training grant from the American Council of Learned Societies. While at the School, I took courses in epidemiology and biostatistics and read broadly in the fields of public health, infectious diseases, and tropical medicine. I am indebted to Dr. Roger Nichols and the Department of Microbiology for having afforded me this opportunity. Dr. Nichols has since passed away, and I deeply regret that he is unable to see the completion of this study.

Over the seven years during which I collected research materials and wrote this book, I have benefited from the advice, guidance, and what I would term "constructive skepticism" of numerous health professionals. Among those who have been particularly helpful are: Drs. Jonny Myers, Department of Community Health, University of Cape Town Medical School; Rodney Erlich, Health Information Center, Johannesburg; Neil Andersson, London School of Tropical Diseases and Hygiene; Douglas Shennan, former director of Tuberculosis Control Program, Swaziland; Oliver Martiny, Chief Medical Advisor to The Employment Bureau of Africa (TEBA); T. F. B. Collins, Director of the South African National

Tuberculosis Association (SANTA); Paul Epstein, Cambridge City Hospital; David Sanders, Department of Pediatrics, University of Zimbabwe Medical School; David Saunders, former epidemiologist with the South African Medical Research Council; Mary Jane Ferraro, Director of Bacteriology, Massachusetts General Hospital; Robert Moellering, Professor of Medicine, Harvard Medical School; Claudio Schuftan, Department of Pediatrics, Tulane University; C. C. Jinabhai, Department of Community Health, University of Natal; Peter Matthews, former director, Malaria Control Program, Swaziland; Derek Yach, Institute of Biostatistics, South African Medical Research Council; and Allen Herman, Visiting Fellow in Epidemiology, Sergievsky Center, Columbia University. From my many conversations with these men and women I have learned a great deal. Most important, I have learned that while patterns of sickness and health are profoundly affected by the wider political and economic environment in which they occur, medical and biological facts do not always fit conveniently with political and economic theories of causation. The relationship between social and biological processes is often complex and seldom clear-cut. I have tried to incorporate these and other insights into the present study, and I apologize in advance for any failure on my part to accurately reflect in my work the knowledge conveyed by these professionals.

Though I have benefited from the advice of medical professionals, this book is a study in medical history and political economy as well as health. Thus I have also relied on the advice and council of a large number of social scientists and historians in this book's preparation. Among those to whom I owe a particular debt of thanks is Dr. Shula Marks, who from the beginning of this research has provided me with unflagging encouragement and support, as well as the benefit of her unique understanding of South African history. I am similarly indebted to Dr. Charles van Onselen, who not only shared his knowledge of South African social history but provided considerable assistance in arranging my research visits to southern Africa. Numerous other scholars have at various times shared with me insights gained from their own researches in southern Africa. These include: Philip Bonner, Alan Jeeves, Jonathan Crush, Alan Booth, Francis Wilson, Ngwabi Bhebe, Leroy Vail, Jeanne Pennvenne, Frederick Cooper, Alan Mabin, Hilda Kuper, Juliet Aphane, John Daniels, Fion DeVletter, and Allen Issacman. Finally, my understanding of the history and political economy of health and medicine has benefited from discussions with Steven Feierman, Ben Wisner, Marc Dawson, Tom Bossert, Michael Watts, Ivan

Karp, Alaghna Raikes, Philip Curtin, Barbara Rosenkrantz, Virgina Drachman, Howard Solomon, and Howard Malchow. Though all these men and women have influenced my thinking, they are clearly not responsible for the conclusions reached in this book.

The historical and medical materials upon which this study is based were collected during several research trips to southern Africa between 1982 and 1988. This research was supported at various times by The Fulbright–Hays Faculty Training Program of the Department of Education, the Council for the International Exchange of Scholars, and the Social Science Research Council. I wish to express my appreciation to these organizations for their support. In addition, I wish to acknowledge the assistance of several individuals who helped me in gaining access to important research collections. Perhaps the most important of these was Dr. Oliver Martiny, Chief Medical Advisor to TEBA. Because of his commitment to gaining a better understanding of the problem of tuberculosis within the South Africa gold-mining industry and his appreciation of the importance of history for achieving this knowledge, I was able to gain access to the Chamber of Mines Archives, without which this study would not have been possible. I am similarly indebted to the Chamber of Mines and TEBA for allowing me to use their important historical collections and to the staff of the Chamber library for the assistance and hospitality they provided during my work there. I would also like to express my thanks to the directors and staff of the Barlow Rand Archives, the Transvaal Archives Depot, the University of the Witwatersrand Archives, the Swaziland National Archives, the Zimbabwe National Archives, and the University of the Witwatersrand Medical School Library.

Support for the writing of this book was generously supported by grants from the National Endowment for the Humanities, the National Library of Medicine, and Tufts University.

Finally, I am profoundly grateful for the support and understanding of my wife and children who at various times and in numerous ways have had to rearrange their lives to accommodate this work.

Introduction: Industrialization and the Political Economy of Tuberculosis

Tuberculosis was the number one cause of death in Europe and America from the late eighteenth to the early twentieth century.[1] Although the disease was by no means unknown before this time, its impact on human populations increased tremendously during the early years of the industrial revolution. The rise of industrial development and the growth of cities in both Europe and America produced ideal conditions for the spread of the disease. The men and women who flocked from rural communities to find employment in the factories and mills of Manchester and Birmingham, Lowell and Fall River had little prior contact with tuberculosis and as a group possessed limited resistance to it. To this inherent disability was added the physical insults of industrial life. Long hours, intolerable working conditions, atmospheric pollution, overcrowded living quarters, the absence of sanitation, and inadequate diets composed largely of bread, cheap tea, and "drippings," marked the daily lives of the newly industrialized workforce. These conditions undermined the ability of workers and their families to resist TB and facilitated the rapid dissemination of infection among them. Though the disease recognized no class lines, attacking some of the most gifted intellectuals and artistic talents of the day including Keats, Shelley, Emily and Charlotte Bronte, and Chopin, it clearly took its heaviest toll among the laboring classes. The spread of the disease was so great and hope of recovery so small that tuberculosis became known as the "great white plague," an allusion to both the black plague of earlier centuries and the characteristic pallor of victims of the disease.

As industrialization spread from its early centers in Europe and America, so too the white plague found new populations to attack. The correlation between early industrialization and tuberculosis is clearly evidenced by the TB mortality curves of major U.S. cities.[2] In each case, the rising tide of TB parallels the growth of urban industrial development and the recreation of conditions that fostered the disease's spread. So strong was the association between early industrialization and rising TB mortality that tuberculosis became seen by many medical authorities as an almost inevitable cost of industrial growth.

The rise of TB in the newly industrialized societies of Europe and America was followed in every case by a long period of gradual decline. This decline, as Dubos,[3] McKeown,[4] and others have noted, was largely independent of medical intervention. In fact, there was little that medical science could do to control TB prior to the 1950s. It appears instead that improvements in housing, working conditions, and nutrition from the middle years of the nineteenth century played a critical role in the decline in TB mortality. At the same time, the proportion of hereditarily susceptible families in industrial populations declined as a result of their higher mortality rates.[5] This selection process contributed to the overall ability of industrial populations to resist the disease.[6]

The downward trend in TB mortality was not continuous, however. Wartime conditions including malnutrition, physical and mental stress, and overcrowding led to sharp upward trends in TB mortality throughout Europe, overriding whatever level of acquired resistance European populations had previously achieved. Immigration was another cause of TB resurgence. Grigg[7] argues that the immigration of Europeans to Boston and New York, and the movement of blacks from the rural areas of the American south to cities such as Chicago and Cleveland during the nineteenth and twentieth centuries, introduced new populations of susceptibles to these cities and thereby increased TB mortality rates in them. This "immigration effect" was no doubt generated as well by the ghetto conditions under which many immigrant populations lived during their early years of urban settlement.

Despite these setbacks the general trend of TB mortality in the west since the middle of the nineteenth century has been downward, so that by the time effective treatments for the disease were discovered following World War II, the disease was no longer the dreadful killer it had been a century before. Like the association of TB with early industrialization, the subsequent downward trend in TB mortality has been so widespread in western medical experience that it is often described as part of the natural history of the disease.[8]

TUBERCULOSIS AND COLONIAL DEVELOPMENT IN AFRICA

At the end of the nineteenth century, the industrial revolution began to expand outward from Europe and America into the third world under the banner of imperialism. While commercial capital led the way, industrial centers began to emerge in a number of European enclaves in Latin America, Africa, and Asia. The development of gold mines in South Africa, Zimbabwe, and Ghana, copper in Zaire and Zambia, and tin in Nigeria drew large numbers of African workers to emerging industrial centers. At the same time, the expansion of agricultural production and the growth of port cities like Accra, Lagos, Dakar, and Mombassa, geared toward the export of Africa's mineral and agricultural wealth, also drew thousands of Africans into an expanding urban environment. As in Europe and America the growth of industrial and urban centers in Africa was accompanied by sharp rises in TB mortality.

Nowhere was the correlation between industrial and urban growth and TB more evident than in the booming industrial and commercial centers of South Africa. The discovery of gold and diamonds attracted tens of thousands of Africans to the mining centers along the Rand and in Kimberley at the end of the nineteenth century. The mineral discoveries also stimulated the growth of African populations in the port cities of Cape Town, East London, Port Elizabeth, and Durban. The rural populations who flocked to these centers in search of employment, like their counterparts in Europe and America, had limited prior experience with TB and thus little resistance to it. Moreover they entered an environment that in many ways resembled the conditions of London and Manchester during the early nineteenth century. Overcrowded housing, low wages, inadequate diets, and lack of sanitation were the common welcome of newly industrialized African workers. Predictably they suffered extremely high rates of tuberculosis, in some cases exceeding 15 deaths per 1,000 residents per year.

Yet the experience of newly industrialized workers in South Africa has not been identical to that of their European and American counterparts. To begin with, the TB epidemic in South Africa did not fall evenly on the working class as a whole. Rather it fell most heavily on African workers.[9] Although many white workers fell victim to the "white plague," at the turn of the century their mortality rates were uniformly lower than those of African workers. Second, while the TB epidemic among white workers paralleled the experience of their counterparts in Europe and America, with both mortality and morbidity falling off dramatically after an initial epidemic wave, rates for blacks have shown little sign of replicating this downward trend.

African TB mortality did decline dramatically in South Africa, as in most of Africa, following the development of effective antitubercular drugs in the early 1950s. There is little evidence, however, that this decline in TB deaths reflected a significant reduction in the level of TB morbidity. Although South African medical officials claim that a real decline in the incidence of TB has occurred over the past twenty years, the evidence for this claim, as we will see, is of questionable reliability. In fact there are those who have argued that given inefficient treatment programs, chemotherapy has simply produced a growing pool of half-cured and therefore potentially infectious cases that have contributed to a rising tide of TB.[10]

South African medical authorities have tended over the years to attribute both the high incidence of TB among Africans during the early years of industrialization and the failure of Africans to develop resistance to TB to their inherent susceptibility. It was not, they have argued, that the conditions under which Africans lived and worked were so much worse than those experienced by white labor, but that whites have had a long historical experience with both the disease and the conditions of urban industrial life. This experience accounts for both the lower initial rates and the more rapid decline of the disease among white workers. Africans conversely were said to have had little or no experience with either the disease or the conditions of industrial life. They were in effect a "virgin" population and therefore more susceptible to TB. These arguments, as we will see, have been presented in a number of different forms since the beginning of this century and, like the disease itself, have reflected changing political and economic interests within white South African society. The message underlying these explanations, however, has remained constant: the experience of Africans with TB has been different from that of whites because Africans are themselves different.

Critics of South Africa's apartheid system have been equally vocal in arguing that the disparity between the experience of whites and blacks with TB has been a product of racial discrimination in South Africa.

Racism caused the squalid working and living conditions associated with the early industrialization of Europe and America to be reproduced among black workers in South Africa, but not among white workers. Racism and the resulting inequitable distribution of resources needed to sustain health similarly account for the persistence of TB among blacks when the disease has nearly disappeared among whites.[11]

Though these two explanations of the South African experience with TB (the "virgin population" theory versus the racism theory) are clearly at odds with each other, they are similar in one important respect. They both define the South African experience as fundamentally different from that of the west. In one case, this difference is attributed to the racial susceptibility of South African blacks. In the other, South African society is defined as different from western society because of its racist policies.

In contrast with that view, this book will argue that while South African experience with TB has been affected by the particularistic contours of South African history, both the epidemiology of the disease and the history of efforts to control it can best be understood in terms of the same set of political and economic factors that have shaped the history of the disease in the west. More specifically, the history of TB in South Africa and the west has been shaped by the changing alignment of political and economic interests within a rapidly expanding capitalist industrial economy. What is unique about South Africa is the specific way in which these alignments have evolved.

THE POLITICAL ECONOMY OF TUBERCULOSIS IN ENGLAND

Looking at the history of TB and industrialization in England, it is clear that both the rise of TB and its subsequent decline were directly linked to changing political and economic interests within English society. The growth of industrial capitalism in England was preceded and preconditioned by the reorganization of agricultural production accomplished through enclosure and estate clearances from the fifteenth through the eighteenth centuries. This process transformed English agriculture into a market-oriented system of capitalist production in which much of the land passed out of the control of independent owner–occupiers into the monopolizing hands of wealthy landlords, and where large numbers of farm laborers lost control over their own lives to their employers and the poor laws. This transformation meant that the land could not absorb the great increase in rural population that occurred in the late eighteenth century.[12] The resulting surplus labor force fueled the growth of industrial enterprises. It also created the political and economic context that largely defined the conditions under which newly industrialized workers lived and worked within the urban and industrial centers of eighteenth- and ninteenth-century England.

It may be true that neither the municipal authorities nor factory owners of the country's growing industrial towns could foresee the health costs of industrial development during the early years of the nineteenth century, that they were faced, as Anthony Wohl has recently observed, "with a set of problems that were novel not only in their form but in their magnitude."[13] It is equally clear, however, that as the century wore on the persistence of these conditions reflected in large measure the unwillingness of either capital or the state to enact the reforms that were necessary to alleviate the suffering caused by the exploitation of labor.

From the viewpoint of capital the surplus of labor generated through the transformation of agricultural production vitiated the need to initiate reforms that would ensure the reproduction of the workforce. It also undermined labor's ability to press for such reforms.

The state, for its part, was dominated prior to 1832, and only to a slightly lesser degree afterward, by the landed interests that had played a crucial role in generating the industrial workforce. As a class they had little immediate interest in the conditions developing in the squalid urban centers of the country and were concerned primarily with keeping down expenditures for poor relief. Given this alignment of political interests the main response of the state to popular pressure for reform was repression. The long list of brutal laws designed to deal with wandering poor produced by enclosures, and the repressive character of the poor laws, attest to the state's efforts to deal with the social and economic costs of industrialization through social control rather than reform.[14]

In short, the great white plague that ravaged the working and non-working poor was not an inevitable cost of industrial development but a result of the specific pattern of primitive accumulation that laid the basis for industrial growth and for the exploitation of labor, and of the alignment of political interests within the state. As Dubos has noted, TB was "perhaps the first penalty that capitalistic society had to pay for the ruthless exploitation of labor."[15]

Conversely, falling TB rates during the nineteenth and early twentieth centuries did not result from some natural progression of modern society or from the triumph of scientific rationalism, or even from the energetic work of such Victorian reformers as Edwin Chadwick and the Earl of Shaftsbury. They reflected instead the effects of "natural selection" and a growing convergence of class interests within English society around the issue of worker health.

The very conditions that laid the base for the exploitation of labor probably played a significant role in ultimately decreasing the force of the TB epidemic that accompanied early industrialization. The fall in TB mortality rates in England dates from the beginning of death registration in 1838. Although it is impossible to know what the incidence of the disease was prior to registration, it was almost certainly higher. Thus the disease was probably decreasing in its impact throughout the nineteenth century. This pattern cannot be explained by improvements in material conditions, which, as we will see, remained appalling through most of the century.[16] It is likely instead that the early decline of TB in England, and probably in America, was brought about by a rise in overall resistance produced by the early elimination of genetically susceptible families and the survival of more resistant families. This experience, common to the natural history of many infectious diseases, should not, however, be seen as an independent biological process. It was clearly encouraged by the creation of a more or less permanent class of urban working and nonworking poor who lived in constant contact with the TB bacilli. Had the extent of land alienation been less, and the movement of labor into industrial centers more temporary in nature, it is likely that this "seasoning" process would have been delayed.[17] In effect, the so-called natural history of TB was shaped by the degree to which workers were fully proletarianized.

Whereas natural selection appears to have played an important early role in the decline in TB in England, the downward trend was hastened by gradual improvements in working and living conditions. These reforms resulted from a combination of the growing bargaining power of labor and an increase in the concern of employers for improving the efficiency of the workforce during the nineteenth and early twentieth centuries.

The middle years of the nineteenth century saw a dramatic increase in labor organization and the growth of trade unions. Populist calls for reform were further crystalized in the Chartist Movement, that, despite its ultimate demise, galvanized the ruling classes into enacting moderate reforms designed to counteract populist demands.[18] Pressure from below, therefore, contributed to better working conditions and wages, which slowly led to some improvement in the overall ability of working-class populations to resist the onslaught of the tubercle bacillus. It is certainly no coincidence that meaningful reforms did not start, however, until after the Second Reform Act of 1867, which began the process of enfranchising the working class; nor a fluke that reform remained largely unsuccessful until the more broad-based political participation of labor was achieved after World War I. It is clear, too, that working-class pressure by itself would not have produced the reforms begun in the middle nineteenth century without a wider convergence of class interests committed to health reform.[19]

The growing importance of industrial and commercial capital within English society led to a shift in the distribution of class interests represented within the state, marked by the enfranchisement of the middle classes in the First Reform Act of 1832.[20] This shift in political power paralleled a growing awareness by the middle class of the need to improve conditions of health among the urban working classes.

The industrial and commercial interests enfranchised by the 1832 reforms represented not capital as a whole but an elite segment of capital, the major manufacturing concerns whose origins can be traced to the sixteenth century.[21] The interests of this group were not always the same as those of small-scale manufacturers of relatively recent origin. Specifically, established industrial interests were more attuned to the tremendous carnage the ruthless exploitation of labor was having on the industrial workforce and came to see it as being in their interest to discipline capital by reducing the demands on labor in order to increase its efficiency. This was not simply an act of *noblesse oblige* but also of self-interest. Reforms such as the ten-hour day and restrictions on the use of child labor not only helped to ensure the health of labor but also contributed to the rationalization of capital. Such reforms hit small-scale, often undercapitalized enterprises the hardest and thus reduced their competitiveness.

Self-interest no doubt also pushed the parliamentary representatives of major manufacturing families to work for reforms in other areas of working-class life. Housing and sanitation reforms were viewed as essential to protect the middle classes from the ill-health of workers. As Dickens put it, "the air from Gin Lane will be carried, when the wind is Easterly, into May Fair."[22] Four cholera epidemics between 1830 and 1866 demonstrated the reality of this observation and played a significant role in getting Parliament to pass the Public Health Act of 1848.[23]

Although implementation of the act was seriously impeded by a subsequent reduction in the power of the General Board of Health established to supervise it, the act represented a significant movement away, though by no means a complete break,[24] from the repressive Poor Law approach to the working-class conditions that had dominated public welfare laws prior to 1848.[25]

One should not of course see the development of reforms in health and in the workplace as evolving easily out of a combination of worker pressure and capital's self-interest. The drive for reform was long and hard, with each effort to improve conditions deflected by a range of conflicting economic and political interests.

Housing reform was symptomatic of the difficulties urban reformers had in improving the conditions under which the working poor lived. Through much of the second half of the nineteenth century housing was a focus of debate by local and national authorities. This debate produced a number of housing reform acts designed to remove the dangers of overcrowded slums. Yet the unwillingness of local and national legislative bodies to provide funds for the creation of alternative housing, together with obstacles created by the nature of land ownership in cities like London, often meant that housing reform resulted in increased overcrowding in areas adjacent to those cleared and did little to reduce the overall problem.[26]

Improvements in nutrition also came slowly. Although McKeown[27] has argued that improvements in food supply were a major contributor to the decline in TB during the nineteenth century, these improvements do not appear to have had much effect on the diets of the working class before the last quarter of the century. Most diets prior to that time lacked the needed protein and vitamins, let alone adequate calories, to hold off infections.[28] In the end, it is safe to say that improvements in urban living conditions came very slowly and only achieved significant improvements from the 1880s. It was not in fact until after World War I when labor gained a greater voice in the control of the state, that conditions of housing and nutrition improved sufficiently to curtail the spread of TB.

Despite the sluggish pace at which reform occurred, there nonetheless can be little doubt that the demise of TB in England from the middle years of the nineteenth century was encouraged by a convergence of class interests around health. If capital and labor had different agenda, their interests coincided in the need to ensure the reproduction of the workforce and to eliminate the causes of diseases that refused to recognize the social boundaries separating the lower and upper classes of English society.

THE POLITICAL ECONOMY OF
TUBERCULOSIS IN SOUTH AFRICA

Changes in the alignment of economic and political interests have also shaped the history of TB in South Africa. As in England, changing patterns of agricultural production and the alienation of peasant farmers from the means of production generated the industrial workforce needed for the growth of industrial capitalism in South Africa.[29] It is clear, however, that during the period of early industrialization, from the end of the nineteenth century through the 1920s, the process of primitive accumulation was slow and uneven. As a result, the proletarianization of the peasantry was less complete than in England. This more limited transformation of the rural economy resulted from a combination of factors. Landed interests, in this case white farmers, while seeking to transform relations of production within the rural economy and having a significant political voice, faced a more resilient precapitalist social order than existed in England and lacked the coercive force needed to transform this order. Many white farmers, moreover, lacked the capital needed to rationalize agricultural production on their lands and were, therefore, dependent on African farmers who obtained access to land in return for payment in kind or labor.[30] In short, white farmers were either unable or unwilling to follow the lead of landed interests in England in alienating the peasantry from the land and thus in laying the groundwork for the development of a proletarianized industrial working class.

For its part, industrial capital did little more to encourage the development of a proletarianized urban workforce. During most of its early history, the mining industry was handicapped by the high cost of capital investments required for mining operations and by a low and inelastic price for their product on international markets. As a result, mine owners were under considerable pressure to keep down labor costs.[31] During the early years of the mining industry this requirement made it difficult for mines to attract labor. African farmers had few incentives to engage in what was seen as a dangerous occupation. When they chose to do so, often at the behest of local ruling elites, they only stayed for short periods of time.[32] This resistance began to decline during the first decade of this century as a result of the state taking a more active role in encouraging African participation in labor markets, through the imposition of taxes, the control of desertions, and, ultimately, through the passage of legislation that began to restrict African access to the means of production. These policies, combined with the creation of effective mine recruiting organizations, began to ensure a steady, if pulsating, flow of labor to the mines.

By the time this occurred, the mining magnates had come to recognize the value of a migrant labor system in which the African worker retained a rural base. The retention of a rural base, in fact, came to be seen as an essential element in the financial structure of the mining industry. For it saved the industry from having to pay for either the reproduction of labor or for the welfare of workers who were too old, sick, or injured. The need to secure a rural base for migrant workers conflicted with the practice of generating labor by restricting access to the means of production and, we will see, produced a fundamental contradiction in the development of labor policies in South Africa. It led the mining industry, nonetheless, to support the creation of native reserves, constituted by the 1913 Native Land Act, and fueled their consistent opposition after 1913 to policies that would lead to a more complete proletarianization of their African workforce.[33]

The less complete proletarianization of the African workforce and the development of the system of labor migrancy affected the epidemiology of TB in several critical ways. First, the pattern of labor migration, which characterized early industrialization in South Africa, caused the urban-based TB epidemic to spread into the rural areas of South Africa at a more rapid rate than occurred in Europe or America. In fact, by the late 1920s, over 90 percent of the adult population of some parts of the Ciskei and Transkei had been infected with TB.[34] This spread, as we will see in chapter 4, reflected not only the high turnover of labor but also the forced repatriation of workers who were sick or deemed to be unproductive, as well as the gradual impoverishment of rural populations in the face of declining access to the means of production and low industrial wage policies. This impoverishment undermined the ability of rural Africans to resist diseases, such as TB, which were transmitted by returning migrants.

Second, in contrast to the history of the disease in England, labor migrancy may have delayed the development of resistance to TB. Though a sizable population of more or less permanent African urban residents emerged in the major cities of South Africa following World

War I, most workers were temporary sojourners, particularly in the mining industry, and thus there was a high turnover of African workers. In the gold mines, the turnover rate in any given year was nearly 100 percent. This pattern may well have retarded the development of a stable balance between African urban populations and the TB bacilli and thus prolonged the TB epidemic.

By contrast, white workers from the beginning of the industrial revolution formed a more settled industrial population and had a longer prior experience with TB. This may well have contributed to a more rapid adjustment to the disease. The steady flow of white Afrikaners into urban centers following the South African War, however, probably had a retarding effect on this adjustment similar to the arrival of immigrant populations in the United States.[35]

Finally, the fact that African workers were less proletarianized than either their English counterparts or white workers in South Africa, limited the ability of African labor to push for health reforms.

The more rapid decline of TB among white workers than among Africans was not, however, a simple reflection of different levels of proletarianization. It was instead the product of fundamental differences in the alignment of political and economic interests in South Africa over the question of health reform. In the case of white workers, a convergence of class interests around health, similar to that which occurred in England, evolved during the first decades of this century following a period of intense struggle.[36] By contrast, although there have been moments when the interests of African labor, certain segments of industrial capital, and the state have converged over the question of health reform for urban Africans, these have been temporary in nature, fragile in terms of the level of commitment exhibited by either capital or the state, and weakened by the opposition of other powerful sets of economic and political interests within white South African society. As a result, much less reform has been achieved or even attempted in the conditions that contribute to high rates of TB among African workers and their families.

The achievement of health reform for white workers and their families did not evolve easily. However racist South Africa was to become later in the twentieth century, the alignment of political and economic interests at the beginning of the industrial revolution did not automatically ensure white privilege or white worker health and safety.

Political power during the period of early industrialization, prior to the South African War, lay primarily in the hands of farming and commercial interests. This was particularly true in the Transvaal where the discovery of gold had created a boomtown environment along the Rand. The Kruger government represented the interests of Afrikaner farmers in the Transvaal and moved slowly to accommodate the expanding industrial complex on the Rand. Like the landed gentry who dominated English politics in the early nineteenth centry, the farming interests in the Transvaal had little reason to implement health reform or other improvements to insure the well-being of the rapidly expanding industrial workforce, and they were primarily concerned with maintaining order and with rent-seeking activities.[37]

For its part, capital, working under severe financial constraints, had no more inclination to invest in the health of white workers than in that of Africans. Silicosis took a dreadful toll among white mineworkers during the early years of underground mining.[38]

After the war, the Milner administration proved much more sympathetic to the interests of industrial capital.[39] In the absence of any perceived need by capital to improve working and living conditions, however, this led to few improvements. The mine owners continued to treat all labor with equal disdain when it came to health and safety. In the end, the ability and willingness of white workers to mobilize and fight for reforms, their representation within the state, particularly after 1924, and the mine owners' fear that failure to provide improvements for white workers would lead to the development of a broad-based multiracial labor movement, encouraged the mine owners to gradually develop a discriminatory system of wages and benefits.[40] They did so with the support of the state, which was committed to the ideal of a white settler society in South Africa. This led to the emergence of the color bar in industrial relations and to a growing disparity in the working and living conditions of white and African workers.[41]

In effect, the needs of white labor, capital, and the state came together in an uneasy alignment of political and economic interests which, while not completely crystalized until the political empowerment of white labor had been secured in the 1920s, ensured that improvements were instituted in white working and living conditions.[42] As a result, TB among white workers exhibited the same downward trend experienced by workers in England following a similar convergence of political and economic interests. In fact the TB mortality rates of white workers in South Africa dropped much more rapidly than those of their European counterparts, reflecting the shorter history of their struggle with capital and their more rapid empowerment within the state.

For Africans there was no such convergence of interests. Although the withdrawal of African labor from the mining industry, in the face of declining wages and expanding opportunities outside of mine employment, created a labor crisis on the Rand following the South African War, the crisis did not encourage self-interested reform on the part of mine owners. This was because, as mentioned above, the state chose to support the mining industry by permitting the introduction of Chinese labor, and later by facilitating the development of a more efficient and geographically expansive labor recruitment system based on migrant African labor.[43] These actions, combined with a decline in non-mine employment after 1906 and the crushing of the Bambatha rebellion, which pushed thousands of Zulus onto the labor market, contributed to the creation of a labor surplus that undermined African labor's ability to organize and push for reform. Mining capital, as a result, was neither impelled nor drawn to make reforms that would have ensured the health and reproduction of the African workforce. The mining industry did make some reforms in order to cut down on mortality rates, for which they became financially liable, and to increase the productivity of the workforce. Yet as we will see in chapter 6, these reforms left a good deal to be desired in terms of both working and living conditions.

The interests of the state did not always coincide with those of industrial capital. As the industry continued to grow, however, the two sets of interests seldom conflicted to a degree that undermined the ability of capital either to acquire labor or to make profits. In the area of health reforms especially, the state, despite much rhetoric on the part of the Native Affairs Department (NAD), only rarely intervened to enforce improvements in working and living conditions in the mines prior to World War II. The most dramatic, and in fact the only, time in which the state seriously defended the interests of African labor, was when appalling death rates among tropical workers became a political embarrassment just prior to World War I (see chapter 6). For the most part, the state, regardless of its political complexion, was sympathetic to the needs of the industry that was seen as the backbone of the South African economy.

In the absence of strong pressure from African workers, of self-interested reform on the part of the owners of capital, or a willingness of the state to enact legislation that might harm the mining industry, the only voice advocating urban and industrial health reform prior to World War II—other than that of the emerging African bourgeoisie, who lacked political power—came from the white residents of the growing urban and industrial centers of the country and from middle-class white reformers.

Like their middle-class counterparts in England during the middle nineteenth century, white urban residents were enfranchised and increasingly vocal about the danger posed by the ill health of poor, and in this case black, workers. This fear was heightened by the plague epidemic of 1902 and later by the Spanish influenza epidemic of 1918. As we will see, both episodes, like the cholera epidemics in nineteenth-century England, led to calls for urban reforms. In theory, these reforms were suppose to benefit African workers by providing them with better housing in regulated "Native locations."[44] But South African housing reform in practice resembled its counterpart in England during the 1890s in that it involved little more than the removal of black urban workers from the centers of white settlement. Little effort was made to actually ameliorate the conditions of African life, and in many cases conditions grew worse in the overcrowded locations that grew up around the white-dominated urban centers following the implementation of sanitary segregation. Slum clearance was in fact little more than a rationalization for racial segregation based on the metaphoric equation of Africans with disease.

The white urban middle class showed even less concern for the health of the rural population from which they drew their labor. Removed from the view of most white voters, the rural reserves were seen as primitive and yet essentially healthy backwaters from which an endless supply of cheap labor could be drawn. This view belied a growing reservoir of poverty and disease within the reserves and by doing so laid the basis for the future expansion of TB within the urban and industrial centers of the country.

Not all whites shared these views and, as in England, there were middle-class reformers—medical men, missionaries, certain officials within the NAD and other state agencies, and Joint Councils of Europeans and Africans,—voluntary associations founded in the 1920s "to promote interracial co-operation and to investigate, and make representations on, matters affecting the welfare of Africans, under the aegis of the liberal South African Institute of Race Relations."[45] During the 1920s and 1930s these reformers were highly critical of the conditions under which Africans were forced to live and work. Their numerous commissions produced reports that clearly identified the problems faced by African workers and their families and made recommendations for eliminating them. Yet the recommendations of these advocates received little support. The white electorate resisted any reforms that would threaten their own economic interests, either directly through taxation or indirectly in the form of competition from an increasingly stable African workforce.

Lacking a mandate for reform and facing significant opposition from the white electorate, the state either did nothing or enacted policies, such as the Native Urban Areas Act of 1923 and the Slum Clearance Act of 1934, which were riddled with contradictions and ineffective as instruments of urban reform. Such reforms, like the white electorate whose interests they reflected, continued to ignore conditions in the rural areas.

During the late 1930s and early 1940s the conditions that had inhibited a convergence of political and economic interests over the question of social reform began to change. This change reflected transformations in both the supply of labor and in the nature of industrialization in South Africa. By the mid-1930s contradictions embedded in the system of capital accumulation which had developed over the previous half century were becoming apparent. The rural support base, meant to provide for the reproduction of labor, showed signs of breaking down under the stress of policies that had been designed to generate labor. As we will see in chapter 4, malnutrition and disease were becoming widespread in the reserves, and employers began complaining about the fall-off in a healthy labor supply.[46] The structure of industrial development began at the same time to change from extractive industries dominated by mining to manufacturing. This shift, which started following the Depression and accelerated during World War II, necessitated the establishment of a more skilled and permanently settled African workforce.

Combined with the failure of earlier reform efforts, these changes resulted in the movement of thousands of African workers and their families into urban centers that had made little effort to accommodate them. This set the stage for a major rise in black TB mortality and led to increased recognition by industrial capital and the state that the new labor force could not be created without significant improvements in the conditions under which African workers lived and worked. At the same time, African labor found itself for the first time in a position to organize and apply pressure for reform. Much of the pressure was focused on the issue of housing, which as we will see was woefully inadequate for the growing African urban population. Highly politicized squatters' movements emerged and were involved in disturbances and riots in several major cities.[47] In short, the period during and imme-

diately after World War II saw the emergence of converging class interests around health and welfare issues paralleling those that had emerged
in England during the second half of the nineteenth century and among
white workers of South Africa at the beginning of the century, in both
cases contributing to health reforms and a declining mortality rate.

This coalition of interests, however, despite a great deal of discussion
about health reform that culminated in the recommendations of the
Gluckman Commission for the creation of a National Health Service,
produced very few substantive changes in the area of African public
health, housing, nutrition, or sanitation. The reasons for this failure will
be discussed in chapter 8, but the basic cause lay in the existence of
significant class interests in opposition to the underlying assumptions of
urban health reform and in the failure of the coalition of interests advocating reforms to mount a significant challenge to the structural basis of
ill-health. The white electorate continued to view African urbanization
as a threat to their interests and refused to support the reform movement. White workers feared increased competition for employment, and
the landed interests in the platteland decried the loss of farm labor. In
contrast to nineteenth-century England, these rural interests remained
dependent on large bodies of cheap labor and opposed policies that
threatened the security of that workforce. Even more moderate middle-
class whites, concerned by the growing radicalization of African labor,
were less than enthusiastic about policies that threatened the tradition
of urban segregation. In addition, whereas large-scale manufacturers
advocated the creation of a more stable African workforce, many
smaller, undercapitalized employers, even in the urban sector, were
unprepared to pay the cost of such a move. Finally, the mining magnates
were opposed to any reform that would interfere with the migrant labor
system. In the end, the Smuts government was unwilling to oppose these
interests and failed to provide resources needed for health reform.[48]

Following the war, the electorate turned its back on the reform
agenda of manufacturing capital and the Smuts government and rejected the demands of African workers, choosing instead to side with
the Nationalist Party and increased repression in the 1948 election. The
Nationalist victory halted the drive for meaningful health reform and
replaced it with a renewed commitment to the policy of urban segregation and labor control designed to relocate the problems of African ill-
health rather than eliminate them. To placate capital, the state worked
to reestablish the supply of cheap African labor through the creation of
a system of more efficient state-run labor bureaus and the expansion of

recruiting areas. By this action, the Nationalists were able to win the support of manufacturing capital for their apartheid policies and undermine industry's earlier commitment to meaningful health reform. In addition the expansion of mining capital into manufacturing, combined with the continued dependence of the former on migrant labor, may have deflected pressure toward urban reform on the part of manufacturers. Finally, by reinstituting earlier patterns of labor migrancy, undermining labor movements, and cleaning out squatter camps, the state greatly reduced the structural basis for popular dissent and thus reduced grassroots pressure for reform.

The withdrawal of the state and, to a large degree, industrial capital from the limited coalition of class forces pushing for health reform, and the repression of labor movements symbolized by the state's crushing of the 1946 African mine workers strike, meant that effective reforms that would have provided a base for the decline of TB and other diseases among blacks were not enacted. The state, to the contrary, can be seen to have resurrected earlier models of disease control based on sanitary segregation. This time, however, it was carried out on a much greater and more tragic scale through the policy of grand apartheid.

This turning back the clock was facilitated by the development of medical technology that promised to solve major health problems. The late 1940s and early 1950s saw the development of INH, streptomycin, PAS, and other effective weapons for fighting TB. It also saw the introduction of DDT in the fight against malaria and typhus. These developments raised the possibility of a relatively simple solution to three major health problems. They were solutions, moreover, that could be implemented without massive investments in social and economic reform and thus freed the state and capital from some of the costs inherent in reducing the disease burden undermining the efficiency of labor. This reliance on medical technology consequently deflected the drive for environment l reform that had arisen during the war. Medical science, in effect, ameliorated and disguised some of the health costs of the Nationalists' political and economic agenda. It did not, however, eliminate those costs. TB control efforts, as we will see in chapter 9, have been seriously hampered by the wider social and economic policies of the Nationalist government. Moreover, the government's failure to enact more broad-based reform has meant the underlying causes of TB have gone largely unchecked, resulting in the production of new cases at a rate that equals or in some areas exceeds the rate of patients being cured.

Although recession and the rising labor militancy of the early- and mid-1970s spurred capital and the state to push for limited reforms in working and living conditions and triggered a resurgence of African labor movements, the resulting fragile convergence of interests produced only limited improvements for a small percentage of African workers. Failure to make more broad-based reforms, together with efforts to further restrict the majority of Africans to the so-called homelands, has limited these benefits to a few while the vast majority of Africans continue to live in abject poverty with all the health costs this condition entails. The health reforms of the mid-1970s were in reality part of a wider strategy designed to preserve the privileges of the white minority rather than to bring about a radical transformation in African health.[49] The consequences of this failure of the state and capital as we will see in the epliogue to this study, is a rising tide of rural disease that is beginning to spill over into white South Africa.

CONCLUSION

By arguing that the history of tuberculosis in South Africa resembles its earlier history in England in that both histories have been shaped by the changing alignment of political and economic interests associated with the early growth of industrial capital, the present study suggests that the South African experience with TB has not been produced by a unique set of social and biological phenomenon (either the racist state or the racially susceptible African). It must be seen instead as a product of a particularly pathological intersection of political, economic, and biological processes that have a much wider distribution.

This book builds, then, on the insights provided by earlier studies that have explored the political economy of health within the context of expanding capitalist relations of production in Africa and elsewhere.[50] These studies have highlighted the complex ways in which changing patterns of sickness and health are linked to the emergence of specific sets of political and economic interests operating at the local, national, and international level. In doing so, they have revealed the inadequacies of more narrowly defined approaches to understanding the causes of ill-health and the development of health care. With few exceptions, however, these linkages have been painted with broad strokes and lack specificity in terms of the historical development of specific health problems. For example, except for John Ford's classic study of trypanosomiasis in Africa,[51] there have been no sustained studies that have tried to relate the history of a specific disease to broader patterns of political and economic development in Africa over an extended period of time. More often studies on the political economy of health have dealt with a number of health issues with limited attention to the specific linkages that exist between biological and social processes. The political economy of disease literature has, in fact, been stronger on political economy than on the linkages between political economy and specific disease patterns.

A number of studies have linked the history of specific disease episodes—malaria epidemics,[52] outbreaks of typhus,[53] or of small pox,[54]—to wider patterns of political and economic change. Yet in limiting their time frame they have been unable to describe how these linkages have evolved over longer periods of time and how realignments in specific sets of political and economic interests have shaped the longer history of both health and health care.

The present study attempts to overcome the limitations of earlier works by exploring in depth the evolution of both a specific health problem and efforts to control it within the changing political economy of South Africa from the middle of the nineteenth century to the 1980s. It is hoped this book will thus provide a richer and more nuanced analysis of the changing relationship between health and society, not only in South Africa but more broadly within industrializing capitalist economies. At the same time, by linking the history of health and disease with the wider study of political and economic development in South Africa, the study throws fresh light on the changing contours of this wider history and, more specifically, on the high cost in human lives this history has inflicted upon the black population of South Africa.

The degree to which this or any study of health and disease is successful, of course, depends to a large measure on the availability of data on the changing health status of the population under view. In dealing with the history of disease in Africa this is a particular problem. The collection of vital statistics in most of Africa has been at best uneven and at worst nonexistent. In South Africa, the longer history of western medical care has meant that there have been more people collecting data over a longer period of time and that there is, in fact, a richer data base than is available in the rest of sub-Saharan Africa. The distribution of this data has been highly skewed, however. We know a great deal about health conditions in the mines, somewhat less about changing health patterns in the cities, and virtually nothing about the health of rural blacks. This distribution of data is not haphazard but, as will be suggested at several points in this study, is, like the health problems the data describes, a reflection of changing political and economic interests in South Africa. For example, although the mining industry and other sectors of industrial capital were concerned about the health of their workforce within narrowly defined limits having to do with the efficiency of labor, they showed a studied disregard for the health of workers' families who lived in the rural areas of South Africa. When the deepening impoverishment of these families began to threaten the reproduction of labor in the 1930s, however, they initiated a series of investigations into health conditions in the rural areas and funded, to a limited extent, the development of rural health services. These studies provided the first clear view of the state of rural health.[55] In the urban centers of the country, similarly, we have health statistics for diseases among the whites and those Africans, coloreds, and Asians who fell within the narrowly defined statistical boundaries of "white" cities, but only occasionally do we get glimpses of health patterns in the segregated townships and peri-urban slums that surrounded these cities. Such momentary flashes of light have not been serendipitous but corresponded either to a growing self-interest among white residents over the threat of black ill-health or, as noted above, to broader transformations in the nature of capitalist development during the 1940s and then again in the mid-1970s, which necessitated the creation of a more permanent, and therefore healthy, workforce.

The exclusion of the majority of blacks from the statistical record has been part of an effort to remove black health problems from view. As we will see in the history of TB control in South Africa, there has been marked effort to eliminate the problem through the application of exclusionary policies that both physically removed blacks from centers of white settlement and expunged any record of their sickness from official health statistics.

As a result of the unevenness of the health record, it is impossible to explore the complex relationship that evolved between changing sets of political and economic interests, on the one hand, and patterns of sickness and health, on the other hand, with the same degree of specificity for all areas and all times. For some areas and periods of history, and especially for the rural reserves or bantustans during much of the period under study, we are often looking through a glass darkly. Occasionally, however, we are able to pierce the darkness created by the biased distribution of South African health resources and statistics and explore, in some detail, the ways in which political and economic development have intersected with biological processes and given rise to the white plague in South Africa.

Preindustrial South Africa: A Virgin Soil for Tuberculosis?

Western-trained medical authorities who have studied the epidemiology of tuberculosis in South Africa have been nearly unanimous in asserting that the African populations of the region were, for all practical purposes, free from the disease prior to their contact with Europeans. Africans in effect represented, like island populations in the Pacific, a virgin soil for TB.

The absence of tuberculosis among African peoples was noted in a number of medical writings and travelers' accounts from the eighteenth and early nineteenth centuries. In the latter half of the nineteenth century, as TB began to appear more frequently among Africans, it was noted that it occurred with greatest frequency among Africans living in close contact with Europeans but rarely among those living in relative isolation. Physicians working in various parts of southern Africa in the late nineteenth century reported that while they were beginning to see numerous cases of TB among Africans, such cases had been rare when they had begun their work in these areas. These facts led Dr. Neil McVicar of the Lovedale Mission Hospital to conclude in his 1907 thesis on the early history of TB in South Africa, that TB had been introduced into South Africa by the Europeans.[1]

McVicar's conclusion was taken up in the 1910s and 1920s by white medical authorities trying to explain why Africans appeared to be more susceptible than Europeans to TB. They concluded that African susceptibility to TB was due to their recent exposure to the disease. Europeans by contrast were said to have developed resistance to TB as a result of their longer history with it. This conclusion was presented in the final report of the Union government's Tuberculosis Commission in 1914. It was also accepted by the Tuberculosis Research Committee, which conducted exhaustive research on the epidemiology of TB among Africans during the 1920s and published a massive report in 1932.[2] Viewed both within and outside of South Africa as the most authoritative study to date on the subject of TB among blacks, the influence of the report played an important role in popularizing the virgin soil theory.

Although the development of effective chemotherapeutic treatments for TB after World War II reduced interest in the causes of African susceptibility to the disease, the virgin soil theory continued to dominate discussions of its history in South Africa.[3] The popularity of the virgin soil theory has in fact been strengthened by writers who have employed it as part of a wider critique of South African social and economic conditions—the prior absence of TB being clear evidence of the costs the development of racial capitalism has imposed upon the African population of South Africa.[4]

What is curious about all these arguments is that they are based on extremely limited evidence concerning the health status of Africans prior to the late nineteenth century. They ignore evidence, moreover, that is contradictory to the virgin soil hypothesis. The validity of the virgin soil theory as it applies to the history of TB in South Africa, therefore, needs to be examined carefully in order to define the extent to which Africans were exposed to the disease prior to the late nineteenth century and to assess the impact that patterns of political and economic development, associated with the early industrialization and the rise of racial capitalism, had on their subsequent experience with the disease.

Evidence for the absence of tuberculosis among black South Africans prior to the middle of the nineteenth century is extremely limited in both quantity and quality. There were very few western-trained medical professionals within South Africa, and those that visited or settled in the region had very little experience in treating Africans. Moreover, in assessing the evidence of medical men prior to the last decades of this century, one must be aware that the collection of medical data was at best passive. Few physicians went looking for the disease. As a district surgeon in Botswana would later speculate, the absence of TB cases among his patients probably reflected the hesitance of "native" TB cases to seek European care.[5]

Even where European physicians did have contact with Africans, the reliability of their observations must be questioned, given the limited nature of medical knowledge on the pathology of tuberculosis and of the technology available for diagnosing the disease. Most diagnoses were made on the basis of clinical symptoms by physicians who often had a very imperfect understanding of the range of infectious agents operating within the African environment. It was not, in fact, until 1884 that Robert Koch discovered the tubercle bacilli and that western medical science acquired a means of clearly identifying the disease through its isolation. The introduction of radiography during the early years of this century provided an additional tool for diagnosing the disease. Despite these advances, however, most early diagnoses of African patients continued to be based on clinical symptoms and were of questionable reliability. Thus the testimonies of western physicians regarding the absence of TB among the region's African populations is of limited value in assessing the validity of the virgin soil theory.

It should further be noted that the opinions of medical personnel on this question were not unanimous. McVicar, despite his overall conclusion that TB was a relatively recent disease within the region, cites a number of local physicians experienced in treating African patients who claimed the disease had a long history among the people with whom they worked. Such reports were particularly prevalent among physicians working among the Zulu in Natal. The 1905 report of the medical officer of health (MOH) for the Natal Colony, in fact, concluded:

> "[A]lthough the evidence points to an increase it would be a grave error to suppose that tuberculosis in Natives dates only from European occupation of Natal; or that it was an unimportant circumstance until quite recently. I am recently informed, by the courtesy of Dr. Ward, District Surgeon of Maritzburg . . . that the disease has been recognized as a distinct disease by Natives as far back as can be traced, and is distinguished by the name, "Mzimbamubi."[6]

Likewise, a Doctor William Addison, district surgeon for Umlazi, commented that "If a Zulu is asked the question, he answers, 'It has always been with us.' "[7]

McVicar, in arguing that the disease was new to the region, did not discount these reports. He suggested, however, that the uneven distribution of such reports was consistent with a history of recent introduction. Specifically, he argued that if the disease had been present before European contact, the distribution would have been more even, as it was in other countries where the disease had existed for many centuries. Although this may be true, the wide distribution of an infectious disease within a population does not simply reflect the length of time it has existed within it; distribution also reflects the conditions under which the population lives and the opportunities for transmission those conditions create. Thus the absence of a more widespread distribution of TB may reflect the relatively scattered pattern of settlement that existed within most of the region and the absence of opportunities for wider transmission of the disease rather than its recent introduction. We might also suggest that the uneven distribution of the disease may have had something to do with the uneven distribution and diagnostic abilities of the European medical personnel upon which McVicar based his survey.

Dr. Peter Allan, who conducted extensive TB survey work in the Transkei and to a somewhat lesser extent in other regions of South Africa during the 1920s, was also convinced that the disease had a long history among Africans and that they were by no means "virgin soil" for the disease. Dr. Allan based his conclusions on both the testimonies of local European physicians and on the fact that rural Africans appeared to be able to resist TB to the same degree as whites. It is interesting to note that while many of Allan's findings concerning the distribution of TB among rural Africans were incorporated into the 1932 Tuberculosis Research Committee (TBRC) report, his opinions concerning their long experience with the disease were ignored. The reasons for this will become apparent later.[8]

Tuberculosis may in fact have existed at a low level of occurrence among Africans in South Africa for centuries. The TB bacillus can survive in a "dormant state" within a human host for long periods of time. The host may not develop symptoms until he or she grows old and the infection is reactivated as a result of the aging process, producing active TB. When this occurs the host may become infectious to kin and close neighbors, and the infection may be transmitted to other members of the group. Some of these newly infected hosts may develop active symptoms immediately if physiological or environmental factors reduce their resistance. Yet in most cases, the disease will remain dormant. In this way the disease may survive without infecting large numbers of people. This pattern can continue almost indefinitely, and no doubt did in many parts of the world. As McNeill notes, tubercle bacilli are among the oldest and most widespread microparasites on earth. Stone Age and Egyptian Old Kingdom skeletons have been diagnosed as exhibiting signs of tubercular damage.[9] The possibility exists, therefore, that tuberculosis was present in southern Africa, and elsewhere on the continent, at a low level of endemicity for centuries before Europeans arrived and that its introduction to the region dates perhaps from the period of Bantu migrations. In this regard, it is worth noting that Africans appeared no more susceptible than other racial groups living under similar conditions when the diseases of small pox and bubonic plague hit South Africa in the eighteenth and early nineteenth centuries. This would support the view that Africans in southern Africa had been exposed to most of the diseases associated with the unified disease pool that had developed in the Old World by the fourteenth century and that they were not "virgin soil" for these diseases.[10]

If tuberculosis did exist at a low level of endemicity among the Bantu-speaking peoples of southern Africa, why does it appear in the historical record of certain areas, particularly Natal and the Eastern Cape, and not others? One explanation of course has already been suggested: the uneven distribution and quality of medical personnel. There may also be an historical explanation, however. In both cases, larger concentrations of population began to emerge toward the end of the eighteenth century. In Natal this eventually led to major social and political transformations culminating in the creation of the Zulu state under the leadership of Shaka and his successors. Within the Zulu state, much of the population was resettled into large military barracks on an unprecedented scale. This reorganization provided opportunities for cross-infection not previously existent in the region. This in turn greatly increased the probability that cases of TB would occur, particularly during periods of environmental stress brought on by civil war, drought, and famine in the years following Shaka's death.[11]

Although population concentrations of the type that emerged within the Zulu state did not occur in the Eastern Cape, population densities did increase, especially during the early years of the nineteenth century as the frontier began to close and land for settlement grew scarce under pressure from both African and white colonists. This provided more frequent opportunities for the transmission of infection. The frontier wars and the deprivation they created, moreover, may have reduced the ability of the peoples living along the frontier to resist infection and contributed to an increase in the number of TB cases and deaths which occurred in the region.

It is also possible that the TB was reintroduced into these areas as a result of early contacts with European traders during the eighteenth and nineteenth centuries. This "reseeding" may help explain why the disease was more prevalent in coastal areas than in the hinterland.

Yet if tuberculosis existed in the region prior to the period of intensive European contact, how do we explain the pattern the disease took at the end of the nineteenth century when large numbers of cases began to occur among Africans? As we will see in chapter 2, the disease often appeared in an acute form at this time, leading to a rapidly fatal conclusion within a period of months. In Johannesburg during the early years of this century, 20 percent of African cases died within thirty days of diagnosis. Similarly in the mines the average length of time between admission to the mine hospital and death was thirty-three days; 18.9 percent died within the first week.[12] In addition the disease attacked organs throughout the body rather than settling in the lungs, as is common in populations in which the disease has existed for long periods and a host/parasite balance has been achieved.[13] This same pattern was observed among Africans in the South African Labour Contingent during World War I. The unit suffered an incredibly high TB mortality rate of 22 per 1,000. Similar experiences were observed among other African peoples brought into contact with Europeans.[14]

By contrast, TB among whites appeared to take a chronic course, often being limited to the lungs. Case mortality rates were lower and the time between initial diagnosis and death longer. For western-trained medical authorities working in South Africa these facts were prima facie evidence that they were faced with a "virgin soil" epidemic of tuberculosis among the region's African population.

There can be little doubt that given the limited and uneven distribution of TB among rural Africans, a significant number of rapidly fatal cases involved genetically susceptible individuals who had not been previously exposed to the disease. Yet, as noted above, Africans do not appear to have been an isolated population that, like Pacific islanders, had no experience or resistance to this disease. We therefore need to ask whether other factors may have contributed to the observed pattern of rapidly fatal cases at the turn of the century.

In their seminal study of the history of TB in Europe, Rene and Jean Dubos noted that so-called galloping consumption was a relatively frequent occurrence among Europeans during the nineteenth century. The poet John Keats died within a year after becoming sick, for example, with both lungs completely destroyed. For many observers this was emblematic of the type of mortality one sees at the beginning of a TB epidemic in a "virgin soil" population. Yet the Dubos go on to note that, "whenever information is available, it takes little ingenuity to recognize that the tubercular process has been going on for several years before diagnosis was made." In effect, what was seen as galloping consumption was often the tail end of a pathological process that had been going on for some time and which was no doubt exacerbated by the fact that tubercular cases "continued to live a life of normal activity almost to the end, . . . spoiling any chance of arresting their disease." The Dubos conclude that "Galloping consumption was probably more the result of medical ignorance than of high susceptibility to infection."[15]

The Dubos also note that TB mortality and the frequency of rapidly fatal forms of tuberculosis increased among Europeans during wartime even though the disease had been present in Europe for a long time. They suggest that this pattern indicates the critical role environmental conditions play in shaping host responses to TB.

> Wars usually bring into sharp relief the failure of hereditary resistance and of immunity when environmental conditions become too trying. Tuberculosis mortality increased suddenly and dramatically in Paris during the siege by the Prussian Army in 1871. Similarly it increased everywhere in Europe within a very few months after the beginning of the two world wars . . . . In many places forms of tuberculosis with a rapid course and without any tendency to healing became very common. The tuberculosis mortality rates soared to levels even higher than those reached in the 1830s . . .[16]

Finally, the Dubos note that apparent racial differences are also affected by changing environmental circumstances.

> During peacetime in Warsaw, the disease was less severe among the Jews than among the Gentiles; moreover, it remained so during the First World War, although the mortality figures had increased sharply in both groups. Very soon after the beginning of the Second World War, however, the relation changed. From 71 per 100,000 in 1938, the tuberculosis death rate climbed to 205 in 1940 and 601 in 1942 among the Jews, whereas the respective figures were 186, 337, and 425 for the Gentiles. The resistance acquired during centuries of urban life in the crowded ghettos of Central Europe proved little help to the persecuted Jew when his tragic load of ordeals became too heavy.[17]

In short, the Dubos suggest that what may appear to be hereditary susceptibility or resistance is often a product of either the quality of medical surveillance or the environmental conditions under which a group lives.

What was true for the peoples of Europe was no doubt equally true for the peoples of South Africa. The limited availability of western medical care for Africans, the tendency for many Africans to avoid such treatment, often ineffective, in any event, and the limited ability of western medical practitioners to diagnose the disease in its early stages, meant that in most cases the disease was well advanced by the time an African consumptive came to the attention of a western medical authority. This, combined with the poor working and living conditions under which Africans lived within the urban areas of South Africa and the adverse affect these conditions had on their ability to control their infections, may well account for the rapid course the disease appeared to take among them. Conversely, whites as a group had both superior access to medical care and were more predisposed to seek it out early in their illness. They were thus likely to be diagnosed at an earlier stage than were Africans. The majority of whites also lived and worked under better conditions than Africans and thus were better able to control their infections.

If one looks at the experience of mineworkers on the Rand at the beginning of this century this pattern becomes clearer. There were no provisions for the periodic medical examination of African workers employed in the mines prior to 1916, and then only if they exhibited a marked loss of weight (see chap. 3). In the vast majority of cases the only time an African worker saw a medical officer was when he was initially employed, for a cursory examination, or if he became too ill to work. Moreover, an African worker who began to experience the early symptoms of TB—fatigue, night sweats, a loss of appetite—was often hesitant to seek out treatment for fear of being repatriated and losing his opportunity to earn much-needed income. The high case mortality rates of hospitalized African workers must also have served as a disincentive to reporting ailments. Thus the likelihood of a African mineworker being diagnosed early for TB was very small. In the absence of an early diagnosis, the diseased worker would continue working under circumstances that could not have been designed better to exacerbate his condition. Inadequate rations, long working hours in extreme heat and humidity, lack of sanitation, overcrowded housing, and exposure to chill were the common parameters of life on the mines. When the African mineworker finally became too ill to work and drew the attention of the mine medical officer, his disease was often well advanced and the duration of his illness from the time of diagnosis to death extremely short.

By contrast white workers were subjected to periodic physical examinations and received better medical treatment if found to be sick. They also had much better working and living conditions. Instead of living in overcrowded compounds they lived with their families or in boarding houses. They worked shorter hours, were provided with changing houses, and generally consumed better and more frequent meals. Their chances of early detection and being able to control their infections were thus greatly improved. It should also be noted that the physical demands of mine work on white workers was much less than on African workers.

Similar factors may account for the high rates of TB mortality experienced by the South African Labour Contingent. The experience of Africans in the SALC was similar to the Senegalese Africans who served in the French army during World War I. Both groups suffered much higher rates of TB than their European counterparts and the disease frequently took a rapid course. Borrel[18] and Cummins[19] looked at the experiences of these two groups. They concluded, in separate studies, that the response of African troops in Europe to TB was dictated by their lack of prior contact with the tubercle bacillus. They were in effect virgin soil for TB. A later study of the Senegalese troops by Bezancon and Arnould, however, questioned this conclusion. They noted that the high mortality rates in Borrel's soldiers in 1917–1918 were found in contingents that had arrived in 1914 and 1915, and had thus been in France for a long time. The cases would have occurred earlier had this been a "virgin soil" epidemic. Bezancon and Arnould suggested that this time lag indicates the soldiers who broke down in 1917–1918 had been infected for some time and that they simply collapsed under the stress of extremely adverse environmental conditions, including the harsh winter climate to which they were not accustomed.[20] Similar conclusions were reached by Dr. Allan in his discussion of the experience of the SALC.[21]

Finally, in regard to the apparent rapidity of African TB cases, it is important to remember Allan's observation during the 1920s that Africans suffering from TB who were not subject to the physical and mental assaults associated with urban and industrial life, were in general able to control their infections and experienced the disease in the same way that Europeans did. This is hardly what one would expect in a virgin soil population.

The resistance of rural Africans to TB was well recognized by European medical authorities working in the urban and industrial centers of the country by the third decade of this century and, as will be discussed in chapter 7, was used by mining authorities to rationalize a system of migrant labor in which the health of African workers was said to benefit from regular periods of "rest and relaxation" in the rural areas. It did not, however, lead these same authorities to the conclusion that it was the conditions of urban life and industrial employment, and not African inexperience with the disease, which caused Africans to break down rapidly within the urban areas. In this way the implications of medical findings were defined by the economic and social interests of industrial capital.

CONCLUSION

The evidence supporting the virgin soil theory is hardly conclusive. There is, in fact, reason to believe that TB has existed in South Africa, albeit at a low level of endemicity, for a very long time, dating perhaps to the earliest periods of African settlement in the region.

There can, at the same time, be little doubt that in most areas cases of the disease among Africans were relatively rare prior to the late nineteenth century. As a result, African populations in the region must have contained a higher percentage of individuals with a hereditary susceptibility to TB than did the population of European immigrants who arrived in large numbers from the middle of the nineteenth century. The high mortality rates and the fulminating course of many early cases of TB among Africans may, therefore, have reflected in part a relative lack of experience with the disease. Yet this group susceptibility was not racial and would have been shared to a significant degree by the native-born Afrikaner population.

It is equally clear, moreover, that the susceptibility that Africans exhibited as a result of their relative inexperience with the disease, was exacerbated by the extremely adverse conditions under which they were made to live and by their lack of access to medical attention. As the century wore on, moreover, and TB infection spread widely among the African population, inexperience became a negligible factor in the epidemiology of TB and conditions of life rose to paramount importance. Ironically, it was during the 1930s, when medical evidence suggests that inexperience had ceased to be a significant causal factor in African susceptibility to TB, that the popularity of the virgin soil theory reached its peak.

Finally, we need to ask why the virgin soil theory came to be so widely accepted within Western medical circles, given the absence of definitive evidence concerning the existence of TB in preindustrial South Africa. Although this question will be explored in detail in chapter 7, it can be noted here that the evolution of medical ideas concerning the history of TB among Africans did not occur in an intellectual vacuum but was shaped by wider currents in the political and economic history of South Africa.

Medical facts, like any other data, have no intrinsic meaning. They are rather the materials with which physicians and others construct hypotheses, theories, and conclusions. Although these interpretive processes are often viewed by medical practitioners and the communities they serve as involving impersonal and objective distillations of medical facts, they are unavoidably shaped by the social and intellectual environment in which they occur. As Charles Rosenberg notes about medical definitions of disease, "A disease is no absolute entity but a complex intellectual construct, an amalgam of biological state and social definition."[22] In the case of the virgin soil theory, this book argues that its popularity and longevity have had less to do with its basis in historical fact than with its usefulness as an instrument for promoting opposing sets of political and economic interests within South African society. On the one hand, it has provided defenders of the status quo in South Africa with a means of deflecting attention from the appalling conditions under which Africans lived and worked. On the other hand, it has offered those who have attempted to challenge the status quo, an equally convenient instrument for highlighting those conditions. In both cases, the virgin soil theory appears to have been accepted more for its instrumentality than for its basis in historical fact.

CHAPTER II

Urban Growth, "Consumption," and the "Dressed Native," 1870–1914

INTRODUCTION

Until the 1870s the South African economy was dominated by herding and agriculture. Its African population was primarily rural, living on farms and in kraals and small towns scattered over the African veld. Few Africans, other than those residing in royal homesteads, lived in large concentrated settlements and only a small number of European towns, such as Grahamstown (1856) and Uitenhage (1836) in the eastern Cape, possessed a sufficiently large African population to warrant the establishment of an African location. In the Transvaal, the Volksraad went so far as to decree in 1844 that no African could settle near a town without official permission.

The absence of large urban centers with sizable African populations limited the spread of tuberculosis in South Africa and no doubt accounted for the infrequent occurrence of the disease among Africans prior to 1870. The discovery of diamonds in 1867 and gold in 1886, however, dramatically transformed the social geography of the region and with it the epidemiology of tuberculosis.

Between 1891 and 1911 the urban population of South Africa increased by 200 percent. Much of the increase was caused by the introduction of thousands of unskilled African workers and by the rapid urbanization of coloreds. By 1890 there were roughly 20,000 Africans working on the diamond fields at Kimberley and nearly 60,000 working in the gold-mining industry on the Witwatersrand. The number of Afri-

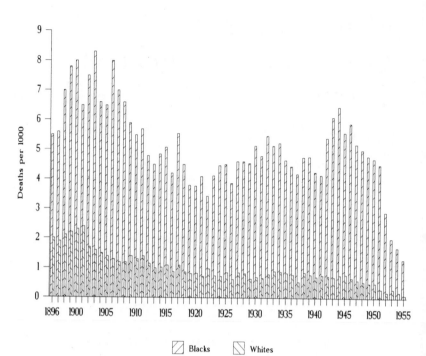

Graph 1.   TB Mortality, Cape Town, 1896–1955
  Source: Cape Town, *Reports of the Medical Officer of Health, 1896–1955.*

can mineworkers on the Rand had grown to over 200,000 by 1910, eliminating for the moment any hope the Transvaal Volksraad had of keeping Africans out of the urban areas. The mineral revolution also stimulated the growth of other population centers in South Africa. The port towns of Durban, East London, Port Elizabeth, and Cape Town grew in size as commerce swelled. In 1879 there were officially 2,984 African men, women, and children living within the whole of the western Cape. By 1907 the recorded African population of Cape Town alone had risen to 7,492.[1] Even the African populations of small rural communities expanded in response to increased opportunities for trade in agricultural commodities spurred by the growth of urban and industrial centers.

The rapid urbanization of Africans and coloreds was accompanied by a killing epidemic of tuberculosis. Black TB mortality rates in Cape Town rose from 5.5 to 8 per 1,000 between 1896 and 1906. In Port Elizabeth the situation was even worse, with rates as high as 15 per 1,000 being recorded at the turn of the century. In the smaller towns of

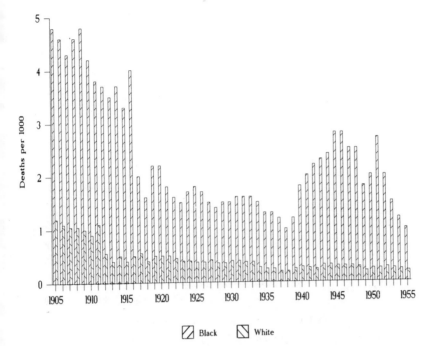

Graph 2.   TB Mortality, Johannesburg, 1905–1955
Source: Johannesburg, Reports of the Medical Officer of Health, 1905–1955.

the western Cape, such as Stellenbosch, Malmesbury, Robertson, and Outshoorn, black death rates exceeded 10 per 1,000, while in the so-called health resort towns of Beaufort West and Cradock, which served as "sanitoriums" for a large number of European tuberculotics, rates between 12 and 14 per 1,000 were common during this period.

TB mortality rates for Africans living in Johannesburg were consider-ably lower than those for Africans in the Cape municipalities. This was no doubt due to a combination of factors, including a shorter history of black proletarianzation and exposure to TB and the mining industry's policy of repatriating diseased workers before they could die. Johannes-burg rates were nonetheless high, running around 5 per 1,000.

African mortality rates in Durban were considerably lower than those of any other major urban center of South Africa at the turn of the century. The reasons for this are unclear, but a number of factors may have been at play. White's in Durban were in general healthier than their counterparts in either the Cape cities or Johannesburg. This re-flected their greater affluence and the relative absence of a class of poor

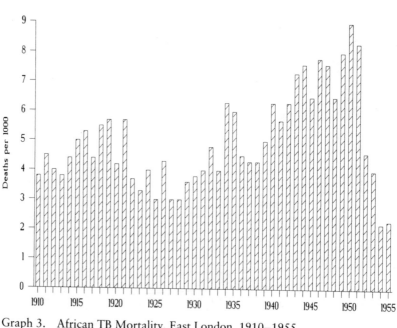

Graph 3.   African TB Mortality, East London, 1910–1955
Source: East London, *Reports of the Medical Officer of Health, 1910–1955.*

whites. As will be noted below, poor whites with tuberculosis were a primary source of infection for blacks elsewhere in South Africa early in this century. In this respect the earlier establishment of residential segregation in Durban, which restricted opportunities for the transmission of infection from whites to Africans, may also have played a role in keeping African TB rates down. It is probable that Africans in Durban also had greater access to the rural areas and to food from rural areas during this period than did Africans in other urban centers. Women came frequently into town with beer and other food for male workers. To the extent that bad diets contributed to the early spread of TB, this rural–urban link could have increased the resistance of Africans in Durban.[2] Finally, the lower recorded mortality rates for Africans in Durban may simply reflect poorer identification of TB cases.

In all urban centers the disease appeared to run a fulminating course among Africans showing little sign of localization. Case mortality rates ran as high as 90 percent with death occurring in some cases within a matter of weeks after initial symptoms were reported. Describing this pattern in Port Elizabeth in 1904, the Acting District Surgeon David Rees observed that tuberculosis

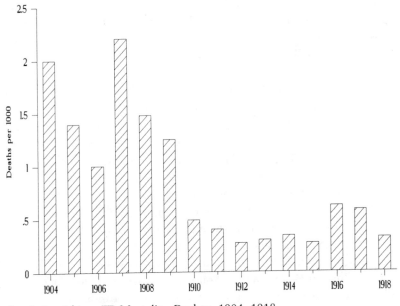

Graph 4.   African TB Mortality, Durban, 1904–1918
Source: TAD, GES 611 6/17, Peter Allan Reports, Natal.

continues to give rise to the greatest mortality, particularly in the case of the Coloured and Native populations. The disease in these classes being virulent and, generally speaking, rapidly fatal. I have not infrequently seen whole families decimated by it in the course of a few months.[3]

White TB mortality rates were comparatively low, as shown in the rates for Cape Town and Johannesburg (see graphs 1 and 2). As noted in the last chapter, moreover, whites generally showed more resistance to the disease, which often took a more chronic course. It should be noted, however, that rapidly fatal cases did occur among whites as well as Africans. The thousands of impoverished rural Afrikaners who flooded the major urban centers of South Africa following the South African War represented, like Africans, a relatively inexperienced population. In this regard it is worth citing an observation of the 1914 TB Commission: "From the evidence given by medical practitioners, it would appear that, in the experience of many, the disease tends to run a more rapid course in the South African-born than in the foreign-born."[4] As described below, many of these poor Afrikaners also lived together with thousands of east European immigrants, on meager incomes in overcrowded slums, alongside African workers and their families. These conditions may explain why 21 percent of the whites in Johannesburg who died of TB in 1903–1904 died within thirty days of being diagnosed, a point largely overlooked by white medical authorities in their quest for an explanation for the high prevalence of acute TB among urban Africans.

The origins of this epidemic can be traced initially to the spread of infection from European immigrants, who settled in South Africa during the second half of the nineteenth century, to the relatively inexperienced populations of Africans, coloreds, and Afrikaners who flocked to the towns and cities during this period. Yet, as in Europe and America, the epidemic was greatly exacerbated by the constellation of adverse social and economic conditions that existed in these urban and industrial centers. These conditions were not an inevitable consequence of urbanization but, as argued in the Introduction, a product of the specific sets of economic and political interests that accompanied the expansion of industrial capitalism in South Africa. In examining the experiences of workers and their families in South Africa we will look first at the conditions existing in urban municipalities and locations, and then, in chapter 3, at the specific conditions that existed in the mining industry, the dominant employer of labor during this period and a primary center for the dissemination of TB in southern Africa.

IMMIGRANTS AND DISEASE

The European immigrants who flocked to South Africa's urban and industrial centers at the end of the nineteenth century came from many parts of the world and from every social class. Two groups, however, played a particularly important role in the history of tuberculosis. These were European consumptives, primarily from England, who came to South Africa in hopes that their health would benefit from its climate, and eastern European refugees escaping poverty and persecution.

Consumptive immigrants seeking a climatic cure contributed to the spread of TB in South Africa even before reaching the subcontinent. For they not infrequently infected their fellow passengers on shipboard. As the Medical Officer of Health (MOH) for the Cape Colony noted in 1906, consumptive passengers most frequently traveled second or third class: "it is, therefore, not an uncommon thing for them to be accommodated in small cabins, not the best as regards light and ventilation, and occupied by several unaffected passengers." He cites the case of two consumptives on board the SS *Medic* bound for Australia. While one of the passengers was isolated, the other was in a cabin with seven other passengers.[5]

Immigrant consumptives began arriving in Natal following the British annexation in 1843.[6] By midcentury the Cape had become a sanatorium for the officers of the Indian Army. The Hotel Cogill, Drake and Rathfelder in the southern suburbs of Cape Town was a famous rendezvous for these consumptives. It was not long before the commercial exploitation of the Cape's climate had begun. Advertisements appeared in the *Illustrated London News,* and articles by Cape medical authorities, extolling the virtues of the Cape's climate, were published in British and South African medical journals.[7] As a result, the colony, and particularly the drier inland communities such as Cradock, Beaufort West, and Burgersdorp in the Karoo attracted large numbers of fresh cases of tuberculosis during the 1870s and 1880s. The 1914 Tuberculosis Commission noted the growing popularity of the Karoo towns during this period, describing the experience of Dr. J. McCall Frehrsen, who reported that when he first began practice in Cradock in 1874,

> "There were no cases of tuberculosis among the indigenous white population," and there were few scattered cases among the Hottentot and Bastard races in the town location. At the time, consumptives began coming pretty frequently from England, travelling up to Cradock by coach. There were about six such cases when he arrived, but twenty years later there was always an average of thirty or forty in the town . . .[8]

Some consumptive immigrants who arrived in South Africa possessed the means or skills needed to establish themselves in business or to take up a trade. For such fortunate men and women, of whom Cecil Rhodes was perhaps the most successful,[9] the sunny temperate climate of South Africa proved beneficial and they remained free of the disease for the greater part of their lives. Many others, however, were not so fortunate. Some who arrived too ill to work and without resources died soon after their arrival. Others who were able to work but lacked resources were forced to seek employment in low-paying, physically demanding jobs that further weakened their condition. In addition they frequently lived in cheap tenements and overcrowded boarding houses, and there they became sources of infection to other residents who shared their economic condition, and eventually their disease.[10] The differential benefit of South Africa's climate for different classes of European consumptives led one physician to observe that "no one but the absolutely leisure class gets substantial benefit."[11]

The threat such imported cases of TB represented for the native-born populations of the colony, both black and white, was not appreciated prior to 1895. The infectious nature of tuberculosis was only discovered by Koch in 1884 and even then was not widely accepted within the western medical establishment. The absence, moreover, of legislation requiring the registration of deaths in the Cape Colony or elsewhere in South Africa before 1895, made it impossible to assess the force of tuberculosis on mortality rates. Unaware of the potential consequences of the immigration of consumptives, town officials in the Cape Colony made no effort to curtail the spread of infection among the town's noninfected inhabitants. Thus the chairman of the 1914 Tuberculosis Commission remembered seeing at Beaufort West during the 1890s, "the consumptives at the chief hotel, and of whom there were a number, sitting all day on the stoep, expectorating into an adjacent open water-furrow which was the only source of water supply of many dwellings and of the extensive coloured location just below."[12]

A good number of male immigrant consumptives made a living by serving as tutors for the children of local white farmers, thereby becoming sources of infection within these families.[13] Infection may also have been spread among the colored and African residents of the towns by the common practice of servant girls taking leftover food from consumptive employers and using it to feed their own families.[14]

With the establishment of compulsory death registrations, medical authorities in the colony came to recognize the high toll that tuberculosis was taking among both native-born white and black populations of these resort towns.

In his annual report for 1897, the district surgeon for Aliwal North warned,

> Suffers from phthisis continue to be attracted to Aliwal North from Europe, and it is much to be desired that steps be taken to prevent the spread of tuberculosis by these invalids. . . . Unless this is done, it is to be feared that tuberculosis will spread in this country, as it has in the health resorts of Europe, for want of simple sanitary precautions.

The district surgeon estimated that the mortality rate for whites in Aliwal North was 19.9 per 1,000 in that year. The death rate among the native-born white population of the town was 13.6 per 1,000. For the African population, there were 37 reported deaths from TB out of an estimated population of 600, or an annual incidence of 62 per 1,000. This is an extrordinarily high figure, which probably reflects some

overdiagnosing of cases or an underestimation of the size of the population at risk. It nonetheless indicates the high toll Africans were paying
for their exposure to imported cases of tuberculosis in the resort towns
of the country.[15]

A similar pattern was observed in the other consumptive resorts of
the colony. Writing in the Annual Report for 1905, the medical officer
of health for the Cape Colony noted,

> It is a significant fact that the centres of the Colony, such as Beaufort West,
> which we formerly knew to be free from disease and which, owing to their
> particularly favorable climatic conditions, have been chosen as health resorts
> by immigrant consumptives, should at the present day be the most severely
> affected by the disease, its incidence falling not only on the native but also on
> the European portion of the population.[16]

The death rate from TB among Africans and coloreds in Beaufort
West in 1896, the first full year of registration, was 8.7 per 1,000. By
1903 it had reached 18.5 per 1,000. The average between 1903 and
1906 was 14.3 per 1,000.[17] Though some of this rise can be attributed
to increased compliance with registration regulations, the observations
of medical men leave little doubt that a good part of the increase was
caused by an actual rise in TB mortality.

Alongside the Europeans who came to South Africa to improve their
health were thousands of impoverished eastern Europeans, and most
prominently Polish and Russian Jews who flocked to the Rand in the
mid-1890s to escape crushing poverty and persecution at home. By
1899 it was estimated that there were over 7,000 "Russian Jews" on the
Witwatersrand. These "Peruvians," as they were called on the Rand,
came from countries with a high prevalence of TB, and the majority had
been infected with tuberculosis at some point in their lives.[18] Like the
poor consumptives who arrived without means of support, seeking a
climatic cure, the prospects of most of these eastern European refugees
were poor. As Van Onselen notes, these poorest of eastern Europeans,
possessing neither mining skills nor the capital needed to follow the
petty-bourgeoisie path of early groups of European immigrants, were
pushed into the life of the lumpenproletariat.[19] Prevented from making
a reasonable living, forced to live on the margins of white society, and
unable to properly care for and feed themselves or their families, these
less fortunate settlers often suffered reactivation of their disease and
became open sources of infection within the community.

During the early years of urban growth in South Africa there were few restrictions on social interaction among the racially and ethnically diverse populations drawn to the Rand and the major port cities of the Cape Colony. This lack of restriction facilitated contact and social interactions across color lines, especially among the poor, to a degree that would not be permitted later in the century. This in turn provided a unique opportunity for the transmission of tuberculosis within these urban centers.

The "toleration of colour and social admixture" permitted in Cape Town at the turn of the century shocked an observer from Natal, where lines of racial segregation had been drawn more clearly during the nineteenth century.

> [I]t is evident in the streets, on the tramcars, in the railway stations, public offices, and in the places of entertainment. . . . The doors of the Bioscope entertainment are open, and the crowd awaiting admission and jostling each other as they get tickets, includes representatives of every colour . . . and if he enters the overcrowded room and braves the foetid atmosphere, he will find no distinction made, all and every colour occupy the same seats, cheek by jowl, and sometimes on each others knees.[20]

Among Cape Town's poorer classes interracial cohabitation in overcrowded slum tenements was quite common, as noted by the attorney general of the Cape Colony in 1902:

> The condition of affairs which . . . prevailed in Cape Town was a disgrace to any country in the civilized world. Whole streets were inhabited by Natives, and in some houses close to the leading thoroughfares the cellars were occupied by large numbers of men—Europeans, Malays and raw Kaffirs—all sandwiched together, living in a state of utmost neglect, disease and vice . . .[21]

Similar patterns of intercourse occurred among the poorer classes of unskilled workers and unemployed in Johannesburg. The early boomtown environment of the Rand defied efforts at residential segregation. With the flood of both Africans and whites into Johannesburg following the South African War and the rapid buildup of an unemployed lumpenproletariat, racially mixed slum warrens sprung up in the various parts of the city. One such slum, the Malay location, was described by Dr. Charles Porter, MOH for Johannesburg, in 1902.

> It consists of congeries of narrow courtyards, containing dilapidated and dirty tin huts without adequate means of lighting and ventilation huddled on an area and constructed without any regard to sanitary conditions of any kind. In the middle of each slop sodden and filth bestrewn yard is a well from which the people get their water supply and as in other places they choose their well for washing purposes. .[22]

In 1904 the population of the Malay Location included 1,752 Asiatics, 252 Natives, 937 Mulattos, and 405 Europeans.[23]

In addition to these interracial slums there was a tendency for the poorer sections of the white working class to congregate in close proximity to the unemployed slum residents, particularly in the southwestern quarter of the city where parts of Fordsburg, Vredesdorp, the Brickfields, and the Indian location merged into one another.[24] The Milner administration, recognizing the potential political ramifications of this situation, pushed for both the elimination of slums and the creation of housing for white workers and their families in segregated suburbs. Although these efforts gradually bore results, as late as 1911 the western half of the city was still dotted by " 'slum-warrens' housing Europeans of various nationalities—Indians, Chinese, Arabs, Japanese, Kaffirs, and miscellaneous coloured people of every hue."[25]

The growing industrial and commercial centers of South Africa thus provided an ideal setting for the rapid spread of tuberculosis. Newly urbanized Africans, coloreds, and Afrikaners, with relatively little prior experience with tuberculosis and thus containing members who had little resistance to it, came in close contact with an infected population of European immigrants, with whom they often lived in common poverty in overcrowded slums. Without adequate medical attention or the means to support themselves, many of these newly urbanized poor succumbed quickly to this disease. Those who survived for longer periods provided new sources of infection for their family and neighbors within the growing urban workforce.

BOVINE TB AND THE DAIRYMEN'S ASSOCIATION

Although the means of TB transmission within the growing urban centers of South Africa was primarily airborne and thus associated with overcrowding, infected milk may also have played a role. Risk of infection through the consumption of milk from tubercular cows was established in British medical circles by the beginning of this century. A British Royal Commission after ten year's investigation reported in 1911 that bovine tuberculosis was a very serious source of human infection, especially among children.[26] In South Africa, at the same time, medical and veterinary authorities in Johannesburg and other major urban centers began drawing attention to the existence of bovine tuberculosis among local dairy herds. Yet the history of bovine tuberculosis and its role in the human epidemiology of TB in South Africa remains clouded by a lack of data on both the incidence of TB among South Africa's dairy cattle and the occurrence of bovine TB in humans. This absence of data reflects the role of economic and political forces in shaping public health.

Until 1905 it was generally assumed that for all practical purposes, bovine TB did not exist in South Africa. In that year, however, William Robertson, a government veterinary officer in the Cape Colony, tested a number of well-known dairy herds in the Cape peninsula. The tests revealed a high rate of TB infection and led Robertson to conclude that 60 percent of the dairy cattle in the Cape Division were affected. The source of the infection was believed to be imported highbred dairy stock from Europe. The subsequent testing of milk from Cape herds revealed that 12 percent of the samples tested were contaminated with tubercle bacilli.[27]

In 1906, the Cape Act No. 16 amended the previous "Animals Diseases Act" of 1893 and gave the colonial Veterinary Department powers to test animals that had been in contact with infected beasts and to slaughter those found to be positive reactors. The owners of the destroyed cows would be paid a compensation of one-fourth the value of the destroyed animal, but not more than £15. Similar laws were passed in the other colonies, and in 1911 the policy of destroying infected animals and the rate of compensation were embodied in the Union Disease of Stock Act.

Following the passage of the Cape Act some 16,796 animals were tested, uncovering 429 reactors (or 2.5 percent of the total). In certain herds, however, up to half of the animals were infected. The divisions of the Cape, Malmesbury, Stellenbosch, and Paarl were subsequently declared infected areas from which cattle could not be transported without a veterinary certificate indicating that they had been tuberculin tested and found free of tubercular infection.[28]

This precaution, designed to prevent the spread of TB to herds in other colonies, was only partially effective. The Cape had for years been a source of breeding stock for neighboring colonies, and the restrictions came too late to prevent the spread of the disease out of the Cape. In addition, imperfections in the application of the law and in testing procedures resulted in cattle that had been identified as tuberculin negative being found to suffer from TB after admission to one of the other colonies. Finally, there is some evidence that certain stock raisers in the Cape chose to illegally dump herds known to contain infected cows in the Transvaal or Natal, rather than incur the loss of having them destroyed and then being compensated at a mere fraction of their true value. Low levels of awareness of the problem among stock raisers and dairymen in the interior may have facilitated this practice.[29]

For whatever reason, bovine TB appears to have spread into the Transvaal and Natal and, to a lesser degree, into the Orange Free State (OFS) during the first decade of this century. Inquiries into the prevalence of TB among dairy herds in Natal turned up infection rates of 25 percent in a number of cases. In Johannesburg, the municipality established public abattoirs in 1910. This provided the first real opportunity to determine the extent to which infection existed among the Transvaal herds. Between October 1910 and June 1912 no TB was found in local Afrikaner cows. Of the 130 other dairy cows presented by local dairymen for slaughter, however, sixty-eight or 52 percent were found to be infected. This discovery led to the testing of the herds from which these infected cows had come. A large percentage of these cows were subsequently also found to be infected (ranging from 3.9 to 87.5 percent and averaging 33.7 percent) and were destroyed. As a result of these investigations and the subsequent financial losses suffered by the owners of the destroyed cows, no more dairy cows were sent for slaughter, curtailing for the moment the collection of further data on the prevalence of the disease in the Transvaal.[30]

The conjuncture of growing evidence of high levels of TB infection among South African dairy herds and recognition of the possibility of transmitting TB between these cows and humans through the consumption of infected milk, led medical authorites in the major urban centers to push for more aggressive testing of the dairy herds that provided milk for urban consumption. Dr. Charles Porter, MOH for Johannesburg, for example, began a campaign to test all of the dairy herds within the Johannesburg Municipality and the destruction of all cows found to be infected in 1911.

The dairy owners were quick to react to this campaign. In a memo submitted to the Union minister of agriculture, members of the Witwatersrand Dairy Farmers Association noted their appreciation of the need to control the spread of infection but objected strongly to the actions of Dr. Porter. They claimed that the policy threatened to destroy their businesses, which, raising the specter of unemployment, distributed "a very large sum in wages each month." They further argued that they had invested considerable sums to build up their herds, containing some of the finest dairy cattle in South Africa, and that the maximum compensation of £15 for such valuable cows simply spelled ruin "for many men who have spent the best years of their lives building up their dairy herds and dairy businesses, men, many of whom are advanced in years and have wives and families dependent on them."[31] The memo also noted that a large quantity of milk sold in Johannesburg was drawn from the OFS and Natal as well as from different districts of the Transvaal. The cows producing these supplies were not subject to the same restrictions, giving their owners an unfair advantage. Finally, they claimed that they were being made to suffer for the Veterinary Department's failure to prevent the transport and sale of infected animals.

The cause of the Transvaal dairymen was taken up by their representatives to the Transvaal Provincial Council:

> In view of the statement made by the Medical Officer of Health of this Province "that what danger *may* exist in regards to tuberculosis in dairy stock *can* be avoided by using only boiled milk," and the fact that the tuberculin test is only successful where animals are slightly affected, whilst those in an advanced stage do not react, and consequently remain in the dairy, will . . . [the Honourable Administrator] recommend to the Minister of Agriculture the advisability or otherwise of stopping the unwarrantable slaughter of valuable cattle, and thereby allay to a great extent the unrest and unsatisfactory state of affairs which at present exists among the dairymen of this Province?[32]

With these counterattacks, the stage was set for a conflict between the economic interests of the dairymen and the health of urban consumers, represented by municipal medical officers. The Veterinary Department and agriculture minister were caught in the middle. They were sympathetic to the interests of the dairymen and objected to the policy of wholesale testing of herds and slaughter of infected cattle, which would destroy the dairy industry, and which in any case could not be carried out given the manpower available. Many of the Veterinary Department's officers were involved at the time in the control of another animal infection, East Coast Fever.[33] Yet they recognized the need to control the spread of TB and did not wish to be seen as putting obstacles in the path of municipal medical officers who were trying to protect the health of the public. They thus sought an arrangement that would allow them to eliminate infected cattle without ruining the dairymen. Though the obvious solution was to increase the level of compensation paid to the dairymen, that would make the control of the disease very costly.[34] In the end the Union government adopted a voluntary policy in which cattle would only be tested at the request of the owner or if the milk from the cattle was found to be contaminated.

This policy predictably failed, as dairymen in South Africa, like those in England, adopted a noncooperative stance in the face of low levels of compensation. Outbreaks of TB among their herds were not reported and in some instances, where more active case finding was initiated by local health authorities, dairymen illegally injected their herds repeatedly with tuberculin. This practice desensitized the cattle so that subsequent testing by veterinary authorities would produce a negative result.[35]

Lack of cooperation on the part of dairymen seriously hampered the medical and veterinary authorities in their efforts to control the spread of TB. Data on the prevalence and distribution of the disease became impossible to acquire. As a result the spread of the disease went largely unchecked. The Tuberculosis Research Committee in addressing the issue in their 1932 report noted that "Little exact information is available as to the incidence in dairy herds but the indications, so far as they go, are that the incidence amongst these stall-fed cows is higher (perhaps much higher) than among cattle generally."[36] Although isolated efforts were made by local municipal authorities to eradicate infected cows during the 1930s, bovine TB went largely unchecked in South Africa until after World War II.[37]

Thus despite an early awareness of the possible spread of TB through human consumption of cow's milk and the sure knowledge that a large number of infected cows existed in South Africa, little was done by veterinary authorities to eradicate the disease. For their part, municipal medical authorities, while advocating the pasteurization of milk as a defense against bovine TB, had little success in implementing the policy. As late as 1954 there was no compulsory heat treatment of milk sold in Johannesburg, and it was estimated that only about half of the milk supply was pasteurized.[38]

The absence of greater control was due in part to manpower shortages. There simply were not enough trained personnel to carry out compulsory heat treatment of all milk supplies.[39] Yet the absence of a more concerted control effort was also encouraged by the fact that bovine strains of TB were seldom isolated in human subjects. Writing on bovine TB and its relationship to the milk supply in 1947, Gillies de Kock observed that, "It is most significant that tubercle bacilli of the bovine type have only once or twice been isolated in tuberculous lesions emanating from human beings in South Africa . . ."[40]

The failure to isolate bovine TB in humans, however, need not indicate that infection by M. bovis bacillus did not occur. Rather it is likely
that it simply did not appear in those who were tested or alternatively
that it was not looked for. During the period prior to World War II the
diagnosis of TB was often made without sputum cultures, particularly
among blacks. Whites were more likely to be sputum-tested, yet a substantial number of cases, particularly among the poorer classes, were
diagnosed on the basis of clinical observations alone. Moreover, whites
were in any case less likely to develop TB. The one black population
regularly subjected to sputum testing as part of the diagnostic procedure
was black mineworkers. Yet milk was not part of the standard mine
rations. It is also likely that those who might have been infected with
bovine strains of TB were also infected with human TB bacilli. Thus,
unless special efforts were made to identify M. bovis bacillus, a procedure that had no clinical value, its presence could easily have been
missed. The fact that M. bovis occurred in humans and could be found
if special efforts were made, however, was demonstrated by a study
carried out in the mid-1950s.[41]

In conclusion it would seem highly probable that some of the tubercular cases that occurred prior to World War I did result from the consumption of infected milk. The extent of this phenomenon, however,
and the role it played in the overall epidemiology of TB, is impossible to
assess given the social and economic forces that shaped medical research
and public health initiatives during this period.

MEDICAL RESPONSES: CIVILIZATION AND
THE "DRESSED NATIVE"

The rising tide of tuberculosis among urban Africans did not go
unnoticed among white health authorities. Nor were they unaware
that white workers and their families suffered lower rates of TB mortality and were apparently better able to control their infections. The
apparent susceptibility of Africans to TB and their inability to localize
infections, in fact, became a topic of considerable discussion among
white health authorities during the first decade of the century. Little or
no research was carried out on the question, however, and much of the
discussion reflected wider prejudices and assumptions about racial differences. Although a number of theories were put forth at this time,
the weight of both medical and lay opinion on the subject favored an
explanation that stressed the "natives'" incomplete and inadequate

adjustment to the conditions of urban life, their ignorance of sanitary habits, and their adoption of European patterns of dress and behavior, symbolized by the wearing of European clothing. In this regard, it was alleged that the so-called dressed native, who was making the transition to "civilized life" was particularly susceptible to the disease. Dr. George Turner, chief medical officer for the Transvaal, who later became a medical advisor to the Witwatersrand Native Labour Association (WNLA) and served on the 1914 Tuberculosis Commission, noted in 1906:

> If there has been an increase it is almost certain that it arises from the use of European clothing. The native gets wet in his clothes, either from rain or perspiration, does not change them and is chilled; this leads to chronic bronchitis, etc. which, reducing his powers of resistance, lays him open to the inroads of the bacillus tuberculosis.[42]

The South African Native Affairs Commission Report of 1903–1905 echoed this theme:

> European clothing which is coming more and more into general use has not been an unmixed blessing. It has promoted public decency, but, *not being adopted in its entirety,* and being necessarily of inferior material, it has not proved equally conducive to the promotion of health. The use of cotton shirts by the men and the habit of allowing wet clothing to dry on the person have been particularly harmful . . . and a marked increase in consumption, pleurisy, inflammation of the lungs and rheumatism have been the result. European clothes, too, require much more frequent cleansing than their ancestral garb, *a fact which, unfortunately, is not sufficiently realized by the natives who have partially adopted our style of dress; but the hard school of experience will teach them as it has taught us to use greater care in these matters.* The evils are not inseparable from European dress, but arise from an *imperfect understanding of the laws of health* [emphasis added].[43]

Though the etiological relationship between European-style clothing and TB contained in these quotations is clearly absurd, there may have been an empirical observation behind this ideological statement. Africans who adopted European clothing were those in closest contact with whites and thus at greatest risk of being infected with TB. Second, those wearing European dress were more likely to have developed other western consumer needs that, given low wage levels, could only be acquired at the expense of basic needs such as housing and diet. Finally, these individuals were more likely to develop western food tastes but, with limited incomes, would be unable to afford the more nutritious elements of such a diet. As a result they were more likely to suffer from malnutrition. For all these reasons, newly westernized Africans may have been particularly susceptible to TB. Thus early Christian converts who adopted western dress as a mark of their new enlightened status were among the first to feel the vice of poverty and suffered high rates of TB.[44]

Other reports pointed to the unsanitary conditions in which urban Africans lived, their habit of living in overcrowded houses, of spitting indiscriminately, of sleeping with blankets pulled over their heads, and "habits of inebriety and depravity" as other indications of their maladjustment to civilization and reasons for their susceptibility to TB.[45] Conversely, the native in his natural surroundings was repeatedly said to lead a healthy life style and to observe a number of practices that reduced the spread of TB.[46]

Though some writers suggested that Africans had a racial predisposition to disease and possessed "an inferior constitutional power of resistance"[47] this opinion was not widely held.[48] Several prominent physicians, in fact, explicitly rejected a racial explanation. Thus Dr. Neil McVicar, whose 1907 thesis on the history and prevalence of tuberculosis among natives in South Africa argued that TB was absent among Africans prior to European contact, stressed the importance of environmental factors and rejected the primacy of race.

> If racial predisposition be a factor in the spread of tuberculosis among the Native races of South Africa, I think it can be safely relegated to a secondary place, and the sanitary reformer may comfort himself with the reflection that, difficult though his task may be, *he is at least not fighting against fate* [emphasis added].[49]

The behavioral explanation for African susceptibility to TB can be seen as a logical extension of earlier medical opinion, which ascribed the relative absence of tuberculosis among Africans during the eighteenth and early nineteenth centuries to their lack of exposure to the unhealthful habits of European life.[50] Where once the "native" had lived a healthful rural existence free from the stresses and excesses of modern civilized life, now he was being exposed to these conditions as part of his journey along the path from a "barbarous to a civilized condition." Being inexperienced with civilized life, moreover, he was ignorant of its pitfalls and of how to protect himself from them. Tuberculosis was the high cost he paid for his incomplete adaptation to a civilized existence.[51]

This viewpoint underlay early efforts to control the spread of tuberculosis. On the one hand, it was argued that African resistance to disease would improve with time through education and experience. Thus European missionaries and African ministers, along with leaders of the social and cultural associations of the African petty bourgeoisie, encouraged their parishioners and members to lead a temperate lifestyle and provided information about how TB was spread and how it could be prevented. A flier distributed by the South African Native and Coloured Health Society, for example, informed blacks that TB could be prevented by *avoiding* overcrowded housing and eating good food (emphasis added).[52] Neil McVicar, in an article in the *South African Medical Record*, argued in a similar vein:

> I think the main effort of our profession and everyone working for the reduction of tuberculosis should be to rouse the people concerned, i.e. the natives themselves, to a sense of the gravity of the situation, and to the need for effort on their part. Let us give them all the information we can. . . . Let us educate them by means of every agency we possess, by means of dispensaries, schools, health societies and literature.[53]

Similarly the 1906 Conference of Principle Medical Officers of Health of British South African Colonies recommended as part of their proposals for combating the spread of TB, "That it is desirable to disseminate among the population information as to the cause and means of spread of Tuberculosis with simple rules for preventing the spread of the disease . . ."[54]

Although ignorance of "civilized conditions" no doubt played some role in the spread of TB among Africans, the theory blissfully ignored the economic realities that underlay the Africans' lack of proper housing and diet. Africans were chastized for living in overcrowded slums and eating nonnutritious foods as if they chose to do so out of perversity rather than economic necessity. Even when poverty was recognized as a causal factor, it was attributed to the "natives' " laziness and lack of a civilized work ethic. For example, an irate town councilor for Worcester told the TB Commission,

> Why does not the government come in and say to these people, "Go out and work"—compel them to go out to work and earn money, and then there will be very much less sickness. It is this continued overcrowding among them, and we have no power over it. They bring upon themselves these wretched conditions, as a result of their idleness. Bad feeding, bad housing, bad clothing, all come from their poverty; and yet they continue to loaf instead of going out and earning a decent living.[55]

Thus, belief in the "natives' " lack of experience with civilized ways of life blamed the victim for his disease and deflected attention away from the political and economic conditions that shaped the world in which African workers and their families lived.

The dominant response to the behavioral explanation for African susceptibility to TB ultimately was the establishment of rigorous social controls designed to halt the spread of disease by enacting and enforcing sanitation laws. This strategy was embodied in the recommendations of the 1906 Conference of Principle Medical Officers of Health of British South African Colonies, which concluded,

> That in the opinion of this Conference the spread of Tuberculosis is especially marked amongst Natives and Coloured persons living in or near towns, or employed in towns, or living in compounds or labor communities: that this incidence of a preventable disease is largely due to unhealthy housing and general insanitary conditions in which such persons *are allowed to live,* and that in order to remove this danger to the entire population of South Africa, bye-laws or regulations must be enacted and efficiently enforced, *compelling* Natives and Coloured persons in such places to live in dwellings constructed of suitable materials and so as to admit adequate cleanliness, lighting and ventilation, and especially a minimum cubic air space of 300 cubic feet per inmate should be fixed and enforced [emphasis added].[56]

This injunction, like the statements quoted above, placed responsibility for the conditions under which Africans lived on the Africans themselves. Africans had to be forced to live under healthful conditions for their own good and for that of the rest of the community, that is, for the protection of whites. The need to protect the health of both whites and Africans underlay the policy that came to be the centerpiece of efforts to control the health of urban Africans: sanitary segregation.

URBAN SEGREGATION: RELOCATING THE TB EPIDEMIC

Municipal health authorities began advocating the creation of segregated locations for African workers and their families at the turn of the century, in response to the insanitary conditions and high disease rates occurring among urban blacks. In this campaign they were joined by white religious and civic leaders who saw uncontrolled urban settlement as undermining the moral well-being of the "natives," as well as that of those whites who were living in close association with Africans. The health authorities were also supported, as Maynard Swanson has convincingly shown, by municipal leaders who viewed "native locations" as a means of controlling the flow of Africans in search of urban employment.

Spurred to action by the outbreak of bubonic plague in 1902–1903, this coalition of interests pushed through a series of health acts resulting in the forced removal of thousands of Africans and coloreds to what were often hastily constructed ghettos on the periphery of Cape Town, Port Elizabeth, and Johannesburg. The establishment of the so-called native locations failed to achieve complete racial segregation in the urban areas of South Africa. In Port Elizabeth, for example, some 7,000 Africans out of a total population of nearly 10,000 were removed from the city in 1904. Pressure from employers for domestic, dock, and commercial laborers, and the exemption of an estimated 600 Africans with the franchise, left some 3,000 Africans within the municipality. This population increased, moreover, following the loosening of plague restrictions in 1905. The health acts went a long way, nonetheless, toward establishing a pattern of segregated housing in South Africa.[57]

Whereas the new locations may have achieved the goals of those who wanted segregation for moral and economic reasons, as well as those who were concerned about the health of whites, they were largely a failure as a means of improving African health conditions. Few municipal authorities, and even fewer white rate-payers, were willing to allocate the resources needed to improve the conditions under which Africans lived within the newly created locations. Thus slum clearance did not mean slum removal in the sense of eradication but simply the physical transfer of slum conditions beyond the city limits.

Many of the locations created prior to World War I offered African residents little more than a plot of leasehold land to rent. Neither housing nor sanitation facilities were provided unless paid for out of rents and other fees collected from the location residents. Thus despite lofty statements about the need to improve African health conditions, few attempts were made to alter the conditions under which most Africans lived in the new locations.

Left to their own economic resources, often reduced by the increased burden of higher transportation costs, location residents created slum conditions frequently much worse than those that had existed in the areas from which they had been removed. As a result, health conditions often deteriorated. The Tuberculosis Commission generally condemned the conditions they observed within the African urban locations, stating that "the majority of such locations are a menace to the health of their inhabitants and indirectly to the health of those in the town."[58]

The housing in the locations was described by the commission as being mere shanties, often nothing more than hovels constructed out of bits of old packing case lining, flattened kerosene tins, sacking and other scraps, and odds and ends. They are put up on bare ground, higgledly-piggledly, without any sort of order, often propped up against one another. . . . The dwellings are low, dark, and dirty, generally encumbered with unclean rubbish, mud floors are the rule, often below ground level and consequently sometimes apt to be flooded in wet weather.[59]

Overcrowding was encouraged by the inadequate supply of housing, low wages, and by the high rents location residents were required to pay for their plots or houses. In New Brighton, for example, the rent charged per month for housing was equal to what residents had paid per year in Port Elizabeth. A married man paid monthly fees as high as thirty shillings plus six shillings for transportation, while wages averaged only sixty to ninety shillings per month. Subletting to reduce expenditures was a common practice that further encouraged overcrowding.[60] The commission concluded that "altogether one could hardly imagine more suitable conditions for the spread of tuberculosis."[61]

Most municipal by-laws provided that a person renting a plot should erect a dwelling to the satisfaction of the location superintendent, but the regulation was frequently ignored. In many cases the minimum standard required was so low as to be of no practical value. The TB commission found that abandoned dwellings, deemed unfit for habitation, had been taken over by the location authorities and, without improvement, rented out to new tenants.[62]

The poor quality of most location housing reflected not only the poverty of location residents but also the insecurity of their tenure. Most location by-laws limited plot tenancy to a month at a time, renewal being at the discretion of the local authority and dependent on the tenant not falling in arrears on his or her rent, licenses, or other fees. Tenants also had to be of good character and not have been convicted of any breach of the law. Such restrictions, arbitrarily enforced by location authorities, hardly encouraged location dwellers to invest in better housing.[63]

Some municipal authorities attempted to improve housing conditions by constructing an "improved class of housing" to satisfy the needs of the "better class of natives." In keeping with the general location policy of requiring residents to pay for any improvements, however, these houses were rented at market rates, which meant that they were out of reach of all but the wealthiest of location residents.

While the poor quality of location housing contributed to the spread of tubercular infections, lack of sanitation and changes in diet undermined the ability of location residents to control infections and increased their likelihood of developing active disease.

Very few locations possessed adequate sanitary facilities. There were normally no private facilities, and public latrines were few in number or entirely absent. The facilities that were provided were often inaccessible and therefore not used. In the native locations of East London, for example, there were no latrines located within the location boundaries in 1912. Instead the 8,500 residents had to use latrines that were constructed around the outside of the location. This policy, which reduced the cost of servicing the latrines, hardly encouraged sanitary behavior on the part of location residents.[64]

A special committee appointed to look into location conditions in Grahamstown observed that,

> There is no proper system of sanitation carried out in the locations. The use of pails and the removal of night-soil is optional. And where there are infectious diseases (when they happen to be found out), there appears to be no regular method of removing or burying the excreta, or of supplying and using disinfectants. The sick and dying crawl out and defecate as near as possible to the hut they live in, and when they get beyond the strength of that, they lie in their filthy clothes, or use rags which are thrown out into the streets, or hidden in the aloes or prickly pear bush.[65]

The committee noted in addition that refuse was in most cases not collected and removed by local authorities despite the fact that location residents were charged for these services. When the services were carried out, they were usually performed in slipshod manner, leaving much refuse behind.[66] On the Rand, early locations were located near rubbish dumps, as was Ndabeni, the first location located outside Cape Town.

The absence of adequate water supplies created additional health hazards in the locations: "in most cases the inhabitants have to fetch their water from the irrigation furrow after it has run through the town, or from some neighboring sluit. Public washing places are seldom if ever provided." Where water supplies were available residents were frequently charged exorbitant rates far exceeding the actual cost to the municipality. In Grahamstown, for example, the residents payed ten shillings a year and received perhaps two paraffin tins of water per week, from tanks opened only twice a week. The municipality made a profit of £1,694 on the waterworks account in 1912. Bloemfontein made a profit of £1,400 from water charges in 1913.[67]

Though poor sanitary conditions did not contribute directly to the spread of tuberculosis, they certainly encouraged the spread of other diseases, especially water-borne and parasitic diseases such as enteritis, dysentery, and hookworm. The parasite load of urban Africans was frequently commented upon by white medical authorities. The average death rate from "diarrheal diseases," a rather broad category that includes a range of parasitic and bacterial disorders frequently associated with inadequate sanitation, was 2.68 per 1,000 for Africans and coloreds in Johannesburg between 1903–1904 and 1913–1914. The figure for whites during the same period was 2.20 per 1,000. The difference is rather small and reflects the absence of adequate sanitation in all sections of the community at this time. There is a marked difference, however, in the age distribution of deaths from this cause. Among whites, 90 percent of the deaths in 1913–1914 were in children under five and most certainly represent cases of gastroenteritis. Whereas in Africans and coloreds only 57 percent of the cases occurred in this age group, reflecting a higher incidence of other intestinal diseases among older children and adults. It is worth noting that "diarrheal deaths" continued to take a significant toll among whites until the early 1920s when the provision of water-borne sanitation to the white areas was completed. By contrast, as will be shown in chapter 5, the rates for African areas, where such facilities were absent or inadequate, remained high and, in fact, increased during the 1920s.[68]

The parasitic infections of African workers and their families may well have contributed indirectly to the development of TB. Parasites drained an individual of the limited quantity of nutrients provided by a diet that was already deficient in proteins and vitamins. This decreased nutritional status lowered individual resistance to TB and thereby encouraged TB infections to develop into active disease. In this way, lack of sanitation contributed to the growing pool of infectious cases and thus to the dissemination of disease.

The failure of municipal councils to provide more adequate housing and sanitation facilities in the newly constructed African locations reflected the unwillingness of white rate-payers to subsidize these improvements and the legal requirement that all improvements had to be funded by the location residents themselves out of the rents, licenses, and fees collected by the location authorities. Yet the balance sheets of several locations reveal a rather different explanation: municipal councils not only refused to subsidize African housing but were *themselves* being supported by surplus revenues coming from the rents and fees paid by location residents. In Cradock, for example, the municipal council gained a surplus of nearly £3,000 between 1911 and 1912. This surplus

TABLE 1

MUNICIPAL REVENUES AND EXPENDITURES, 1912–1913

Municipality	Revenue Collected from Native Locations (in pounds)	Expenditures on Native Locations (in pounds)	Surplus Revenue
Pretoria	1,594	764	829
Bloemfontein[1]	7,614	6,569	1,044
Grahamstown	6,119	4,277	1,842
Graaff-Reinet[2]	1,156	905	251
Kimberley	2,984	1,780	1,203
Beaufort West	368	253	144
Uitenhage	2,010	900	1,110
East London[3]	4,116	2,774	1,342

[1]The TB Commission estimated that the actual profit was £2,500. The additional £1,400 was hidden by overcharging the water account. The actual cost of supplying water to the location was £915, while the amount charged was £2,322.

[2]The commission estimated the actual profit to be closer to £600. Part of the £349 represented charges for soil removal in the town which were charged to the location account.

[3]Represents amounts for ten months only in 1911.[71]

covered roughly 12 percent of ordinary municipal expenditures. The native location was, in short, subsidizing the cost of services for whites.[69] The African TB mortality rate in Cradock in 1912 was 13 per 1,000.[70]

The profits earned by some other municipalities for 1912–1913 are shown in table 1. Of the 217 towns reporting to the secretary for native affairs for the year 1916–1917, no less than 191 derived more from native revenues than they expended on native services.[72]

Urban settlement, whether in locations or within the boundaries of a municipality, frequently led to a shift in dietary practices that had an adverse impact on nutrition. There exists relatively little data on the diets of urban Africans at the beginning of the century, compared to what we know about later periods. The role of nutrition in the maintenance of health was not in general given much attention, and few inquiries were made into African diets. In addition, white authorities lacking knowledge of "traditional" African diets assumed that Africans were used to living on mealie meal. Thus the first effort to establish a minimum ration for African workers in 1905 resulted in a diet that was wholly inadequate, being composed almost exclusively of mealie meal and containing few foods that build resistance to sickness.

There appears to have been a noticeable shift in the types of food consumed by urban Africans in comparison with their rural counterparts. Descriptions of rural African diets from the nineteenth century cite the frequent consumption of a variety of beans, pumpkins, millet, sorghum, and a variety of fruits. Meat and milk (either fresh or soured) were also commonly consumed.[73] Urban diets were much more limited by comparison. Fresh fruits and vegetables, peddled by African women in the locations, were seen by many Africans, especially those at the lower end of the economic spectrum, as expensive luxury items. Although some early locations provided garden plots on which Africans could grow their own vegetables, these were converted to house plots as the locations became more crowded.[74]

Urban Africans also tended to substitute relatively unnutritious white bread in place of maize and other grains. In addition, coffee frequently replaced soured milk as a staple beverage. As will be seen from an analysis of food consumption patterns during the 1930s, the extent to which more nutritious, resistance-building foods such as meat, milk, and fresh vegetables were included in African urban diets was closely tied to income levels and therefore sensitive to shifts in household income. Thus during periods of hardship, the range of foods consumed narrowed and the more nutritious foods were excluded. More generally, removal to the locations meant residents faced increased transport costs, which cut into household budgets and thus the quality of diets. Inadequate nutritional levels, marked particularly by the loss of animal protein and vitamin A and C, may well have lowered African resistance to TB infections as well as to other diseases. The Dubos suggest that, "inadequacies in protein and ascorbic acid retard healing and thereby become one of the determinants of the exudative type of disease through their interference with the production of fibrotic tissue."[75]

NEW BRIGHTON: A CASE STUDY

Although it is possible to document the inadequate housing, sanitation, and dietary conditions under which Africans lived in the newly created "native" locations of South Africa—and there can be little doubt that these conditions were detrimental to the health of their residents—it is difficult to document the precise impact of these conditions on incidence of tuberculosis. The 1914 TB Commission was convinced that conditions in the locations fostered the spread of TB among Africans and coloreds, yet they produced very few statistics to support this contention. Health statistics for native locations were rarely kept prior to World War I. There were few locations with medical officers to report on health conditions, and municipal health authorities conveniently excluded locations from their own record keeping. This exclusion explains the noticeable drop in the black TB mortality rate in Cape Town in 1901, following the removal of 6,000 to 7,000 Africans to Uitvlugt (later Ndabeni). African TB mortality rates for Port Elizabeth dropped similarly, from 15 per 1,000 in 1903 to 5.2 per 1,000 in 1904, as a result of the removal of 7,000 Africans beyond the city limits. Interestingly, these rates climbed back up rapidly in both cities following the relaxation of plague restrictions and the reentry of many Africans into the city.

In the absence of better records we must be cautious in indicting location housing and sanitation conditions as the factors responsible for the spread of TB during this period. To the contrary, statistics from the one location for which records were kept, New Brighton, outside Port Elizabeth, suggest that the movement to location housing brought about an initial reduction in TB mortality among Africans. The experience of New Brighton was in fact cited by white health authorities as an example of the health benefits of "native locations." For example D. P. Marais, in an article on the prevention of consumption presented to the Congress of Municipal Health Officials in 1911, stated:

> The remarkable fall in the death-rate from tuberculosis amongst natives in Port Elizabeth due to their removal by the plague authorities to a new location outside the municipality (from 15/1000 in 1903 to 5/1000 in 1904) proves at once the importance of better housing and the destruction of infected localities.[76]

Just as it is perhaps too facile to equate location conditions with rising TB rates, however, it is be equally simplistic to credit locations conditions with improving TB rates. A closer examination of both the statistical evidence from New Brighton and its early history suggests that the relationship between the creation of locations and the epidemiology of TB was extremely complex and that the changing incidence of TB within locations was dependent on a range of social and economic variables.

The New Brighton location, like those of Cape Town and Johannesburg, was created to control the outbreak of plague in 1902 and to provide greater control over the flow of migrant African labor. In contrast to the Cape Town and Johannesburg locations, municipal authorities in Port Elizabeth provided houses within the location and assigned a medical officer to supervise the health of location residents. In both respects conditions in New Brighton were better than those in most locations established at this time. Though this difference may help account for the apparent reduction in TB mortality indicated by New Brighton records, three other factors may have played an equally important role.

To begin with, the majority of Africans who were forced out of Port Elizabeth did not move to New Brighton. Instead they moved into Korsten and other private lands free of government control just beyond the limits of Port Elizabeth. Rents in these unregulated settlements, while often highly exploitive, were still cheaper than in New Brighton. Transportation costs were also lower in the unregulated areas since they were much nearer places of employment. In addition there was less control over liquor brewing and other commercial activities upon which urban African families depended for their survival.[77] As a consequence, the poorest of the poor, the unemployed and underemployed, who were often the most susceptible to disease, could not afford to reside in the government housing at New Brighton and flocked instead to the unregulated areas. The location authorities in fact evicted rent defaulters from the location, despite their avowed interest in encouraging Africans to settle there for health reasons. These evicted residents moved to the unregulated areas. The African population of Port Elizabeth in effect was disaggregated along economic lines in 1903–1904, and the population of New Brighton, although hardly well off, was at least separated for the moment from many of their poorer, more disease-ridden brethren. There are few TB statistics for Korsten and the other unregulated areas, but medical reports suggest that conditions in Korsten were appalling. Landlords purchased plots and constructed boarding houses in which rooms were rented at high rates of profit. These slum tenements were unregulated and quickly became jammed with residents who could not afford to rent rooms singly and so split the cost among several tenants. The overcrowded tenements were a hothouse for infectious diseases including TB.[78] The reported two-thirds reduction in TB mortality rates associated with the movement of Africans from Port Elizabeth to New Brighton was therefore achieved in part by the weeding out of the more susceptible members of the African population.

Not all residents of Korsten were poor, however. Many Africans who possessed the means to purchase land moved to Korsten because land could not be purchased in New Brighton. Thus many of the more permanent African residents of Port Elizabeth moved to Korsten. The population of New Brighton appears in fact to have been largely made up of employed migrant workers, who were not interested in purchasing land.[79] This predominance of migrants may also have helped lower TB mortality rates in New Brighton. For migrants were more apt to return to their rural homes when they became ill than were the more permanent residents of Korsten. Their deaths from TB would therefore not appear on New Brighton records.

The disaggregation of the African population of Port Elizabeth may well have influenced TB mortality rates in New Brighton in another way. The high rents charged to married men, together with low wages and restrictions on activities such as beer brewing, by which women frequently supplemented household incomes, discouraged many African families from settling in New Brighton.[80] Thus in 1904 the population of New Brighton was made up primarily of male workers. Women composed only 28 percent of the population. From the records of TB mortality between 1904 and 1912 it is apparent that women were at greater risk of dying from TB than were men. For the period as a whole the mortality rate for men was 5.3 per 1,000 while that for women was 6.8 per 1,000.[81] This difference, common during the early stages of a TB epidemic, when women between ages fifteen and fifty generally suffer higher mortality rates then do men of the same age,[82] may have been excentuated in South Africa by the differential application of pass laws. African men over sixteen were required to carry a pass indicating their place of employment. If a man contracted TB he would inevitably lose his job and not have the proper stamp in his passport. This made it difficult for male TB cases to continue living in the urban areas. By contrast women were not required to carry passes at this time and may therefore have been more likely to remain in the urban area.[83] If this is so, then female TB deaths would more likely be recorded than those occurring among men. Whatever caused women to have higher TB mortality rates than men, the tendency for married couples to avoid New Brighton reduced the percentage of women within the location's population below that of either Korsten or Port Elizabeth, and contributed to the lower level of TB mortality recorded in New Brighton in 1904.

A third factor that may have contributed to the recorded drop in New Brighton TB rates was the government's increased ability to control African settlement and movement within the newly created "native location." This control allowed for the collection of more accurate demographic data than was possible in the uncontrolled environment of either Port Elizabeth or Korsten and thus rendered a more accurate estimate of the actual population at risk of TB. African urban population figures during this period tended to underestimate the actual number of African residents, due to the frequent entry of unregistered African job seekers, and thus underestimated the population at risk.[84] For example, according to Port Elizabeth's city engineer, the population of the city remained stable between 1904 and 1918. Water usage, however, increased from 535,000 to 2 million gallons per day, indicating that the actual population had increased during this period.[85] There was thus a tendency for mortality rates to be inflated, since the denominators were too small. With better influx control the denominators would more accurately reflect the size of the population at risk and, in all likelihood, the resulting mortality rates would have been deflated. The lower TB mortality rates among Africans who moved to New Brighton may therefore simply reflect better record keeping. In short, better housing conditions and the provision of minimal health care was only part of the explanation for the initial decline in New Brighton's TB mortality rates.

Between 1904 and 1912 TB mortality rates in New Brighton fluctuated considerably, rising to 6.7 per 1,000 in 1905, then dropping sharply in 1906 and 1907, only to rise again to over 8 per 1,000 between 1908 and 1910. During the final two years the rate declined, reaching 4 per 1,000 in 1912. The average overall mortality rate was 5.9 for the nine-year period.[86] Although lower than the recorded rates for Port Elizabeth in 1903, this was still a very high mortality rate, indicating that conditions in New Brighton, while perhaps better than in some other locations, were still unhealthy. The provision of houses may have eliminated the shanties that characterized other locations, but it did not necessarily eliminate overcrowding since the high rents encouraged subletting. High rents and transportation costs, moreover, reduced food budgets and may have encouraged the consumption of less nutritious diets.

The fluctuations in New Brighton's TB mortality rate provide additional insights into the relationship between location conditions and the epidemiology of TB. Although the fluctuations may reflect variations in record keeping, they may have been shaped by changes in the composition and economic status of New Brighton's population.

Given the equation between overcrowding and the spread of TB, these fluctuations may reflect changes in availability of housing. In 1905, for example, in response to the conditions created in Korsten and other unregulated areas, legislation was passed (Native Reserves Location Amendment Act no. 8, 1905) which permitted the municipal authorities of Port Elizabeth to extend their control over these areas and to force more Africans into New Brighton. The population of New Brighton now grew from 2,332 in 1904 to 3,710 in 1905. Yet municipal authorities refused to make the necessary investment in location housing that this increase in population required. Pressure on the existing housing stock increased as a result, and overcrowding followed. TB mortality rose from 5.5 per 1,000 in 1904 to 7 per 1,000 in 1905. The population of New Brighton continued to grow, however, in 1906 and 1907, when the TB mortality rate dropped. Moreover, when the TB rate shot up again in 1908 and 1909, the population of New Brighton was declining, and when the population rose again at the end of the period, the TB rate dropped. It would thus appear that overcrowding may not have been a critical factor in determining fluctuations in the TB mortality rate.[87]

One factor that may have helped shape the TB mortality curve in New Brighton was the changing proportion of women in its population. Given their higher TB mortality rates during the period, increases in the proportion of women in the population would have led to increases in overall TB mortality rates. Conversely any decrease in the percentage of women in the population would have lowered TB mortality rates. There are, in fact, similar patterns in the changes in proportion of women in the population and in the overall mortality rate from TB in New Brighton. (Graph 5)

Related to the proportion of women in the population is the number of children. A large portion of the people contracting TB during this period were children. Although death rates were not divided by age, the medical officer for New Brighton reported in 1912 that 45 of the 107 cases of TB he had seen were children under fourteen years of age. This equals 42 percent of the cases. In the same year, children of this age made up only 27 percent of the African population.[88] This heightened risk for children is again common in the early stages of TB epidemics. Changes in the proportion of children in the location population, like changes in the percentage of women, would have affected overall TB mortality rates. One can assume that as the proportion of women in the population changed so did the population of children, and thus that the above relationship between percentage of women in the population and

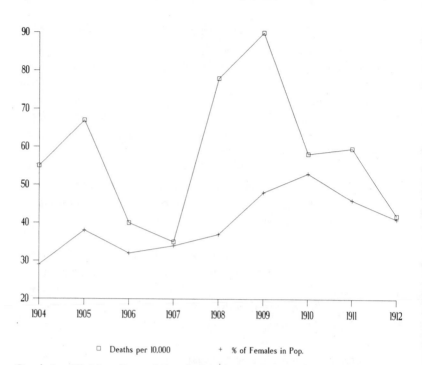

Graph 5.   TB Mortality and Female Population New Brighton, 1904–1912
   Source: U.G. 34–14, *Report of the Tuberculosis Commission,* Cape Town, 1914, p. 144.

TB mortality may reflect, in part, the changing proportion of children in the population. Unfortunately there are no figures to support this assumption, and a certain proportion of women may have been single or childless.

The sharp rise of TB mortality between 1907 and 1909 almost certainly was affected by declining economic conditions in Port Elizabeth. This decline was brought on by the depression in the mining industry on the Rand and the subsequent recession in shipping and related economic activities in Port Elizabeth. Similar rises occur in the figures for Johannesburg, Cape Town, and Durban at this time.

The relationship between economic downturns and rising TB rates, however, is complex. On the one hand, the overall rise in TB mortality during these years may have been caused in part by an increase in the proportion of women in the location population. This increase was caused by the movement of male migrant workers out of New Brighton, due presumably to unemployment associated with the recession, while the number of women in the population remained stable. On the other hand, the rates of both men and women rose dramatically during the recession, indicating that other factors were involved in the overall rise in TB mortality.

Declining employment opportunities and income during the depression made it more difficult for location residents, already living on a thin margin between income and expenses, to meet their financial requirements. Evictions increased and many residents fled the location, moving back into Port Elizabeth or into other less-regulated areas. For those who remained, food budgets were further reduced and with them the ability to resist tubercular infections. It is also possible, although no data is available on this, that declining incomes encouraged overcrowding as a means of making ends meet and that overcrowding may have increased despite an overall drop in population. As conditions improved after 1909, residents returned to New Brighton and TB rates declined, in part because of better conditions and in part due to a decrease in the proportion of women in the population. The sensitivity of TB rates to changing economic conditions within the urban areas of South Africa is a pattern we will observe again at several points in the history of TB and reflects the particular susceptibility of urban residents living on inadequate wages to even small fluctuations in the economy.

Finally, it is worth noting that although TB mortality rates for both men and women rose during the recession, the female rate rose much more sharply (a 121-percent increase for females versus a 72-percent increase for men). This suggests that women suffered more than men from recession conditions. The reasons for this difference, however, are unclear. It may be that women sacrificed their food for their children and therefore lowered their own resistance, while men may have had more access to food provided by employers. It should be noted that women in general have higher demands for resistance-building foods than men, especially during childbearing years; thus even if the decline in their food consumption was the same as that of men, they would have suffered more from the loss of important nutrients.

All in all an examination of TB mortality rates in New Brighton between 1905 and 1912 suggests that a number of factors shaped the epidemiology of TB in the newly created African townships of South Africa. Although overcrowding, lack of sanitation, and malnutrition may have played a role, shifts in age, sex, and socioeconomic status of location populations may have been of equal importance.

TB mortality rates for both Africans and whites began to tail off in

TABLE 2

AFRICAN TB MORTALITY WITHIN FIRST MONTH AFTER
DIAGNOSIS, JOHANNESBURG, 1906–1914

Year	Total TB Deaths	Deaths within First 3 Months	%
1906–1909	1129	241	21.0
1909–1911	810	109	13.4
1911–1912	433	31	7.1
1912–1913	374	39	10.4
1913–1914	410	31	7.3

the major urban centers toward the end of this period. There appears also to have been an improvement in the ability of Africans to control their infections. Data on the percentage of Africans diagnosed with TB who died within the first month after diagnosis collected by the chief medical officer of Johannesburg reveal a steady decline in early case mortality between 1906 and 1914.[89]

Although the increased longevity of African TB cases could have resulted from earlier diagnoses and better medical care, there is no evidence that such improvements occurred during this period or in fact until well after World War I. A more likely explanation is that in the wake of the depression years there was some improvement in employment opportunities and living conditions on the Rand and that Africans were better able to cope with their infections. At the same time, with the exception of mineworkers, the African population living in and around Johannesburg in 1912 was a relatively stable population, having settled on the Rand in the wake of the South African War. It may therefore have represented a more resistant population due to the loss of hereditarily susceptible members.

The tailing off of TB mortality among whites was more or less permanent, but the decline in African mortalities was temporary. With the onset of World War I and the rise of manufacturing industries, African urban settlement expanded, bringing thousands of new residents into urban centers that were unprepared for the rising tide of newcomers. This expansion was accompanied by a rise in African TB mortality.

CHAPTER III

Black Mineworkers and the Production of Tuberculosis, 1870–1914

Although the major urban centers of South Africa provided important foci for the initial spread of tuberculosis in southern Africa, it was the mines in Kimberley and especially on the Rand that were the major producers of tuberculosis prior to World War I.[1] The immense size of the mine labor force, over 200,000 on the Rand alone by 1910, together with the appalling health conditions that existed on the mines, ensured that they would play a central role in the early development of TB in southern Africa. Though African mortality rates from TB were generally lower on the mines than in Cape Town or Port Elizabeth during this period, reported mortality rates underestimate the actual toll TB took among African mineworkers. The mines repatriated African workers who fell ill, and thus much of the actual mortality from TB went unrecorded. By contrast African urban residents were more likely to die in town. In addition, a significant number of TB deaths were misdiagnosed as simple pneumonia during the early years of this century. The high incidence of pneumonia among African mineworkers, combined with the rapid progression of many TB cases, led medical authorities, who had little experience with rapidly progressing forms of TB, to diagnose TB deaths as cases of pneumonia.[2]

Almost every aspect of the industrial process that evolved in the mining industry prior to World War I, from the recruitment of labor, to the housing and feeding of the workforce, to the conditions under which the miners worked, contributed to the production of tuberculosis. These conditions in turn were shaped by the specific relationships that developed between mining capital, the state, and various segments of labor during the early years of the industry's existence.

LABOR RECRUITMENT AND WORKERS' HEALTH

The rapid expansion of the mining industry, from the end of the nineteenth century up to World War I, caused the demand for labor on all mines to exceed the available supply. As numerous studies have demonstrated, this generalized labor shortage was produced by African resistance to low wages and to the unhealthy, life-threatening living and working conditions on the mines, rather than by an absolute shortage of potential workers. These conditions and wages, in turn, were the product of the high capital costs of underground mining and the efforts of mining companies to reduce their overall expenditures by restricting their wage bills and other labor costs.[3] In order to acquire an adequate supply of African workers, mine owners employed a range of recruiting agencies, contractors, and touts to round up potential workers. Although efforts were made to regulate and centralize this recruiting process, they met with limited success in the face of intense competition among mining houses for a portion of the available labor supply. Intense competition, combined with the absence of centralized control over the recruitment process, led to the employment of workers who were unfit to cope with the physical assaults of mine life and who often succumbed to diseases, including tuberculosis, during the first months of their contracts. This was particularly true within the gold-mining industry.

During the early years of the gold-mining industry, mine managers frequently complained about the poor condition of the African recruits who arrived in their compounds. Scurvy, malaria, pneumonia, and general exhaustion were common problems among newly arrived workers. Those from the more distant tropical areas to the north, who traveled far distances and underwent a change in climate, were often in the worst shape. The poor health of newly recruited African workers was sometimes caused by conditions in their home areas. During 1903–1904, for example, drought destroyed the maize crops of African farmers in many areas of the northern Transvaal and Mozambique.[4] Recruits coming from these areas during the period arrived in poor condition and subsequently suffered high mortality rates from disease. More generally, however, the poor health of recruits was caused by the shortage of available labor and the failure of recruiters, who were competing for a share of the limited labor pool, to insure that the workers they sent were fit for mine work. This was a chronic problem throughout the period. Few labor contractors took the trouble to have their recruits examined by district surgeons, and most sent all but the most obviously sick and lame, including many recruits only marginally fit for mine labor. Although the recruiter's capitation fee depended on a recruit completing a minimum number of shifts, recruiters often took risks, sending unfit men in the hope that they would survive long enough to earn the recruiter his fee. As a district surgeon in Pondoland explained,

> Their attitude is more or less that of a gambler, and what they say in effect is this: "If the boy is rejected now the money advanced is (or may be) irrecoverable, so we may as well risk a little more (viz. the boy's railway fare), and perhaps, by some lucky chance he may work out his time, if not the usual six months, well then, two or three months, in which case if I make no profit at least I make no loss."[5]

Contractors who required their recruits to be examined by a physician before being forwarded to the mines may have reduced their losses, but it is unlikely that they improved the overall quality of labor going to the mines. The extreme competition for labor meant that a man who was rejected for medical reasons by one recruiter could almost always find employment through another recruiter who was less particular about who he put forward. In addition, recruits who were rejected on the mines were often forwarded again by another recruiter. Poor record keeping and an insatiable demand for workers discouraged efforts to eliminate this practice.[6]

The conditions under which African workers traveled to the Rand often compounded the problems created by recruiters failing to select their recruits carefully and contributed to the poor health of labor arriving at the mines. African workers who were sent in good health from the WNLA (Witwatersrand Native Labour Association) compound in Ressano Garcia, for example, often arrived sick in Johannesburg.[7] The poor condition of many recruits was caused by inadequate feeding. WNLA recruits were only given minimun rations during their journey to the Rand. Those recruited by contractors and touts were often not fed at all, expected instead to feed themselves out of their advance. Inasmuch as the advance was frequently used for other purposes, such as the payment of taxes, it was not uncommon for men to make the journey to the

Rand on an empty stomach. Reports of newly arrived workers gorging themselves on mealie meal in the WNLA compound attest to their deprivation during their journey.[8] Lack of food was particularly harmful to recruits who had to travel long distances by foot where no rail lines existed. Additional health problems were caused by overcrowding in train cars, steamers, and rest camps. The intermixing of healthy and sick recruits encouraged the spread of influenza and pneumonia as well as TB. Failure to provide adequate clothing for recruits from tropical areas coming to the Rand in winter also contributed to these diseases.[9]

The poor condition of many recruits arriving at the WNLA compound forced the Association to establish a hospital at its Johannesburg depot to care for sick newcomers. In addition, it adopted the practice of holding back weakened recruits from a fortnight to a month to increase their strength before forwarding them to the mine compounds. In many cases this precaution may have saved the life of a recruit weakened by his trip to the mines. Yet even a month's recuperation was not enough for some recruits. Such weakened recruits were often sent onto the mines anyway. According to the chief medical advisor to WNLA, this practice was justified on the grounds that keeping a sickly recruit in the WNLA compound too long was detrimental to his health, whereas the "regular work, good food and contentment" of the mines would make the "weakling strong."[10] In reality, of course, the cost of repatriating an unfit worker and the fear that high mortality rates within the WNLA compound would alarm both government officials and potential recruits, dictated sending unfit workers forward. Moreover, far from making the "weakling strong," exposure to the physical stresses of mine labor often caused such unfit recruits to succumb quickly to disease.

Men recruited by private contractors were brought directly to the mines and did not enjoy this recuperative period. Instead they were either rejected on the spot or put to work immediately, since the mine managers were generally unwilling to support the convalescence of an unfit and thus unproductive worker.[11]

Ultimately, a recruit's fitness for mine work was determined by medical officers on the Rand. Yet this line of defense, even during the best of times, was only partially effective in eliminating unfit workers. During periods of labor shortage it was totally ineffective.

Prior to the establishment of WNLA in 1900, the medical examination of recruits on the Rand was left up to individual mine managers who employed part-time medical officers to examine their workers. There was no established criteria for certifying the fitness of workers, and standards fluctuated greatly between mines as well as at individual mines over time in line with the mine's current labor needs. A worker who was rejected by one mine would simply seek work at another where the medical officer was less demanding or the mine manager in greater need of labor.

With the establishment of the WNLA compound at Johannesburg in 1902, an effort was made to require that all recruited workers undergo a standardized physical examination and meet a minimum level of fitness before being allotted to individual mines. This attempt to control the quality of labor was largely unsuccessful, for several reasons. First, voluntary workers were not required to pass through the WNLA compound and thus avoided the examination process. Second, individual mines continued to employ private recruiters and touts to secure workers. These non-WNLA recruits also bypassed the WNLA compound. Third, the standard of fitness required of workers who passed through the WNLA compound was not particularly high. The association, after all, was in the business of providing recruits and, having laid out the expense of transportation, feeding, and advances, costs often irrecoverable, WNLA was reticent to reject workers who arrived in its compound. Dr. W. H. Brodie, medical advisor to WNLA, observed for example that he did not keep back African workers who were suffering from scurvy, "for if they are fit otherwise they can work and are as well fed at the mines as in your compound."[12] The high mortality rate from scurvy on the mines, noted later, suggests that the diets in neither place were adequate. The willingness of WNLA to pass on recruits of questionable fitness led on numerous occasions to disputes between the WNLA medical officers and individual mine managers, who wished to avoid hiring workers who might succumb quickly to disease. For example, in 1904 Dr. Miller, medical officer of East Rand Property Mines (ERPM), received an allotment of 106 Africans workers who had been passed as fit for underground employment by the WNLA medical officer. Dr. Miller complained that the workers were in poor condition and only fit for surface work and that ten were suffering from "phthisis pulmonalis." The ten workers in question were then returned to the WNLA compound, where they were again certified as fit and sent out to another mine.[13]

WNLA's attempt at creating a centralized examination procedure, flawed as it was, broke down completely by 1907. A sharp downturn in the number of African recruits coming to the mines from September 1905 to July 1906, combined with the formation of the Liberal government in England, dedicated to ending the use of Chinese labor, raised the specter of a labor crisis in the minds of Chamber of Mines officials. This in turn set off a scramble for labor and a major rise in both recruiting by individual mines and the use of private recruiting companies. By the end of 1906, WNLA recruiters had been largely driven out of their recruiting areas in the South African colonies.[14] The perceived labor shortage also made mine managers less particular about the quality of mine labor, and the overall standard of labor declined. TB mortality rates on the mines at the same time rose dramatically, though as will be seen, other factors were involved in this rise.

The decline in quality of recruited labor and the rising mortality of African labor on the mines was one factor that caused the Transvaal government's Native Affairs Department to enter the recruiting field after 1907, leading to the establishment of the Government Native Labour Bureau (GNLB), created to supervise the recruitment of labor in British South Africa. The GNLB established agreements with the Cape Colony for the recruitment of African labor from the heavily populated Transkei and Ciskei areas and worked to reestablish a degree of centralized control over the recruitment process. In line with this effort, it established labor depots at Germiston and Driehoek for the reception of all recruited labor.[15] As in the WNLA compound, which continued to serve as a clearinghouse for Mozambican and tropical labor, recruits were subjected to a medical examination before being sent out to individual mines. Though this reintroduced some degree of standardization in the examination process, examinations at the government depots were cursory at best. As Dr. B. G. Brock, government medical officer at Driehoek, stated in testimony before the Tuberculosis Commission, he sometimes examined up to nine hundred recruits a day. He was often under pressure, moreover, to pass the workers on to the mines as fast as possible and had to get through all the examinations in as little as three and a half hours. That worked out to one examination every twenty seconds![16] Yet even this cursory exam appeared to suit the needs of most mine managers during this period. When asked how the system worked, he replied that "I get very few back."[17] This however was less a measure of his superior ability to detect defective workers than the fact that the mines, in line with their increased effort to reestablish centralized control over recruitment, had agreed to allow the government medical officer (GMO) to have final word in determining the fitness of recruited workers. Mines that rejected workers passed by the GMO had to pay for their repatriation. This did not eliminate the role of individual mine medical officers, but it certainly limited their ability to act as independent examiners. Such a system could not have worked, however, without some sort of understanding between the GMOs and the mine managers as to the latter's labor needs and fitness standards. Although Brock claimed he made no adjustment in the standards he applied to the labor of particular mines—and in fact felt it was safer not to know where workers were sent after the examination— he noted in later testimony that, "You get boys back before you get to know the standards of medical officers and before they get to know your standards."[18]

All in all, medical examinations on the Rand prior to World War I failed to prevent the employment of physically unfit workers whose resistance to disease was from the outset compromised. There can be little doubt, moreover, that the willingness of recruiters to gamble on recruiting unhealthy workers was encouraged by their knowledge that the medical standards applied to new recruits on the Rand were at best flexible. With time the successful recruiter would learn just what standards were being applied at particular mines or in the WNLA or GNLB depots.

The poor condition of recruits when they arrived at the mines helps explain the high incidence of TB among African mineworkers during their first months of employment. In a follow-up study of 1,200 cases of TB between 1912 and 1914, 25 percent of the cases occurred within the first three months of mine employment.[19]

Yet the poor physical condition of African mine recruits when they arrived at the mines does not by itself account for the high toll TB took among African mineworkers prior to World War I. Conditions on the mines played an equally important role in the production of TB.

MINING CONDITIONS AND TUBERCULOSIS

New recruits who arrived on the Rand and in Kimberley throughout this period ran a high risk of being infected with TB. Though it is impossible to state with certainty how TB established itself on the mines, it is likely that it arrived along with the skilled European miners who came to work them. Like other Europeans of their day, immigrant miners often carried with them tubercular infections acquired in childhood. Under the conditions of gold mining, described below, many of these miners developed silicosis, a disease characterized by fibrosis of the lungs due to the inhalation of silicious dust. This condition contributed to the activation of dormant foci of tubercular infection.[20] Although the conjunction of silicosis and TB was originally believed to retard the active spread of tuberculosis within European miners, many broke down and developed infective cases of the disease. In the vast majority of cases, in fact, it was the tuberculosis that ultimately killed the silicotic white gold miner. Before he died, however, he often became a source of infection to his fellow miners, both African and white.

Mine managers naturally objected to any claim that African workers acquired their infection while on the mines, arguing instead that TB was common in the rural areas from which African workers were recruited and that recruits who came down with TB had brought their infections with them.[21] This theory not only ran counter to general medical opinion (that Africans in their rural homes were relatively free of the disease) but also conflicted with the results of tuberculin surveys conducted between 1910 and 1912 among men from Basutoland, Nyasaland, and Mozambique. These tests indicated that men who had worked the mines had higher positivity rates than men who had not.[22]

Conditions in the mineshafts facilitated the spread of TB between infected and noninfected workers. Laboring closely together in narrow, poorly ventilated stopes, for long hours, provided ample opportunity for tubercular miners who were coughing and expectorating bacilli-laden sputum to infect their fellow workers. In 1910 axial water-fed

TABLE 3

TB INFECTION RATES AND EXPOSURE TO MINE WORK,
1910–1912[23]

Sample	No. Tested	No. Positive	% Positive
Basuto (mine experience)	222	81	36.0
Basuto (no mine experience)	181	28	15.5
Mozambique (mine experience)	63	11	17.5
Mozambique (no mine experience)	415	7	1.7
Nyassa (mine experience)	52	10	19.0
Nyassa (no mine experience)	129	6	4.0

drills were introduced, designed to reduce the incidence of silicosis by emitting a fine moist spray that cut down on atmospheric dust. The new drills further facilitated the transmission of tubercular bacilli, however, by increasing the humidity of the air in the stopes.[24]

African mineworkers who acquired tuberculosis in this manner be-came foci for the further spread of TB within the overcrowded barracks typical of the vast majority of mining compounds during this period. Tuberculosis, it must be remembered, is not a highly infectious disease, and thus the rate at which it spreads within a host population is directly related to the frequency with which unaffected individuals are exposed to sources of infection. The type of sleeping arrangements provided in the mine compounds of the Rand and Kimberley insured that healthy workers were subjected to multiple exposures and thus ran a high risk of becoming infected.

At Kimberley during the early years of compound construction the authorized space per man in a barracks was 600 cubic feet and the minimum space required for good health was estimated to be 300 cubic feet. Actual space provided, however, was often much less and was identified as a primary cause of the extraordinarily high mortality rates from disease experienced by African workers in the compounds. Dennis Doyle, the sanitary inspector for Kimberley Central, estimated that 1 in every 15 miners in the barracks was sick in 1883. With the introduction of closed compounds designed to establish greater control over the mobility of African labor and to reduce illicit diamond buying, over-crowding grew worse and overall death rates climbed from 80 per 1,000 in 1878 to over 100 per 1,000 ten years later.[25] By 1913, when the TB commission visited the DeBeers Diamond Mines at Kimberley, the situa-tion had apparently not improved despite claims to the contrary by compound managers. The commission noted that there were more in-mates than bunks in the barracks they visited, "so that many had to sleep on the floor or else outside in the open."[26] At the Jagersfontein Diamond Mine in the Orange Free State, the commission also found extreme overcrowding in the compounds.

> A large proportion of the boys have to sleep outside in the yards, but even then they could not accommodate all of the boys, but for the fact that there are always a third or a half, as the case may be, out on shift. Thus day and night they are always overcrowded . . . [27]

The official capacity of the Jagersfontein compound was about 1,600, whereas the actual number of workers housed was 3,900. The mine managers noted that the overcrowding of the mine compound resulted from the commencement of underground mining following the exhaustion of surface deposits in 1910. As an underground mine, Jagersfontein was subject to Cape labor regulations that reduced the length of shifts from twelve hours to eight hours. In order to maintain production, the mine owners simply hired more workers so that they could run three shifts of eight hours instead of two of twelve hours each. This resulted in a one-third increase in the workforce without any increase in compound space.[28] Respiratory diseases, including TB and pneumonia, took a significant jump following these changes, the annual incidence of TB going from 4.03 per 1,000 between 1903 and 1909 to 6.22 per 1,000 in 1911–1912. Though part of the increase may have been due to the changed nature of work, it was no doubt also related to overcrowding.[29]

From a respiratory-disease viewpoint the Kimberley compounds were also detrimental to the health of mineworkers due to inadequate heating. This problem also affected miners on the Rand.[30]

As Jeeves, Wilson, and Johnstone[31] have all noted, the housing of African mineworkers on the Rand during the early years of this century was hardly better than that at Kimberley. Early compounds were little more than wood and iron shacks that housed as many as twenty to fifty workers sleeping on concrete or wooden bunks built like shelves without any partitions between them. The arrangement was almost ideally suited for the transmission of tubercular infection.

Staggering mortality rates, exceeding 100 per 1,000 among tropical workers in 1902 and 1903—together with the prospect of importing a large number of Chinese workers to counter African resistance to mine work and the British government's concern that the mortality experience of African workers not be repeated with the Chinese—led to the establishment of a commission to look into the working and living conditions at the mines in 1904. The Coloured Labour Commission was primarily concerned with housing conditions, particularly with the cubic air space to be allotted to black laborers in the mine compounds of the Witwatersrand District.[32]

The commission went to great lengths to measure carbon dioxide levels in various types of huts at the mines and to determine the relationship between those levels and the cubic air space provided for each inhabitant. This inquiry was based on a theory of contagion that wrongly linked the spread of disease to high levels of carbon dioxide. A minority report authored by George Turner, MOH for the Transvaal, argued that a limit of 300 cubic feet per occupant should be established for compounds on the Rand, noting in addition that the proximity of inhabitants to one another was as important as cubic air space.[33] This view was staunchly opposed by the Chamber of Mines for obvious financial reasons. As Sam Evans of H. Eckstein and Co., holding company for Rand Mines Ltd., noted at the time:

> I believe there is a majority on the Commission opposed to Turner's views. Of course, if 300 cubic feet of air space has to be provided in the compound for the Chinese, the Kaffirs will soon have to be treated in the same manner, with the result that every mine on the Rand will be put to enormous expenditure in providing additional compound accommodation.[34]

The general manager of Rand Mines, where the average cubic air space per inhabitant was 107, estimated that the cost difference between meeting a 200 cubic foot requirement versus a 300 cubic foot one was £50,236. To achieve a basic air space of 150 cubic feet per occupant would cost £23,408. Overall, it was estimated that the 300 cubic foot requirement would have cost the mining industry one and a quarter million pounds.[35]

Fortunately for the mine owners, the majority report of the commission concluded that 200 cubic feet per occupant was adequate and that the high mortality rates at the mines in 1903–1904 were less a product of overcrowding than of other factors including a particularly harsh winter, the large number of new "raw" recruits, poor nutrition, and exposure to cold after coming up from the ground. The report advocated the recruitment of more experienced miners who had been acclimatized to the conditions of mine work and appeared to have a lower death rate. It also recommended a more gradual introduction of tropical recruits into mine work.[36] These conclusions focused attention away from the problem of overcrowding and permitted the mines to continue their standard of 200 cubic feet per occupant.

The findings of the majority report concerning the role of overcrowding and the minimum level of space required for good health were both misguided and founded on a fundamental misunderstanding of the problem. Measurements of cubic air space per occupant as noted above were a product of a prebacteria era theory of contagion,[37] of little relevance when, as was the case in all compounds, the occupants slept in close proximity to one another in stacked bunks, or huddled together for warmth on cold nights because barracks were inadequately heated.[38] The Chamber of Mines, in a classic example of "victim blaming," cited the latter practice as evidence of the futility of increasing the cubic air space standard: "It is a well-known fact that the natives prefer a crowded room, and, however much air space is provided, insist upon huddling together."[39]

The same theory of contagion, with its fetish for reducing carbon dioxide levels, caused medical authorities to require that compounds be adequately ventilated. As Alan Jeeves notes, the construction of the "Rand Hut" with large ventilators at either end[40] produced cold drafts during the winter months and was a contributing factor in the epidemiology of respiratory diseases in the compounds. It encouraged, moreover, the practice of huddling together for warmth noted above and thus further facilitated the transmission of infection. It is interesting to note that sickness rates were frequently lower in the older barracks. From the Commission's point of view these were unfit for habitation, yet in fact they were much less drafty than the newer, better constructed, but "ventilated" huts.[41]

In 1913 when Colonel William Gorgas was invited by Sam Evans, chairman of the Crown Mines Company, to inspect conditions on the Rand and make recommendations for lowering mortality rates, overcrowding remained a major problem. Gorgas strongly criticized the housing of large numbers of men in close proximity to one another and, citing his experience in fighting pneumonia in Panama, suggested that mineworkers be housed with their families in separate huts so that there was no close contact between infected and noninfected workers. This idea was rejected for reasons to be discussed in chapters 6 and 7, and improvements in the housing of workers would only begin to occur after the war.

While overcrowding in mine compounds facilitated the transmission of tubercular infections among African mineworkers, pre–World War I diet and working conditions at the mines undermined the ability of infected workers to control their infections, thus contributing to the production of TB cases and deaths.

Patterns of food consumption among the African mineworkers, like housing, reflected the mine owners' efforts to reduce labor costs as far possible. During the early years at Kimberley, mineworkers purchased their own rations from local merchants. With the creation of closed compounds, self-rationing continued. The African mineworkers were required to purchase their provisions from company stores, however, which in turn were supplied by local merchants. This arrangement was established by the Labor Wage Regulation Act of 1887, the product of a compromise between the mine owners' desire for closed compounds and the interests of local white merchants who feared that closed compounds would lead the mines to develop their own sources to feed their workers and thereby eliminate the merchants' lucrative market in food sales.[42] The compromise resulted in the elimination of competition and an increase in the price that mineworkers paid for rations, despite the mines ability to purchase in bulk.

The TB commission estimated that the cost of an adequate diet for an African mineworker at Kimberley in 1912 was one shilling per day. This represented, at the time, roughly one-third of an African worker's wages. Many mineworkers felt they could not afford to spend such a large portion of wages on food and chose to reduce their consumption in order to save money for other uses. According to the superintendent of the DeBeers Ltd. compound, the unwillingness of mineworkers to spend their wages on food was indicated by their refusal to patronize a restaurant he established to sell "well-cooked meat-meals" for six pence. The compound restaurants had to be closed down for lack of patrons.[43]

The impact of reduced outlays for food on the health of diamond miners is difficult to determine without more information on the composition of diets and on the cost of various diet staples. There does appear to be a correlation, however, between the unwillingness or inability of certain groups of workers to allocate money for food and the incidence of scurvy, which was high throughout this period, occasionally reaching epidemic proportions.[44] Thus the TB commission found that the three groups that were the "meanest" in terms of purchasing food supplies— Africans from Bechuanaland, Basutoland, and the Cape Province—were also the three groups with the highest incidence of scurvy. In addition, the overall incidence of scurvy among underground workers at DeBeers between 1903 and 1912 was 478 per 100,000, while that for surface workers, who worked in less strenuous jobs, was 510 per 100,000. The higher incidence of this disease among surface workers may well reflect their lower wages and a corresponding reduction in their food consumption, though it should be noted that mines often placed less fit recruits in surface jobs.[45]

In contrast to Kimberley, mine managers on the Rand from the outset chose to feed their African workers and include the cost of food as part of their overall wage package. This practice was resented by many mineworkers since it reduced their spendable income. The mine owners, however, argued that from a medical standpoint the distribution of standardized rations ensured that mineworkers received an adequate diet and did not skimp on food expenditures.[46] Although this policy made good sense in theory, in actual practice, mine diets were notoriously inadequate for the needs of mineworkers throughout this period.

Prior to 1905 there was no regulation of the rations provided by individual mines. The average diet consisted of little more than mealie served in the evening after the shift with perhaps coffee and a biscuit in the morning prior to going into the shaft. No mine provided a midshift meal, although some attempted to provide their workers with food to take underground and eat during the shift. At the Crown Mines, S. K. McKenzie experimented with several different rations during this period. Hot cocoa and army biscuits, beans and mealie, flour and fat dumplings, and sandwiches were all tried. The mineworkers generally rejected these efforts, stating that they did not wish "to eat in a hole like rats." They complained, moreover, that the food was affected by the noxious mining gases and tasted of the mines. Thus the only way mine managers could provide their workers with a midshift meal was to treat them like white workers and bring them to the surface. This was considered too costly in terms of lost shift time and was rejected as unfeasible.[47]

The pattern of food consumption and the poor quality of the diet meant that most mineworkers were woefully underfed and often worked for long hours on a near-empty stomach. As a result, the high-energy demands of mine labor, especially toward the end of a shift, were not being adequately met, causing physiological stress. In at least one case, mine managers were reported to have withheld food as a punishment.[48] More generally, "compound-police boys" who supervised the distribution of food were reported to use the distribution of food to enforce their own authority, rewarding their supporters with additional rations and punishing those who met their disfavor with smaller rations.[49]

The absence of fresh vegetables and meat from the average Rand diet led to serious vitamin deficiencies and, as at Kimberley, to a high incidence of scurvy. Between November 1902 and April 1905 there were 186 deaths from scurvy among African mineworkers on the Rand.[50] Mine managers argued that much of the scurvy on the mines during the early years of this century reflected the inadequacy of kraal diets. Scurvy resulted, in effect, from mineworkers arriving at the mines in a subscorbutic condition. The mine managers argued further that the mineworker was consequently better off from a dietary point of view on the mines than in his kraal. There may well have been some truth to these claims during years of drought and famine in the rural areas, such as occurred in the northern Transvaal and Mozambique during 1902–1903. Yet data on the incidence of scurvy at the mines suggested that in most years it was the mine diet, in conjunction with excessive energy requirements of mine work, that was the main cause of scurvy on the Rand.[51]

As with all sickness, the mines attempted to repatriate workers with manifest scurvy before they died, arguing, as we will see later, that the sick "native" did better in his home surroundings. The argument in this case directly contradicted the claim that mine diets were better than those in the kraals and lays bare the underlying reason for quick repatriation—the desire to keep mortality rates on the mines down. As a result of this policy, many African mineworkers arrived in their home district with advanced cases of scurvy or died from the disease before reaching home.[52] The following testimony, taken from an African worker returning to Lesotho in 1902, vividly describes what was a recurrent experience.

> I am a labourer and have until lately been working in Johannesburg. . . . On Thursday 11th instant I, accompanied by deceased Matebo Ramapiai and 2 other natives left Johannesburg en route for Basutoland. Deceased was ailing when leaving and grew rapidly worse on journey [sic]. On our arrival at Bloemfontein Station on morning of 12th instant he was unable to descend from carriage and we carried him, intending to take him to some shelter, where he could remain till departure of the train for Sannah's Post. We laid him down at the corner of the wire fence near the goods shed, here he grew rapidly weaker and expired at 2 pm. We reported it to the Native Railways Constables, who conducted us to a I.R.C. who ordered the removal of the body to the hospital.[53]

A second witness reported that the deceased had worked for the Henry Nourse G. M. Co. and that they had been fed on "mealie meal and meat once a week."

In 1903 a committee of mine medical officers headed by Drs. Irvine and Macauley made recommendations for lowering mortality at the mines. Among their suggested reforms was a proposal to establish a minimum standard diet. Appealing to the mine owners economic interests, they argued that "provision of an adequate diet is a matter of the simplest commercial economy, in that it not only reduces the incidence of disease . . . but it secures the maximum output of efficient labor from those who are at work."[54]

The recommended diet was largely adopted as a standard scale by the medical officer of the Native Affairs Department and gazetted in June 1906. The diet established under this regulation included the following provisions.

2 lb mealie meal, or 1½ lb of army biscuits per day

2 lb of bone free meat, or 2 lb of fish per week

1 lb soup meat per week

1 lb of vegetables per week

1 lb of sugar or treacle per week

½ oz salt per day.

Although this diet represented a considerable improvement over earlier ration scales, mine rations remained woefully inadequate in relation to the high-energy demands of mine work. As Gorgas noted in his report to the Chamber of Mines in 1913:

> I have never seen so large a portion of the ration supplied by one article as is here supplied by mealie meal. The two chief components of the daily ration are 2 lbs. of mealie meal and 6.85 oz of meat. This I think is too large a portion of carbohydrates for men doing hard manual labor that the natives do.[55]

It was particularly deficient in fats and protein.[56] Moreover, the bulk of the diet continued to be consumed in one meal.

The continued lack of adequate amounts of fresh vegetables meant that scurvy remained a problem, even though deaths from scurvy declined. For every case of manifest scurvy that occurred, moreover, there were undoubtedly hundreds of cases where a subscorbutic condition existed. As noted in chapter 2, vitamin C deficiency has been shown in a number of studies elsewhere to be a significant cofactor in the etiology of TB.

The deficiencies in the dietary intake of African miners may have been exacerbated by the inadequate sanitation in the mine compounds and the absence of sanitary facilities within the mines themselves. This encouraged the transmission of intestinal parasites that, as we have seen, reduced the nutritional level of those infected.

In the mines themselves, mineworkers had no choice but to defecate in corners. Parasites in their stools were released into the surface water that had been introduced to reduce dust levels, and the parasites were transferred to new hosts. Hookworm was a particular problem during these years. It was estimated that between 50 and 60 percent of the recruits from tropical areas were infected with ankylostomes when they arrived on the Rand. During the early years of outcrop mining the acidic character of water in the mines, together with relatively low temperatures, are said to have prevented the development of hookworm larvae and thus reduced chances for transmission. With the onset of deep-level mining, however, these conditions changed. The water in deep-level mines was more alkaline and temperatures were higher. As a result the incidence of hookworm rose dramatically as the depth of mining operations increased in both Kimberley and the Rand. Infected miners developed a progressing anemia along with dyspepsia, possible vomiting, and constipation followed by diarrhea. In many cases hookworms were found in association with both pneumonia and tuberculosis upon autopsy.[57]

Other parasites were transmitted as a result of the mineworkers drinking contaminated surface water in the mines. These parasites drained nutrients from infected miners and were thus possible cofactors in the etiology of TB. The failure of most mines to provide safe sources of drinking water encouraged this practice.[58]

Along with dietary deficiencies exacerbated by parasitic infections, working conditions in the mines further undermined the ability of African mineworkers to control their tubercular infection. These conditions grew progressively worse, moreover, as the depth of mining operations increased.

Data on the relationship between overtime employment and the incidence of TB on the coal mines of the Transvaal suggests that the number of hours worked underground by the average African mineworker was an important factor in the etiology of TB. The average shift on the coal mines, as on the gold, was twelve hours. Drillers could usually complete their task in less time, while those involved in filling and tramming seldom worked less than twelve hours. During periods of heavy production or labor shortages, moreover, workers frequently put in overtime, meaning shifts could reach fifteen to eighteen hours. Periods in which overtime was worked appear to have produced higher TB rates than periods for which little or no overtime was worked. (Table 4)

Although these classifications are rough, they suggest that excessive hours of labor were detrimental to the health of African mineworkers and contributed to the incidence of TB on the mines. In this regard it is worth citing the TB commission's observation that up until about 1910 African workers on the Rand frequently worked double shifts.[59] Ideally, one would like to have data on the TB rates of different occupational groups since it appears that drillers, or "hammer boys" were usually able to complete their task in the shortest period of time and would be expected to have lower TB rates if length of shift played a role. This effect might be obscured, however, by the drillers' higher exposure to

TABLE 4

EFFECT OF OVERTIME ON TB INCIDENCE, TRANSVAAL
COLLIERIES, 1909–1911
(Repatriations and Mortality per 1,000 Employed)

	Repatriations	Mortality
Witbank Colliery		
1909 (Overtime very heavy every month)	16.31	7.85
1910 (No overtime last six months of year)	8.52	4.59
1911 (Overtime frequently worked)	14.02	8.01
Transvaal and Delagoa Bay Colliery		
1909 (No overtime)	1.77	3.54
1910 (Overtime last six months)	6.62	1.32
1911 (Overtime continuous)	17.88	7.15

a. The low mortality rate for 1910 may reflect the residual effect of overtime on TB. In other words, overtime weakened workers who fell victim to TB but did not die during this year. Thus overtime during the last six months of 1910 may have contributed to both the repatriation and mortality rates for 1911.

b. *Report of the Tuberculosis Commission*, p. 191.

siliceous dust. Like most of the adverse working conditions in the mines, length of actual work day, measured from the time a worker left the compound till he returned, grew as the depth of mining operations increased.

Simply getting to the shaftface on the Rand could be an arduous experience, lowering a worker's resistance to disease, especially in winter. In a number of cases mine compounds were located at some distance from the mineshaft. At New Modderfontein, for example, the shaft was a fifteen- to twenty-minute walk from the compound. On arriving at the mineshaft, workers in deep mines often waited an hour or more before entering the cages to be lowered down the shaft. Since few mines provided shelters prior to 1911, this waiting was done in the open, exposing the mineworkers, who wore little clothing because of the high temperatures underground, to the risk of chill.[60] At older outcrop mines, the mineworkers could descend directly without this waiting period.

Once underground the mineworkers began their shift by clearing debris from the previous days blasting. When this was done and the white miners had arrived, the drilling of holes for dynamite charges began. Prior to the introduction of machine drills this was done by hand by African mineworkers, who were paid for completing holes that met a minimum depth requirement. Minimum depth averaged thirty-six inches, but prior to 1910 it was occasionally as much as forty-eight inches. Miners who drilled more than the minimum were paid a bonus, thus encouraging African mineworkers to labor longer hours. Workers who failed to meet the minimum were given a "loafers" ticket and not paid for the shift. The work, involving the hammering of sharp steel bits into the ore face, was carried out in hot, poorly ventilated stopes and was generally exhausting.[61] The process produced considerable amounts of dust, moreover, which in the long run contributed to the development of silicosis. While these conditions were bad, they became worse after 1890 with the introduction of machine drills and the increasing depth of mining operations.

Prior to 1910 machine drills were used primarily for development work. Based on a reciprocating-piston principle, they produced large quantities of atmospheric dust, specifically silicious dust that hung in the air of the poorly ventilated mineshafts. The increased use of reciprocating drills from the turn of the century was accompanied by a rise in the incidence of silicosis. During the early years of this century this disease was identified primarily in white miners and was not associated with Africans. This racial division did not, however, reflect differences in exposure to siliceous dust. Whites had better access to medical care and thus were more likely to be diagnosed as having the disease. In addition white miners worked much longer periods of continuous service in the mines; Africans for the most part worked relatively short contracts from three to nine months separated by extended periods away from the mines. Thus, although all mineworkers were exposed equally to the risks of silicosis while working on the Rand, the period of exposure to this risk was normally much greater for white workers than for Africans. Mozambican workers, who often worked for longer contracts and spent less time at home between contracts, had predictably higher rates of silicosis than other groups of African mineworkers during this period.[62] Whether or not a mineworker was diagnosed as having silicosis, exposure to siliceous dust increased the risk of developing TB. As the report of the 1938 Conference on Silicosis in Geneva noted, "the effective occupation of the lungs by silicious dust not only leads to fibrosis but facilitates the development of tuberculosis, either at sites of pre-existing dormant foci of tuberculosis, or at sites where silicotic lesions are developing or have developed at which tubercle bacilli may arrive and become arrested."[63]

The problem of atmospheric dust grew as the depth of mining operations increased. For there was a tendency for deeper mines to decrease the number of shafts in proportion to the number of claims being worked. As the secretary of mines noted in 1906,

> This practice . . . is no doubt largely the result of the enormous cost attendant on sinking shafts to great depths, but, on the other hand, it has increased and will continue to increase the difficulty experienced in effectively ventilating the miners working in these mines.[64]

The problem of silicosis together with pressure from white miners led the mine managers to employ large quantities of water to wet down operations and reduce dust levels in the mines. This was difficult, however, when working on the upper surfaces of the stopes and with the winches. In 1910 axial-feed water drills began to be introduced. These emitted a fine spray of water that reduced to some degree the dust produced by the drills. Yet the extensive use of water, as noted above, increased the humidity of the mines. This in turn increased opportunities for the spread of tubercular infection as well as the incidence of heat stroke.[65] It also caused the mineworkers clothing to become soaked from both perspiration and water. This became a serious health problem once the mineworkers left the mine face to return to the surface. The mineworkers would frequently have to walk several hundred feet up an incline to the foot of the mineshaft, sometimes carrying drills weighing thirty pounds. This further increased their overheated condition.[66] Once they reached the foot of the shaft they had to wait to be hauled to the surface. This could take several hours since in many cases the cages that lowered and raised mineworkers were replaced with skips for raising ore during the day. In order to avoid delays in switching back and forth from cages to rock haulers, black workers were not hauled back to the surface until the rock was removed.[67] This delay exposed the overheated miners to cold downdrafts and predisposed them to chill.

Where possible, miners sometimes preferred to climb out of the mine rather than face the delay in hauling. This, however, was an exhausting exercise. Describing the effects of this practice on the health of African workers at the Robinson Mine, where African workers at the thousand-foot level could walk out of the mines, the TB commission noted,

The condition of some boys arriving on the surface was one of very marked physical stress. They were staggering, breathing rapidly and with obvious difficulty, nostrils expanded, pupils dilated and pulse very rapid. . . . A boy brought to this extremity would not return to his normal condition for a long time, and while in this state is not in a fit state to take his evening meal and would be liable to go down under an infection which normally he would be able to resist.[68]

Even if the mineworkers did not have to wait in the drafty mineshaft and were transported immediately to the surface in a cage, the temperature differentiation between the interior of the mines and the surface air, especially in winter, and the soaked conditions of the miners clothing, created a serious threat of chill. Again, the absence of shelters or changing houses at most mines prior to 1911 meant mineworkers had to wait until they got back to the compound to change into dry clothes and escape the exposure to cold air. This was delayed, however, by the practice of stamping work tickets on the surface following each shift.

The use of changing houses became an issue in 1906 in line with the wider inquiry into colored labor health regulations. A special committee was established to investigate the problem of changing houses at the mines. Composed of Dr. Charles Samson, nominated by the NAD, and Drs. L. Irvine and H. Ross Skinner, nominated by the Chamber of Mines, the committee took testimony from mine managers concerning the feasibility of requiring all mines to provide changing houses.[69] Although most managers agreed that some form of shelter was useful for reducing the problem of exposure, few were willing to recommend that shelters provide facilities for bathing or changing into dry clothes. Changing houses were said to be unworkable, since the "native worker" would not make use of them, and it would be both difficult and costly, in terms of both supervision and lost shift time, to organize a change of clothing for each of several thousand workers every day. Changing houses were also problematic because many mineworkers did not have adequate supplies of clothes. Requiring mines to provide changing houses therefore would demand the provision of adequate clothing, for which few mine managers were willing to pay unless the cost was deducted from the mineworkers' wages. This deduction, they argued, would make the system difficult to enforce because the African miners would refuse to spend their own money on the extra clothing. Some managers further argued that changing houses were simply unnecessary since the men could change once they got back to the compound. As for the problem of traveling a considerable distance in inclimate weather, one manager observed that this could be avoided by simply having the workers run back to the barracks.

> I do not agree with the change house [sic] at all. The Natives themselves are not in accord with it. They have no use for it . . . get the nigger out, let him come out of the shaft and keep him on the move until he gets home.[70]

The fact that running already-exhausted workers to the compound would increase their risk of contracting pneumonia or other respiratory conditions, was blissfully ignored.

As a result of these discussions, the idea of changing houses was dropped and a regulation requiring the provision of simple shelters was implemented in 1911. The problem of chill was therefore left largely ignored until after World War I.

The chill factor was particularly debilitating for workers coming from tropical areas, whose numbers increased significantly between 1906 and 1912 in order to overcome shortages in local labor supplies. These workers suffered greatly from respiratory diseases, and particularly from TB and pneumonia.

The problem of inadequate ventilation, dust, high heat and humidity, length of shift, exposure to chill, as well as risk of hookworm infection, all increased as the depth of mining operations increased from an average stoping depth of 800 feet in 1889 to 1600 feet by 1916. It is not surprising therefore to find that the incidence of TB among African workers appears to have been greater in the deeper mines.

The incidence in 1916 of TB in mines with an average working depth of less than 2500 feet was 6.73 per 1,000, while the rate in mines of a depth exceeding 2500 feet was 10.77 per 1,000. The latter figure, however, is skewed by one mine with a rate of 24.79 per 1,000. If this mine is eliminated the mean for mines with a depth over 2500 feet was 8.44 per 1,000, which is still 25 percent higher than for mines under 2500 feet. The figures for 1917, which are more consistent, show a greater difference: 6.37 per 1,000 for the shallower mines compared to 11.91 per 1,000 for the deeper mines. In 1917, therefore, the risk of contracting TB while working the mines was 87 percent higher if one worked in the deeper mines.[71] A comparison of TB rates at outcrop and deep mines during the period from 1910–1912 suggests a similar relationship. These figures indicate that while there was little difference between the TB rates of outcrop and deep mines in 1910, the rates for 1911 and 1912 were 43 and 35 percent higher, respectively, at the deep mines. For three years the average incidence of TB at the deep mines was 25 percent

TABLE 5

COMPARISON OF DEATHS AND REPATRIATIONS (PER
1,000 WORKERS) ON DEEP AND OUTCROP GOLD MINES,
1910–1912

	TB Deaths	TB Repatriations	TB Total	Pneumonia Total	All Diseases
1910					
Outcrop	5.10	5.46	10.56	11.9	51.2
Deep	4.95	5.44	10.39	15.07	58.9
1911					
Outcrop	5.16	6.56	11.72	13.4	50.6
Deep	6.30	10.53	16.83	18.4	88.2
1912					
Outcrop	5.28	8.63	13.91	12.8	58.7
Deep	5.56	12.93	18.17	15.3	90.0
Mean for 3 years					
Outcrop	5.18	6.88	12.06	12.7	53.5
Deep	5.60	9.63	15.13	16.2	79.0

a. U. G., Report of the Tuberculosis Commission, 206.

higher than for the outcrop mines. Similarly the risk of contracting pneumonia was 27.5 percent higher in the deep mines during these three years, while for all diseases the risk for deep mineworkers was 47 percent greater than that for outcrop mineworkers.

It should be noted that the distinction between "outcrop" and "deep" mine in this comparison does not necessarily indicate differences in depth. A few outcrop mines were actually deeper than some of the deep mines during the early years of this period. In general, however, the deep mines were deeper than the outcrop mines. "Deep mines" had vertical shafts that cut the reef, moreover, and miners could not walk out of them. Employment at deep mines therefore meant a mineworker was subjected to the adverse conditions associated with hauling and, particularly, longer working days and increased risk of chill.

The apparent relationship between deep mining and increased risk of disease needs to be modified somewhat, however, since the composition of the deep mine labor force was not the same as that of the outcrop mines. Specifically, a higher percentage of miners from tropical areas worked in the "deep mines" than in the "outcrop mines." As noted above, workers coming from tropical areas of British Central Africa and Mozambique had the highest rates of TB, pneumonia, and all other diseases, whether working outcrop or deep mines. Workers from these two areas together made up 46 percent of the total labor force but represented 65 percent of all cases during this period. The percentage of Mozambique and tropical workers on the outcrop and deep mines from 1910 to 1912 were as follows:

TABLE 6

PERCENTAGE OF MOZAMBIQUE AND TROPICAL MINERS
IN OUTCROP AND DEEP MINES, 1910–1912

	1910	1911	1912	3 Year Mean
Outcrop	46	44	41	44
Deep	50	50	50	50

Thus over the three-year period there were roughly 13 percent more tropicals and Mozambicans working in the deep mines than in the outcrop mines, which accounts in part for the higher disease rates at the former. If the higher susceptibility of tropicals and Mozambicans is adjusted for, the total TB rates for outcrop and deep mines for 1911 are 12.7 per 1,000 and 14.8 per 1,000 respectively. The territorially adjusted rate for deep mines was thus 16.5 percent greater than that for outcrop mines.[72] This difference may not in itself be statistically significant. When viewed together with the figures for mines deeper than 2,500 feet, however, it does suggest that deeper mines were less healthy mines.

The higher percentage of tropical and Mozambican workers in the deep mines reflects the poorer working conditions of these mines and their consequent unpopularity with African workers. Voluntary labor preferred to work in outcrop mines because labor conditions in them were often better. Of particular importance was the fact that the workers could walk to and from the workface and did not have to wait around to be lowered or raised.[73] Outcrop mines, because of their popularity, generally had an easier time acquiring a full complement of labor. The deep mines, being less popular, had a more difficult time attracting workers and were dependent on recruited foreign labor, workers with no choice about their place of employment. Thus the relationship between deep mining and TB was direct in that working conditions increased the risk of developing the disease, and indirect in that these same conditions caused the deep mines to be more dependent on foreign workers who were more susceptible to disease. It should be noted, however, that for domestic labor working in deep mines, the higher percentage of foreign labor at these mines and their higher susceptibility to TB, probably increased the risk of TB infection since there was likely to be a higher percentage of infectious workers in these mines.

The adverse health conditions associated with deep mining together with the particular susceptibility of tropical workers to these conditions, helps to explain why TB incidence on the mines rose between 1906 and 1912 when both the average depth of mining and the percentage of tropical workers on the mines increased. Conversely, as described in chapter 6, the cessation of recruitment of tropical workers in 1913, in light of their high overall morbidity rates, played a significant role in the subsequent decline in TB on the mines after 1913.

Migrant Labor and the Rural Expansion of Tuberculosis, 1870–1938

Just prior to World War I, a settled urban African population was beginning to emerge in the towns and cities of South Africa. Yet most Africans who lived and worked in urban centers were temporary sojourners, moving back and forth between the towns and the countryside. Within the gold-mining industry, where temporary employment for periods of six to nine months was the norm, the turnover of employees was nearly 100 percent within any given calendar year. By 1910 this meant that several hundred thousand men a year moved back and forth between the mines and their rural homes. This general pattern, in combination with the desire of sick migrant workers to return home and the mining industry's practice of repatriating all diseased or injured miners, guaranteed that the epidemic of urban-based TB quickly spread to the rural hinterlands, infecting the rural households from which industry drew its labor. As a result of this process, TB infection rates among the rural African populations most heavily involved in migrant labor reached extremely high levels by the late 1920s.

THE MINING INDUSTRY AND THE RURAL SPREAD OF TB

There can be little doubt that urban "native locations" produced a considerable number of the tubercular migrants, who returned home to infect their kin and neighbors. It was the mining industry, however, that was most frequently cited in the medical reports of this period as the primary disseminator of tubercular infection within the rural areas of southern Africa.

The Public Health Report for the Cape Colony in 1906 noted,

> Noticeable and singularly coinciding with the figures given us from Johannesburg, is the general testimonies of district surgeons that the disease is mainly spread by Natives returning from the mines.[1]

An even stronger condemnation of the role played by the mining industry in the rural spread of TB was made by Dr. Grant Millar, district surgeon in Pondoland in 1908.

> Pondoland is one of the chief recruiting fields for the gold mines of the Transvaal . . . [and] I have no doubt that this is the primary cause of tuberculosis among the Pondo . . .

> A young man goes up from this district to work in the mines at Johannesburg. After working there for some six months or a year—where, it must be remembered the conditions of life are totally different to what he is accustomed to . . . he happens to contract phthisis [TB], as likely as not from a fellow worker, after which he returns home to Pondoland, where the manner of living is pre-eminently calculated to favour the spread of the disease. . . .

> Time and again one native returning from the mines infects almost the entire occupants of a hut previously quite healthy.[2]

Specific examples of this pattern were also reported by Dr. Peter Allan who conducted research on TB in the Ciskei and Transkei during the 1920s. The research as noted in chapter 1 was part of a much larger inquiry into the prevalence of TB among Africans in the Union, and particularly in the mining industry, carried out by the TB Research Committee jointly funded by the Union government and the Chamber of Mines. Allan concluded that by the late 1920s TB infection was so rife in the Transkei and Ciskei that returning tubercular mineworkers were no longer a major health threat. He nonetheless cited a number of cases in which returning mineworkers had apparently infected members of their families.[3]

One such case involved a thirty-one-year-old man who was seen at Victoria Hospital in the Ciskei on November 24, 1927, having been repatriated from the mines in September of that year without compensation. He was seriously ill with abdominal tuberculosis and also slight lung involvement. He died in January 1928. While he was working on the mines, a brother aged thirteen years, a sister aged twenty-seven, and his father all died of tuberculosis within the space of a year. Another sister had developed tuberculosis and was then in an advanced stage, and another had developed tuberculous glands.[4]

The history of the Mapukata family from the Idutywa District in the Transkei is illustrative of this same pattern and suggests that the process of transmission could last for years.[5] The father, who had worked on the mines, died of chest trouble in 1923. His daughter, aged twenty-two, died from chest trouble soon after the father. His son Ntsentse, aged thirty-five, was repatriated from the mines suffering from tuberculosis and died in early 1927.

Another son, James Mapukata, was repatriated with TB on July 7, 1927. He was about thirty years of age and married; he had worked on the mines for a total of forty-five months at different times. Prior to his repatriation he had spent seven days in a mine hospital and thirteen days at the WNLA Hospital. At the time of his release he was said to be in fair condition, without a temperature but with tubercule bacilli in his sputum. Dr. Allan visited his home in November 1927 and found that he was away but was told that he was still well.

James' oldest brother, age forty, was repatriated from the mines in October of 1928 and was seen by Dr. Allan in June of 1929. He could not work, was coughing up blood, and could hardly walk. By December of 1930 he was bedridden and had a bad prognosis.

In total five members of the family were either sick or dead from TB. Dr. Allan concluded:

> In this family there is the possibility that the father contracted the disease on the mines and infected the family. The three sons were apparently healthy when they went to the mines, but broke down under industrial strain.[6]

Reverend H. P. Junod, who worked in Gazaland, Mozambique, between 1922 and 1929, provided the Fagan Commission with similar evidence in the 1940s:

> ... any man who has a real knowledge of the life of Gazaland, or probably any other big reserve of mine labour, will seriously question the advisability of going on purely and simply with migratory labour as it is today, if only for the number of cases that have come to his knowledge of complete deterioration of health through mine labor and frequent deaths in the reserves, directly caused by the effects of tuberculosis, silicosis, and other diseases contracted on the mines. In Gazaland the people sing a most pathetic complaint which goes:—"There is a disease ... the doctors can do nothing against it ... It is the *ndere* (tuberculosis) ... The sun has gone down for me ... O! father, I die."

> This is not a single experience. . . . During my stay in Manjacaze, Gazaland, quite a number of men serving our Church, who could not be paid sufficiently, went to the mines in order to get more ready cash, and I know of seven who died of pulmonary tuberculosis.[7]

Some of the criticism of the role played by the mining industry in the dissemination of tuberculosis may have been exaggerated, and occasionally one can discern jealousies over the economic dominance of the Transvaal underlying the finger-pointing exercises of Cape officials. The Cape Public Health Report cited above, for example, goes on to conclude that the resulting spread of TB among Cape Africans is "decimating the Colony's most valuable labour asset" and to question whether "from a human life point of view . . . we ought to waste *our* Bantus over mine labour" (emphasis added).[8]

Yet the vast numbers of men involved in the mining industry, the conditions of mine employment, and the industry's laissez-faire attitude toward the effects of repatriation on rural populations, must have made the industry a major contributor to the spread of TB. Prior to World War I, African workers who became ill were repatriated without regard to the consequences this would have on the rural populations from which the mines drew their labor. As TB became viewed as a serious health problem on the mines after the war, however, more attention was paid to the question of how repatriation was affecting the spread of the disease in the rural areas. These discussions seldom resulted in any concrete action being taken to prevent the spread of disease. Unwilling to bear the high cost of sanatorium care for affected workers, mining authorities adopted the somewhat self-serving argument that Africans disliked being placed in a hospital and preferred returning to their own homes when they became ill. This rationale surfaced repeatedly in the discussions of medical officers and mine managers. It was presented most clearly in the following statement by the president of the Transvaal Mine Medical Officers Association in 1926, as reported in the proceedings of the association.

> The President pointed out how anxious natives with tuberculosis were to go home, because they had a feeling that if they could get home their own native doctors might cure them. Although that might not be the case, they had that feeling. If one stopped them they very often died out of sheer disappointment.[9]

Mine medical officers also pointed to the absence of accurate health statistics for the rural areas and the impossibility of knowing what effects repatriated cases were having on the general prevalence of the disease. Finally, they argued, with little or no supportive data, that Africans who became ill did better in their home environment.[10]

There was no doubt some truth to the claim that Africans did not wish to be hospitalized, but then given the poor quality of the medical care provided in most mine hospitals during the early years of the mining industry, and the high mortality rates within these hospitals, an aversion to hospitalization was not unreasonable. The absence of rural health statistics was no doubt also a real problem. The mines did nothing, however, to encourage the collection of statistics until the late 1920s, by which time, as noted above, much of the damage had been done. And although some Africans clearly did improve once they returned home, others simply deteriorated and died. Allan estimated that 60 percent of African miners who were repatriated with TB died within two years of repatriation.[11]

Although it is difficult with available records to provide exact figures for the number of TB cases repatriated during this period some idea of the scale of the practice can be gained from a study conducted in 1914 by Dr. George Turner. He found that the number of African workers repatriated due to TB in 1910, 1911, and 1912 was 6, 11, and 18 per 1,000 of the total African workforce. This works out to roughly 7,500 workers over the three-year period.[12] Some of these may have been repatriated twice, given the inadequate record keeping and medical screening of new recruits that occurred at the mines. The TB commission, however, also found cases of tuberculosis in the rural areas which had been repatriated under the general term "debility."[13] Whether this represented poor diagnostic procedures or an effort to underreport TB cases is unclear. The actual number of repatriated TB cases may in fact have been greater than 7,500. In any case the number of repatriated tuberculous mineworkers was high and must have represented a significant factor in the spread of TB within the rural areas of southern Africa.

To this number must be added countless others who were infected while working at the mines but who were not identified as having TB before their contracts were completed. Prior to World War I there was no procedure for screening African workers at the end of their contract. Even after the war, when termination physicals were begun, they consisted of little more than weighing workers to see if they had lost a significant amount of weight during their contract. If they had, they were given a somewhat more thorough examination by the mine's medical officer. The failure of this procedure to pick up cases of TB is discussed in chapter 6.

Recent research conducted by Dr. Colin McCord in Mozambique indicates that returned mineworkers who had not even been infected with TB while at the mines might subsequently become a source of infection to their kinspeople and neighbors as a result of their mine working experience. McCord found that men who had worked the mines but not developed TB were at greater risk of developing TB later in life than men of the same age who had never worked the mines. He suggests that this delayed risk may be due to the mine workers' exposure to silica dust while on the mines, since silicosis is a progressive disease that (as we have seen) predisposes a person to TB.[14]

VARIATIONS IN THE RURAL TRANSMISSION OF TB

It is clear that returning workers were responsible for the spread of tuberculosis into the rural areas of southern Africa. Yet the rapidity with which the disease spread, once introduced into the rural areas, varied considerably from household to household, area to area, and within a single area over time. In the western Cape, McVicar estimated that the TB mortality rate for Africans and coloreds in Paarl District was already over 7 per 1,000 by 1906. This may have had more to do, however, with the rapid urbanization of coloreds in the towns of the western Cape at the end of the nineteenth century than with the effect of African workers returning from other urban centers. For other districts in the western Cape, McVicar estimated the rural mortality rate from TB among Africans and coloreds to be around 3 per 1,000.

Though statistics for other areas of the Cape Colony are either nonexistent or of questionable value, the reports of district surgeons in the eastern Cape echo those of Dr. Millar, quoted above, in indicating an alarming increase in the incidence of TB during the first decade of this century, especially within the heavily populated districts of the Ciskei and Transkei.[15] The district surgeon for Stutterheim for example considered phthisis "unquestionably the cause of the greater part of the high (Native) mortality," accounting for over 30 percent of the notified deaths for the years 1904 and 1906. The disease was taking a particularly high toll among the colored population, leading him to warn that "If preventive measures are not constituted, I am of the opinion that the whole of the Hottentot race in Stockenstrom will in a short time be wiped out."[16]

Similarly the district surgeon for Tsomo in the Transkei observed in 1905 that

The disease is rapidly on the increase in the district, especially in two wards, Lutuli and Qutsa. It is attacking young adults who have not been away from home. . . . In one case a man came back from work and died shortly afterwards; his wife and child, also his mother, all previously healthy, came to me within two months, the two adults far advanced in Phthisis, the child commencing. The adults died within a few weeks. . . . I believe the above is being repeated daily among us.[17]

Information collected by McVicar in 1906 from other areas of the Transkei and Ciskei, such as Hershel, Tsolo, and Bizana, suggests that the rapid spread of TB was not, however, a universal phenomenon among the African populations of the eastern Cape.[18]

In Natal tuberculosis also appears to have become a major problem by the turn of the century, in association with the Rinderpest epidemic that killed vast numbers of cattle, the destruction of crops by locusts, and the effects of the South African War. As many as five TB cases a day were reported among the Zulu attending the native dispensary at Eshowe. By the early 1920s, however, the disease began to become less prevalent, with some physicians reporting a 50 percent decrease in number of cases seen.[19] Overall the rural spread of TB in Natal after the initial attack, appears to have been slower than in the Transkei and Ciskei until World War II.[20]

We have virtually no reliable data on the spread of TB within the reserve areas of the Transvaal or in the Orange Free State, where the vast majority of Africans lived on white-owned farms, removed from the supervision of even missionary doctors. One can only surmise, for reasons discussed later, that the spread of the disease was somewhat slower than in the Ciskei and Transkei at least up to the 1920s.

The spread of TB from the urban centers of South Africa to surrounding rural areas was of course not confined within the country's borders. For as we have seen mine labor was recruited from a number of neighboring colonies, with over one-third of the workers prior to 1920 coming from Mozambique. Reporting on Mozambique in 1906, Turner claimed that he could find little evidence of the disease in his tour of the recruiting areas. He concluded, moreover, that "it is a disease which is certainly not being spread throughout the country by labourers returning to the East Coast from the mines."[21] Though we may wish to question Turner's opinions on these points, given his role as medical advisor to WNLA, there is evidence that TB had not spread very far among rural Mozambicans by World War I. A tuberculin survey of 415

Mozambican recruits in 1912, using the Calmette method of placing tuberculin on the conjunctiva, found only 1.7 percent of the new recruits had positive reaction, while 17.5 percent of "old boys" reacted positively.[22] By comparison, as noted in chapter 3, a survey in Basutoland using the same method found that 15.5 percent of the adult men who had never been out of Basutoland reacted positively while 36 percent of those with mine experience tested positive. By the late 1920s, a tuberculin survey of Mozambique recruits found a positivity rate of between 65 and 70 percent.[23] This survey used a method of testing different from the earlier study and therefore is not directly comparable. The study also did not break down the results into new recruits versus old hands, so it is not possible to determine the extent to which this rate reflects conditions in the rural areas from which these recruits were drawn. The rates for Mozambique in the latter study were equal, nonetheless, to those of recruits from areas of British South Africa, suggesting that the disease had made considerable inroads within Mozambique by the late 1920s.

Although Basutoland appears to have been more affected by the spread of TB during this period than were the recruiting areas of Mozambique,[24] the disease was still less pervasive in either Basutoland or Swaziland than in the eastern Cape. Tuberculosis in fact attracted little attention in either protectorate prior to the late 1920s, despite the fact that as many as 5,000 men a year were working outside of Swaziland and 20,000 outside of Basutoland by 1911. By the 1930s, however, medical authorities in both protectorates were expressing alarm over the rise in TB cases.

Reports from Bechuanaland Protectorate during this period suggest that TB was relatively rare in the northern areas of the protectorate, though, as noted in chapter 1, local district surgeons felt this was partly because tubercular cases seldom came to white physicians for treatment. By contrast the disease appears to have begun making serious inroads in the southern areas by the 1920s.[25]

FACTORS AFFECTING THE RATE OF TB
TRANSMISSION IN THE RURAL AREAS

The reasons for these variations in time and space are both diverse and difficult to sort out. In general, however, the rate at which the disease spread in the rural areas of southern Africa was determined by

the same set of factors that controlled its spread in the urban areas—
conditions that increased opportunities for infection and factors that
lowered the ability of the host population to cope with infection.

Looking first at factors affecting the rate of infection, it appears that
the extent to which tuberculosis spread within any given rural area prior
to World War I was directly proportional to the extent to which the
area's population had been involved in migrant labor and thus exposed
to the risk of outside infection. Thus, the TB commission's inquiry into
the prevalence of TB in the rural areas of southern Africa, although
limited in scope, concluded:

> The amount of tuberculosis in women and children . . . is greater in propor-
> tion to the length of time and extent to which resort to labor centres has been
> taking place. . . . So that the number of affected women and children is
> smallest among the Northern Transvaal tribes, greater among the Basuto-
> land Basutos and greatest among the Cape Natives and of these last greatest
> among the natives in the districts of the Cape Province proper.[26]

The role of labor migration in the spread of TB may help explain the rise
in TB cases that occurred among the Basuto during the 1930s. As late as
1921 only 8.7 percent of Basuto men and women were absentees. By
1936 the number had jumped to 15.3 percent. Although the rising tide
of TB in Swaziland during the 1930s does not correspond to any increase in Swazi involvement in labor migration, the 1931 annual medical report for Swaziland indicates that a larger number of reported cases
of both TB and syphilis occurred in the southern areas of the country
than in the central and northern areas and attributes the difference to
the greater involvement of men in the south in migration to the mines.[27]
Similarly the 1933 annual medical report from Bechuanaland contains
the following observation:

> The distribution of pulmonary tuberculosis was fairly even in the Southern
> districts of the Territory while in the northern districts (Mangwato and Tati)
> it was lower than in the South. The distribution may be of some significance
> in that up till the end of 1933 native labourers have not been recruited from
> north of Latitude 22 for work on the Gold Mines in Johannesburg. (Most of
> the Bamangwato Reserve and the whole of the Tati district is north of that
> latitude.) It would therefore appear that Tuberculosis is met with more
> frequently in those tribes south of Latitude 22 from which labour for the
> mines is recruited.[28]

The relationship between increased involvement in migrant labor and a
rising prevalence of TB, however, must be viewed against the background of other factors that both encouraged Africans to engage in

migrant labor and decreased their resistance to disease. These will be discussed below.

Length and frequency of contact would not appear to explain the situation in Mozambique. Mozambique workers had been traveling to various labor centers in South Africa since the 1850s.[29] By the turn of the century, tens of thousands of Mozambicans were working on the mines every year. Moreover, as noted above, Mozambique workers experienced high rates of TB morbidity and mortality in the mines. If intensity of contact was a critical factor in the epidemiology of TB in the rural areas of southern Africa, southern Mozambique should have been experiencing a considerable increase in TB during the early years of the century. Yet this appears not to be the case.

A number of factors may account for this apparent contradiction, some of which will be discussed below, but one difference may have been the long contract periods that Mozambique labor worked. Mozambican workers represented a relatively stable element in the Rand working population, since their contracts averaged from twelve to eighteen months. Cape workers by contrast contracted for periods of between three and nine months on average. Thus while the mean annual strength of Mozambique labor in the mines was large, equaling between one-third and two-thirds of the total mean annual labor force between 1903 and 1913, the number of men who actually worked the mines during any given year may have been less than the total number from the Cape, despite the fact that as a percentage of the annual mean labor strength, Cape recruits represented only between a tenth and a third of the Rand labor force. If we take the years 1910–1912, for example, the mean annual strength of Mozambique labor over the three years was 77,072 while that of Cape labor was 55,116. However, if we calculate that the average contract of a Mozambican worker was fifteen months[30] while the average Cape contract was six months, then during the three-year period the number of actual workers (some on repeat contracts) who came and left the mines would have been 184,973 from Mozambique as compared to 330,696 from the Cape. In other words the intensity of contact, measured in terms of numbers of workers migrating to and from the mines, would have been 78 percent greater for the Cape than for Mozambique. Opportunities for employment outside the mining industry and thus the total number of men and women involved in labor migration were, moreover, far greater for the Cape Colony than for Mozambique. Still, the number of Mozambican men migrating to the mines was substantial and certainly greater than the number of men from Basutoland, where infection levels were evidently higher prior to World War I. Other factors must therefore have been involved in the relatively low infection rate among nonmigrating men in Mozambique at this time.

One crucial factor must have been the opportunities for infection within the rural areas themselves. The risk of a tuberculous worker infecting his family and neighbors was determined in the rural areas, as in the urban locations and mining compounds, by the extent to which housing and sanitation conditions either facilitated or prevented the transmission of infection.

In this respect there is considerable evidence that overcrowded housing, though certainly not as severe as in congested urban locations and mining compounds, was indeed a growing problem in certain areas of the Ciskei and Transkei during the early years of this century. In Pondoland, where the disease appears to have spread very rapidly among the families of returned mineworkers, Millar describes excessive overcrowding:

> The overcrowding is probably worse than anything that can be found in an East End slum of a great city at home. One may see some 20 people—men, women, and children—crowded into a small hut, the door of which is carefully blocked up and which contains no other opening or ventilation of any kind. The overcrowding is very much the rule, it being quite the exception to find a hut not overcrowded. Now imagine the phthisical patient one of this crowd, constantly spitting on the floor and on the walls of the hut, and can it be wondered that the disease spreads.

Millar ascribed this condition to the system of taxation imposed upon the Pondo by the colonial authorities.

> In regard to the overcrowding, there is a very serious practical difficulty to be surmounted, that in order to lessen the overcrowding there would require to be a great building of huts. This is a serious matter, not only in regard to the actual putting up of huts, but still more because it means an increased payment in the shape of the hut tax. All the Pondos contribute in the way of taxes is 10s. per annum for each hut they have, hence the more huts the more tax they have to pay.[31]

Thus, ironically, a taxation policy designed in part to generate labor may have undermined the social reproduction of labor in Pondoland by encouraging overcrowding and the spread of tuberculosis.[32]

If the hut tax encouraged overcrowding in Pondoland and elsewhere in the Transkei and Ciskei, exemptions to the hut tax may have had a similar ironic effect in Natal. The exemption was for Africans who built square huts in "the European style" "containing a modicum of European furniture such as tables and chairs, and in which the occupants lived on 'European lines.' " The exemption was designed to benefit the "better class of educated natives" and, as Slater has suggested about regulations requiring Africans to wear European clothes during the nineteenth century,[33] was aimed at encouraging African consumer demands. Constructing "European-style huts" cost more than building ordinary thatch huts and deterred household heads from building additional houses to accommodate their families. As a result large families would occupy a single hut, producing serious overcrowding.[34] Changing house styles may also have encouraged the spread of TB in another way. Thus the MOH of Swaziland in 1931 observed that the gradual adoption of European-style huts by the Swazi was a threat to their health and noted that the traditional beehive huts

> are much more wholesome than the rooms built after the European pattern, because the uneducated native sleeps with all the openings closed. In the common hut smoke and used air can pass through the thatch, and so a very steady effective stream of ventilation is always going in without any severe draughts, whereas in the closed room the air soon becomes vitiated.[35]

By the 1930s, deforestation as well as declining access to grass for thatching may well have exacerbated the situation, making it more difficult to construct huts and encouraging the housing of more people in fewer huts.

Overcrowding seems to have been less a feature of rural life in the recruiting areas of Mozambique during the earlier years of this century and may help explain the slower spread of TB there. Similarly, in Swaziland, health officials frequently commented on the role of dispersed settlement and absence of overcrowding in forestalling the spread of all infectious diseases. It is also worth noting that colonial authorities in Swaziland based their tax structure on the number of wives a man had, not on the number of huts, and thus did not encourage overcrowding. Finally, in assessing the impact of overcrowding in various regions one must keep in mind that these general patterns often obscure local variation within specific regions. Disparities in wealth and access to building materials, which increased during the 1920s and 1930s, meant that some families lived in much more squalid conditions than others and the spread of TB was always uneven.

Differences in the treatment of tubercular cases and in household sanitation may also have affected the rate of transmission in different rural areas. In the Transkei and Ciskei, medical officers repeatedly ascribed the spread of TB to the African's complete lack of attention to the danger of spitting, the use of one another's clothing, and lack of ventilation. By contrast, G. A. Turner's report on the prevalence of infectious diseases in Mozambique noted that, "As regards tuberculosis, certain cases are isolated in the bush by the Native doctors and are not permitted to enter the Kraal proper." He adds that "the attendants on a patient who for some reason, has not been isolated in the bush, are careful in many cases to remove the sand on the floor on which the patient has been spitting, within a few minutes of its being contaminated, not only outside the hut, but outside the Kraal."[36] Although such characterizations often reflect an imperfect understanding of African cultures and indigenous therapeutics, as well as broader racial and ethnic stereotypes—"the filthy Pondo," being a phrase that occurred frequently in the popular discourse of whites during this period—there may have been differences in the Africans' treatment of disease which affected the spread of tuberculosis. Further research on African reactions to diseases introduced by European contact is clearly needed before we can determine how much weight should be placed on this factor.

The pace at which tuberculosis spread within the rural areas of southern Africa prior to World War I was also determined by the ability of members of the rural population to control their infections and avoid the development of open cases of active TB. Yet the relationship between resistance levels and the speed at which infection spreads is complex. The various relationships existing between resistance, morbidity, and mortality can be arranged along a continuum. At one extreme we have a population such as that found today in the western industrial world and among whites in South Africa. For the most part, such westerners who are exposed to TB during their lives often are unaware they have been infected. This is because their immune systems are strong and they are generally resistant to the disease. As a population they have, in addition, a long historical experience with the disease. At the other extreme are people whose immune system has been compromised by stress, malnutrition, or disease. In this category are the growing number of AIDS cases who are currently developing TB in the United States, Europe, and Africa. At this end of the spectrum as well are populations that historically have had little or no exposure to TB, the so-called virgin-soil population. In between these two extremes lie a wide range of intermediary conditions in which people have greater or lesser resistance to TB. A society's position relative to this spectrum depends on both the general health and nutrition of its members and, to a somewhat lesser degree, on its experience with TB. Obviously within any society there may be a wide variation in the former criterion.

The relationship between a population's level of resistance and the spread of TB can be defined in terms of this same continuum. At one end, where a population has a high level of resistance, very few active cases or deaths from TB will occur. At the other end, we find a large number of cases with a high mortality rate. In terms of incidence rates, however, this population may have a lower rate than a population with a somewhat greater level of resistance for the simple reason that the cases will die before they are able to infect many of their kin and neighbors. In a population with a fair amount of resistance, the disease, conversely, may take a more chronic course allowing greater opportunities for the spread of infection.

As one moves from low resistance to high resistance on the spectrum, mortality rates will fall but morbidity rates will continue to rise as a result of the more chronic nature of cases and the heightened opportunity for transmission. As one approaches the high-resistance end of the

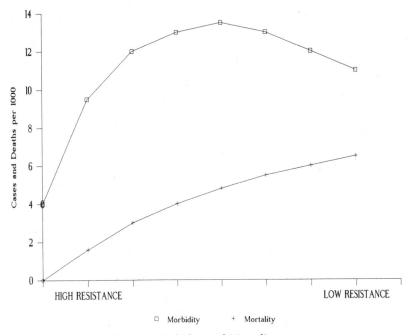

Graph 6. Host Resistance, Morbidity and Mortality

spectrum, however, the incidence rate will eventually begin to fall since fewer and fewer open cases occur. Thus the rate of transmission is highest for groups with limited resistance but tails off with both increased and even decreased resistance.[37]

Looking at the populations of southern Africa during the first three decades of this century, it would appear that very few people, regardless of race or social class, fell within the high-resistance/low-mortality category at the beginning of the century. A sizable portion of black workers and poor whites in the urban areas, however, fell within the low-resistance/high-mortality grouping—though as indicated in chapter 2, there is some indication that in the years between the 1907–1909 depression and World War I, there was some movement of urban Africans toward the high-resistance/low-mortality end of the spectrum. This pattern did not persist, however, and mortality rates began to rise again during and after World War I.

Returning to the rural areas, the situation is difficult to sort out. It would appear, as noted above, that in some areas of the Cape Colony, Ciskei, Transkei, and Natal, TB mortality rates were fairly high during the first decade of this century, with a certain number of rapidly fatal cases, though in comparison with urban centers mortality was still relatively low. By the 1920s TB *mortality* appeared to be declining in Natal and certain areas of the Ciskei and Transkei. In all three areas one finds repeated references to the fact that Africans seem better able to resist their infections and are developing more chronic forms of the disease. At the same time, however, there appeared to be an increased TB morbidity, that is, in the prevalence of active cases.[38] This is impossible to quantify, yet the opinion of many physicians is that TB cases increased during the late 1920s and 1930s. This is what one would expect given the decline in TB mortality.

The picture that emerges of the changing epidemiology of TB from this admittedly subjective data fits well with what we know about changing social and economic conditions within the reserves, the general health and nutrition of reserve populations during this period, and the relationship between TB resistance, morbidity, and mortality described above.

AGRICULTURAL TRANSFORMATIONS AND DECLINING RESISTANCE TO TB

Conditions at the turn of the century were marked by extreme deprivation in many rural areas of South Africa. Droughts and the effects of the South African War and the rinderpest epidemic, which eliminated upward of 90 percent of African cattle, combined to undermine the health and well-being of rural populations in many parts of the region. The acute form that TB took in the rural areas at the turn of the century no doubt reflected the impact of these conditions on populations that had only limited prior experience with the disease.

Rinderpest may have been particularly important in reducing the resistance of rural Africans to TB during the early years of this century. The immediate consequence of the rinderpest epidemic was a loss of important nutrients from rural diets, including animal fats, protein, vitamins A and C, and calcium. The removal of these elements may well have reduced African resistance to TB. Dr. Peter Allan, in his 1924 TB survey, concluded that the epidemic of TB among the Zulu at the turn of the century was directly related to rinderpest and the inability of the Zulu to obtain "amas" (soured milk). He writes: "The children born during the years following the rinderpest were then attaining puberty, and by not getting sufficient nourishment, fell easy victim to tubercular infection."[39] The outbreak of East Coast fever on the heels of the epidemic contributed further to this pattern.

The recovery of herds after the war and the enforcement of dipping regulations may have briefly reversed this effect and increased the ability of rural populations to resist infection. The resulting decline in TB mortality rates, however, would have contributed to the more rapid spread of infection, therefore explaining reports of an increase in TB incidence despite somewhat improved economic conditions. As a consequence of this spread, TB infection rates achieved very high levels in the Ciskei and Transkei and moderately high levels in many other areas of the region by the late 1920s (see below).

Had conditions remained as they were in the early 1920s, mortality rates might have continued to decline. This would have been followed after a decade or so by a gradual lessening in the number of new cases per annum and, eventually, of infection rates. Conditions unfortunately did not remain static but in fact deteriorated rapidly from the late 1920s onward. Although the causes of this decline have been described by numerous studies,[40] they need to be outlined here in order to understand both their effects on the rural transmission of TB and the connection between this spread and the changing political economy of South Africa.

The period between 1870 and 1913 saw the gradual incorporation of wide areas of southern Africa into the periphery of industrial development centered on the mining industry. This incorporation produced significant transformations in the social relations of production within the rural areas, redefining social relations within households and the distribution of land, labor, and cattle among households. Ultimately incorporation undermined the productivity of many rural households and made their reproduction dependent upon access to wage employment outside the rural economy. Both the rate of incorporation and the nature and timing of these subsequent transformations varied widely within the region as a whole. By World War I incorporation, and the destruction of rural household economies, was well under way in many areas of the Ciskei, Transkei, and Natal, while in Pondoland, Basutoland, Zululand, and Swaziland the process took longer, the majority of rural households remaining viable and productive through the 1920s. Yet even in these areas the foundations for eventual impoverishment were laid down prior to World War I. The pace at which these transformations occurred helped determine the rate at which TB spread within particular rural areas. On one hand, growing impoverishment encouraged participation in migrant labor and thus increased opportunities for the transmission of infection. On the other hand, it reduced the ability of the rural inhabitants to resist infections and thus increased the incidence of active cases of TB.

The incorporation and transformation of rural households began in some areas of the Cape and Natal during the middle years of the nineteenth century, as farmers took advantage of expanded commodity markets and became actively involved in maize production. Maize was not only marketable but produced a higher yield in good years than either millet or sorghum, previously the primary sources of starch in most rural diets. In addition maize required less labor than either millet or sorghum and was particularly attractive to families who were also participating in migrant labor or whose children were attending mission schools, since these children had played an important role in protecting millet and sorghum from birds. These factors also made maize an attractive crop for farmers who were unable to participate in market production but wished to increase their food supplies. As a result of these immediate advantages, maize became a primary source of both nutrition and income within the rural areas of South Africa by the end of the nineteenth century.[41]

In the long run, however, the shift to commodity maize production entailed liabilities that would contribute to the impoverishment of many rural households and prepare the ground for the spread of TB. To begin with, maize provided fewer protective nutrients than either sorghum or millet, despite its higher protein and calorie content. In a diet largely composed of a single starch, sorghum is a more nutritious source of calories than maize. As long as maize was supplemented with a variety of other vegetables there was little disadvantage to replacing sorghum. When these other vegetables ceased to be consumed on a regular basis, however, then a maize-based diet became inferior to one based on sorghum or millet. For reasons discussed later, this elimination of supplemental vegetables became common in certain areas of the Ciskei and Transkei during the first decade of this century and occurred more broadly in many maize-growing areas of South Africa in the period after World War I.

The second liability associated with a growing reliance on maize production was the demand it made on available land resources. Maize production quickly depleted the soil of nitrogen, phosphorus, and potassium and thus required either extensive crop rotation or intensive fertilizer use. Alternating maize with nitrogen-restoring legumes helped but was insufficient to counteract long-term deterioration of the soil. Cattle manure could replace both nitrogen and phosphorus but did not replenish potassium loss. Yet even this source of fertilizer was gradually eliminated as population growth placed pressure on existing sources of energy and led to the widespread use of manure as fuel.[42]

Most African farmers who shifted to maize production employed shifting forms of agriculture that provided substantial fallow periods to restore the soil. This produced high yields of maize as long as land was available. By the end of the nineteenth century, however, access to land was declining in the Ciskei and certain areas of the Transkei. The Glen Grey Act, which introduced individual land tenure in the Ciskei, and the later, more pervasive 1913 Native Land Act severely limited access to land, and by 1915 the Beaumont Land Commission estimated that the so-called native areas supported only half the African population, the remainder living and/or working outside the reserves.[43] Restrictions on land forced farmers who had become dependent on growing maize for food and income to concentrate their available acreage in maize production. Intercropping became less frequent, narrowing the range of foods consumed. Fallow periods were also reduced, taking a toll on the productivity of the soil and reducing yields per acre. In a desperate effort to maintain production levels, many farmers attempted to compensate for reduced yields per acre by increasing the number or acres planted, often at the cost of further reducing fallow periods.[44]

Land restrictions also took their toll on African cattle herds. African herds, as noted earlier, recovered rapidly following World War I. Between 1918 and 1930 the cattle population increased by 132 percent, with the average number of livestock per family increasing from 6.5 to 10.7. In the Transkeian territories alone the cattle population increased by 240 percent,[45] while Swazi herds increased by 400 percent between 1911 and 1936.[46] Yet this rapid increase in herd size in combination with the growth of human populations[47] and no increase in grazing areas following the 1913 Land Act, led to overstocking, overgrazing, and soil erosion.

The deterioration of grazing land was accelerated by the droughts of the late 1920s and early 1930s and by the rapid expansion of sheep raising. From 1912 to 1936 the number of sheep rose from a few thousand to 3 million. Though some observers saw the shift to small animals as a positive response to deteriorating grazing conditions, it was in reality a primary contributor to these conditions. In effect it was the sheep that were driving the cattle off the land.[48]

Conceivably income from sheep herding could have offset the loss of cattle, yet the vast majority of sheep were owned by a relatively small group of elite African farmers; the impoverished families whose herds were being threatened owned few sheep. Only 20.7 percent of the family units in the Transkei in fact owned sheep. Thus a small group consisting of Bunga councillors, headmen, and chiefs were earning income from wool at the expense of the food supplies of the majority of reserve families.[49]

The deterioration of grazing lands during the early 1930s led to the rapid impoverishment of African herds and increased stock mortality. Between 1931 and 1935 the livestock population decreased by 13 percent. The average number of cattle owned by a family declined from 10.7 to 6.7.[50] The quality of the herds also declined. Thus the Union director of native agriculture reported in 1933 that,

> The native cattle in many parts are the worst for conformation that can be seen anywhere in the world. They are very bad, both from the trek-ox point of view and the milk and beef point of view.[51]

Loss of cattle was directly linked to declining agricultural production as well as to declining food supplies. As Beinart shows, access to draft animals became critically important for household food production after 1912 as a result of increasing participation in migrant labor and a resulting decline in the availability of household labor supplies and household size. Households with few or no cattle found it difficult to maintain production levels.[52] In 1936 it was found that Transkei families on average owned 2.3 oxen, while a minimum of 6 was considered necessary for operating a single-furrow plough. Although the lending of oxen occurred, some plot owners were only able to cultivate half their lands. Even in a good season, those without access to oxen and plows were often too late with their crops and failed to reap any gain.[53]

Those farmers with better access to land or capital, allowing them to crop more intensively or raise cattle or sheep, were able to maintain production. Those who lacked these resources saw their production drop as their land became exhausted. Before long these less fortunate farmers were unable to produce surpluses for market and, in many cases, could no longer meet their household food demands even in good years. In bad years they faced severe hunger. Such disadvantaged families were drawn increasingly into wage employment to meet their financial needs and became dependent on purchased food. Although migrant labor was by no means the exclusive reserve of households that lacked sufficient land to support themselves, these families provided a large percentage of the migrant workers coming from the eastern Cape during this period. These families were at greatest risk of TB infection from returning workers and least able to control their infections due to poor nutrition.

This pattern of social differentiation explains the apparent contradiction between recurrent reports of widespread malnutrition and disease in the Ciskei and Transkei from the late 1920s onward (described below) and the argument set forward by Charles Simkins[54] that total agricultural production in the reserves was stable and met a constant proportion of requirements between 1918 and 1955. Simkins conclusion reflects aggregate measurements and does not reveal the emerging disparity between richer and poorer families in the region. Aggregate production figures, moreover, do not reveal significant shifts in dietary intake and nutrition associated with the transformations in the agricultural production outlined earlier. These shifts are discussed below.

Reliance on maize production carried with it two additional liabilities that, like those already discussed, were felt first in the eastern Cape prior to World War I and more broadly throughout South Africa during the 1920s and 1930s. Maize was less resistant to drought than sorghum. African cultivators were well aware of this limitation and in many areas planted the two crops together so that if the rains failed, the sorghum would provide an insurance against famine. Under pressure to raise commodity crops and faced with declining land resources, however, sorghum production decreased. Farmers in need of cash but with limited land available, or land that was declining in productivity, took risks and planted maize on land set aside for sorghum. This trend was reflected in production figures for Pondoland. Between 1895 and 1920 maize production grew steadily from 121,000 bags to over 300,000. Sorghum production, by contrast, peaked at 105,000 bags in 1898 and then declined to 16,872 in 1920. Although it increased to 70,000 in 1929 and 1930, it averaged between 20,000 and 30,000 bags through the 1930s. Beinart's informants attributed this shift to the superior yields per acre provided by maize and changes in the workforce that made it more difficult to protect sorghum from birds.[55] These calculations, however, must have been shaped implicitly by the need to increase commodity production and the willingness to take chances on losing one's means of subsistence to drought. The costs of this decision were brought home to an increasing number of farmers as the century wore on and took a wide toll during the drought years of the late 1920s and early 1930s.

Ultimately, the willingness to invest resources in a more vulnerable crop reflected the final liability of maize production: dependence on markets for subsistence needs. Farmers who became involved in commodity production and reduced their food reserves became dependent for their subsistence needs on cash reserves earned through maize production or wage labor, and on traders to sell them grain when their crops failed or were reduced by low rainfall levels. This dependence worked well when maize prices were high and opportunities for employment plentiful. Both labor and maize markets were volatile, however. The depression years following the South African War drove both markets down and caught farmers whose livelihood was tied to one or the other, or both, in an economic vice. This experience was repeated again in the early 1920s and most dramatically in the 1930s.[56] Over the long term, moreover, the movement of white farmers into large-scale maize production in the Orange Free State, Natal, and Transvaal, with the assistance of the South African state, co-opted maize markets and made it difficult for smallholder producers to compete. When this happened, the full costs of dependence on commodity maize production came crashing down on the shoulders of African farmers throughout South Africa.[57] Again, the roots of this problem were laid down and began to take their toll on Transkei and Ciskei farmers prior to World War I. It grew in intensity, however, and together with recurrent drought and declining land resources created a tidal wave of economic adversity that came crashing down on African farmers during the 1930s.

DECLINING NUTRITION AND THE RURAL
SPREAD OF TB

By the mid-1930s the health costs of rural impoverishment and differentiation, well marked in the Transkei and Ciskei, were becoming apparent elsewhere in the region. Declining conditions in the reserves had progressed so far as to affect the quality of mine labor. This led the Chamber of Mines to initiate several inquiries into rural conditions. The most extensive and important of these was carried out in the Ciskei and Transkei by Dr. F. W. Fox and D. Back.[58] The resulting report, submitted to the chamber in 1938, provided the first clear picture of conditions in the reserves. Although the report noted the prosperity of a small group of Bunga councillors and other elites, the overall portrait was one of declining production, widespread destitution, malnutrition, and disease.[59]

Health authorities during the 1920s and 1930s were fond of comparing the monotonous starch-based diets of urban workers to the more varied "traditional diets" of rural Africans. Fox and Back found, however, that most rural families had come to rely heavily on maize meal by the 1930s, with very limited quantities of resistance-building or high-quality foods. The most critical change in rural diets during this period was the sharp decline in the consumption of milk and other animal fats and proteins.

As noted above, the loss of milk in rural diets began at the end of the nineteenth century with the decimation of cattle stock caused by the rinderpest epidemic. Although herds recovered following World War I, they declined again during the 1930s. Overstocking, due primarily to declining pasturage and a reluctance on the part of cattle owners to sell their cattle at the low prices typical of the depression years, increased the mortality rate for cattle. Disparities in access to cattle continued and in fact increased, moreover, so that many families possessed few if any cattle while a small group of elite farmers possessed many. As a result access to milk supplies for many families were seriously undermined. Fox and Back found that in Umtata 25 percent of the households possessed no cattle and 58 percent of the remaining households had herds too small to meet their milk requirements. In another district, 3 out of 1,000 stock owners owned 70 percent of the sheep and 50 percent of the cattle.[60] The average number of milk cows per African family in 1936 was 0.63. Viewed in terms of the number of persons per milk cow, the average ranged from between 5 and 6 in Pondoland to upward of 20 or more in Ciskei. In one district of the Ciskei, Sterkstrom, Fox and Back estimated there were 73.6

persons per milk cow! Overall they calculated an average of one cow with average milk yield of one to two pints per day in the summer and less than half that in the winter, to every three children and four adults.

To make matters worse, it is clear that having a milk cow and having access to milk were not the same thing.[61] Another survey in the Transkei found that only 25 percent of the milk cows were capable of producing milk above the amount needed for their calves. It also reported that of 663 children examined in the Flagstaff area of Pondoland, only 54, or 8 percent, consumed milk.[62] Fox and Back noted that "there are areas where milk is almost unobtainable for long periods, whilst in times of drought the position becomes desperate."[63] The rate at which this loss of milk supply occurred, like the general process of rural impoverishment, varied considerably. Thus, on one hand, a survey conducted by the Ciskei Missionary Council concluded that in only 13 percent of the districts was the regular diet of maize "commonly supplemented by milk."[64] On the other hand, Monica Hunter found that milk was still consumed by the average Pondo family in the early 1930s.[65]

The limited milk supply available to rural Africans was reduced further by the establishment of "native creameries" to which Africans were encouraged to sell their milk beginning in the 1930s. The policy was designed to relieve some of the economic problems faced by rural Africans with a minimal amount of government expenditure. Though highly successful from the point of view of their white owners, the creameries represented a threat to the already compromised nutritional status of many African families, especially the poorer ones, who sold their milk to the creameries in order to obtain much needed income. The creameries were widely criticized by medical authorities who rightly saw them as contributing to the ill-health of the rural African population. Describing the impact of native creameries on the diet of the Swazi, the chief MOH of Swaziland observed, "If the native is going to depreciate still further his already defective diet by sending his milk to the creamery and either doing without it in the kraal or using it in the condensed form, he will be establishing just those conditions that are most favorable for the development of the tubercle bacillus."[66]

The absence of milk in the diet of rural Africans adversely affected their health in numerous ways. For infants, it was critical. Frequently mothers were unable to provide breastmilk either because of their own malnourished condition or because they needed to find employment in order to support the family. In such cases *inembe*, a thin porridge made from mealie meal, thoroughly cooked and strained, was substituted. It resembled milk but had little of its nutritional value. Moreover, it frequently led to gastrointestinal problems, a major cause of infant mortality. Fox and Back estimated the infant mortality rate (IMR) for the Ciskei and Transkei to be 25 percent.[67] The removal of milk from rural diets in general greatly reduced intake of animal fats, vitamins A and C, and calcium, elements that played an important role in supporting resistance to TB.

Other protective foods were also in short supply for many families. Declining productive capacity within the reserves led to a narrowing of the range of foods produced as poorer farmers took land that had been used to grow nutritionally important supplementary foods like beans, leafy vegetables, and pumpkins and used it to grow maize in order to maintain income levels. By 1936 nine-tenths of the cultivatable land in the Transkei was taken up by either maize or sorghum, with the production of the former outpacing that of the latter by a ratio of nearly ten to one. This practice reduced the amounts of fresh vegetables and pulses (beans) that were available for household consumption and thus the amounts of vitamins, iron, and protein in the family diet. Nutritional edema, or kwashiorkor, caused by protein deficiencies, was commonly met with among African babies and smaller children in the Transkei and Ciskei in the mid-1930s. Evidence of vitamin deficiencies and particularly scurvy were also not uncommon. Commenting on the absence of vitamin C, Fox and Back noted:

> Next to a seasonal shortage of calories and an inadequate supply of good quality protein there can be no doubt that a low intake of anti-scorbutic vitamin is the outstanding deficiency in the diet of the average Territory Native. There are few, if any, medical men we met who had not seen their cases of scurvy, whilst some had many such cases.[68]

One food that did provide an important source of vitamins C and A as well as calcium and iron was *mfino* or wild spinach, made from the shoots and leaves of various wild plants. This was consumed widely by women and young children, though it was rejected as effeminate by men and older boys and generally by so-called dressed natives. Yet the extension of both cultivation and grazing eliminated many of the plants used in *mfino* so that this resistance-strengthening food was becoming less easy to procure by the 1930s. This difficulty explains the willingness of African women to trade their labor for the right to collect these plants on white-owned farms.[69]

Men and older boys acquired vitamin C and B supplements from beer drinking. On the basis of an analysis of African beers collected from all over the Union, Fox and Back concluded that, "the amount of ascorbic acid present in one quart of beer would be equivalent to that supplied by a pint of milk, half an ounce of orange juice, or one tenth of an ounce of fresh lucerne leaf."[70]

As the decline in productivity of land continued, households became increasingly dependent on wages and on purchased food to get them through the year. For many rural households, seasonal food shortages toward the end of the year requiring the purchase of food was common by the 1920s. By the 1930s these shortages were occurring earlier and earlier. In addition, families who needed to purchase maize at the end of the year often found themselves in debt to local merchants. This forced them to liquidate any surplus food grown during the next year shortly after harvest, when prices were low, and to buy back maize later in the year when prices were high. Finally, purchasing maize rather than growing it had additional nutritional consequences. For by the 1930s, the mealie meal distributed by traders was becoming highly refined and lacked important nutrients found in the unrefined maize meal African farmers produced for themselves.[71]

The nutritional status of rural African consumers was further undermined by the various marketing and agricultural subsidies instituted by the Union government during the 1920s and 1930s to encourage the development of white farming, reduce the wage differential between urban and rural whites, and increase the country's food exports and revenues.[72] For Africans living in the reserves, the most destructive of these measures was the 1936 Maize Marketing Act. Although designed to benefit all maize producers, for the small African farmer who lacked access to maize markets and was increasingly a consumer of purchased maize, the act quickly proved to be a hardship. Under its terms African farmers had to pay tax on every bag of maize they sold. This tax was suppose to pay for state-funded improvements in agricultural production and marketing. Very little of this money went to African farming areas, however. At the same time, the act imposed a levy of five shillings (reduced to four shillings in 1937) on every bag of maize purchased.[73] As a result, consumers in the Transkei paid a levy of five shillings per bag during the drought of 1935–1936 when 1,068,860 bags of maize were imported in order to meet local needs. This represented a tax of £267,215 imposed on a population suffering from famine![74] Commenting in 1937 on the act's effect on the health of African families in the Mount Fletcher area, the district surgeon noted:

This district has never been able to produce enough grain for their consumption and with the mealie quota have to pay for their food as much as 18/– to £1 a bag, with the consequence that in the majority of cases they are always underfed and this is having an effect on the physique of the young men presenting themselves as labourers for the mines and farms and the young children suffer in great numbers from the dietetic insufficiency.[75]

The nutritional consequences for rural Africans of the Maize Marketing Act was not lost on the Chamber of Mines' investigators. Dr. Fox wrote to Dr. Orenstein, chief medical advisor to the Rand Mines, in July of 1938 imploring him to get the chamber to intercede on behalf of Africans living in the reserves in upcoming hearings on a new Maize Act. He wrote,

> I do feel strongly that if the Chamber really wants to take up the question of Native health in the Reserves seriously they should lose no time watching these new proposals and support efforts . . . to persuade the Control Board to take the Native producer–consumer into proper consideration . . .
>
> Out of self-interest alone it seems to me so short sighted and foolish to be running Commissions on Labour shortage and Tuberculosis and at the same time arranging these schemes which ignore the basic necessities of such a large group of the population.[76]

The South African government was by no means alone in the application of such callous policies during this period. In Swaziland the British government imposed a levy of four shillings per bag on imported maize in the midst of a famine in order to protect the interests of local white growers.[77]

By the mid-1930s, Fox and Back had come to two conclusions: that the diet of African families living in the Transkei and Ciskei was at best barely adequate for the maintenance of good health, and that a narrow margin of safety separated this simple, nearly inadequate diet from one bound to lead to ill-health, if long continued.[78]

That margin of safety was frequently eliminated by the occurrence of drought in combination with the high price of purchased grain. In 1915, 1919, 1924, 1927–1928, and 1933–1936, much of South Africa was hit by severe droughts, the effects of which were increasingly severe as a result of the growing marginalization of many rural households. During these years the price of maize skyrocketed, and reports of near starvation and cases of scurvy were frequent. In severely hit areas the government provided some famine relief and prevented more widespread starvation. It should also be noted that the government put pressure on the Chamber of Mines to increase the employment of Africans from the

South African reserves and to cut back on foreign recruitment.[79] These measures, however, must be seen against a background of agriculture and marketing policies that placed most African farmers in a state of nutritional vulnerability at the same time that they protected the interests of white farmers and ranchers. The perversity of government relief policies during such crises was highlighted by Fox and Back, who noted that in 1936, "while Natives in the Ciskei area were paying 18/– to 25/– per bag for maize as food for families, many of whom were reported to be in a state of semi-starvation, a munificent government was supplying maize to white farmers in the same district for cattle feed at a subsidized price of 7/– per bag." The authors concluded, "There seems some justification for the remark made to us by an intelligent Native that 'at least in the Reserves, it is often an advantage to have four legs rather than two.' "[80]

The growing severity of nutritional problems faced by Transkeian and Ciskeian Africans, and increasingly by Africans in the rest of South Africa, produced a fertile breeding ground for TB infections carried by returning migrant workers. Although the absence of morbidity or mortality data makes it difficult to measure the spread of TB within the rural areas of South Africa, a number of studies conducted by individual district surgeons, together with the more extensive research by the Tuberculosis Research Committee (TBRC), provide strong evidence that TB was well established in the Transkei and Ciskei and expanding rapidly in Basutoland and Natal by the late 1920s and early 1930s. It can in fact be stated that by the beginning of World War II and probably a good deal earlier, the rural and urban areas of South Africa formed a single pool of widespread tubercular infection.

As part of his research for the TBRC, Dr. Peter Allan carried out a series of tuberculin surveys to determine the extent to which the rural populations of the Transkei, Ciskei, and Basutoland had been infected with TB. In the southern Butterworth area of the Transkei, Allan found that 88 percent of both men and women over twenty years of age reacted positively. Among children under ten years of age, 54 percent were positive. The average for all those tested was 74 percent. In the Flagstaff area of Pondoland, 97 percent of adults over twenty and 57 percent of the children under ten tested positive. The overall rate was 78.5 percent.[81] These are very high rates, comparable with rates recorded in European and American cities earlier in the century and in many African cities today. They are, in fact, probably too high, for no allowance was made for the possibility of nonspecific reactions. The report, moreover, does not indicate what measurement criteria were used in distinguishing a positive from a negative reaction. The fact that the rates for women were the same as those for men, despite their relative lack of experience in the urban labor centers, nonetheless indicates that the disease had become endemic within these two areas. The high infection rates for children under ten also suggests that the disease was spreading rapidly.

Prevalence data from the Butterworth area add further support to the conclusion that TB was widespread at this time. These data come from hospital records and must be used with care for two reasons. First, diagnoses of TB were made primarily on the basis of clinical examinations and in many cases did not include either x-ray exams or sputum tests. The resulting estimates may therefore be too high. Second, the number of cases seen in hospitals almost certainly represented a small proportion of the total number of cases in the population, since most Africans neither sought nor had access to western medical services. Even today with more extensive medical services, the ratio of seen cases to those identified by prevalence surveys is roughly one to four (see chapter 9). Although the two problems may in fact cancel each other out, they must nonetheless be kept in mind when evaluating the reliability of prevalence estimates based on hospital data.

Allan reported that of the 5,000 patients seen per year by two physicians working in the Butterworth area, about 450 had TB, or 9 percent. When this figure is divided by the total population of the district, estimated to be 23,000, it gives a TB prevalence of 1,950 per 100,000. Dr. Fennell, district surgeon for Butterworth, produced records showing that out of 3,360 African patients he had seen in the previous twelve months, 298 were suffering from TB. Using the same base population figure, this works out to a prevalence of 1,295 per 100,000.[82] These exceptionally high figures may include cases from outside the Butterworth area. They may, moreover, include urban location and institution cases along with cases coming from the kraals, and thus they may not reflect rural conditions. Yet the figures are consistent with the infection rates recorded above. They are supported, moreover, by figures from the Butterworth office of the Native Recruiting Corporation (NRC) which indicate that 0.79 percent of men examined for mine work were rejected for having TB in 1927. This works out to a prevalence of 790 per 100,000. Although a lower figure than those based on hospital statistics, it must be remembered that unlike the hospital sample, this was a population of mostly young men who felt fit for mine employment. In addition, one would expect that given the age distribution of tuberculosis in the early stages of an epidemic, the prevalence of the disease within the wider population from which these men were drawn would have been substantially higher. It should also be noted that NRC examinations were not noted for their thoroughness or accuracy and that many cases may have been missed.[83]

Dr. Allan, observing that most of the cases he saw were of a chronic nature, concluded that under their own conditions Africans showed considerable powers of resistance. He described a number of cases that had lasted for years, including one extraordinary case of a woman who had originally been diagnosed as having TB in 1896. At various times she had apparently suffered relapses, having experienced severe coughing and the spitting up of blood in 1911, 1916, and 1928. Examined in November of 1928, she was said to have a chronic cough and to be having trouble catching her breath. She also had tubercle bacilli in her sputum but was found to be in fairly good condition overall.[84] The presence of such chronic cases again squares with the high attack rate reflected in the infection rates of children under ten, for chronic cases may have frequent opportunities to infect others. One can only guess, for example, how many kin and neighbors were infected over the years by this one woman. Finally, Allan noted that many of the cases he examined had no connection with industrial employment, reinforcing the picture of a disease that had achieved a self-sustaining level of cross-infection within this area.[85]

Allan found that infection rates were somewhat lower, by contrast, in the Matatiele area of the northern Transkei and in Basutoland. In Matatiele, 70 percent of men, 58 percent of women over twenty, and 19.9 percent of children under ten tested positive, with an overall infection rate of 40 percent. In Basutoland 70 percent of men and 59 percent of women over twenty were positive reactors along with 9 percent of children under ten. The overall rate in Basutoland was 50 percent.[86] Again these rates may be too high due to nonspecific reactions, though the effect of nonspecific mycobacteria may have been less given the higher altitude of these locations. The lower rate for children under ten and the differential in the rates for men and women over twenty indicate that TB was not as prevalent and was spreading more slowly in these two areas. Though even these comparatively lower rates reveal a high level of infection for a rural population. No prevalence data was available for these two areas.

Reports that TB was making serious inroads into the rural African population of the Transkeian territories and was particularly severe among schoolage children led the Department of Public Health to conduct a survey of school children in the Bizana District in 1936. The survey, conducted by the district surgeon of Bizana, Dr. Westlake Wood, included 2,252 children. The results were staggering: 4.5 percent of the children were found to be suffering from TB, and 3.9 percent had pulmonary TB. Overcrowded, poorly ventilated classrooms evidently provided an ideal setting for the transmission of TB among rural African school children.[87]

For Natal we have a clearer picture of the state of TB in the rural areas at the end of the period. This is based on an extensive survey of several African reserves directed by Dr. B. A. Dormer in 1937. This survey employed sputum tests and clinical examinations to identify active cases of TB. On the basis of these surveys, Dormer estimated that the prevalence of active TB cases in mission reserves ranged from 0.6 percent (600 per 100,000) in the Adams Mission Reserve to 0.98 percent (980 per 100,000) in the Groutville Mission Reserve. (About one-third of the cases identified by clinical means produced positive sputum.) By contrast Dormer found that in the "native reserve" 0.25 percent (250 per 100,000) of those screened had active TB.[88] The higher rates in the mission reserves may reflect the more crowded conditions of these areas, the more extensive use of poorly ventilated European-style houses, and a greater reliance on migrant labor. In describing conditions in the mission reserves Dormer noted that while most of those screened had sufficient food, 82 percent lacked basic resistance-building foods such as milk and fresh vegetables in their diet. Ten percent had neither sufficient food supplies nor food of adequate quality.[89] As noted earlier, Christian Africans were often the first to feel the yoke of poverty around their necks.[90]

Together, the above figures strongly suggest that by the late 1920s tuberculosis had established itself in those rural areas from which the mines as well as the major towns and cities drew their labor supplies.

Before completing this discussion on the rural transmission of TB during the early industrialization of South Africa, we should briefly look at the conditions under which several hundred thousand Africans lived on white-owned farms. By 1936, 60 percent of rural Africans lived on white farms.[91] A recent World Health Organization study of apartheid and health noted that today this group is probably the most disadvantaged and discriminated against in South Africa.[92]

The origins of this situation can be traced to the capitalization of white agriculture during the early years of industrial expansion. Industrial growth greatly increased the demand for maize and thus the profitability of farming in many areas of South Africa. This encouraged the expansion of capital into agricultural production, which in turn transformed relations of production within the white farming areas of the country. Prior to the expansion of capital into agriculture, production in the white farming areas had been based primarily on a system of farming "on the halves," or sharecropping, which had evolved over the previous century in many parts of the Orange Free State, Transvaal, and the Cape. This system, though varying widely in detail, had provided African farmers with land on which to grow their crops and herd their livestock. In exchange for these rights, African farmers paid a portion of their produce to the white landowner. For large-scale white farmers, however, this system represented an inefficient use of land and labor, and they pushed to eliminate it through the passage of the 1913 Native Land Act, which greatly restricted the practice. Although sharecropping continued to exist on a reduced scale in many parts of the country for decades after the passage of the act, it was increasingly replaced by a system of labor tenancy: African farmers were given a small plot of land and the right to keep a limited number of livestock in return for providing labor without a cash wage for a certain number of months each year.[93] Labor tenants and their families were also provided with some food rations, consisting primarily of mealie meal. Like sharecropping the terms of labor tenancy varied considerably. In general, however, it represented an advantage to most white farmers, since it allowed them to exercise greater control over their labor force and to maximize their use of land resources. For the African farmer, by contrast, labor tenancy often represented a significant reduction in his control over the means of production and a corresponding increase in his economic dependency.

During the 1920s, the terms under which African farmers lived and worked on white-owned farms deteriorated still further as white farmers strove to maximize production in the face of rapidly expanding commodity markets, buttressed by the Union government's protectionist policies. Restrictions on land use and on the number of cattle an African farmer could keep were increased along with the length of service demanded for these benefits. Africans who resisted this trend were frequently evicted and, in some areas, replaced by wage laborers who had no access to agricultural or pastural land. Yet the movement toward full proletarianization of the workforce was generally resisted by white farmers since it was seen as leading to an overall increase in the cost of labor. By maintaining a system of exploitative labor tenancy some costs of labor could be borne by other industries, and particularly mining, which employed members of farm workers' families during periods in which their labor was not required by the labor tenancy contract. African farmers were thus increasingly caught in an ultraexploitative system in which they were paid no wages but at the same time were not provided with enough land to support themselves or time to cultivate what little land they had.[94]

The situation grew even worse during the depression years as a result of the lengthening of farm labor contracts and the extension of the minimum mining contract to 270 shifts (roughly nine months). This made it extremely difficult for African farm workers to earn income on the mines and still complete their work obligation on the white farm. The departure of members of a tenant's family before the family had completed its labor obligation became a source of tension between white farmers and African tenants during this period.[95] At the same time the conflicting demands of farm owners and mine managers may help explain the rise in desertions the mines experienced between 1933 and 1938.[96]

By the late 1930s when the Native Farm Labor Committee was created, it was abundantly clear that Africans working on white-owned farms were in many cases living under desperate conditions, driving many to abandon rural employment in favor of the cities. The committee observed that African tenant farmers were unable to grow sufficient amounts of food for themselves and had become largely dependent on the food rations provided by the white farmer. These rations were deemed to be clearly inadequate. The primary, and in many cases the only, food provided by the white farmer was mealie meal. In the northern provinces the number of employers who provided meat represented only 20 percent of the total. In the Cape the figure was 60 percent, but even there it was not issued more than once a month. Except where dairy farming predominated, milk did not constitute a significant supplement to the diet. Employers did not provide it and restrictions on herding prevented African farmers from producing their own. So too the value of vegetables was ignored. The majority of African witnesses to the committee claimed that mealie meal was "virtually the only food supplied, except in rare instances." The committee report concluded that for the greater part of the year, the worker and his family were reduced to the narrowest margin of those resistance-building foods essential for their well-being.[97]

Although the committee provided little direct evidence to support their conclusion that malnutrition was widespread among workers on white farms, they observed that,

> Much of the evidence of farmers was to the effect that their Native employees, both resident on the farms and from the reserves and elsewhere, exhibited no zeal, energy, intelligence or initiative in the performance of their work, and they adversely contrasted the service now rendered to that given by the Natives in the olden days. The medical and other expert evidence points with some emphasis to these features being not inconsistent with a condition of impaired vitality due to malnutrition.[98]

Though one must consider the real possibility that the performance and attitude of African farm workers was a calculated worker response to the exploitative conditions of employment, Dr. E. H. Culver, secretary of public health, testified before the committee that, "When Natives are malnourished they can just keep healthy when leading lazy lives, and rest becomes increasingly important as nutrition diminishes."[99]

Scattered reports existed of TB among farm workers, but we have no way of gauging how widespread was the disease among this group of rural Africans. One can only assume that given the spread of disease in reserve areas plus the dependence farm families had on off-farm income, which brought them in contact with urban and industrial labor centers where TB was endemic, that there were frequent opportunities for farm workers to become infected. Given inadequate nutritional levels, moreover, infected workers were likely to develop active cases of TB. It is highly probable, therefore, that the disease had made sizable inroads among farm workers by the mid-1930s.

The absence of medical data on farm workers is a problem that continues today, another product of the political economy of medical knowledge in South Africa. The only reason we know anything about the health condition of Africans in the rural reserves is because the deteriorating health of African mineworkers began to be noticed by the mines' medical officers and managers during the 1920s. This, as noted above, led the Chamber of Mines to support a series of inquiries into conditions in the reserves, as well as to support the training of African medical personnel.[100] White farms by contrast were removed from even the limited network of medical services existing in the reserves. In many cases the only source of western medical treatment was the farmer's wife. Cases of TB would either not be recorded or appeared in the medical records of district surgeons or mission hospitals in the reserves.[101] Until the late 1930s, moreover, the response of white farmers to labor shortages was not to improve conditions but to call for increased coercion on the part of the state. This pressure led to the passage of the Native Services Contract Act of 1932 and the Native Laws Amendment Act of 1937, both attempts to control the movement of African women and children and extend the period of labor due to white farmers.[102] These measures helped the farmers maintain labor supplies and deflected any need to improve conditions. By the late 1930s, however, the expansion of industrial employment and African discontent over farm conditions led to a serious shortfall in farm labor. This time the state, seeing the urban flow of labor as necessary for the expansion of manufacturing, was less responsive to the farmers' renewed calls for coercive farm labor legislation. The government instead attempted to assess the conditions causing the labor shortage by establishing the Native Farm Labour Committee. This provided the first real glimpse of conditions on the farms.

CONCLUSION

The establishment of TB in the rural areas of South Africa during the first decades of this century not only undermined the health of rural populations, it also provided a catalyst for the expansion of the disease within the country's growing industrial centers after World War I. The creation of a growing reserve army of infected men, women, and children meant that workers who entered the workforce during the 1920s and 1930s increasingly carried with them the seeds of tubercular disease. Although white medical authorities would argue that this earlier "tubercularization" provided African workers with added protection against the ravages of TB, this proved to be no more than wishful thinking, as previously infected workers exhibited a higher susceptibility to the disease than uninfected ones. Under the stresses of urban and industrial life marked by severe overcrowding and malnutrition, the infections these workers carried with them became active cases of TB and contributed to a rising tide of TB mortality.

Slumyards and the Rising Tide of Tuberculosis, 1914–1938

World War I marked the beginning of a period of rapid industrial growth in South Africa centered on the development of secondary industries and accompanied by a dramatic expansion of urban populations. These changes were paralleled by a steady rise in TB mortality. African TB mortality rates peaked during World War I and then, following a brief period of remission after the war, rose again through the mid-1930s. The increase in postwar TB mortality indicates that the conditions under which Africans lived and worked in the urban centers of South Africa became progressively worse during the 1920s and 1930s. This deterioration occurred despite a growing awareness of the need to deal with the slum conditions under which Africans lived and some movement toward urban reform. The relationship between these efforts to clean up urban areas and a rise in TB mortality was not coincidental. Not only did the rise in TB encourage slum clearance efforts, but the efforts themselves contributed directly to the rising tide of TB since they were directed primarily at removing African slums beyond the purview of white society, reflecting the political and economic interests shaping urban reform. Far from dealing with the root causes of African health problems, this pattern of urban reform simply transferred these problems to the increasingly overcrowded "native" locations and sprawling peri-urban slums that grew up around the major urban centers of the country. These segregated areas provided ideal breeding grounds for tuberculosis.

World War I ushered in a new phase of industrial development in South Africa. Stimulated by wartime shortages in consumer goods, manufacturing industries began to emerge in the nation's major urban centers. On the Rand, for example, the number of industrial establishments increased from 862 to 1,763 between 1915–1916 and 1921–1922.[1] The growth in manufacturing greatly increased the demand for labor. Since many of these industries were undercapitalized, moreover, and during their early years operated on the margins of profitability, they shared the mine owners' preference for low-wage African labor. By 1920 there were 20,000 Africans working in manufacturing on the Rand, primarily in light consumer industries. Industrial expansion also meant more jobs in commerce and construction and a need to expand the municipal workforce. As a result, the size of the African workforce engaged in nonmining activities on the Rand swelled from 67,111 in 1918 to 92,597 by May of 1920.[2] Similar patterns of growth occurred in the other major urban centers. In Cape Town the African population grew from 1,569 in 1911 to 7,466 in 1921. In East London the population grew from 8,000 to 12,000 while in Port Elizabeth and Durban the African population doubled in size.

The structure of the African urban population also changed. The earlier movement of Africans into wage labor within the urban centers had been primarily a male migrant phenomenon, but now a growing number of African urban workers began moving to the cities with their wives and children. In Johannesburg, for example, the number of African women in the population rose from 4,357 in 1911 to 12,000 by 1921.[3] This equaled a 180 percent increase in the female population. During the same period the number of African men increased by only 5 percent.

Although the recession years of 1921 and 1922 slowed the pace of growth, urbanization resumed in the mid-1920s, sparked not only by the continued expansion of industry but increasingly by declining economic opportunities for Africans within the country's rural areas. There was thus significant pressure for rural Africans to seek urban employment. Added to this growing reserve army of African labor were Africans who had already made the transition to wage employment in the mining industry but saw better opportunities in the manufacturing sector. Manufacturing offered wages that, although low by white standards, were by the end of the war slightly higher than those on the mines, and working conditions that were less life threatening. These experienced migrants were also attracted by the relative freedom of location life as compared to the more regimented conditions that existed in the mining compounds. For some, the opportunity to live with their wives and families was a major enticement.

Overall African urban populations grew by 94 percent between 1921 and 1936.[4] Looking at specific centers, the African population of Cape Town increased by 36.5 percent, Johannesburg by 83 percent, Durban by 38 percent, East London by 44 percent, and Port Elizabeth by 21 percent.[5] As before, this growth reflected the movement of women and families into the urban areas. Nationwide the number of women living in urban areas increased by 142 percent between 1921 and 1936, while the number of men increased by only 78 percent. In Johannesburg alone the number of women rose by a phenomenal 245 percent, while the number of men increased by 45 percent.

The growth in African urban settlement was accompanied by a rise in black TB mortality rates in the cities of South Africa. In Cape Town, African and colored TB rates peaked during the war and then declined in the immediate postwar period, only to begin a slow but steady rise from 1922 to 1934. In both East London and Port Elizabeth, the pattern was the same but with a steeper continuous rise from 1924 through the depression years to 1935. In Johannesburg, after an initial peak during World War I, TB mortality rates rose less evenly, with an initial rise during the mid-1920s followed by a decline in 1926 and then a second more gradual rise from 1927 to 1933 (see graphs 1–3). White rates in these cities, by contrast, leveled off or decreased during the early part of the period. The depression, however, brought an increase in white TB mortality as well.

The upward trend in black TB mortality needs to be examined carefully in order to understand the connection that existed between the changing epidemiology of TB and the shifting political economy of South Africa during this period. Such an inquiry must begin with a consideration of the very real possibility that increases in TB mortality recorded during World War I and after 1921 were a statistical illusion, resulting from the inability of municipal authorities to control, much less accurately enumerate, the urban influx of Africans. If the actual African population rose at a faster rate than the estimated population, the denominators used to establish TB mortality rates would have been too low and the rates themselves would have risen without any increase in the actual mortality rate. There is reason to believe that this phenomenon may have played some role in shaping mortality rates. If one looks at the mortality curves for Cape Town and East London one can see that the rates dip downward following the census years of 1921, 1936, and 1946. These appear to represent statistical corrections based on more accurate estimates of the populations at risk. (A similar, much greater correction occurred in the white rates for Johannesburg as a result of the 1911 census.) Yet in each case the TB rates jumped back up in the year following the population correction. Even with the correction, moreover, the general trend in TB mortality between 1922 and 1946 was upward. In effect, the statistical error appears to have altered the overall height of the mortality curves, rather than their trajectory. The reality of the upward trend in TB mortality in Johannesburg during World War I is supported by a second set of data collected by Dr. Charles Porter, the medical officer of Johannesburg. As noted in chapter 2, Porter followed the progress of patients who were diagnosed as having TB and recorded how long they survived after diagnosis. The percentage of patients who died during the first month after diagnosis declined dramatically from roughly 20 percent during the period 1904–1909 to 7.3 percent in 1913–1914. This same rate jumped to 31 percent in 1914–1915, 36.7 percent in 1915–1916, and 36.2 percent for the years 1916 to 1919.[6] This dramatic jump in rapidly fatal cases is consistent with an overall increase in TB mortality.

The rapid growth of urban populations during this period also raises the possibility that the rise in TB mortality reflected what E. R. N. Grigg calls the "immigration effect," the introduction of new urban residents who had not been previously exposed to TB and thus represented a susceptible population. Limited prior exposure to TB may have played a significant role in the initial rise in mortality rates prior to World War I. The Africans who arrived in the cities of South Africa during the 1920s and 1930s, however, were, as noted in chapter 4, coming from areas in which TB had become endemic. They were not for the most part an unexposed population.

This prior exposure did not, however, mean that the Africans who poured into South African cities between the wars were more resistant to TB. There is evidence, in fact, that, contrary to what white medical authorities believed about the relationship between prior infection and susceptibility, previous exposure may have increased African susceptibility to TB when subjected to the conditions of urban life. In a follow-up study of 93,979 African mine recruits who were tuberculin-tested in 1928, it was found that 566 developed TB between April 1 and September 30. Of these cases, 452 occurred among workers who were initially positive reactors (61,115) while 114 occurred among negative reactors

(32,864). This worked out to an incidence rate of 738 per 100,000 for positive reactors compared to 347 per 100,000 for negative reactors. The study also observed that initially negative reactors were more likely than positive reactors to develop a rapidly fatal form of tuberculosis (miliary tuberculosis). Several conclusions can be drawn from these findings. First, they suggest that previous exposure to TB contributed to the elimination of individuals with a hereditary susceptibility to TB. Thus individuals who had been exposed to TB and survived (the tuberculin-positive reactors in this study) were less likely to succumb later in life to a rapidly fatal type of TB than those who had not been previously exposed (the tuberculin negatives). Second, prior exposure did not, however, protect workers from developing TB when subjected to malnutrition, concurrent diseases, and physical stress within the urban areas of the country, since these conditions undermined their ability to control their infections. In fact, previously infected workers were likely to develop TB sooner than were previously unexposed workers, simply because the exposed workers were already infected. In other words, within the conditions that existed in the urban and industrial centers of South Africa, previous exposure to TB reduced the virulence of the disease but not the risk of developing it. Moreover, given these conditions and the absence of effective medical care, the odds were that once urban Africans developed TB they would die whether or not they had been exposed to the disease earlier in life. The only difference was in how long it would take for them to die. Commenting on the protection afforded by previous exposure to the disease, the TBRC observed, "The gain does not amount to much; if compelled to choose between dying in four weeks or in forty, most people would choose forty, but they would not be particularly grateful for this much of a choice."[7] Finally, it needs to be stressed that this data clearly supports the argument made in chapter 1 that the resistance afforded to a population through exposure to TB and the elimination of hereditarily susceptible individuals and families could be overwhelmed by environmental stresses. Thus, as noted in the last chapter, rural populations appear to have been becoming better able to control the disease during the 1920s as a result of this "seasoning" process. When these rural Africans were exposed to the conditions of urban life, however, or when conditions in the rural areas began to deteriorate, this protection was of little value.

In conclusion, it appears likely that the rising tide of urban TB mortality during the 1920s and 1930s resulted more from the earlier spread of TB infection to the rural areas of South Africa and the subsequent

movement of infected Africans from these areas into the harsh conditions of urban and industrial life than from the introduction of a new
wave of previously unexposed immigrants.

Related to the question of inexperience and susceptibility is the role
played by women in the rise in TB mortality. As observed in chapter 2,
the higher TB rates of women during the earlier years of this century,
together with their increasing numbers in urban areas, helped elevate
urban TB mortality rates during the period up to World War I. The
possibility exists, therefore, that part of the rise in urban TB mortality
rates from World War I was caused by the large urban migration of
women during this period. Yet, evidence for the period between 1921
and 1936 suggests that women were not more susceptible than men.
Gender specific mortality data from Ndabeni township outside Cape
Town, for example, reveal that TB mortality rates for men and women
were virtually the same, with men having slightly higher rates for most
years between 1924 and 1936.[8] (graph 7) It is impossible to determine
from the available data whether the similarity of gender-specific TB
mortality rates during this period reflects an increase in male susceptibility to the disease or a decrease in that of females. Grigg, however, notes
that it is common for the differential in male and female TB mortality to
decrease as a population becomes more exposed to the disease.[9] The
increased percentage of African women in the urban areas of South
Africa from World War I may therefore have played a very limited role
in the overall rise of TB rates.

Although the TB mortality rates of men and women in Ndabeni were
generally equal during the interwar years, the rates for women were
markedly higher during the Depression, just as those in New Brighton
had risen during the recession of 1906–1909. TB *notifications* for
women in East London also rose during the recession years of the early
1920s. (graph 8) The occurrence of higher female rates during periods
of economic recession, reinforces the suggestion made in chapter 2 that
part of the higher susceptibility of women to TB was environmental and
related to differences in the ability of men and women to survive the
oppressive conditions that existed during periods of economic decline.

Although underestimations of the size of the population at risk and
changes in the composition of the African urban population may have
played some role in the rising tide of TB mortality that occurred in
South African cities between the wars, much of this increase was undoubtedly due to the fact that conditions of life for the majority of
urban Africans, coloreds, Asians, and a small percentage of poor whites,

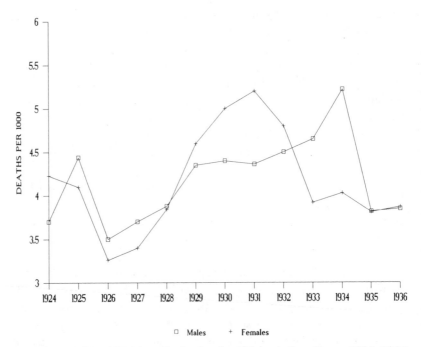

Graph 7.   African TB Mortality by Gender, Ndabeni, Cape Town, 1924–1936
Source: Cape Town, *Reports of the Medical Officer of Health,* 1924–1936.

deteriorated significantly during this period. This decline in living conditions in turn reflected the inability of the growing number of urban poor
to obtain adequate housing, sanitation, food, and medical care. Yet
ultimately, this lack of resources was the end result of a series of conflicting social and economic policies that were designed to benefit a wide
range of interests within white society, at the expense of black workers
and their families.

TB AND THE POLITICAL ECONOMY OF
HOUSING

Factory owners welcomed the influx of African workers during
World War I, but they made little effort to insure that they were properly housed or fed. Existing location housing was quickly saturated, and
efforts to build new locations were blocked by the rising cost of building
materials and by opposition from white rate-payers to both the expense
of providing housing and the prospect of having African locations near

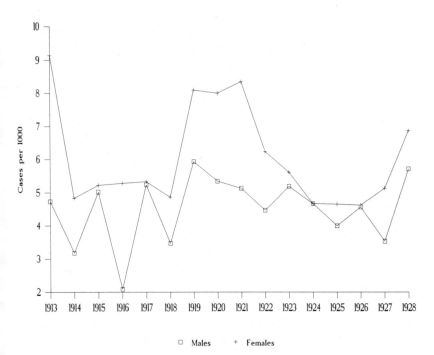

Graph 8.   African TB Notifications by Gender, East London, 1913–1928
Source: CMA, TBRC, Allan Reports (b), file 1b, Progress Report 15.

their homes. On the Rand, the situation was further complicated by the refusal of mining companies to sell the municipality surface rights on which to construct a new location. This prohibited the construction of housing on the broad strip of land that ran from east to west, just south of the city. It was not until 1918, in response to the influenza epidemic, that construction was begun on the Western Native Townships at Newlands. Like the earlier Klipspruit location, the new townships were situated adjacent to a refuse dump.[10]

To meet the needs of their workers, employers applied for licenses from the city council to construct compounds on the grounds of their factories, warehouses, and foundaries. These, like the slumyard properties white landlords rented out to African workers, consisted of rows of poorly constructed small rooms without adequate sanitation or water supplies and rented out at rates as high as twenty-five to thirty shillings per month. The high rents and low supply of housing encouraged extensive overcrowding. By 1918 there were some 10,000 African workers and their families living in conditions such as these in Johannesburg.[11]

Similar conditions developed in East London, Port Elizabeth, and Cape Town, though to a somewhat lesser degree.

The influenza pandemic that hit South African cities in 1918 contributed to a peaking of urban TB mortality rates and threw into sharp relief the appalling housing conditions under which the majority of blacks and an embarrassing number of whites lived. Influenza reactivated existing lesions converting previous infections into active cases of TB. For Africans who were already suffering from TB, moreover, the overlay of influenza brought on a more rapid death. In Cape Town, seventy-four blacks whose official cause of death was influenza, also had TB.[12] Ironically the influenza epidemic may also have contributed to the decline in TB mortality which occurred in the years immediately following the epidemic. The epidemic undoubtedly killed off a large number of blacks and poor whites who might have otherwise died of TB in subsequent years, since it hit hardest among those groups who lived in overcrowded, malnourished circumstances and were thus at greatest risk of TB. This early die-off may explain why the wartime rise in TB was not sustained during the recession years following the war, when social and economic conditions would normally have taken a heavy toll in TB deaths.

The appalling mortality accompanying the influenza epidemic sparked a debate over the need to provide adequate housing for the country's growing population of urban black workers and to eliminate the slums that dotted most urban areas. The debate culminated in the passage of the Native Urban Areas Act in 1923. Like much of the social legislation passed during this period, the act was the product of a compromise between conflicting social and economic interests operating within white society.

There was widespread consensus among whites that urban segregation was a desirable goal. There was in addition a significant element of the African petty bourgeoisie who saw in segregation an opportunity to separate themselves from the poor working-class Africans among whom they were forced to live in squalid conditions. Yet the terms upon which segregation would be established, and the question of who would bear the expense it would entail, were greatly disputed.[13]

The representatives of industrial capital appreciated the need for better housing conditions both to enhance their workforce and in order to eliminate slums. They did not wish to pay the cost of constructing alternative housing, however, arguing instead that housing should be provided by the municipalities or the state, or by the African workers themselves. To this last possibility they acceded to the proposition that Africans should be allowed freehold rights to urban land in their own locations. Finally, the factory owners objected to too stringent an application of influx controls since this would restrict their labor supply and increase wage bills.

Municipal councils represented the interests of white rate-payers, many of whom were newly proletarianized white workers whose economic position was threatened by the growing influx of low-wage African labor. They thus objected to bearing the cost of constructing segregated native locations and were adamant in their call for stiffer influx control laws. Embracing the Stallard Commission's position that Africans should only be allowed in the urban areas to serve the needs of whites and that their natural place of habitation was in the reserves, they rejected the provision of freehold rights to land for Africans since that implied a permanence of occupation they would not tolerate.[14]

The Union government for its part was sympathetic to the labor demands of the manufacturing sector. Even after the victory of the Pact government in 1924, efforts to generate white employment focused primarily on preserving the position of white workers already entrenched in the mining industry and on creating jobs in the railways, postal services, and municipalties. Manufacturing was given a relatively free hand to employ African workers. The government therefore was reluctant to apply strict influx control measures. At the same time, they insisted on retaining control over the administration of influx regulations and thus prevented the municipalities from enacting their own restrictions on urban migration. As for housing, they were no more willing to pay the bill than were other interest groups, arguing that these costs should be borne by those who benefited from the presence of the African workers.[15]

These conflicting views of segregation and slum clearance, led to the passage of a bill riddled with contradictions. Though the resulting Native Urban Areas Act imposed influx control measures as a way of restricting the entry of Africans into the urban areas, it left control of these measures in the hands of a government hesitant to apply them lest it undercut the labor needs of the nation's emerging manufacturing sector. The act allowed municipal authorities to proclaim portions of their land for white settlement only, halting further settlement by Africans. It also provided the legal basis for removing blacks from areas proclaimed "white" as well as for slum removals. Yet it required that the municipalities provide alternative housing for those who were to be removed *before* proclamations or removals could be initiated. The act allowed municipal councils to restrict the issuance of freehold titles to Africans but permitted existing titles to remain in force. Finally, and perhaps most importantly, although much of the act depended on the construction of new housing, it contained no provisions for funding this building program. The government steadfastly refused, moreover, to hand over revenue obtained from African taxation and the registration of passes to municipal authorities for the construction of African housing and other social amenities. As a result of these contradictions the Native Urban Areas Act did little to improve and in some ways further exacerbated the already critical housing problem.

The limitations of the act were quickly made apparent to the City Council of Johannesburg when, in November of 1924, it proclaimed the city a whites-only area. The proclamation was struck down by the Supreme Court because the 8,500 houses available in the native locations were said to be totally inadequate for the needs of the city's existing African population. Efforts were made to provide alternative housing where funds were available, but these measures could not keep up with the continued influx of Africans whose presence could not be limited by the municipal authorities. By 1927, 16,200 Africans were housed in three locations and two hostels, yet the number of African males, many with families, still requiring accommodation was conservatively estimated at 11,500.[16] As a result slumyards and overcrowded, disease-ridden locations continued to grow. In 1925 the slumyard population of Johannesburg was estimated to be 9,000. By 1927 the figure had reached 40,000 and a belt of slums stretched across the western, central, and eastern suburbs of the city. Conditions in the other major urban areas, as noted below, were little better.[17]

Clearly the influx of new African residents was proceeding faster than the municipal authorities could construct new housing, given the limited resources they were willing to spend on this construction and the state's unwillingness to help. This led to calls for an amendment to the 1923 act. The government was slow to react, but in 1930 it passed an Amended Act allowing the municipal authorities to restrict the further influx of Africans into the areas under their jurisdiction and to require that all new residents settle in designated "native locations." Although the law continued to insist that Africans who were already living within proclaimed areas could not be removed until alternative housing was provided, it allowed the authorities to begin dealing with existing slum properties without having to cope with a continual increase in the number of such properties. Yet, continually hampered by lack of funds, attempts to provide alternative housing in the end did little more than transfer the slum problem from one part of the city to another.[18]

In Johannesburg, the Municipal Council moved ahead rapidly with the proclamation of various sections of the city and construction of alternative housing in the new location of Orlando. By 1931, 93 out of 103 of the city's suburbs had been proclaimed. Although the removal of existing African dwelling cleaned up slum conditions in the newly designated white areas, it did not improve overall housing conditions for Africans. The reasons for this have been described by a number of authors, and we need not do more than outline them here.[19]

To begin with, few African residents were willing to move to the location housing being created for them in Orlando, despite the fact that the new houses were often superior to those they currently inhabited. Africans feared that the locations would provide municipal authorities with greater control over residential rights and thus restrict their ability to live with their families. The Municipal Council had in fact passed an amendment allowing them to restrict the settlement of wives and families within the towns. They also feared that within the locations the authorities would be in a better position to control the illegal production of beer, which by 1930 had become a major source of supplemental income for many families (see below for a discussion of the importance of beer brewing for urban Africans). Location housing in addition was situated further away from sites of employment and thus imposed an additional cost for transportation. The distance from the center of town also restricted the informal economic activities of women, removing them from their customers for beer as well as making it more difficult for them to take in the laundry of white families.

Although the cost of location housing was somewhat cheaper than comparable accommodations within the city, the addition of ten shillings per month for transport negated this advantage. The cost of location housing was in fact artificially high as a result of the use of white labor. As the Smit Committee would note in 1942, color bar restrictions prohibiting the use of African labor for housing construction in African locations created the anomaly of white workers who earned somewhat over three shillings per hour constructing houses for African laborers who earned not much more than three shillings per day.[20]

As a result of these obstacles, African families removed from proclaimed areas chose to move to areas that had not yet been proclaimed rather than to the houses being constructed in the locations. By 1933 only 9,000 of the estimated 30,000 Africans who were removed had taken up housing in the locations. This had two effects. First, location housing often stood empty for want of occupants.[21] This permitted the municipal authorities to continue carrying out clearance without having to invest large sums in new housing. In the long run, this slowdown in construction would create an even greater housing crisis in the 1940s. Second, the unproclaimed areas to which Africans moved, places like Prospect Town, Malay Location, Newclare, Martindale, and Sophiatown, became increasingly congested. Newclare had a population of 2,660 in 1921. By 1938 it had grown to an estimated 35,000. Sophiatown grew from 12,000 to 17,000 between 1928 and 1931.[22]

As Andre Proctor shows, the demand for housing in the areas in which the newly removed Africans settled pushed rents upward. In Sophiatown, where the estimated average monthly wage was seventy shillings, the cost of a single room rose to forty shillings per month in the mid-1930s.[23] This high cost increased the practice of subletting and greatly increased the frequency of overcrowding. Conditions grew worse during the depression with the creation of an expanding population of unemployed men and women who could not afford to pay rents. In Pimsville it was estimated that there were six persons per household by the mid-1930s. When the estimated 15,000 lodgers were added to the calculation, however, the average occupation ratio was twelve per house.[24] The 1932 Native Economic Commission estimated that the average number of occupants per room in slum properties was nearly eight and that the population density in the cities slumyards was an incredible four million per square mile.[25]

Elsewhere, the ability of municipal governments to exclude Africans from settlement within the proclaimed urban areas, combined with their failure to provide alternative housing and the continued buildup of African populations deprived of a living on the land, resulted in a similar increase in poorly housed urban Africans and the growth of slum conditions in the locations and uncontrolled peri-urban areas.

In Port Elizabeth the African population increased by 1,961 people between 1921 and 1928. During the same period, only 162 new dwellings were constructed. This was clearly inadequate in that it only provided one dwelling per 12 persons. The shortage in housing resulted in the illegal construction of wood and iron shacks in the backyards of dwellings. As the MOH noted, a considerable number of these shacks were created ostensibly as kitchens or storage sheds but were rented out by the owners to workers who could not find housing elsewhere. The rent charged for these inadequate shelters was said to be out of proportion to the cost of constructing them.[26] The lack of accommodation in Port Elizabeth also resulted in an ever-growing number of Africans settling in Korsten, which remained outside municipal control until 1932. As in the unproclaimed locations of Johannesburg, this movement caused rents to climb and led to a similar pattern of slumyard construction, subletting, and general overcrowding. A survey of housing in Korsten in 1932 found that the average occupancy rate per dwelling, many of which contained only one room, was 6.19 persons. The senior assistant health officer described one such dwelling as follows:

> I was taken to see some of the overcrowded premises. One four-roomed dwelling, which was owned by a native, consisted of a well built brick house . . . with only only two families living in it. The yard, however, was lined with 7 single small rooms, each about 8' by 8', with a separate family in each room. Each family on average consisted of 4 persons . . . [27]

In Durban, the African population increased from 29,000 to 40,000 between 1921 and 1930. Of those 40,000, only 9,000 were provided with housing by the municipality, primarily in unisex hostels. Of the remainder, some 10,000 to 15,000 were domestics housed by their employers. An unknown number of industrial workers were provided housing by their employers under conditions reported to be marked by overcrowding. An estimated 10,000 workers, including virtually all workers who wished to live with their families, had to find housing in uncontrolled peri-urban slums outside the borough. In many cases housing consisted of slumyards similar in character to those in Johannesburg and Port Elizabeth. The conditions existing in these peri-urban areas in 1930 were described by the Joint Council of Europeans and Africans.

> We entered by a narrow passage off the main street and found ourselves in a courtyard with rows of one-roomed houses on each side; in the center were back to back very small kitchens. . . . The first house we entered was occupied by a native shoemaker, with a respectable Coloured wife and three children 16, 13 and 12 years of age. Wages I was told were £1.10.0 a week and rent £1 per month. The area of the room was 10ft by 10ft. . . . We saw another area where small shanties were planted down behind the store higgledy-piggledy. . . . I entered one of these houses, not a bit bigger than a fair sized bathroom. . . . This room contained about 800 cubic feet and was inhabited at night by a man, wife and three children.[28]

In East London, the number of coloreds and Africans living in the two municipal locations rose from 8,500 in 1912 to nearly 13,000 by 1926. In the larger East Bank location there were 11,068 residents (10,142 Africans and 926 coloreds) who occupied 1,111 private and

153 municipal dwellings. The average number of occupants per privately owned dwelling was 8.89 while that for the municipal dwellings was only 4.33. The high ratio of occupants per dwelling in the privately owned homes reflected the regular practice of subletting rooms and the failure of the East London authorities to either provide an adequate supply of municipal housing or to enforce housing regulations within privately owned properties.[29]

By 1931 the number of privately owned dwellings had increased by 387 or 34.8 percent while municipal housing had increased by only 15 dwellings or 9.8 percent, an example of the extent to which municipal authorities had delegated responsibility for providing housing to local entrepreneurs through their own inactivity. Meanwhile the population of the location had grown by roughly 6,000 or 8.3 percent.[30] If the total population was distributed equally among the 1,666 available houses, the resulting ratio of occupants per house would have been just over 10 per dwelling. Regulations controlling overcrowding in municipal housing, however, and significant economic differentiation among location residents, meant that the vast majority of new residents were housed in overcrowded private houses with an occupancy ratio of nearly 12 per dwelling.

The rapid buildup of location residents outside East London, Port Elizabeth, Johannesburg, and other growing urban centers not only outpaced the growth of housing and led to excessive overcrowding, it also overwhelmed the limited sanitation facilities provided by residents or location authorities. In Korsten there was no waterborne sewage until the mid-1930s and nightsoil was still collected in wooden buckets. The pail closets that did exist, moreover, were insufficient for the number of people using them. This resulted in the frequent overflow of raw sewage within the slumyards. The assistant MOH noted one yard inhabited by sixty people which was "served by two dilapidated and dirty pail closets."[31]

While waterborne sewage systems were installed in the two locations of East London in 1927, they only served a limited number of installations. In 1931 there were a total of 175 toilets, 50 showers, and 175 washtubs located in 25 sanitary blocks, provided for a population of approximately 20,000 residents. The number of residents per latrine was 114! Commenting on this situation the MOH noted that the "lack of individual sanitary conveniences results in the use of street gutters after dark with the result that the storm water drain is now a sewer."[32] A study of the bacterial and parasitic egg content of dust samples collected in East London in 1930 predictably revealed considerably higher levels of soil contamination in and around the locations than elsewhere. Among the parasites identified in the study were the cysts of amebic dysentery and hookworm.[33]

Such lack of sanitation contributed to the spread of parasitic diseases within the locations and to very high rates of diarrhea. In East London 153 deaths were attributed to diarrhea in 1931.[34] This was the equivalent to roughly 7.6 deaths per 1,000 residents. Since most of these deaths would have occurred among children, however, the rate of diarrhea-related deaths among location children would have been considerably higher. In Johannesburg, where diarrhea-related deaths began slowly to decline among whites from 1921 following the provision of waterborne sewage, rates for Africans rose sharply in the face of population growth and the inadequate provision of sanitation.[35]

The health cost of inadequate sanitation, however, was not limited to diarrhea-related deaths. Parasitic infections, as noted in chapter 2, have an adverse effect on nutritional levels, particularly on protein absorp-

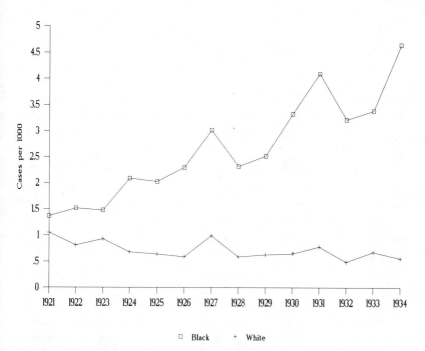

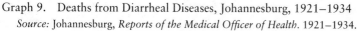

Graph 9.   Deaths from Diarrheal Diseases, Johannesburg, 1921–1934
Source: Johannesburg, *Reports of the Medical Officer of Health.* 1921–1934.

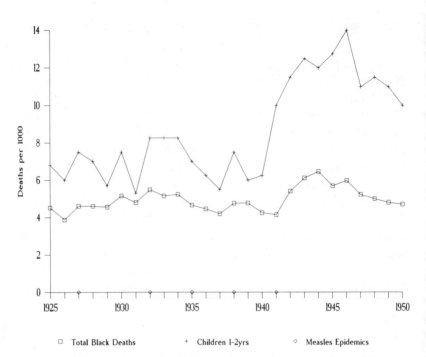

Graph 10.   TB Deaths, Black Children 1–2yrs, Cape Town, 1925–1950
Source: Cape Town, *Reports of the Medical Officer of Health,* 1925–1950.

tion, and are a significant cofactor in the production of tuberculosis. Thus lack of sanitation facilities in the urban locations may have contributed to the rise in TB that occurred among urban Africans between 1922 and 1934.

A second synergistic relationship may have been set up by the rapid increase that occurred in overcrowded housing. Measles, like TB and other infectious diseases, found a fertile ground for transmission within the overcrowded urban locations, and outbreaks of the disease occurred regularly between 1921 and 1941. Although measles by itself accounted for a considerable number of deaths among infants and young children, the disease, which often acts as a catalyst to TB infections in such children, appears to have contributed to increased TB mortality among black infants under two years of age in Cape Town.[36]

The deteriorating conditions that developed in the locations and periurban areas surrounding South Africa's cities as a result of segregation and slum removal efforts between 1923 and 1933, led to renewed calls by municipal authorities, health officials, joint European and African councils, and white rate-payers for both increased authority to clean up slum locations and greater government financial support for these efforts. This pressure led to the passage of the 1934 Slum Clearance Act. The act provided the municipal authorities with new powers to force the removal of slum properties. It also provided for the first time government financial support for slum clearance in the form of low-interest loans for constructing new location housing.

The new act did not solve the African urban-housing problem. It did provide for an increase in the removal of slum properties from municipal areas, but it failed to insure the provision of an adequate supply of housing. There were several reasons for this. First, despite the providing of low-interest loans, white rate-payers were still resistant to allocating funds for new housing. Even at subeconomic rates there was concern that the cost of housing would result in rents that Africans could not afford, and that ultimately the rate-payers would be left paying for the new housing.[37] This did not of course lead to pressure for higher African wages but for greater government financial support. The act in addition did nothing to change the existing pattern of influx control designed to benefit manufacturing interests. Combined with the continuing deterioration of the rural areas, punctuated by the widespread drought during the mid-1930s, these factors generated a continual influx of new impoverished urban residents. Although the Native Urban Areas Act, as amended in 1930, allowed the municipal authorities to restrict the settlement of these new residents within the proclaimed municipal areas, illegal structures sprang up in the surrounding native locations. The municipal authorities worked to remove these structures, but the flow of Africans continued unabated and new structures replaced the ones that were torn down. The municipal authorities, seeing themselves faced with a losing battle, were highly critical of the government's policies.

The antipathy of local white rate-payers to the provisions of the Slum Clearance Act and their view that the solution to the problem lay in controlling the influx of black labor rather than in better sanitation laws was clearly expressed at a meeting between the secretary of health for the Union and the Port Elizabeth Council in 1934. Reporting on the meeting, the secretary of health noted,

> I commenced by referring to the passage of the Slums Act and the increased responsibilities of the Council in connection therewith. It was at once evident that I was in for a hostile reception as I was interrupted on several sides and was asked what financial responsibility the Government was going to shoulder.

The secretary went on to suggest the need for an additional story on the existing infectious disease hospital to treat TB cases.

> This was altogether too much for several members who then got up and delivered addresses on the Government's labour policy, on the poverty of the rate payers and expressing the opinion that the Government should pay the whole cost of dealing with tuberculosis and so on . . . [38]

The combination of increasing urban settlement and the continued unwillingness of white rate-payers, government officials, or the owners of industry to support housing projects undermined the effectiveness of the Slum Clearance Act. Although the act does appear to have contributed to a fall in urban TB rates in Cape Town, Johannesburg, Port Elizabeth, and East London, this fall, like that which followed the initial construction of location housing at the beginning of the century, represented for the most part a displacement effect generated by the forced removal of Africans out of the municipal areas included in urban health statistics. This effect was reinforced by the 1936 census, which caused a downward adjustment in rates.

The effects of slum clearance measures and population removals on TB mortality rates can be seen in graph 11, which compares the African TB mortality rates for Port Elizabeth with those of its official native location, New Brighton. In general TB rates for New Brighton during the 1930s were higher than those for Port Elizabeth. This is particularly true for 1935, a drought year during which the population of New Brighton rose from 6,658 to 7,430. Although the rate fell in 1936, it rose steadily between 1936 and 1940 following the enactment of slum clearance measures that got underway after much foot dragging in 1935. During this period the population of New Brighton increased from 7,827 to 16,574 as a result of removals from Port Elizabeth and a growing migration of rural migrants to the city.

Commenting on conditions in New Brighton, the medical officer for Port Elizabeth observed in his annual report for 1934–1935 that there was a "comparatively healthy labor supply at New Brighton" and that,

> I think we have in New Brighton, Port Elizabeth, a practical example of the value which accrues to a community from a comprehensive medical service to the poorer classes.

In terms of TB, however, this benefit clearly was not being shared by the residents of New Brighton.

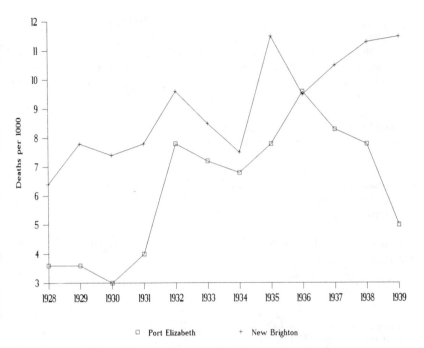

□ Port Elizabeth   + New Brighton

Graph 11.   African TB Mortality, Port Elizabeth vs. New Brighton
Source: Port Elizabeth, Reports of the Medical Officer of Health, 1928–1939.

TB rates for Port Elizabeth, by contrast, declined after 1936 as a result of slum removals. Slum clearance in effect shifted Port Elizabeth's TB burden to New Brighton. Interestingly, the downward pressure slum removals had on TB mortality rates in Port Elizabeth after 1935 was mirrored in the earlier rise of TB mortality rates between 1930 and 1936, and especially the dramatic rise from 1931 to 1932. That rise reflected the city's incorporation in 1932 of Korsten, a notorious breeding ground for TB. Long resisted by Port Elizabeth's white rate-payers, this incorporation added to the municipality's TB caseload. In short, the TB mortality rates for both Port Elizabeth and New Brighton reflected policies that did little to affect the actual death rate from TB but instead shifted the burden of the disease from one area to another.

The Slum Clearance Act, therefore, continued the process begun at the turn of the century—that of transferring TB deaths beyond the view of urban whites. This process was facilitated by the terms of the Slum Clearance Act, which specifically excluded location housing from restrictions that defined minimum standards for housing within the white urban areas. As the Smit Committee would later observe,

[M]any of the houses being built for Natives under the Housing Acts, themselves primarily designed to prevent or eradicate slums, are from the first day of their occupation overcrowded and therefore slums as defined in the Second Schedule of the Slum Act and escape condemnation as such only by reason of the specific withdrawal of Native locations from the purview of the ... Act.[39]

Commenting on the overall effect of slum clearance on the health of Africans, the MOH of East London observed,

Though slums may disappear from European Urban areas, segregation has resulted in overcrowded unhealthy slum areas in locations, hot beds of Tuberculosis and Venereal Disease removed at some distance from the town, or separated from it, and under the eyes of officials alone.[40]

It was this exclusionary process, rather than improvements in black health, that was largely responsible for the recorded drop in urban black TB mortality after 1934.

THE POLITICAL ECONOMY OF URBAN FOOD CONSUMPTION

Although deteriorating housing and sanitation conditions played a major role in the epidemiology of TB in urban South Africa after World War I, malnutrition undoubtedly contributed to the TB death rate. As noted in chapter 2, urban diets before the war were heavily dependent on starches and generally lacked vitamins, fats, and protein. This pattern continued after the war, exacerbated first by rising food prices and then during the depression by declining buying power. As with housing and sanitation, inadequate food consumption was the product of a set of economic policies designed to benefit specific sets of economic and political interests within white society at the expense of African consumers.

Reports of malnutrition and inadequate urban diets in the annual reports of medical officers sparked a series of studies on African dietary patterns conducted by both individual researchers and groups such as the Joint Councils of Europeans and Africans (JCEAs) which emerged during the interwar years. These studies provide rich sources of data on urban African nutritional patterns during the 1920s and 1930s.

The Johannesburg JCEA in 1927 prepared a minimum monthly budget for an African family of five, covering rent, transportation, taxes, burial society fees, fuel, food, candles, and school and church fees. No amounts were included for clothing or furniture. The budget ranged from £6.1.2 to £6.11.8. The council's budget exceeded the mean wage paid to Johannesburg location residents by £1.14.6 to £2.5.0 per month.[41] Dr. Orenstein, in evidence presented to the 1932 Native Economic Commission (NEC), similarly estimated that the lowest cost of a diet consistent with the maintenance of good health in Johannesburg for a family of four—consisting of a man, his wife, and two children (one five years of age and the other two)—was 60 shillings, or the equivalent of roughly 70 percent of the average African wage.[42] Ellen Hellmann, in her 1934 survey of families living in a Johannesburg slumyard, found that only two of the family budgets allowed enough money for food to maintain reasonable health as determined by several recommended minimal diets.[43] In 1938 the chief medical officer of Benoni calculated the cost of a nutritious diet based on the ration provided by the Crown Mines to the families of its married employees. The cost of this diet, which did not include allowances for fruit or milk, came to 85 shillings if purchased in the Orlando location and 70 shillings if purchased in the city.[44] At the time the average monthly wage paid to a resident of Orlando township was 70 shillings.

Other examples could be given. In fact, estimating the cost of "urban native diets" seems to have been a popular pastime of white liberals during this period. But the point that is made by all of these studies is that Africans were not paid a wage that permitted the purchase of an adequate diet. As a result diets consisted largely of lower-priced starches, mealie meal, and bread, with few resistance-building foods such as milk, fresh fruit, and vegetables. Ray Phillips, commenting on African urban diets in the 1930s, noted,

> Reports of wholesalers and personal observations led to the conclusion that mealie meal, bread and sugar are the staple articles of diet, accounting with candy and mineral water, for well over fifty percent of total grocery purchases. A little milk and meat go a long way. Vegetables and fruits provide a taste only . . . [45]

A more detailed evaluation of the nutritional value of African urban diets was conducted by Dr. F. W. Fox in 1940. Working from the food budgets collected from nearly a thousand African families living in four African townships around Johannesburg, he constructed the average purchased diet of an adult male. He then calculated the nutritional value of each component in this purchased diet and compared this with optimal standards of nutrition as well as with "marginal standards," defined as "an amount that will maintain health . . . for a limited period." The resulting comparison revealed that the average purchased diet was seriously deficient in a number of important nutrients. From the perspective of resistance to TB, deficiencies in calcium and vitamins A and C were particularly significant, since these nutrients appear to play an important role in controlling TB infections. Commenting on the amount of vitamin C in the average purchased diet, Fox noted that the estimated thirty-seven milligrams probably erred on the generous side.

> for although meat and vegetables in the quantities purchased will undoubtedly contribute appreciable amounts of this vitamin, it is doubtful how much will survive the drastic methods of cooking that are likely to be employed. A 50% reduction would not be unreasonable, and this would barely leave enough to protect from actual scurvy.[46]

Fox stressed that while these deficiencies were serious for men, they were an even more serious problem for women and children who generally needed higher levels of these protective nutrients.

Although calculations of average diets indicate that serious nutritional problems existed for all urban Africans, an analysis of the food budgets collected by Phillips in the mid-1930s indicates that both the quantity and quality of African diets deteriorated as income declined. There were thus marked differences in the nutritional levels of different segments of the African population. More important, nutritional levels were highly sensitive to economic shifts. The budgets that Phillips recorded were collected from relatively well-paid workers. The lowest recorded monthly income was 150 shillings, whereas the average worker's salary at the time was just above 86 shillings. Thus Phillips' data reflects the food consumption habits of the African petty bourgeoisie. There are marked differences, nonetheless, in the consumption patterns of the highest-paid group as opposed to the lowest-paid as calculated on the basis of per capita income.

Table 7 divides the budgets of forty-six families[47] into three groups on the basis of per capita income. For each group, the percentage of total food expenditure allocated to the purchase of various food items is recorded. The table suggests that as per capita income decreased the composition of family diets changed. Families in the lowest third spent a larger portion of their food budget on starches and particularly on bread and maize, which together made up 23 percent of the food expenditures of this group, than did families in the upper third whose combined expenditures on bread and maize made up 18 percent of their

TABLE 7

AFRICAN FOOD CONSUMPTION AND PER CAPITA
INCOME, JOHANNESBURG, 1935

	Highest Third	Middle Third	Lowest Third
Meat, vegetables, fruit, and milk	43%	45%	34%
Mealie and bread	18%	19%	23%
Tea/coffee/sugar	16%	18%	19%
Other food items	23%	18%	24%

purchases. Conversely, the lowest group spent a smaller percentage on so-called protective foods—fruits and vegetables, fresh milk, and meat. The combined expenditure of the lowest group on these foods was 34 percent while the higher-income groups spent 43 percent of their food budget on these higher-quality foods. Difference in the amounts spent on fresh milk by the three groups, 11, 9, and 7 percent respectively, as compared to their expenditures on tea and coffee, support the observation made in chapter 2 that poorly paid workers tended to substitute less nutritious beverages for milk in their diet.

If one calculates the amount of each food item consumed per capita on the basis of the amount each family spent on a particular item together with the average price of that item, the decline in protective foods in the diets of lower-paid workers is clearly evident. Graphs 12 through 15 correlate per capita income with per capita consumption of milk, meat, maize, and bread using all forty-six budgets. These show that although there is some decline in the quantity of bread and maize consumed as per capita income declines, milk and meat consumption is more clearly sensitive to income shifts.

One can assume that the trend toward a more monotonous, less-nutritious diet as per capita income decreased was much more marked among common laborers, who made up the vast majority of the urban African working class. Phillips, in fact, notes that on average African workers in Benoni consumed smaller quantities of protective foods than did the forty-six families cited above.

Of every 4/6d spent on food by Africans in Benoni location only 4d or 1/12 [6.6%] is spent on vegetables, fruit milk and fatty foods, while 2/6d [55%] is spent on starch foods and 1/2d [25%] on meat.[48]

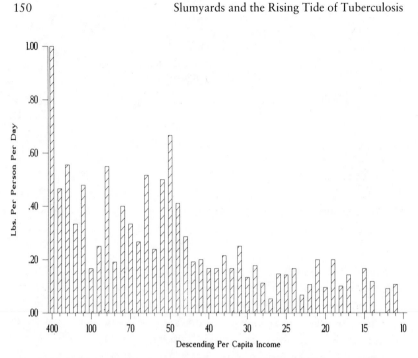

Graph 12.   African Meat Consumption, Johannesburg, 1935
   Source: R. E. Phillips, *The Bantu in the City* (Lovedale, S. A.: Lovedale Press, 1938).

The MOH of Benoni estimated that the average per capita consumption
of fresh milk by Benoni residents was one-tenth of one pint or 1.6
ounces per day.[49] In East London a study carried out in 1929 estimated
that the average consumption of milk per head was about double the
Benoni figure or 3.1 ounces per diem.[50] Yet given the disparity in milk
consumption indicated above, many families clearly went without milk.

In some locations milk was simply not available. There were no
established outlets for fresh milk, and producers found it more profit-
able to sell their milk to producers of butter, cheese, and condensed milk
than to location consumers. In Germiston location, for example, there
was no regular milk supply prior to 1940. The milk supply that did exist
consisted of occasional deliveries of surplus milk left over after white
needs had been met. This surplus never averaged more than 50 to 100
gallons a day. In 1936 the African population of Germiston was estimated to be just over 40,000.[51]

Condensed milk was sometimes purchased by families who could not
obtain fresh milk. When diluted to a strength equal to fresh milk, however, it cost six to eight pence per pint or twice the price of fresh milk

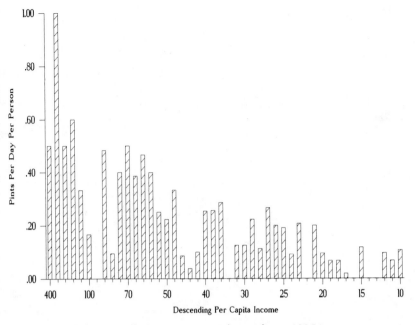

Graph 13.   African Milk Consumption, Johannesburg, 1935
   Source: R. E. Phillips, *The Bantu in the City* (Lovedale, S. A.: Lovedale Press, 1938).

when available. The high cost per pint of condensed milk meant that it was frequently diluted to much weaker strengths, all but eliminating its nutritional value.[52]

The absence of milk together with the need for women to find some kind of employment, and the early weaning of children from breastmilk to nonnutritious substitutes accounted for much of the infant mortality from gastric troubles in African locations and was undoubtedly a contributing factor in infant and child TB deaths.[53] Like women, the TB mortality rates of young children rose at a faster rate than the general population during periods of economic hardship, brought on either by depression or high inflation (see graph 10).

Evidence of changing nutritional patterns associated with declining per capita income suggests not only that a range of nutritional patterns existed among urban African families but also that the dietary patterns of any one family varied through time. The loss of income through unemployment or wage cutbacks, such as occurred during the depression, or a decline in buying power produced by inflation, such as occurred during and immediately after World War I, could lead to signifi-

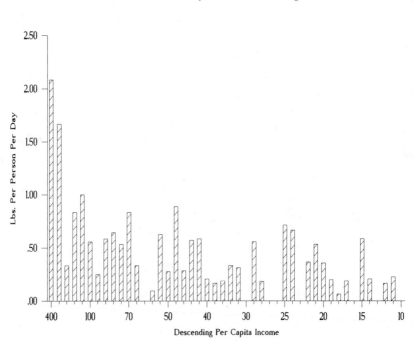

Graph 14.   African Maize Consumption, Johannesburg, 1935
Source: R. E. Phillips, *The Bantu in the City* (Lovedale, S. A.: Lovedale Press, 1938).

cant dietary shifts involving the loss of protective foods. This in turn
made a larger portion of the African workforce vulnerable to TB infections. Even a slight rise in the price of a food item such as milk or fresh
fruit, considered luxuries by the average working family, could put the
item out of reach. For example, the inspector of urban locations in
Johannesburg noted in 1936 that in one location where there was a high
demand for milk when it sold for two pence per pint, demand dropped
to zero when the price rose to three pence.[54] The demand for even basic
starches like bread could drop quickly with an increase in price. Thus
the MOH of East London reported in 1932 that the sale of bread
plummeted when bread that had sold at three pence per one-pound loaf
was replaced by half-pound loaves selling for two pence each.[55]

    There can be little doubt that declining nutrition resulting from loss
of income or decreasing buying power had an adverse effect on TB
mortality rates. Medical reports attest to the malnourished condition of
the majority of the TB cases treated in hospitals. In addition, a follow-
up study of 100 African TB cases in East London in 1931 revealed that
unemployed Africans had a higher than average case mortality rate.

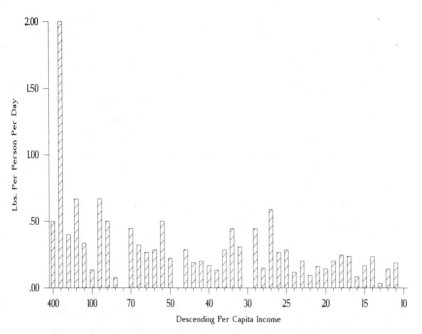

Graph 15.   African Bread Consumption, Johannesburg, 1935
  Source: R. E. Phillips, *The Bantu in the City* (Lovedale, S. A.: Lovedale Press, 1938).

Whereas the overall African case mortality rate was 44 percent, the rate for unemployed Africans was nearly 54 percent.[56] Interestingly the same study revealed that the rate for domestic servants was 69 percent. This contradicts the view that domestic servants did better in terms of health because they had access to food from their employers.[57] As Jacklyn Cock[58] and others have shown, most African women in positions of domestic service lived lives of quiet desperation in which they were paid low wages, worked long hours, and were separated from their children for long periods of time. Most of their meager wages were sent to support their children, not spent on personal items. The few scraps from the madam's table hardly compensated for the physical and mental stress involved in such employment. The pressure to continue working even when ill, moreover, must have contributed to their high case mortality rates.

   Although the inability of poorer African families to purchase adequate amounts of high quality foods was directly related to the low-wage policies of employers, it was also the product of government policies designed to benefit white food producers at the expense of urban food consumers. These policies kept the price of food, particularly of resistance-building foods like milk, butter, fruits, and vegetables, high and in relative low supply. As noted in chapter 4, the Union government put into place an agricultural production and marketing policy in the 1920s and 1930s designed to increase the agricultural productivity of white farmers and raise the country's food exports. Among the programs established by the government to accomplish these goals was a system of levies imposed on dairy products such as cheese and butter to generate revenue that could be used to improve the quality of dairy production among white farmers. The government also began paying bounties to farmers to encourage them to sell their produce to export rather than domestic markets. (This in part explains the preference of dairy farmers for selling their milk to cheese and butter manufacturers rather than to urban consumers.) In some cases export quotas were imposed on white farmers for the same purpose. As a further incentive to white producers, domestic prices for agricultural products were set above international levels. In order to make the resulting produce competitive on international markets, the government sold the produce at a loss, absorbing the difference between the price paid to the producer and the price paid by international buyers. The same service, however, was not provided to the domestic consumer, who paid the artificially high price paid to the producer plus the cost of transport and marketing. Finally, to insure that this artificially high price was not undercut by cheap imports, tariffs were imposed on imported foods and marketing boards were established to restrict food imports. The price of slaughtered beef for example, was kept high by the establishment of a meat marketing board that not only controlled the number of cattle slaughtered each day but also carefully restricted the importation of beef cattle from neighboring territories.[59]

Although these policies encouraged the expansion of white agricultural production, this growth was accomplished at the expense of urban consumers who paid artificially high prices for their food. Even during the depression, when agricultural prices tumbled in the face of unemployment and declining demand, the government's protectionist policies continued to buoy domestic consumer prices. Thus whereas the value of South Africa's agricultural commodities sold on international markets in 1932 was barely 36 percent of their 1928 value, the corresponding average value of internal prices was 60 to 70 percent of their 1928 value.[60] The urban consumer was thus caught between declining income and high food prices. Referring to the effect of the Maize Control Act of

1937 that imposed a levy of four shillings per bag on traders who wished to purchase maize, an editorial in the Lovedale Mission *Outlook* observed:

> Consider what this levy means to the multitude of poor people who live on mealies but who have no land, the very poor White and Coloured people and the many thousands of Native labourers scattered about the Union, in the docks, in the cities and elsewhere, doing useful and necessary work. A Native family living on mealies uses, at a conservative estimate, ten to twelve bags a year, and for each bag purchased 4/- has been paid to the Mealie Industry Control Board. In other words, *each of these landless Native labourers is supporting the maize industry by a contribution of 40/- to 48/- a year.* And this on top of the poll tax! The thing is iniquitous . . . [61]

Like maize, the cost of wheat bread, a major staple among the urban poor, was kept high by the imposition of a tariff on imported wheat. The Wheat Importations Restriction Act of 1930 prevented the importation of wheat into the Union for less than twenty-two shillings six pence per bag, and wheatened meal and flour for less than thirty-seven shillings per bag. This in turn kept the price of domestic wheat artificially high.[62] Heavy fees for licenses to bake bread (in East London the fee was £5) served in addition to restrict the establishment of African-run bakeries. This resulted in Africans having to purchase bread baked by white bakers at white prices based on white costs. In effect an informal color bar increased the cost of bread in the same way that the formal color bar in construction increased the price of housing.[63]

Reviewing the marketing and subsidy policies of the South African government in 1938, liberal academic and politician J. D. Reinhalt-Jones concluded,

> The whole of our legislation, control boards and marketing acts have the effect of limiting internal consumption. We grant monopolies to millers and restrict the issue of licenses to producers and distributors as if we are dealing with liquor instead of protective foods.[64]

The control of liquor was in fact of questionable value in terms of protecting the health of African urban residents. The adverse effects of alcohol on Africans living in towns and working in the mines was frequently referred to by health officials and mine supervisors, especially at the turn of the century. For the mines, the consumption of "rotgut" liquor, initially viewed with some ambivalence because it was seen as a form of labor control and an enticement to African workers, became a critical problem by the mid-1890s. The Chamber of Mines claimed that between 15 and 25 percent of the workforce was disabled each day because of alcoholic consumption. As a result the chamber moved to strictly control the consumption of alcohol at the mines.[65] Later, urban authorities, starting with those in Durban, saw in the control of beer a means of raising revenue through the creation of municipal beer halls. This led to a series of laws restricting the manufacture and sale of alcoholic beverages by Africans. The prohibition ranged from a complete abolition, to the restriction of sales to municipal-run beer halls, to the limiting of manufacturing to small amounts of home-brewed beer for personal use. In general, however, the laws prevented Africans from manufacturing beer for sale within the urban areas.

Although the prohibition on alcoholic consumption was presented as a means of protecting the health of the "native" while insuring the productivity of the urban workforce, it is doubtful that it did either, and it may well have contributed in a number of ways to the production of TB. Prior to the prohibition the primary alcoholic beverage consumed by urban and rural Africans alike was one or another form of so-called kaffir beer or *utshwala,* produced by fermenting either sorghum alone or a combination of maize and sorghum. The alcoholic content of the drink was relatively low, between 3 and 4 percent, although on occasion brown sugar was added to the recipe to speed up the brewing process and increase its alcoholic content. Beer was brewed by urban women for their husbands and friends and was sold to single men. The sale of the home-brewed beer provided women with a separate income that could in fact represent a substantial addition to a family's household budget. E. Hellmann noted in 1933 that women in the Rooiyard slumyard of Johannesburg earned between £3.17.6 and £4.16.0 per month from beer sales. This income often made up the difference between the high cost of living and the low wages paid to male workers. It did so, moreover, in a way that permitted a woman to stay at home and care for her children, reduced the need for early weaning, and may have generally improved their children's chances of survival.[66]

In addition "native beer" contributed to the nutritional content of urban diets. As nutritionist F. W. Fox noted before the Native Farm Labour Committee in 1939,

> A Native living on mealie meal alone is much better off when he is allowed to make kaffir beer because fermentation substances are produced, more particularly yeasts and anti-scorbutic vitamin which are not available to him otherwise. These same substances can, of course, be equally well supplied in other ways, but the point is that in nine cases out of ten they are not supplied.[67]

While the consumption of "kaffir beer" produced some drunkenness, and when made primarily of mealie was of limited nutritional value, the 1932 Economic Commission, after taking a great deal of evidence on the subject, was of the opinion that the drink was not particularly harmful and that, "unless substitutes are provided, its absence deprives the Native of an essential article of food."[68]

By attacking the manufacture and sale of beer, the urban authorities undermined both the nutritional value of urban diets and the economic viability of African households, whose survival depended on the supplemental income from beer brewing. The attack on beer brewing did not, however, prevent it from occurring. The practice was too ubiquitous and the demand too high for it to be completely eliminated. It did, however, contribute to a transformation of manufacturing and consumption patterns that undermined the nutritional benefits of beer brewing and increased its harmful side effects.

The attack on beer brewing helped to transform the production process and led to the manufacturing of new varieties of drink that had a higher alcoholic content, contained harmful substances, were of no nutritional value, and led to an increase in drunkenness among urban men. The production of these new varieties of beer were stimulated by the prohibition of home beer brewing and the need to avoid detection. Commenting on the impact of secrecy on the production of beer, the Native Economic Commission notes,

> In this respect utywala has serious drawbacks. It is required in bulk, from a view point of economical manufacture and of producing the desired stimulating effects. It is therefore difficult to hide. Moreover, the process of production takes a considerable time, and its smell readily betrays its presence. The problem, therefore, arose of inventing a drink which could be made and stored in small quantities, easy to hide, which could be matured in a few hours, and could have its alcoholic effect quickly. These qualities are possessed only by a drink of high alcoholic content. The prohibition of utywala, therefore, led to the consumption of the very article which the Europeans desired . . . to prevent.[69]

Thus, although the shift to more, and more varied, alcoholic beverages like *skokiaan* and *shimeya* also reflected changing urban tastes, the pressure of prosecution played a significant role in the changeover.

In terms of the health of urban Africans, the shift in consumption patterns, resulting from the active prosecution of beer brewing, reduced the nutritional content of male diets and thus their ability to resist infections, and specifically TB. It may in addition have contributed to increased drunkenness and alcoholism. To the extent that alcoholism threatened a man's employment, it could place his health and that of his family at increased risk. More directly, expenditures for alcohol reduced a family's food budget thereby contributing to malnutrition. Finally, alcoholism may act in a synergistic manner with TB, speeding the progression of the disease by suppressing the immune system.

CONCLUSION

It is possible to attribute the rise of African TB mortality in South African cities during the late 1920s and early 1930s to the cumulative effect of industrialization and rural impoverishment. Yet this general relationship needs to be refined if we are to understand the specific linkages that existed between the changing epidemiology of TB and the shifting contours of South African society. Thus the present chapter has argued that increases in TB mortality among urbanized or partially urbanized Africans were the human cost of a series of economic and social policies that evolved in response to a conflicting set of economic interests within white society rather than the product of an impersonal set of economic and social processes.

These interests not only contributed to a rising tide of TB mortality, they also prevented the formulation and implementation of progressive housing and nutrition policies that might have reduced the impact of TB among urban Africans. In addition they precluded the provision of adequate medical and sanitation services. As we will see in chapter 7, medical services for urban Africans were rudimentary at best, and any attempt on the part of municipal medical authorities to improve health services was met with fiscal roadblocks created by municipal councils that steadfastly refused to accept financial responsibility for the welfare of Africans.

In the end, municipal authorities did little more than attempt to build social barriers against the rising tide of TB, hoping that time and the effects of natural selection would solve the problem of African TB. The cost of this inactivity would be brought home during the late 1930s and 1940s when a second wave of industrial expansion and large-scale African urbanization produced a second epidemic of urban TB and revealed the failure of earlier efforts to control the disease.

CHAPTER VI

Labor Supplies and Tuberculosis on the Witwatersrand 1913–1938

INTRODUCTION

Although tuberculosis morbidity and mortality rates rose steadily for blacks living within both the urban and rural areas of South Africa from World War I through the mid-1930s, they dropped dramatically within the country's gold-mining industry. TB rates on the Rand, in fact, mirrored the mortality rates of the major urban centers, excluding those of Johannesburg, where TB rates were shaped by the experience of the mining industry. Whereas urban TB mortality rates rose during World War I and then again from the mid-1920s to the mid-1930s, TB incidence on the mines fell during both of these periods. Overall between 1913 and 1935 the average incidence of TB among African mineworkers fell from roughly 18 per 1,000 to just over 2 per 1,000. This remarkable decline in TB morbidity was attributed by mining officials and medical authorities, both on and off the Rand, to the mining industry's success in providing its black workers with better housing, food, working conditions, and medical services. The mining industry was in fact widely viewed as a model of enlightened worker management by the mid-1930s.

There can be little doubt that improvements in working and living conditions account for some of the decline in TB incidence that occurred during this period. The standard mine ration was improved with the addition of more resistance-building foods and by more frequent meals. Housing also underwent significant improvements, and overcrowding

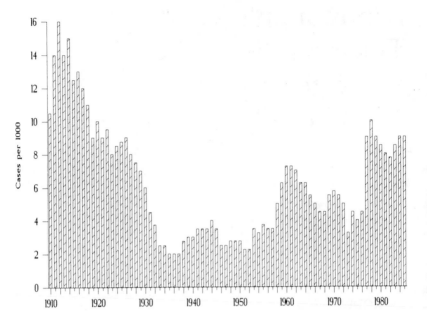

Graph 16.   TB Incidence among African Mineworkers, Central Mining–Rand
Mines, 1910–1985

Source: Central Mining–Rand Mines, Department of Sanitation Annual Reports and
Health Department Reports, 1915–1985.

was reduced. Though working conditions proved more difficult to
change, and in some ways grew worse, certain improvements were
made during this period. Most important among these were the changing houses erected at the head of the mineshafts and the distribution of
clothing, both of which reduced the risk of chill. Medical services, still
inadequate in terms of the numbers of doctors and nurses employed to
care for the workforce, were nonetheless expanded. Part-time physicians were replaced at many of the mines with full-time medical officers.
The number of hospitals at the mines increased and a Mine Medical
Officers Association was established to help coordinate medical knowledge and care available at the mines. The Central Mining/Rand Mines
group, to which roughly half the mines belonged, went even further,
establishing a coordinated medical service under the leadership of Dr.
A. Orenstein. With the improvement in medical services, greater care
was taken in the examination of recruits, thus reducing the number of
infective or susceptible Africans who entered the mining industry. Finally, the Chamber of Mines funded the establishment of a medical
research center, the South African Institute for Medical Research, to

carry out studies into ways of improving worker health. The institute was established in 1913 to develop a vaccine for combating pneumonia, at the time the number one cause of death on the mines. It later played a major role in the investigations carried out by the Tuberculosis Research Committee into the epidemiology of TB among Africans in South Africa. Not all mines improved conditions to the same degree, and a comparison of TB statistics for any given year reveals a remarkable range of incidence rates. All in all, nonetheless, the mining industry could and did take pride in its efforts to reduce the toll TB was taking on its workforce.

Yet as significant as these achievements were, they did not by themselves produce the dramatic decline in TB rates noted above. The reformed conditions, as we will see, still left a good deal of room for improvement. Much of the decline in TB morbidity, moreover, resulted from the industry's ability to eliminate particularly susceptible groups and individuals from the mines. Although the weeding out of the susceptibles resulted in part from improvements in medical services and examination procedures, it was accomplished primarily by changes in the composition and availability of labor, resulting from the forced withdrawal of tropical labor after 1913 and the abundant supply of labor created by the depression of the early 1930s. The reduction in TB morbidity that occurred at the mines during this period was in fact as much the product of historically specific forces as it was the result of long-term improvements in mining health conditions. It is important for two reasons to understand the nature of these forces and the role they played in the declining incidence of TB on the mines. First, it was largely on the basis of this decline and the claim that it was produced by improved living and working conditions, as well as by better health services, that the Chamber of Mines was able to overcome government objections to the recruitment of tropical labor. Second, understanding the role these forces played in the declining incidence of TB on the mines before 1935 helps to explain the steady rise in TB incidence that occurred on the mines after 1935.

IMPROVING CONDITIONS AND THE
ECONOMICS OF HEALTH ON THE MINES

Serious efforts to improve the conditions under which African miners lived and worked only began in 1911–1912 when, in response to the appalling mortality rates experienced by tropical workers and the complaints of health officials and administrators in the native territories and protectorates from which tropical labor was being drawn, the Union government presented the mine owners with an ultimatum: either drastically improve mine conditions and reduce mortality rates or face the possibility of losing access to tropical workers.[1] Though tropical workers represented only 11 percent of the total African workforce in 1911, they along with Mozambican labor were viewed as critical for the future expansion of the mining industry, since domestic manpower had proved to be both unreliable and insufficient for the industry's needs. The government's concern with mortality on the mines had been expressed earlier, and the mine owners had responded with token efforts to improve conditions. The threat of losing access to an important labor supply, however, sparked a new round of more serious reform efforts. Changing houses were built at the shaftheads and special clothing was provided to tropical workers to reduce the effects of chill. A policy prohibiting tropical workers from carrying their drills up from the mineface and thus reducing exhaustion was put into place. Efforts also were made to reduce drafts created by the overventilated compounds in which the tropical workers were housed. In the end, however, the unwillingness of mine managers to spend the money needed to bring about these reforms, combined with the mine owners' belief that the government would not undermine the industry by eliminating access to tropical labor, meant that reform efforts were both limited in scope and incomplete in their execution.[2] Mortality rates remained unacceptably high, and in March 1913 the government made good its threats and prohibited both the recruitment and employment of African workers from areas north of twenty-two degrees south latitude. The official number of tropical workers on the mines dropped from 19,394 in 1913 to 6,732 in 1914 and to 2,046 by 1918.[3]

The withdrawal of tropical labor had a sobering effect on many of the mining houses on the Rand. For some it meant that the era of total worker neglect was over. The costs of continuing to consume labor as if it were a kind of raw material were becoming too high. As Sam Evans, chairman of the Crown Mines Company, noted in a memorandum to Sir Lionel Phillips, chairman of Rand Mines Limited, "If we let things slide we shall lose the Portuguese natives as well as the tropicals."[4] In addition the loss of shift time due to accidents or disease was proving very costly. In a survey of mine conditions in April of 1913, the Native Labour Bureau found that 10 percent of the men were incapacitated every day. This amounted to 191,343 lost shifts, or nearly one shift per worker.[5] In an effort to initiate more substantial improvement of mining conditions, Evans recommended that the Chamber of Mines undertake a serious reassessment of mining conditions. He then invited Colonel William Gorgas to visit the Rand and make recommendations for lowering mortality rates. Evans had been highly impressed with reports of Gorgas' success in lowering mortality rates among tropical workers on the Panama Canal and had in fact visited the canal in 1912.[6] Gorgas, along with two of his medical officers, visited the Rand in December 1913. He carried out an inspection of the mines over the next three months and presented his report to the chamber on February 25, 1914.

Gorgas' recommendations, though hardly startling by today's standards, were radical by those of the mining industry in 1914. His major recommendations concerned the need for reducing overcrowding, improving diet, and expanding and centralizing medical services. Gorgas criticized the industry for not providing adequate accommodations for its workforce and recommended a minimum of fifty square feet per man in every room. As noted in chapter 3, he proceeded to propose an even more radical solution to the housing problem, the creation of family housing. He also criticized the mine diet and proposed that the ideal system for feeding workers was in a family setting. He recommended that the workers be paid cash to buy their own food, which their wives could prepare in their huts.[7]

On the matter of health services, he concluded that the current practice of each mine having its own medical officer and health services was highly inefficient, involving both duplication of services and the absence of specialized medical services. He recommended that instead of each mine caring for its own sick, a centralized hospital be created. "You could afford to equip such a hospital with first-class surgical appliances of every kind at a cost less than the moderate supply given to 62 hospitals now in use." Gorgas also concluded that all medical services, curative and hygienic, should be staffed by full-time personnel and centralized under a head directly responsible to the Chamber of Mines and independent of individual mine managers. "If you had this system for the past few years, with a sufficient force constantly devoting its whole time and attention to sanitation, you would have by this time reduced pneumonia to a minimum."[8]

Needless to say, Gorgas' recommendations were not well received by the mining houses. Improvements were made in all three areas over the next twenty years, but they came slowly and were limited in scope.

Conditions underground, moreover, which Gorgas was not asked to report on, remained largely unchanged.

Both housing and feeding arrangements improved significantly following the war. Deficiencies remained in both areas, however. Gorgas' proposal for family accommodations was never accepted. Such a policy, it was argued, would lead to the eventual separation of the mineworker and his family from their rural base and would be detrimental to the mineworker's health. What was not stated was that the localization of their African workforce would place increased pressure on wages by forcing the mine owners to pay for the reproduction of labor. Such a prospect was unacceptable, particularly in the wake of the 1913 strike and the threat of another strike six months later.[9]

HOUSING

Although overcrowding was reduced considerably during the period under study, it was not eliminated. The reasons why were largely economic. Not only did it cost money to provide housing, but there was an economic benefit to keeping an excess number of workers in the compounds. The profitability of gold mining depended on the availability of a full complement of labor.[10] Moreover, because a decrease in the labor supply not only reduced the tonnage milled but increased the cost per ton, small labor shortages produced large profit losses. In one example, the manager of West Rand Consolidated Mines estimated that an 18 percent decrease in his labor complement would cause a 54 percent decline in profits.[11] The manager of Witwatersrand G.M. Co. Ltd. painted an even bleaker picture of the relationship between labor supply and profits. He estimated that with a 23 percent decrease in the mine's labor contingent, the mine would not only show a reduced profit but would in fact suffer a loss of £2,350.[12]

To avoid this situation, mines frequently retained a surplus supply of workers despite the cost of feeding and housing them. This labor was used for development work, such as sinking new shafts, that helped reduce future production costs and increase profits. The cost of housing an additional 150 African workers for one month was estimated by the manager of West Rand Consolidated Mines to be £675, whereas the profits lost due to a one-month reduction in the labor force of the same number would be £1,649.[13] Labor surpluses were not, however, an everyday situation and, from the mine manager's viewpoint, their erratic occurrence did not justify the supplying of additional housing.

Thus, from time to time, housing shortages and overcrowding became a problem. This condition became particularly acute at certain mines during the depression. A survey of sleeping accommodations on various mine compounds in May of 1931 found that one-third of the mines surveyed had labor complements that were at least 5 percent in excess of available accommodations.[14]

Even where the number of men housed in a compound did not exceed that permitted by the mine regulations, the sleeping arrangements continued to place men in close proximity to one another and to facilitate the spread of infection. Although the Chamber of Mines had accepted a recommendation made by Dr. Orenstein in 1916 that dividers be placed between bunks, the adoption of this practice was still incomplete in 1931. In some cases, moreover, the barriers built were only four inches high and thus of little benefit. The delay in adding these barriers occurred largely because they made it difficult to accommodate more workers in the compounds.[15]

Finally, mines viewed as having a limited future were often allowed to run down. In such cases the owners were unwilling to invest in improvements in either existing housing or new housing. Overcrowding was frequently the consequence of this policy. This was the case with the Simmer and Jack Mine, found to have 40 percent more African workers than legally permissible in October of 1930.[16] In general, health inspectors on the Rand were sympathetic to the financial constraints of such mines and did not push too hard for reforms.[17]

It is difficult to assess the impact of this type of overcrowding on the incidence of TB on the mines. While overcrowding was excessive during the depression, TB rates actually fell—though, as will be seen below, this may have been because the effects of overcrowding were offset by other factors that improved the overall health of the workforce. Given the increasing percentage, moreover, of workers on the Rand who had been previously infected, overcrowding probably played a less critical role in the epidemiology of TB on the mines than it had prior to World War I. Still, a significant number of new recruits were evidently still tuberculin negative when they began their contract. And the ability of previously infected workers to control their infections could be overwhelmed by heavy new doses of TB bacilli. Finally, overcrowding may have contributed to the spread of other infectious diseases, particularly influenza, believed to contribute to the "lighting up" of existing tuberculous lesions.[18] It may therefore be significant that the mines in which overcrowding was reported in 1930 had an average incidence of TB without silicosis of 5.92 per 1,000 while those without overcrowding had an incidence of 4.46 per 1,000, or 25 percent lower.[19]

Compound sanitation, although improved, also left a good deal to be desired during this period. Only four mines installed waterborne sewage systems prior to 1938. The rest used bucket systems with their inherent health problems. The continued incidence of enteric fever attests to the inadequate nature of sanitary measures. Between 1918 and 1936 the incidence of enteric fever at Rand Mines Ltd. ranged from 3.89 to 2.65 per 1,000.[20]

DIET

There can be little doubt that the mine diet established during the 1920s and 1930s was a major improvement over that which had existed before the war. Both the variety of foods and their nutritional content were increased. The effect of this improvement on the general health of the African mineworker was directly evidenced by the declining incidence of scurvy deaths.[21]

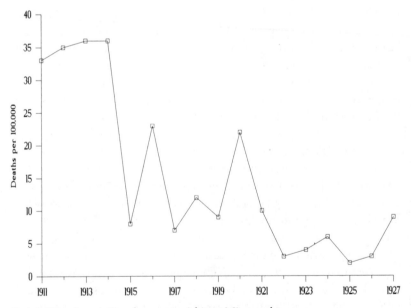

Graph 17.   Scurvy Deaths among African Mineworkers

Source: CMA, 22/1931, Low Grade Ores: Tropical Natives (Central Health Administration), E. N. Thorton to Chairman, Low Grade Ores Commission, Jan. 19, 1931.

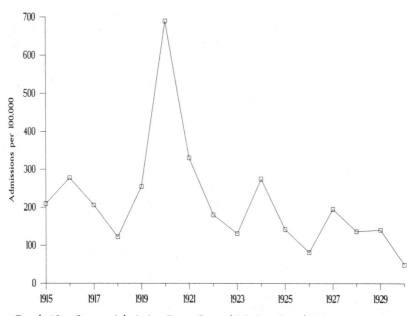

Graph 18.   Scurvy Admission Rate, Central Mining–Rand Mines

Source: CMA, 22/1931, Low Grade Ores: Tropical Natives (Central Health Administration), E. N. Thorton to Chairman, Low Grade Ores Commission, Jan. 19, 1931.

Yet despite this improvement, the feeding of mineworkers remained problematic. Although scurvy deaths had nearly disappeared, scurvy cases and subscorbutic conditions remained. As the acting secretary for public health noted in his testimony before the Low Grade Ore Commission in 1931,

> The Commission will doubtless consider that the mortality from scurvy alone is not in itself alarming, but the fact that deaths still occur from a disease which is preventable and is ordinarily very amenable to treatment must indicate that there is a considerable amount of scurvy present on the mines that is recognized by Medical Officers and doubtless a vast number of boys in a subscorbutic state who have not come under medical care for this disease.[22]

The rate for scurvy cases admitted to hospital by Rand Mines Ltd. averaged around 2 per 1,000 workers between 1915 and 1930 with some fluctuation and a small downward movement over this period. A more significant drop occurred between 1930 and 1940. In addition, a certain percentage of scurvy cases evidently went unrecognized as such and were repatriated under other headings. Doctor E. N. Culver, assistant health officer for the Union carried out a number of investigations into mining conditions in 1930 and 1931. In an inspection of the WNLA compound in December 1930 he reported seeing a number of such cases. This report was supported by Dr. Girwood, medical officer in charge of the WNLA depot, who admitted that there was a good deal of scurvy entering the WNLA hospital under other headings. Finally, Thornton examined eighty-eight workers due for repatriation and found that nine had definite signs of scurvy that had not been recorded on the mine hospital case sheets. He concluded: "It is evident, therefore, that scurvy is fairly prevalent even today amongst boys at the ends of their contracts."[23]

Mine managers and their medical officers continued to argue that scurvy on the mines was due to the scorbutic condition of African workers in their home areas:

A very large majority of territorial natives are scorbutic, as their consumption of anti-scorbutic foodstuffs in their homes is practically nil. Such inherent scurvy is nondetectable on arrival at the mines, but in my experience develops quickly in certain poorly built boys after a month or two of hard work . . .[24]

There was no doubt a certain amount of truth to this claim. The record of both scurvy deaths and hospital admissions indicates that the incidence of scurvy on the mines rose during periods when food production in the reserves was low, for example, following the drought years of 1915 and 1919.[25] What was unstated in this assessment, of course, was the role the mining industry's low-wage policies played in the long-term deterioration of agricultural productivity and nutritional stability in the reserves. So even if scurvy was imported to the mines, it was increasingly a case of one's chickens coming home to roost.

Yet there is also evidence that the recruitment of subscorbutic workers was only part of the problem and that inadequacies in mine rationing in combination with the high-energy demands of mine labor played an equal or greater role in the incidence of scurvy and subscorbutic cases. In 1926 an outbreak of scurvy occurred at the Randfontein Estates Gold Mining Company, involving fifty-two cases and two deaths in November and thirty-two cases with one death in December. The mine's medical officer determined the length of service of each of the men who developed the disease.[26] (See tables 8, 9.) In a larger study of all cases occurring on the Rand Mines Ltd. between 1923 and 1930, A. J. Orenstein found a similar pattern:[27] These figures show that the majority (61 and 71 percent in the former study, 55 percent in the latter)

TABLE 8

SCURVY CASES AND LENGTH OF SERVICE, RANDFONTEIN
MINES, 1926

Length of Service	Percent of Cases	
	November	December
1–3 months	5.7	9.3
3–6 months	32.7	18.6
6–9 months	13.4	25.0
9–12 months	30.7	18.6
Over 12 months	17.3	28.1

TABLE 9

SCURVY CASES AND LENGTH OF
SERVICE, RAND MINES LTD.,
1923–1930

Length of Service	Percent of Cases
1–3 months	18.7
3–6 months	26.4
6–9 months	19.8
9–12 months	10.4
Over 12 months	24.7

of the scurvy cases that occurred in the mines involved workers who had worked for more than six months. Whereas, if the mine manager's hypothesis was correct, a larger proportion of cases should have occurred during the first months of service. What these figures indicate is that scurvy was a product of the conditions existing on the mines. This was in fact the conclusion of Dr. F. W. Fox who reviewed 1,000 records of scurvy among miners between 1929 and 1939: "It is clear that, in the very large majority of cases, the disease breaks out after quite a considerable stay on the mine, as a result of the Native's reaction to mine conditions; in other words, *it must be regarded as a disease of mine life*" (emphasis added).[28]

Although it would appear that the standards laid down by the government in 1922 guaranteed adequate amounts of antiscorbutic foods if properly prepared and consumed, the margin of adequacy was thin, and any alteration in the amounts consumed, if sustained over even a short period, could lead to scurvy. There were several ways in which this occurred on the mines. In some cases, mines simply evaded the regulations. Sir Edward Thornton noted before the Low Grade Ore Commission in 1932 that,

> On the Meyer and Charlton Mine, on the Van Ryan G. M. Estate Company and on the West Consolidated Mines, Limited, germinated beans were not being supplied at all. On the West Rand Consolidated mine of the Albu Group, inferior meat was until recently being supplied. Deliberate evasion of the bread regulations was occurring on at least the Meyer Charlton G. M. Company and the Van Ryan G. M. Estate Company and the West Rand Consolidated Mines, Limited.[29]

In other cases, supplies of vegetables were disrupted due to transport problems or disputes with distributors. In 1926, eighty-nine cases of scurvy occurred on the Durban Deep Mine as a result of a "temporary disruption" of the vegetable supply.[30] An additional problem early on was the habit of mineworkers refusing to eat raw vegetables and in fact picking them out of their food. To overcome this practice mincers were introduced to finely chop the cabbage, carrots, or leeks that were included in the diet, making them difficult to remove. Perhaps the most common cause of vitamin deficiency was the tendency for food to be overcooked. The mines were directed to cook vegetables and germinated beans for no more than forty-five minutes lest they lose most of their vitamin content. Yet overcooking frequently occurred at a number of mines.[31] Delays in hauling men to the surface played a role in this, since it meant that the men who were last to be hauled up were often late for their evening meal. As a result the food they were served had often been simmering for several hours. Twenty-seven cases of scurvy at the Van Ryan Deep Mines in January and February of 1931 were attributed to this pattern of late feeding.[32]

The appearance of scurvy following even temporary losses of adequate supplies of vitamin C strongly indicates that subscorbutic conditions were widespread and that the line between low chronic vitamin deficiency and scurvy was rather thin. As Culver concluded from his investigations in 1930 and 1931,

> What is important is the fact that the continued presence of florid scurvy to even this small extent suggests the very much greater prevalence of latent scurvy among mine employees. Such Natives are not getting the physiologically necessary supply of anti-scorbutic vitamin, and therefore are more susceptible to infections such as pneumonia.[33]

This condition almost certainly contributed to the incidence of TB on the mines, though it is difficult to document the association. On one hand, TB did rise along with scurvy cases on Rand Mines Ltd. mines in both 1916 and 1920. The monthly incidence of both scurvy and TB also peaked during the summer months. On the other hand, while "East Coast" workers had a somewhat higher incidence of pulmonary TB than British South Africa (BSA) workers, they had a significantly lower incidence of scurvy.

Vitamin C deficiencies were not the only problem with the mine diet. The supply of vitamins A and D, both important elements in the body's defense against TB, was also lacking.[34] At a meeting of the TB Research Committee (TBRC) in 1929, Dr. Orenstein noted that the shortage of vitamins A and D in the mine diet was largely a question of economics, since even a slight addition in the cost of an individual ration would aggregate a very large sum.[35] The final report of the TBRC stated that increased vitamin A levels in the diet was "a desideratum to be aimed at."[36]

The timing of meals also continued to be a problem at most mines, with one large meal following work being supplemented by a prework meal varying from no more than coffee or cocoa to meat stew. The mines continued to resist the idea of treating African workers like their white counterparts by bringing them up for a midshift meal. Thus on most mines, much of the work by Africans continued to be performed on empty stomachs.

UNDERGROUND CONDITIONS

As with housing and feeding, working conditions in the mines improved to some degree during the 1920s and 1930s. Most noticeably improved were sanitation facilities. According to the TBRC report, clean water for drinking was layed on at conveniently situated locations and permanent latrines were provided in reasonably close proximity to working places and supplemented by portable installations carried as close as possible to the advancing shaftfaces. In addition the incidence of hookworm was reduced through the use of salt on mine surfaces. Where water used in drilling was found to be contaminated, it was usually chlorinated. Fecal and urinary contamination continued to occur, however, in both the mines and the compounds.

Changing houses, introduced just before the war, were an additional improvement that reduced the threat of chill. Yet the problem still remained. Thus the TBRC report found that,

The mine managements have appreciated the importance of avoiding exposure between the shaft-head and the compound, and there is an adequate
provision of changing rooms and baths on most mines.

It appears to the Committee, however, that there has not been an equal
appreciation of the risk of chill run by the Native during the time spent
(which may be an hour or more) after knocking off work in a hot, damp
place, in waiting to be hauled up out of the mine.

The waiting-places are near the down-casts and comparatively cool and dry.
The contrast between one's temperature sensations in the slow-moving air of
most working-places and in the gales blowing down the underground main
roads must be experienced to be appreciated. At a working place one is glad
to be stripped while in the main road one is just glad to get into clothes,
although the thermometer may be registering the same temperature in each
situation.[37]

In this respect the mining conditions had changed little since 1914.

Other working conditions were either the same or had become
worse. The long working day continued to exist, with most shifts lasting
ten to eleven hours from the time a worker left the compound until he
returned. Commenting on this practice the TBRC concluded:

Whether any man, healthy or infected, can continue for long to do effective
work for eight or nine consecutive hours, without intervals for meals, is an
economic question as to which scientific test must supply the answer; but it
can hardly be doubted that, for the man whose health depends on a delicate
balance between larval tuberculous lesions and tissue resistance, a day's
work of this length, without food, is calculated to swing the balance the
wrong way.[38]

Conditions within the mineshafts were much the same as they had been
before World War I with the exception that the quantity of water employed in the mining process to keep down silicosis-producing dust had
increased considerably.

Not only is all drilling done with axially water-fed drills, but additional
water is sprayed on the exposed rock face when drilling is first commenced—
"collaring" as this is known—and in addition to it, no rock is handled in any
way until it is thoroughly saturated with water by means of a hose. Further-
more, the floor, sides and roof of the working-place are thoroughly sprayed
with a hose. The shafts are also subjected to spraying, and water is atomized
by means of compressed air to form a dense curtain during blasting time.[39]

Commenting on these conditions in a memorandum to the TBRC, Dr.
A. J. Orenstein warned that a saturated high-temperature atmosphere
was deleterious to mineworkers in terms of both their health and effi-

ciency. He noted in conclusion that, "one must inevitably regard that workers in atmospheric conditions prevalent in deep mines are, because of the excessive use of water and consequent high humidity, exposed to conditions which are likely to affect deleteriously their respiratory apparatus and predispose them to the development of the pathological lesions of silicosis and also perhaps to special liability to the development of Tuberculosis."[40]

The moisture in the mines continued to facilitate the transmission of infection, as noted in chapter 3.

> Infection with organisms is immensely facilitated by moist surroundings, because the organisms concerned must be able to live and maintain their virulence outside the body and their ability to do so for any length of time depends upon moisture.
>
> Our moist surroundings are responsible for the fact that much of the silicosis that does arise is readily infected and rendered rapidly progressive.[41]

On this subject the observation of mine doctors Irvine, Mavrogodato, and Pirow is apposite. In their report on silicosis on the Witwatersrand to the ILO in 1930, they observed that the type of silicosis present on the Rand had changed between 1900 and 1930, "viz an increasingly early tuberculosis infection became observed as the volume of water underground increased, turning simple into infective secondary cases of miner's phthisis."[42]

At the same time the excessive use of water contributed to the incidence of TB, its value in reducing the risk of silicosis was open to question. Orenstein, in his above cited memorandum, concluded:

> Bearing in mind the minute size of the particles of silica which are specifically responsible for the development of silicosis, it may seriously be questioned whether these particles can be precipitated and kept at rest by the spraying of water, *once these particles have been released into the atmosphere.*[43]

The chamber's technical advisors held a similar view.

> . . . While water has been an important factor in *preventing the formation* of silicotic dust, its use in many cases for catching or allaying dust which is already escaped is largely ineffective . . . other factors, such as the prohibition of promiscuous blasting, and the blasting of cut and round separately on the same shift, the provision of waiting places free from dust and fumes, improvements in ventilation, and the introduction of a lapse in time between blasting and the commencement of the next shift, have probably contributed more largely to the bringing about of improved condition than has the lavish use of water.[44]

Despite these reservations, most mines continued to apply excessive amounts of water to working areas. This may have been because the alternative methods were more costly in terms of both capital outlays and lost shift time. Consequently, whereas mining regulations ensured the provision of waiting places and the observance of a lapse time between blasting and the commencement of the next shift for white workers, these regulations were seldom applied to black workers. In their place, the mines continued to apply large amounts of water as a cost-cutting method of reducing silicosis among black workers. It was, however, of limited use in this regard and a signficant cofactor in the epidemiology of TB on the mines.

As before the war, many of the working conditions that contributed to TB—long hours, heat and humidity, risk of chill, lack of ventilation—were more severe in the older, steeper and deeper mines, found chiefly on the central Rand than in the flatter, shallower mines of the west and east Rand. With the exception of two mines, in fact, all the deep mines had above-average TB rates. Commenting further on this correlation the TBRC report noted,

> The deeper mines are the hotter mines. There are exceptions but, in the main, the hotter mines are the less healthy, though even this applies to health in general rather than to tuberculosis in particular. The lay-out renders impracticable really satisfactory districting and splitting of the air supply. The more the working force is scattered the better for their health. If there be numerous back-stopes in use the vital statistics are apt to be adversely affected.[45]

In this regard it is significant that as the average depth of workings increased during the 1920s and early 1930s the mines began to narrow the width of the stopes, to reduce costs. This had the effect of creating the type of crowded working conditions associated with ill-health.

HEALTH CARE AND MEDICAL EXAMINATIONS

Improvements in medical services also occurred after World War I, although again within the strict limits dictated by costs and benefits. Though more hospitals were constructed, for example, and the number of full-time medical officers employed on the mines increased, the creation of a single centralized hospital, suggested by Gorgas, was viewed as impractical given the distances involved in transporting patients from the various mines widely spread over the Rand. The mine owners also objected to the high capital cost of such an institution. By 1930 every mine had its own hospital with the exception of the Central Mining–

Rand Mines group (the Corner House group) which established three Central Native Hospitals in order to reduce costs and increase the quality of care.

The recommendation that all medical services be centralized under a health supervisor directly responsible to the Chamber of Mines was also rejected. Despite its cost advantages, it represented a threat to the autonomy of individual mines and mine managers. As would become clear in later years when the same recommendation was made by the secretary of health, centralization was seen as restricting the ability of individual mines to control their labor costs and supplies. It implied uniform standards of fitness that might hamper recruitment and health regulations that might impose additional costs on financially weak houses.[46] For all these reasons, the concept of a centralized health service was strongly resisted by the mine managers.

Central Mining–Rand Mines did implement the recommendation for a centralized health service along with the centralization of hospital care. Dr. A. J. Orenstein, who had worked with Gorgas in Panama, was invited in 1915 to serve as superintendent of sanitation and oversee health conditions at their mines. Under Orenstein's leadership the Central Mining–Rand Mines group took the lead in health reforms on the Rand. Yet even on this more limited scale, it was often difficult to enforce centralized authority over the health conditions of individual member mines. Orenstein had little authority to force mine managers to improve health conditions and, as noted above, his suggested reforms often met with stiff opposition.[47]

Although the Chamber of Mines members rejected the idea of a centralized medical service, an Association of Mine Medical Officers was organized in 1921 in an effort to coordinate medical knowledge and practices on the mines. The association had no authority to direct changes in the policies of individual mines, but it did play a role in introducing changes in mine health services. Perhaps the most important contributions of this group during the period from 1918 to the mid-1930s was in the area of medical examinations. The Transvaal Mine Medical Officers Association (TMMOA), in fact, viewed medical examinations as their primary defense against TB and other diseases. There were, by contrast, almost no discussions of mining conditions, housing, or diet during the association's first ten years of existence, an omission that no doubt reflected an awareness of the mine owner's reluctance to spend money on such improvements.

Procedures for screening out tuberculous recruits and others unfit for underground labor were improved after the war by raising the standard of preliminary examinations. Beginning in 1916, all British South African (BSA) recruited workers, except for those from Bechuanaland and Swaziland, were examined before being attested and sent on to Johannesburg. Local recruiters and their employed medical advisors were, moreover, "discouraged" from forwarding to the mines marginally fit workers by the dissemination of established procedures for medical examination in 1920 and by sending back, at the recruiters' expense, large numbers of workers who failed to meet the mines' standards.[48] Between 1916 and 1922 this practice contributed to a steady decline in the percentage of recruits rejected by the Government National Labour Bureau (GNLB) at its compound where all BSA recruits were subjected to a second examination before being sent to the individual mines, at which time they were examined yet again. This three-tiered system of examinations also applied to East Coast (Mozambique) workers who were examined at Ressano Garcia before departure for the Rand and a second time at the WNLA compound before being screened by the medical officer of the mines to which they were sent. These improvements may explain the reduced percentage of TB cases found in the first three months of service. Between 1916 and 1920, 25 percent of all cases occurred among men in their first three months of work. Between 1924 and 1927 this figure was reduced to 9 percent.[49]

Despite these advances, the value of medical screening as a tool for combating TB was handicapped by several factors. To begin with, the medical standard put in force on the mines by the 1916 Miner's Phthisis Act only applied to underground workers. Recruits and voluntary workers who failed to meet the minimum standard for underground work were often placed in an aboveground job. Although this improved their chances for survival, they were still at risk of contracting TB, and since they were not segregated from underground workers in the compounds, they were a potential source of infection for the entire mine community.

Second, the effectiveness of stethoscopic examinations as a means of preventing cases of TB from reaching the mines was limited. A trained ear might be able to detect chest abnormalities indicative of TB in somewhat advanced cases. It was difficult if not impossible, however, even under the best of circumstances, to detect early cases of TB by this means. In 1943 the medical officer of Robinson Mines argued that 99 percent of stethoscopic examinations were wasted effort since auscultation was unlikely to pick up early cases of TB. "The very nature of tuberculosis in Natives, weights against its detection in an incipient stage by these means."[50]

The conditions under which most examinations were carried out, moreover, were far from ideal and thus further reduced the effectiveness of this method of screening. As was the case prior to the war, mine medical officers continued to work under time pressures imposed by mine managers who wished to process new recruits in a single day. Thus medical officers were still required to examine large batches of recruits within a short period of time. At the GNLB depot at Driehoek in 1921, for example, the medical officer had to process up to 600 recruits, including a stethoscopic examination, in a period of 4 hours. Although this may have been an improvement over the 900 examinations in 3.5 hours reported by Brock in 1912 (see chapter 3), it was hardly commensurate with the need to thoroughly screen new recruits. The impossibility of the task no doubt led more than one medical officer to adopt the confident attitude expressed by Dr. L. G. Irvine of the Miner's Phthisis Bureau:

> I do not think every native needs to be stethoscoped. You can tell almost at a glance a native that has, or is likely to get, Tuberculosis.[51]

Third, there were loopholes in the examination procedures that permitted a majority of recruits to arrive at individual mines without any prior examination for TB. To begin with, while WNLA recruits went through three examinations, the quality of these inspections was questionable. The examination at Ressano Garcia was cursory at best. The examination at the WNLA depot in Johannesburg, moreover, did not include a stethoscopic exam for TB or other respiratory problems prior to 1925, unless a recruit exhibited other clinical symptoms such as low weight. WNLA argued that they did not have enough medical officers to screen the 2,000 or so recruits that passed through their hands each week.[52] Most WNLA recruits were not examined stethoscopically until they arrived at the mine.

Similarly, "voluntary workers," African workers who were not recruited but traveled to the Rand on their own, continued to proceed directly to individual mines. For these workers, the mine medical officer was the first and last examiner. This was a sizable problem, for by the mid-1920s voluntaries amounted to nearly half the total number of workers coming to the Rand.

Finally, even BSA recruits found ways of avoiding preliminary examinations. Mine recruits who knew that they might be rejected for a particular problem occasionally employed surrogates who presented themselves in place of the actual recruit. Since physical examinations within the Union often preceded actual departure for the mines by days or even weeks, this ploy was easy to carry off.[53] Responsibility for screening out possible sources of TB was therefore left to each mine's medical officer, an arrangement that was open to abuse, as we shall see.

Thus, despite the three-tiered examination system, the majority of African workers coming to the Rand were only screened for TB by the individual mine medical officers. In 1924 for example, 211,745 African workers came to the Rand from all sources. Of these only 66,755 were BSA recruits who were examined three times. The remaining 89,485 voluntary workers and 55,496 East Coasters, or 68 percent of the total, were only stethoscopically examined for TB by the individual mine medical officers.[54]

Reliance on mine medical officers undermined efforts to effectively exclude workers who either had TB or who, because of their general physical condition, might be particularly vulnerable to the disease once employed. Standards for evaluating the fitness of labor for mine employment, as before the war, continued to vary considerably from mine to mine and for the industry as a whole over time. Summarizing the situation in 1921, Dr. A. Frew of the East Rand Property Mines (ERPM) stated, at a meeting of the Transvaal Mine Medical Officers Association,

> While it might be possible if we had an unlimited supply of labour at our doors to have an absolutely rigid standard of examination, we have to bear in mind that there are frequently recurring times when any type of "boy" is eagerly sought for, and also due to the varying underground conditions prevailing along the Reef, a boy who may not suit a mine with steep stopes may prove of great utility on a mine working more or less on the flat.[55]

As before the war, workers found to have TB who were rejected by one mine officer were free to seek employment at another mine where the demand for labor was greater or in some other occupation. Though the mines tried to halt this practice by stamping the passes of such rejects with the words "Not To Be Employed in Underground Labor," the practice was of little value. Workers identified in this way simply "lost" their passes and paid the cost of having them replaced. Eventually, the Native Affairs Department (NAD) protested that the stamp prevented a worker from finding any employment. This led mines to adopt the practice of inscribing a small-letter "s" in one corner of the pass of anyone deemed unfit for mine employment. Needless to say, it did not take the worker long to remove the stigma by simply tearing off the corner of the pass.[56]

Speaking in 1925 with regards to East Coast recruits, Frew reportedly observed that,

> They knew that East Coast boys developed tuberculosis more rapidly than others. Whether they examined them carefully or not, they might develop tuberculosis. . . . Those members who were in a position [of being] very hard up for boys, had to take them to keep the mine going. Their standards had to vary from time to time.[57]

Frew may well represent the opinion of a minority of mine medical officers who worked for unpopular mines and were thus under considerable pressure to lower standards of fitness in order to fill the mines' minimum labor needs. He was not, however, alone in this opinion. Commenting on the occurrence of scurvy at the mines, the medical officer for Randfontein Estates, another mine that suffered in popularity, noted,

> In my opinion, scurvy (per se) is often seasonal in incidence, and small outbreaks occur sporadically particularly during periods of shortage of native labor. At the latter time the more robust natives stay at home for ploughing etc. whilst we get both voluntary and recruited natives of a lower physical standard than normally.[58]

Comments by the director of WNLA to the Mine Medical Officers Association concerning the strictness of preliminary examinations, reinforce the image of a flexible standard that changed in accordance with the labor needs of the mining industry and conditions in the labor market.

> If we ask the Medical Officers in the Territories or here to be more strict, I think we will divert labor to other channels. To-day it does not matter, as industry outside the mines is slack and there are a large number ready to come forward, but when the diamond mines and other industries start, if we are going to be too drastic either here or in the Territories we will divert labor from going to the mines. Dr. Welsh tells us he can be stricter, but he may do more harm than by the passing of a few less fit boys to come up here.[59]

Examination standards in short, continued to vary considerably depending on the needs of the mining industry, eroding the effectiveness of preliminary screening as a defense against TB.

Along with efforts to improve preliminary examinations, the Mine Medical Officers Association devoted a great deal of time during the

1920s to discussing ways to further reduce the spread of TB on the mines through the early detection of new cases. The primary method developed to detect early cases of TB among mine workers was periodic weighing, made compulsory in 1916. Initially each mineworker had to be weighed each month. It proved more convenient from the mine managers viewpoint, however, to do the weighing when the workers were assembled to receive their monthly pay. Since this was calculated on the basis of thirty shifts (six per week), the weighing was normally done every five weeks. Any mineworker found to have lost a certain amount of weight between two consecutive weighings was automatically taken aside and given a stethoscopic examination and, if necessary, sent to the hospital for observation and further testing.

During the early years, there was little agreement as to how much weight a worker could lose without being marked for further examination. As with preliminary examinations, mine managers insisted on establishing their own standards, which could vary from two to ten pounds. This variation was justified on the basis that certain mines with steeper slopes and deeper workings took a higher toll in lost weight than flatter, shallower mines. No one seemed to acknowledge that the larger weight losses recorded on deeper mines were indicative not simply of more strenuous working conditions but also of the physiological stress associated with these conditions, or that this stress may have been a contributing factor to the higher incidence of TB recorded on these mines (see above). There was thus considerable variation in what might be considered a normal weight loss. Whether mines with chronic labor shortages employed higher weight limits is unclear from the data available. The Miner's Phthisis Act of 1925 laid down a maximum standard of five pounds lost between any two consecutive weighings and six pounds between any three.[60]

Mine medical officers were convinced that weighing was an efficient tool for detecting early TB and pointed to the decline in TB deaths that occurred following the introduction of weighing. A report of the Miner's Phthisis Bureau based on a study of cases collected over two years prior to July 31, 1926, concluded that, "approximately 66 percent of bacteriologically verified cases of simple tuberculosis in mine Natives show a loss of weight of the prescribed amount at their periodic examinations, and should therefore automatically be made available for special stethoscopic examination."[61] Yet the efficiency of periodic weighing as an instrument for detecting early cases of TB was in actual practice rather low. Thus a survey conducted in 1925 found that only 26.2

percent of the cases that eventually appeared were detected through periodic weighing. The remaining 73.8 percent were discovered following the onset of an acute disease or by "accident" (often the result of hospitalization for some other cause, usually trauma).[62] These studies suggest that at best weighing was an imperfect tool for the early detection of TB (missing 34 percent of the possible cases) and that in actual practice it was ineffective.

The failure of the mining industry to develop more efficient means for the early detection of TB among African mineworkers, such as the use of x-rays, can be explained by the fact that prior to 1925 there was a financial disincentive to doing so. Not only were x-rays expensive, and thus opposed on economic grounds by mine managers, as noted below, but under existing mining regulations a mine could actually save money by failing to detect early cases of TB. Under these regulations an African worker could only be compensated for TB if he was diagnosed and certified by the Miner's Phthisis Bureau before he either died or was discharged. If a mineworker died while on the job, or while in a mine hospital before he had been certified, or if he was discharged and repatriated without being diagnosed and certified, no compensation would be paid. This anomaly helps explain why more was not done to ensure the early diagnosis of TB cases as well as why African TB cases were often retained in mine hospitals for long periods before being forwarded to the Miner's Phthisis Bureau for certification. If the unfortunate worker died while in the hospital, as so frequently happened, no compensation would be paid.[63]

The failure of compensation laws to cover African mineworkers who were discharged before being diagnosed and certified, and the desire of mine managers to limit the payment of compensation, also helps explain the cursory nature of discharge examinations prior to 1925. These only involved weighing to see if the worker had lost weight since his preliminary examination and the examination of those who had. As a result of this procedure many discharged African workers were declared to be free from TB or silicosis when they were not. Some of these cases were caught at the WNLA compound before repatriation. Others were identified when they turned up again for employment. Many were never caught but simply returned home to die.[64] To eliminate this problem the Native Affairs Department (NAD) suggested that central depots be established under the authority of the Chamber of Mines to examine all mineworkers at the end of their contracts. The medical officers put in charge of these facilities would not be influenced by Boards of Directors and Mine Managers, they would have an open mind when making their examinations and would not be confronted with the question as to how much it was going to cost the Company in the event of compensation being awarded.[65]

This proposal, like other recommendations for a centralized health service, was rejected by the mine managers since it threatened their autonomy.[66]

It should be noted that white workers who were eligible for compensation even if they were diagnosed and certified by the Miner's Phthisis Bureau after they were discharged from service, received much more thorough interim and termination examinations, which included x-rays.[67] In the case of white workers the mines evidently found it difficult to avoid their financial responsibilities and thus were more concerned with identifying cases early in order to reduce their liabilities, by limiting both the degree of an individual miner's disability, and the number of additional cases of TB an unidentified tubercular miner might generate by infecting other workers.

Compensation benefits were extended in the 1925 act to former African mineworkers who were found to have TB or TB plus silicosis within six months of discharge. This act eliminated the financial benefit derived from failing to catch early cases of TB among mineworkers and made the benefits of reducing overall TB rates more attractive. The act was followed by a tightening of both periodic and final examination procedures.

The system remained imperfect, however. Attempts to introduce more thorough examination procedures, including more frequent stethoscopic examinations, or reducing the weight standard for periodic weighings, were rejected as impractical given the limited number of medical officers available in the mines.[68] In one study carried out in 1938 it was found that reducing the weight standard to a loss of two pounds between two consecutive weighings would increase the number of early cases detected by 20 percent, but would require a two hundred percent increase in stethoscopic examinations, since more workers would fall within the lower standard.[69] An additional impediment to more thorough periodic examinations was created by the conditions under which examinations had to be carried out. As Dr. Mavrogadato of the South African Institute for Medical Research (SAIMR) observed in 1926,

There are some 160,000 natives, there is about one medical officer to every 6,000 or 7,000 natives. The medical officer has to carry out his routine tuberculosis inspection without interfering with the natives' work and without interfering with the natives' leisure.[70]

Financial constraints limiting implementation of more effective screening methods are perhaps best revealed in the debate over the introduction of radioscopic examinations for African workers. The idea of using x-rays in examining both new recruits and in-service workers was raised early on in the meetings of the Mine Medical Officers Association. Under the 1919 act all white miners were x-rayed both initially and periodically, contributing significantly to a decline in TB rates among them. Dr. Frew observed in 1921 that, "In view of present day knowledge no examination of the chest can be considered complete without the use of the X-rays." He went on to caution, however, that, "While we realize that this is the counsel of perfection, we must also realize that the cost is prohibitive unless an efficient means of examining the chest by screen alone can be evolved."[71]

The issue was raised repeatedly during the 1920s and became a focus of research for the TB research committee during 1926 and 1927. The problem of costs, however, continued to act as a deterrent to any scheme to introduce wide-scale x-raying of African workers. These costs were not simply measured by the financial expenditure installing and operating x-ray equipment required. They also involved costs as defined in terms of compensation payments, described above, and of the availability of labor. In early discussions by the TBRC on the possible use of x-rays in examining recruits, the representative of the Gold Producers Committee warned that the use of x-rays would lead to the exclusion of many experienced mineworkers who showed signs of calcified lesions and ante-primary silicosis but who were free of TB and fit for underground work. He stressed that this type of experienced laborer was particularly valuable to the mining industry and that "any curtailment in the supply of such natives should be deprecated." The chairman of the TBRC objected to this line of thinking, noting that the use of ante-silicotic workers was unprofitable because of their likelihood to become openly tuberculous. In fact a survey of 991 African workers with five years of continuous service had uncovered an astounding TB prevalence of 50.4 per 1,000.[72]

The use of x-rays was also perceived as a threat to the mines' ability to acquire labor because it implied the use of more centralized medical screening. Since not every mine could afford an x-ray plant, it was suggested that centralized centers be created. If this were done, however, it would have reduced the ability of individual mines to adjust their standards of fitness to meet their current labor needs.

The debate over the use of x-rays continued through the 1930s with little effect. Long-term mineworkers (continuous mine work for five years) were x-rayed yearly at some mines from 1926 onward. For the vast majority of mineworkers, however, x-rays remained a diagnostic tool employed only after they had been identified as possibly tuberculous by clinical examination. In the late 1930s, however, attitudes on the mines began to change. The acute labor shortage the mines experienced required mine managers to take on workers who earlier in the decade would have been rejected. In this context x-rays began to be seen by some managers as a means of reducing compensation expenses in the face of a growing reliance on marginally fit workers. The cost-saving value of selective x-raying in preemployment examinations was demonstrated by the results of x-raying at Randfontein Mines between 1930 and 1936. During this period 15,237 recruits were submitted for x-ray, or about 11 percent of the total number of recruits examined during this period. The cost of these examinations was estimated to be £2,444. X-raying, however, saved the mining company an estimated £10,050 in compensation for TB and TB with silicosis.[73] Still, not all managers were convinced of the value of x-rays, and this resistance, combined with wartime financial constraints, delayed widespread use of x-rays in the examination of African workers until the 1950s.

LABOR SUPPLIES AND THE EPIDEMIOLOGY OF TB

It is clear that although overall working and living conditions on the mines after World War I represented a marked improvement over those of the prewar period, they were far from ideal. Deficiencies in diet and occasional overcrowding continued to occur. Many underground working conditions remained the same or were worse, and the system of preemployment and periodic examinations was still woefully inefficient. Given these continuing flaws, it is difficult to accept the mining industry's conclusion that the dramatic drop that occurred in the incidence of TB among African workers between 1912 and 1933 was a reflection of better conditions. Other factors must have been at work.

One factor that may have contributed to the fall in TB incidence was an increase in the resistance level of the workforce brought about by more extensive prior experience with TB. Thus a higher percentage of

Africans coming to the Rand in 1930 had been previously infected with TB than before the war. Postwar labor contingents may therefore have contained fewer genetically susceptible individuals. Yet as noted in chapter 5, the incidence rate for previously infected workers was higher (738 per 100,000) than for workers who were tuberculin negative when they arrived on the Rand (347 per 100,000). Increased experience may not, therefore, have had much of an impact on TB incidence on the mines.

Of greater importance was the changing composition and availability of labor. Seventy-one percent of the decline in TB incidence between 1912 and 1935 occurred within two periods. From 1913 to 1919, the incidence of TB among African workers fell from roughly 18 per 1,000 to 9 per 1,000. Sixty-three percent of this drop, from 18 to 12.5 per 1,000, took place between 1913 and 1915 and coincided with the withdrawal of tropical labor. The percentage of tropical workers in the workforce dropped from 9 to 1.5 percent during this period. The second drop in TB incidence occurred between 1928 and 1933—from 8 per 1,000 to 2 per 1,000—and largely coincided with the depression and with an equally dramatic shift in the composition of the mine labor force.[74]

The withdrawal of tropical labor, as we have seen, was imposed on the mining industry by the Union government in response to the appalling death rates suffered by tropical mineworkers up through 1912. Although pneumonia was the number one killer of tropical mine labor during this period, many tropical workers also died from TB and, as a group, they had the highest TB morbidity and mortality rates, largely because of their vulnerability to chill and other respiratory infections which predisposed them to TB. Twenty-six percent of the total deaths and 23.2 percent of the total number of TB cases occurring on the mines between 1910 and 1912 were suffered by tropical workers who represented only 9.5 percent of the workforce.[75] These figures are probably underestimated since, as noted in chapter 3, many pneumonia cases during this period were actually unrecognized cases of acute pulmonary TB.

The withdrawal of tropical workers would have had an immediate positive impact on TB rates on the mines, though it is impossible to measure the exact extent of this effect. Not only would the cases produced directly by tropical workers have been eliminated, but the cases that were produced as a result of tropical workers infecting nontropical co-workers would have also been reduced. Most of the shortfall in labor created by the withdrawal of tropical workers was made up by an

increase in the number of Cape Africans on the Rand. As a group, Cape
Africans suffered from significantly lower rates of TB than tropical
workers. (Between 1910 and 1912 they represented 28 percent of the
workforce but accounted for only 14.7 percent of the total cases.) Since
the withdrawal of tropical workers was largely completed by 1915, the
remaining decline in the TB incidence rate between 1916 and 1919,
from 12.5 to 9 per 1,000, is likely due to other causes including some
improvements in working and living conditions.

Between 1918 and 1928, the incidence of TB on the mines fluctuated
considerably, with a small overall decline from 9 to 7 per 1,000. Beginning in 1929 and the onset of the depression, however, the incidence of
TB once again dropped sharply, going from 7 to 2 per 1,000 in a period
of only four years. As described in chapter 5, the depression and the
drought years of the late 1920s and early 1930s generated a flood of
surplus labor out of the rural reserves. In addition thousands of Africans
already employed in manufacturing lost their jobs. In the urban centers
of South Africa this flood of unemployed workers contributed to a
rising TB mortality rate by putting pressure on already inadequate housing supplies and by creating a mushrooming population of impoverished job-seekers. For the mines, however, the depression was a wind-
fall. For the first time since the war, the mines found themselves with an
abundant supply of labor from which to choose their workforce.[76] This
situation led to changes in the composition of the mines' African labor
force and, in turn, to a dramatic decline in TB incidence.

To begin with, the abundance of labor allowed many mines that had
been hard up for labor and thus forced to accept many marginal workers to be more choosy about who they employed. As a result, overall
rejection rates at the mines increased. Although mine managers claimed
that the same medical standards had been applied since 1920, and that
the rising rejection rate reflected the declining quality of labor,[77] it is
clear that the mines were being more selective in their hiring. Thus a
report to the general manager of the Native Recruiting Corporation
(NRC) in 1933 noted,

> A disturbing feature which emerges from the present unusual situation in
> South Africa where more labor is seeking employment than can be absorbed,
> is that only the best, or grade "A" labor is being accepted.[78]

The mines were also able to force the recruiting agencies to keep back
marginal labor for additional feeding and rest before distributing them
to the mines. The percentage of BSA recruits kept back in this way

increased from 4 percent in 1928 to 5 percent in 1929 to 30 percent in 1930.[79] Thus whereas the general health of rural Africans may have declined during the depression years, the overall fitness of the mine labor force increased.

Second, the depression and the absence of economic alternatives to mine labor resulted in many workers extending their contracts. By 1932 there were approximately 70,000 time-expired workers on the mines.[80] From the mines' viewpoint, this was an advantageous situation for it meant that their workforce was more experienced, and though the Chamber of Mines was unwilling to give up the financial advantages of a migrant labor system, they went to considerable effort to extend the average number of shifts worked by their African workforce. It was during the depression that the chamber took advantage of the demand for employment to require a minimum nine-month contract for BSA recruits. The number of time-expired Africans on the mines eventually became an issue with the Native Affairs Department, which argued that the mines should encourage a regular turnover of workers in order to provide employment for the large army of unemployed workers in the reserves. The chamber resisted this suggestion, however, stating it was both inefficient and unethical to force experienced, useful workers to return home to be replaced with inexperienced raw recruits. They suggested in addition that experienced miners were more acclimated to the conditions of mine work and less subject to health problems such as heat stroke. That this logic pointed toward the creation of a permanent workforce was needless to say ignored by the mines.[81] The NAD eventually had its own way, however, and the mines began a program of planned wastage, repatriating a minimum of 11,000 BSA workers per month beginning in April 1932.[82]

The experience level of the workforce prior to this, measured in terms of the number of shifts worked on the present job, increased as the percentage of new recruits declined. This change may well have contributed to the overall decline in the incidence of TB, for it was well established that new recruits in their first months of employment were more vulnerable to TB than later on. The TBRC estimated that during the first year of service the TB rate for recruits was 13.4 per 1,000 but that this dropped off to 3.6 per 1,000 in the second year and 1.7 per 1,000 in the third year. The rate for all TB cases in mineworkers with more than one year of continuous service was 2.9 per 1,000.[83] Similarly, a study of over 5,000 TB cases occuring on the mines between 1916 and 1920 found that 45 percent occurred during the first six months of service, whereas only 23 percent occurred during the second six months and 32 percent in workers with more than twelve months' experience.[84] An analysis of 1,218 cases of TB among African workers by Dr. Mavrogadato in 1926 found that among workers with previous mine experience, 49.7 percent of the cases detected occurred during the first six months of service. Among workers with no previous experience (i.e., novices), 72 percent of the cases were detected in the first six months. Overall, 56 percent of the cases occurred in the first six months. These figures all support the conclusion that the first six months of mine work, particularly for novices, was what the TBRC report called "a danger zone for tuberculosis."[85]

During the 1920s, about half of the complement of mineworkers was at any one time in their first year of employment. During the depression years this figure was considerably reduced. Overall in 1932 only 30 percent of BSA workers were in their first year of employment. Table 10 uses figures for the average BSA complement between 1926 and 1929 (105,000) and the average incidence rates per 1,000 for various lengths of service for this same period to calculate the impact that a reduction in the percentage of men with less than one year of service would have had overall on the incidence of TB among BSA mineworkers. It shows that decrease in the percentage of workers with under one year of service from 50 percent to 30 percent could have produced a 25 percent decline in overall TB morbidity on the mines.

The susceptibility of mineworkers, particularly of raw recruits, during their first year of mine service is striking. It suggests that initial exposure to the combination of adverse factors described above overwhelmed whatever natural resistance the new recruit might have and resulted in either a reactivation of existing TB lesions or an inability to localize a new infection acquired on the mines. Yet this raises an important question. Why were mineworkers who survived the first year able to resist the combination of factors that struck down the new recruit? Mine medical officers attributed this reduced susceptibility to acclimatization or "Europeanization." The terms, though not clearly defined, generally referred to a combination of cultural and physiological adaptation to mining conditions. This was commonly associated with the concept of "tubercularization" and the theory of acquired resistance through repeated exposure to the disease (see chapter 7).[86]

This theory may have had some relevance, especially during the early years of mining when new recruits may have included a proportion of hereditarily susceptible individuals. Yet as we have seen, it was the

TABLE 10

IMPACT OF REDUCTION OF WORKERS WITH LESS THAN ONE YEAR SERVICE ON INCIDENCE OF TB AMONG BSA MINEWORKERS

	No. < 1 yr	Cases per 1,000	No. Cases	No. > 1 yr	Cases per 1,000	No. Cases	Total Cases	Cases per 1,000
With 50% < 1 yr	52,500	13.4	703	52,500	2.9	152	855	8.14
With 30% < 1 yr	31,500	13.4	422	73,500	2.9	213	635	6.04

previously infected mineworker who was at greatest risk of contracting TB by the late 1920s. This suggests that learned experience rather than biological adaptation may have played a more central role in the survival of experienced mineworkers. As early as 1911 Maynard observed that,

> The old hands drill their complement of inches in a shorter time than the new boys, and therefore, leave the mine sooner, and thus spend more time in the fresh air. Experience shows, so I am informed, that the old boy spends more money on buying food, and so from every point of view renders himself less liable to disease and death.[87]

Getting to the surface earlier also ensured that one's meal was not overcooked and thus lacking in vitamins. It is also possible that experienced mineworkers learned when to leave the work area in order to reduce waiting to be hauled to the surface and thus exposure to the drafts of the main shaft. In these and other ways, for which a good deal more research on the experience of mineworkers is necessary, the experienced mineworker may have simply learned to survive in the mines.

The composition of the workforce was also changed through the replacement of Mozambican workers with BSA workers. This shift, like that involving the planned wastage of employed workers after 1932, was instituted in response to pressure from the government to find room for the thousands of unemployed workers in the reserves. The number of Mozambique workers was gradually reduced from roughly 75,000, or 36 percent of the total workforce in 1928, to 45,000, or 19 percent of the total workforce at the end of 1932. Conversely the number of BSA workers, primarily from the eastern Cape, increased from roughly 104,000 or 50 percent to 127,000 or 60 percent during this period.[88] This change in the workforce, like the earlier withdrawal of tropical workers, may also have had a positive effect on TB incidence on the mines. Though the TBRC concluded that the susceptibility of Mozambique workers was not universal and that some were much more susceptible than others, the overall difference between the incidence of TB and TB plus silicosis in Mozambique workers compared to BSA workers between 1926 and 1930 was significant: 6.18 per 1,000 for Mozambique workers compared to 3.42 per 1,000 for BSA workers.[89] It is important to note that the withdrawal of Mozambique workers by itself might not have lowered the TB Rate. A similar cutback occurred between 1922 and 1927, yet during this period TB rates rose on the mines. The difference between these two retrenchments seems to be the labor shortage in the earlier case so that the mines were unable to be as selective about the BSA workers they acquired to replace the Mozambique workers. The reverse was true during the later withdrawal.[90]

Those familiar with the recent history of TB on the mines (discussed in the epilogue), will no doubt find curious arguments concerning the different TB rates of novices versus experienced workers and Mozambican versus BSA workers, since in the recent history of TB among mineworkers these relationships have been reversed. In other words, today it is novices, Mozambique, and tropical workers who appear to have lower TB morbidity rates than BSA and experienced workers. This apparent contradiction can be explained in terms of changes in mining conditions and in the etiology of TB on the mines.

During the 1930s and then again after World War II the mines continued to make improvements in living conditions. These included further improvements in diet, elimination of the causes of chill, and a significant reduction in opportunities for the transmission of infection. As a result of these reforms, the susceptibility of both tropical and inexperienced workers was reduced and there were far fewer cases of primary progressive disease that had taken such a heavy toll among these two groups. At the same time, experience on the mines played less of a resistance-building role than it had in the past. To the contrary, experience became a significant risk factor.

By the 1960s the factors most important in the etiology of TB among African mineworkers were the working conditions within the mines— heat, humidity, long working hours, and barometric pressure. These conditions caused previous infections to reactivate. In these circumstances, the population at greatest risk were those miners who, as a result of repeated exposure to the TB bacillus, were the most strongly positive reactors to tuberculin. This group was made up largely of experienced mineworkers from heavily infected areas, located primarily within South Africa.[91] Within this group it was Transkeian workers who were at greatest risk.

It should be noted as well that the increased risk of BSA workers resulted from the more extensive use of these workers in underground work as Mozambique and tropical workers were withdrawn. In short, changes in mining conditions altered the etiology of TB on the mines reversing earlier patterns of susceptibility and resistance.

The surplus of labor during the depression may have reduced the incidence of TB still further by allowing the mines to improve their examination procedures. As mentioned above, nearly half of the labor coming to the mines in the 1920s was voluntary. These workers proceeded directly to the mines where they were examined only once by the mine medical officer. In 1928 the Chamber of Mines instituted the Assisted Voluntary System (AVS), by which potential workers would be provided with transportation expenses by the Native Recruitment Corporation (NRC) but would be free to choose their own mine and not, as was the case with recruited labor, be assigned to one. The movement to an AVS system was instituted both to encourage more workers to proceed to the mines and to bring the system under greater control by the chamber. The voluntary system had in fact become so widespread that individual mines were using it to circumvent the recruiting system and in some cases were employing private recruiters to encourage men to come to their mine. This threatened to increase competition for labor and drive up wages.[92]

The AVS system placed voluntary employment back in the hands of the NRC and thus reduced the threat of renewed competition. During the first two years of the system, a certain number of African workers continued to come forward on their own, perhaps out of fear that the AVS system would restrict their choice of employer. Yet the surplus of labor available to all mines permitted the members of the Chamber of Mines to agree on gradually restricting voluntary employment to AVS workers. The AVS system by 1932 had established a virtual monopoly over the control of voluntary workers.[93]

The advantage of the AVS system for lowering the incidence of TB was that it required AVS workers to be medically examined before departure to the mines. It thus improved the mines' ability to screen out unfit workers.[94]

CONCLUSION

The dramatic decline in TB morbidity that occurred in the gold mines of South Africa during the period from 1912 to 1935 must be seen as the result of a combination of forces. Although there can be little doubt that improvements in working and living conditions and in medical services played a role in this decline, the reduction also reflected the convergence of historically specific forces—the withdrawal of tropical labor and the changes that occurred in the composition of the labor force during the depression. Improvements in the incidence of TB on the mines resulted in both instances from the exclusion of susceptible groups and individuals. The decline in TB in mineworkers was thus similar to that achieved by urban authorities in the mid-1930s through the use of slum clearance acts and sanitary segregation. In both cases the failure to do more to transform the underlying causes of ill-health among African workers and their families meant that the improvements achieved by these measures were ephemeral and in the long run unsustainable. In both cases, moreover, exclusionary policies sowed the seeds for future health problems as the continued exclusion and repatriation of diseased workers, without any regard for their future health or well-being, contributed to the rising incidence of TB in the wider African population from which industries drew their labor. When changes in the labor market occurred in the late 1930s and early 1940s, both sets of authorities lost their ability to restrict TB through social control measures. The result was a rising tide of TB in the urban and industrial centers of South Africa.

CHAPTER VII

Segregation and Racial Susceptibility: The Ideological Foundations of Tuberculosis Control, 1913–1938

For medical officers working on the Rand and in other urban and industrial centers of South Africa, the struggle against TB in the 1920s and 1930s was an exercise in holding back the tide. TB control was based on a policy of exclusion rather than amelioration. Sanitary segregation, slum clearance, and medical screening were instruments for keeping TB off the Rand and away from white urban populations, and had little or nothing to do with improving African health.

The response of white medical authorities to the rising tide of TB during this period represented an extension of health practices established at the turn of the century with the creation of "native locations" and the use of medical repatriation of mineworkers. Yet underlying this continuity of practice, one can discern a significant shift in the ideological foundations upon which exclusionary policies were based. This shift in turn reflected, and ultimately reinforced, a more fundamental movement in white attitudes and perceptions about Africans and their role in South African society.

Sanitary segregation, as formulated and practiced in the first decade of this century, was based on a "progressive" view of African development. This view posited that Africans were susceptible to disease, particularly tuberculosis, because they were inexperienced in the ways of western industrial life. They lacked knowledge about sanitary behavior and about how to cope with a "civilized" life style. With time, it was argued, African individuals would adjust to these new conditions or, in the language of mine medical officers, become "acclimated" to them. Salvation therefore lay in education and was an individual experience. In the meantime, Africans needed to be segregated, not only to protect the health of whites but also to establish stricter controls over the manner in which Africans lived. Segregation would, in the language of the day, protect Africans from the abuses inherent in a population traveling along the road from "barbarism to civilization." This paternalistic view, which grew out of the nineteenth-century liberal discourse about Africans, dominated the thinking of white medical authorities through the first decade of this century. Although other ideas about the causes of African ill health, including theories about the existence of racial traits, coexisted with this theory, they were not widely held or espoused in either the medical or popular writings of the day.

These "progressive" attitudes began to shift during the initial phase of racial segregation in the Cape Colony. The policy of sanitary segregation was carried out along strictly racial lines and did not allow for significant differences in the social class and living conditions of different segments of the African and colored urban populations. Individual distinctions and the view that improved resistance would come through individual advancement or adjustment were incompatible with the interests of those who wanted to create urban locations for economic or social reasons. All blacks had to be removed.[1] The application of the policy of sanitary segregation consequently contributed to a more generalized association of unsanitary behavior with race. Physical segregation heightened racial consciousness and moved conceptions of the causes of African susceptibility to disease toward a more explicit racial conceptualization of the problem. This evolution was completed during the second and third decades of the century in tandem with the expansion of industrial capitalism.

Industrial expansion not only transformed the nature of the South African economy, it also altered in a fundamental way the discourse on race in South Africa. The growth of industrial centers during and after World War I gave rise, as we have seen, to new fears among white workers and farmers about the growing number of urban African workers and families. This led to a heightened consciousness of racial differences and to new calls for racial segregation. Within this environment, progressive ideas concerning the gradual acclimatization of Africans to the conditions of modern industrial life were replaced by Stallardist pronouncements that rejected the very idea of an urban African. The "native" was a temporary sojourner in the city, whose natural home was in the reserves. Not only was the "native's" adjustment to western civilization difficult, it should not be attempted.[2] This new orthodoxy, which crystallized racial distinctions, was reflected in the discussions of white medical authorities concerning the causes and prevention of African ill-health. Within these discussions the behavioral model of African susceptibility to disease was gradually replaced by a biological model stressing the importance of physiological differences in explaining the apparent higher susceptibility of Africans to disease and particularly to TB. Africans were, in effect, biologically ill-adapted to civilization and its diseases. These ideas in turn strengthened awareness of racial differences and further encouraged the physical isolation of Africans from white society. The physiological explanation for African susceptibility to disease in effect increased the social distance between Africans and whites, creating for whites a definition of "the other" which facilitated and justified the physical removal of Africans from "civilized society." Although the argument still stressed both the need to protect white society and to protect Africans from the effects of that society, the underlying terms of the argument had changed.

The physiological explanation for African susceptibility to TB became widely accepted within the white medical community in South Africa during the 1920s and 1930s, but it was the mine medical officers working on the Rand who played a significant role in its emergence and spread. An important actor in the initial development of the physiological model was Dr. G. D. Maynard, medical advisor to WNLA. Maynard's early work on overall mortality rates had led him to conclude that experienced mineworkers had a lower mortality rate than raw recruits due to the old hands' acclimatization to working conditions. In 1912 he directed his statistical methods to the question of tuberculosis and came up with very different conclusions. He read his findings in a paper, entitled "The Relative Importance of Infection and Heredity in the Spread of Tuberculosis," before the Witwatersrand Branch of the British Medical Association.[3] In it, he argued that the TB bacillus was ubiquitous within the population and that the determination of the disease depended not so much, if at all, on the fresh introduction of a few more organisms from a new source, as on conditions that determined the resistance of the body. He went on to argue, following the work of Karl Pearson in Europe, that the conditions that affected resistance of the body were hereditary and related to the presence or absence of "the tubercular diathesis." He did not see it as an environmental problem, that is, that resistance was affected by better diet or sanitation measures.

Maynard's statistical analysis at one stroke resurrected nineteenth-century hereditarian ideas and rejected two basic assumptions that underlay existing efforts to control tuberculosis. First, he strongly implied that efforts to prevent the spread of infection within the population were of little use. Second, he argued that efforts to improve housing and sanitation through public health regulations were also unlikely to reduce the incidence of the disease, arguing correctly that TB mortality in England began to decline before improvements in sanitation and housing commenced. Maynard concluded that increased resistance to tuberculosis could only be achieved through a process of natural selection in which the more susceptible members of a race died off leaving those who were more resistant to the disease to reproduce. This would eventually produce a more resistant population. Maynard argued that this process of natural selection had already occurred among Europeans but was just beginning among South Africa's African population. This difference in historical experience accounted for the higher susceptibility of Africans to the disease.

Maynard's extreme Darwinism set off a major debate within South African medical circles and was ultimately rejected in light of what was felt to be widespread clinical evidence that tuberculosis was infectious.[4] Yet the idea that there was a physiological component to African susceptibility to the disease persisted. In 1913 Dr. D. Traill, in an article published in the *South African Medical Record,* lay the groundwork for a modified hereditary theory that would come to dominate South African medical opinion for the next thirty years. Traill stated,

> I agree with Dr. Maynard in putting it [African susceptibility to TB] down to the breeding of a more resistant stock. But I entirely differ from him as to the way in which the more resistant stock is brought about. He says that the decrease is due to the selective death rate. My explanation is that we are all gradually becoming more and more immune to tubercular disease.[5]

Traill went on to propose a theory of acquired immunity based on the principle of vaccination. He argued that repeated successful encounters with tubercular infection led to an acquired immunity. He further suggested that this acquired immunity was then passed on to the next generation, which further strengthened its resistance through repeated encounters with the disease.

Traill's theory of natural vaccination predated the tubercularization theory of Bushnell[6] and Opie[7] and the related "virgin soil" theories of Borrel[8] and Cummins,[9] all of which were published in the 1920s. Underlying Traill's theory were four related assumptions. First, African susceptibility to tuberculosis was due to their having had limited exposure to the disease and therefore not having had time to build up an adequate immunity to it. Second, African resistance to tuberculosis would only be increased through repeated exposure to the disease over several generations. Third, until this process was completed Africans would be vulnerable to tubercular infections. Finally, in light of this vulnerability, TB control efforts should be directed at reducing the exposure of the vulnerable "native" to the harsh conditions of urban life which limited his ability to survive early encounters with the disease. Traill saw this last conclusion as a call for environmental reform. Within the particular economic conditions of the Rand, however, it became a justification for the use of migrant labor, through which periods of exposure to the conditions of industrial life would be separated by periods of rest and recuperation in the supposedly healthy, open-air environment of the reserves.

The theories of Maynard and Traill were not without merit. As we have seen, increased group resistance through the elimination of susceptible individuals may have played a role in the reduction of African TB mortality during the early years of this century. Yet racial susceptibility, or more specifically a lack of experience with TB, was at best only one of the factors contributing to the problem of TB among Africans. Working and living conditions also lowered the ability of Africans to control their infections and thus contributed to their high rates of TB morbidity and mortality. These conditions played hardly any role in the ideas of Maynard and Traill.

It is not difficult to understand why the theory of tubercularization gained early acceptance within the white medical community working in the Rand, predating its popularity in the wider western medical community by nearly a decade. Whereas the theory of acclimatization had coincided with the mines' efforts to establish an experienced permanent workforce in the face of severe labor shortages following the South African War, it was increasingly incompatible with the interests of the mine owners within the changed labor market of the second decade of this century.

By the end of the first decade of this century, mine owners on the Rand realized that efforts to establish a "permanent clientele" from local labor sources could not meet the mines' growing labor demands. Local African workers were able to take advantage of the higher wages and better conditions offered by other industries and were unwilling to work on the mines or, if they did, refused to take up underground work. Attempts to import Chinese coolies had met with strong opposition from white labor and was abandoned in 1908. The industry responded to this crisis by expanding the geographical limits of the labor catchment area and by recruiting large numbers of "raw" workers from tropical and low-lying areas to the north. These recruits, unlike local Africans, were unable to take advantage of alternative forms of employment and could therefore be made to accept the low wages offered by the mines. The expansion into new recruiting areas was accompanied by renewed efforts to establish a centralized recruiting system that would keep down the costs of labor. The establishment of the NRC in 1912 marked a major step in the achievement of this goal, even though the problem of competing labor-recruitment agencies continued for nearly a decade.[10] The passage of the 1913 Native Land Act, supported by mining interests, further increased the mines' access to a cheap supply of African labor by decreasing the ability of South African peasants to resist recruitment to low-wage employment. By World War I the mining industry was clearly wedded to the propagation of a cheap labor supply based on the extensive use of temporary migrant workers. With the successful establishment of this system the advantages of maintaining a more settled workforce decreased and the social and economic costs of such a workforce became more burdensome.

This shift in the character of the mines' labor supplies brought the economic interests of mine owners into direct conflict with established medical opinion on the Rand concerning African susceptibility to disease. Mine medical officers, prior to 1912, shared the popular view that inexperience with the conditions of urban and industrial life produced African susceptibility to disease and that the establishment of a more permanent workforce would reduce African morbidity. The conflict between this opinion and the increasing reliance of the mines on temporary migrant workers was thrown into stark relief by a marked increase in African morbidity and mortality on the mines following the expansion of the mines' labor catchment area to the north.

Between 1910 and 1912 the rate of combined TB deaths and repatriations rose 50 percent from 10 to 15 per 1,000.[11] As noted in chapter 6, this rise in mine mortality rates brought the industry under fire from the Native Affairs Department and from health officials and administrators in the native territories and protectorates from which migrant labor was being drawn, and it ultimately led to the withdrawal of tropical labor. Although withdrawal reduced overall mortality on the mines, the incidence of TB remained unacceptably high and, in fact, became more noticeable once the tropical workers were removed and pneumonia, the number one killer of tropical workers, began to decline.

For mine medical officers and other health authorities who had argued for a stabilized workforce, the rise in mine mortalities must have verified existing opinion about the causes of African susceptibility to disease. Yet this conclusion and the underlying conflict between medical opinion and the emerging labor recruitment policy were largely unmentioned in the statements of medical authorities working on the Rand during this period. Though in private they may have been critical of the new recruitment policy and its adverse health consequences, in their public writings they made no mention of their concern. What one finds instead is a shift in medical opinion away from the cultural explanations of the previous decade and toward the physiological or racial model of African susceptibility to TB proposed by Maynard, Traill, and others. This new model provided an explanation that did not conflict with the mines' migrant labor policy. Ideas about acquired immunity and "natural vaccination" could, to the contrary, be used to justify the use of migrant labor and to reject arguments in support of a more permanently settled workforce. It was now argued in effect that labor migrancy would limit the exposure of Africans to the adverse conditions of industrial life and provide opportunities for recuperation in the reserves. This would allow African workers to gradually develop a resistance to the disease. Labor stabilization by contrast would increase opportunities for contracting the disease as well as exposure to conditions that reduced the "native's" ability to survive infection.

This argument was in fact used by the mining industry as early as 1913 to reject some of the recommendations made by Col. George Gorgas, who, as seen in the last chapter, was invited by the Chamber of Mines to inspect mining conditions and report on measures for reducing mortality among African mineworkers. Among Gorgas' proposals was the suggestion that African miners be settled in native locations with their families.[12] This suggestion, although very much in line with his own experience in Panama and with earlier recommendations of Rand medical authorities for reducing African mine mortalities, conflicted with the current needs and practices of the mining industry. The proposal was therefore rejected. The reason given, however, was not that native locations were incompatible with labor recruitment policies but that they would have adverse consequences for African susceptibility to TB. The mine owners' position was incorporated in the 1914 Tuberculosis Commission Report, which in general gave voice to the growing acceptance of a physiological paradigm:

> The suggestion has recently been made that, as opportunity offers, the natives should, so far as practicable, be "dispersed" or "scattered" in huts with their families instead of being barracked in compounds. Amongst natives employed on the Panama Canal, this measure is believed to have brought about a permanent drop in pneumonia on the Isthmus. In some instances in the Transvaal it has also answered admirably. . . . But, as regards the Gold Mines of the Rand, we feel that this proposal should be approached with considerable caution. Under present conditions a large portion of mine natives return periodically to their kraals after from 12 to 18 months of work on the mines. If, however, the wives and families of such natives were brought to the Rand, the native would have less inducement to leave work, and often no home to go to. *He would consequently lose the recuperative effect of long rests which he now periodically enjoys, and which we believe to be invaluable.* While, therefore, we do not doubt that his morbidity and mortality from pneumonia would be materially decreased by family life in a location hut, *we think there is reason to fear, that one effect of continued mine work without the intervention of the present long periods of rest and change would be a marked increase in tuberculosis.* (emphasis added)[13]

The advantages of the rest periods provided by a system of migrant labor were stressed again elsewhere in the report.

> [O]wing to the shortness of the period of exposure to the adverse conditions of labour centres, and to the recuperative effect of a return to the free and lazy life of the kraal, any evil effect of such conditions is very much mitigated in the case of the native.[14]

Preventing the spread of tuberculosis became, in effect, a medical rationale for the use of migrant labor.[15]

At the same time, the view that Africans were inherently susceptible to tuberculosis because of their lack of contact with the disease deflected attention away from environmental conditions on the mines and thus undercut calls for environmental reforms. It was argued that environmental reforms were unlikely to have much effect in the face of a racial predisposition to disease. This argument can be seen in the following discussion of the effect of exposure to adverse living conditions in the workplace on African susceptibility to tuberculosis, also taken from the 1914 Tuberculosis Commission Report.

> There appear to be good grounds for believing that . . . the mere change from Kraal life to the environment of the labour centre adversely affects the health of the average raw native. How much of this is due to change in climate conditions, aggregation, often in overcrowded compounds, alterations in dress and diet, restriction of freedom, unaccustomed physical strain, *or exposure to organisms harmless to ordinary individuals, but pathogenic to the uninured raw native,* it is difficult to say. (emphasis added)[16]

In this way, the theory of racial susceptibility, while coexisting with environmental explanations, ultimately had the effect of undercutting the impact of environmental arguments and obviating the need for improving conditions at the mines.

Although the compatibility of the tubercularization theory with the changing production requirements of the mining industry does not necessarily explain the theory's acceptance by mine medical authorities, there is, as we have already seen, clear evidence that while these men might disagree with mining policies they were nonetheless receptive to the interests of the industry that supported them directly or indirectly. As Cartwright notes in his account of the development of the mine medical services, "Mine doctors in those days were regarded by the mine managers as members of their administrative staff and subject to their orders, very much as ship's surgeons are subject to the orders of the captain of the ship."[17]

Medical authorities elsewhere on the Rand, not directly in the employ of the mining companies, were no less sympathetic to the needs of the industry. Thus, as noted in chapter 6, the chief medical officers for Johannesburg and the other Rand municipalities who together with inspectors from the Department of Mines were responsible for overseeing sanitation and safety measures at the mines, seldom pushed the mining houses too hard. This lack of critical oversight on the part of Rand medical inspectors drew the fire of the chairman of the 1914 TB Commission, Dr. John Gregory, and was the subject of considerable acrimony between Gregory and two other members of the commission, Dr. Charles Porter, MOH for Johannesburg, and Dr. George Turner, medical advisor for WNLA.[18]

Needless to say, the medical officers in the employ of the major labor recruiting organizations were unlikely to put forward medical opinions antithetical to the use of migrant labor. Medical authorities on the Rand were, in short, either unable or unwilling to oppose the interests of the mine managers and thus unlikely to maintain medical opinions that conflicted openly with those interests. Thus the growing popularity of the physiological model of African susceptibility to TB among Rand medical authorities from 1912 onward may well have reflected their own susceptibility to the economic interests of the mining industry.

In evaluating this argument it is important to recognize that the shift in medical opinion on the Rand did not coincide with any advance in medical knowledge concerning black susceptibility to disease in South Africa or elsewhere. In fact very little research was done on the epidemiology of TB among blacks in South Africa until the late 1920s. The shift was more in the nature of a leap of faith than an exercise in deductive reasoning. In this respect it was similar to other shifts in scientific paradigms that, according to Thomas Kuhn, are a part of normal science.[19]

It is also important to remember that western medical opinion about the causes of African TB susceptibility was in a state of paradigmatic flux at this time. Although the cultural model had been dominant during the first decade of the century, other paradigms, including the physiological model, coexisted with it and were seen as secondary explanations. Determining which etiological factor was paramount was, in fact, difficult in the face of insufficient epidemiological data and the absence of a clear, established voice of authority on the question. Given the large measure of uncertainty that surrounded the issue, the shift from a cultural to a physiological model did not represent a radical break from a deeply rooted medical paradigm. It was rather a shift of emphasis in which a secondary explanation for African susceptibility to TB became a primary explanation. There were, in fact, significant points of continuity between the two explanatory models. Both models ultimately placed the blame for African susceptibility to TB on the victim, the culturally or physiologically inexperienced "native." By doing so, both models reduced the responsibilities of municipal and industrial health authorities to make reforms. Rand medical authorities therefore found it relatively easy to adjust their theoretical position to coincide with the interests of the mining industry. In fact the only issue that was hotly debated at this time was Maynard's contention that infection was not a major element in the spread of tuberculosis.

By the time of the first meeting of the Transvaal Mine Medical Officers Association in 1921, lack of acquired immunity was well established as the primary cause of African susceptibility to tuberculosis among medical authorities working on the Rand. Reinforced by Borrel's study of tuberculosis among French West African Recruits in Europe during World War I, Bushnell's epidemiological work in America, and Cummins studies of Sudanese soldiers (cited earlier), TB among Afri-

cans in South Africa was increasingly seen as a "virgin soil" phenomenon. Although mine medical officers recognized the benefits of certain
environmental reforms, those who pushed for better living and working
conditions at the mines found that the mining houses were resistant to
any proposal that would increase their labor costs, unless the improvements could be shown to pay direct benefits in terms of direct worker
productivity.[20] The frugality of the mining companies, and the consequent difficulty of improving living and working conditions at the
mines, no doubt increased the mine medical officers' support for the
theory of racial susceptibility to tuberculosis. For the theory not only
justified the mine managers' resistance to reforms, it also allowed the
mine medical officers unwilling or unable to challenge the authority of
the mine managers to rationalize their acceptance of the status quo.

Seeing African susceptibility to the disease as the overriding cause of
high TB rates on the mines, mine medical officers during the 1920s and
1930s argued the health benefits of migrant labor. The intermittent rest
periods provided by a system of migrant labor came to be seen as a key
instrument in protecting African workers from TB, and repatriation to
the "open-air life" of the kraals, the African workers' only hope for
recovery. Medical officers were even critical of the practice of encouraging experienced miners to return to the same mine by providing them
with a bonus if they returned within four months, even though they
seldom turned down such "valued employees" when they returned to
the mines.[21]

For the most part, as we have seen, the mine medical officers concentrated their TB control efforts on eliminating sources of infection on the
mines and thus on reducing the vulnerable African worker's risk of
exposure to the disease. Yet even this imperfect line of defense could be
undermined by the argument that "natives" possessed a physiological
predisposition to tuberculosis. This can be clearly seen in the following
argument put forward by Doctor A. I. Girwood, chief medical officer
for WNLA, during the debate over the use of x-ray machines for examining new recruits described in chapter 6.

> In conclusion . . . we should . . . acknowledge that pulmonary TB is endemic
> in the mines . . . that the natives are going through a period of tubercu-
> larization common to all negroid races and therefore we know that it is not
> possible to eliminate the disease locally. It is better to acknowledge that at
> the start and to regard it as a distressing economic fact, than to embark on
> expensive schemes which in our opinion would seriously handicap the sup-
> ply of labour.[22]

Thus, the use of x-rays, which would detect more tuberculosis cases and reduce opportunities for infection on the mines but would be expensive and restrict the flow of labor by eliminating otherwise healthy recruits, was rejected on the grounds that all efforts at TB control were futile in the face of the "native's" lack of immunity.

It is important to note that, despite these difficulties, the control efforts of the mine medical officers appeared to be effective. The incidence of TB among African miners, as we have seen, dropped dramatically between 1912 and 1935. Although the medical screening efforts of the mine medical officers probably played only a small role in this decline, these men cannot be blamed for having taken credit for the decline and for seeing it as a vindication of their faith in screening and, in turn, in the theory of tubercularization.

The efforts of Rand medical authorities to control TB also included research into the epidemiology of the disease. This research led in 1925 to the creation of the Tuberculosis Research Committee jointly funded by the Union government and the Chamber of Mines. The committee worked for seven years, publishing their findings in 1932. As noted in chapter 1, the report was widely regarded in South Africa and abroad as the most exhaustive inquiry to date into the problem of tuberculosis among Africans. As such, it played a significant role in shaping ideas about the causes and prevention of TB in South Africa.

The report contains a mass of data on nearly every aspect of the problem of TB among Africans and is of tremendous importance to anyone interested in the history of the disease. Yet its conclusions regarding the causes of African susceptibility to TB were to a large degree determined prior to the start of the investigation by the makeup of the TB research committee. The committee was chaired by the head of the South African Institute of Medical Research, an organization established and funded by the Chamber of Mines. Twelve of the seventeen members of the committee were identified in the report as "Representatives of the Chamber of Mines." Thus the interests of the mining industry were well represented, a point that was clearly stated by the committee's chairman at a meeting of the Mine Medical Officers Association in 1927.

> I would like to pay tribute to the mining industry here tonight. We live on the mining industry; there would be no Tuberculosis Committee; there would be no visit of Professor Lyle Cummins; but for that industry, and these men, with broad view and great vision, are not entirely impelled by economic principles. . . . They have enabled us to carry out this investigation, and Mr.

Chairman, they will support us so long as our investigations continue on correct and logical lines.[23]

Just what those lines were to be in terms of investigating the causes of African susceptibility to tuberculosis were made clear by the chamber's appointment of Sir Lyle Cummins to serve as the committee's expert adviser. Cummins, widely known as an expert on tuberculosis, had extensive experience with the disease in both Europe and Africa. More importantly, as noted earlier, his prior experience in the Sudan had led him to develop his own version of the "virgin soil" theory to explain differences he had observed in the TB experiences of Europeans and Africans. The theory attributed African TB susceptibility to their lack of contact with it and the consequent absence of any immunities to the disease. Cummins' views were well known, and his choice as expert witness was not accidental.

Cummins' virgin soil ideas, echoing those of Maynard and Traill before him, were clearly represented in the completed report of the Tuberculosis Research Committee. The report begins with a lengthy historical section that emphasizes the absence of tuberculosis in South Africa prior to white settlement. As noted in chapter 1, this discussion carefully ignores evidence collected as part of the investigation by Dr. Allan which challenged this view. Subsequent sections of the report, which discuss the causes of African susceptibility to tuberculosis, follow upon this basic virgin soil premise and upon the theory that African resistance to TB would develop through the eventual tubercularization of the African population.

> This want of resistance to tuberculosis is . . . a biological character of the African Native which can only disappear with the lapse of time and during many successive generations of industrial contact. This biological lack of resistance exists quite apart from any risk incurred in the mining industry or in any other industries . . .

Moreover, even where the report acknowledges the importance of environmental conditions, it tends to emphasize the African's lack of experience with these conditions rather than the conditions themselves:

> . . . but there can be no doubt that the concentration of Native industrial "recruits" under the conditions inseparable from practically all commercial development in Africa, together with the *unaccustomed hard work and the unfamiliar housing and diet conditions of a new environment,* leads to a state of things in which this liability to tuberculosis ceases to be latent and becomes actively manifested. (emphasis added)[24]

The assumption that Africans were racially susceptible to TB colored the committee's interpretation of data collected during the investigation. This can be seen in the committee's explanation of the positive correlation that was found between raw recruits and TB. For the committee this was clear evidence that Africans lacked immunity to TB. Yet earlier researchers at the beginning of the century, working within a behavioral paradigm, had used this same correlation to argue that new recruits had simply not adjusted to working conditions on the mines.

Similarly, evidence that TB was widespread in the rural areas and that workers with previous infections had higher TB rates than those who arrived at the mines free of TB were not seen as anomalies. Instead they were fit into the physiological paradigm. Thus Cummins argued that the South African situation was one of a "modified virgin soil epidemic." He in fact concluded that Africans were not a virgin soil but had been exposed to TB. This exposure, however, had not been intense enough or lasted long enough to provide them with the degree of resistance that Europeans had achieved from several hundred years of exposure. They thus had a partial resistance, which under the healthy conditions of the reserves allowed them to modify the disease. Under the unaccustomed stress and hard work of industrial life, however, they broke down.

In this assessment Cummins was only partially correct. It is true, as noted in chapter 5, that exposure to TB reduced the occurrence of rapidly fatal cases of TB among Africans. It is also true that this exposure did not protect Africans from TB once they were exposed to the harsh conditions of industrial life. Where Cummins erred was in continuing to ascribe the African's susceptibility to TB on the mines to their as-yet-incomplete tubercularization and in distinguishing between the African and the European in this regard. Although it might take decades for an entire population to be exposed to TB and for susceptible individuals and families to be eliminated, the individual African worker who was infected with TB in childhood and who survived this exposure was just as "tubercularized" as his European counterpart. What distinguished the experience of the European miner from that of the African miner by the late 1920s and 1930s was simply the fact that the African worker was exposed to a constellation of unhealthy working and living conditions to which the European miner was not exposed. By continuing to stress the African's lack of tubercularization, Cummins blamed the victim and reduced the liability of the mining industry.

The TBRC's findings concerning the causes of African susceptibility to TB were thus shaped by the prior assumptions of those in charge of the investigation and did not reflect an objective evaluation of all the data collected. The report, in effect represents a clear example of what Thomas Kuhn describes as "normal science":

> No part of the aim of normal science is to call forth new sorts of phenomena; indeed those that will not fit the box are often not seen at all. Nor do scientists normally aim to invent new theories, and they are often intolerant of those invented by others. Instead, normal-scientific research is directed to the articulation of those phenomena and theories that the paradigm already supplies.[25]

The TBRC report had a tremendous impact on the wider South African medical community and contributed significantly to the popularization of a set of ideas about tubercularization and acquired racial immunities which were only partially correct and which deflected attention from the need for serious environmental reform. This influence can be seen in the articles and reports of municipal medical officers and other white medical authorities up through the 1930s. Although these authorities differed concerning the implications that the physiological paradigm had for the future of TB control efforts, they all accepted its validity.

Acceptance of the physiological paradigm led some authorities to take a pessimistic view of the future of TB control. This view was clearly expressed by Dr. J. A. Mitchell, the secretary of public health,

> As regards the Coloureds and Natives however, the outlook is much less hopeful owing mainly to their susceptibility to the disease and the difficulty of enforcing precautions against its spread. . . . It seems doubtful whether it is practicable, humanly speaking, to prevent tuberculosis from decimating the Native races.[26]

Dr. Mitchell's only hope lay in the "native's marvelous fecundity." The same position was taken by the high commissioner for South Africa:

> The increase in tuberculosis among the natives is somewhat disquieting but the susceptibility of South African natives to the disease is well known and there is little that can be done to help them at present.[27]

Others adopted a more optimistic perspective. D. P. Marais, for example, a major critic of Maynard's work, concluded in 1933 that, "Urbanization and tubercularization go hand in hand, and with satisfactory control an increasing immmunity is slowly acquired by hereditary evolution." Marais went on to highlight the distinction that existed between his positive view, "which is fraught with such hope for the future," and earlier, more negative views.[28]

Whether optimistic or pessimistic, however, the emerging dominance of the physiological paradigm imbued white medical authorities with a sense of fatalism—that the problem of tuberculosis among Africans would work itself out and that there was little medical authorities could do to modify this natural evolution.[29] In extreme cases, it was even argued that environmental improvements could be counterproductive. This was suggested by a Dr. Strachan in 1913 at the South African Medical Conference: "It might, in the future, be possible to reinforce natural by artificial selection, but the trouble [is] that the more we [improve] the environment, the less play we [give] to natural selection."[30]

Most municipal medical officers, however, were less fatalistic and tried to improve the environmental conditions that contributed to TB. Yet they, like the mine medical officers, faced severe restraints on their ability to implement public health measures that might have improved African access to food or housing and thus increased their resistance to tubercular infections. As a result, they must have found the theories of Maynard, Traill, and Cummins compatible with the fiscal realities within which they worked. Unlike the mine medical officers, however, they lacked the resources to mount even the imperfect effort at worker screening achieved at the mines. Municipal efforts at TB control were for the most part limited to slum clearance and to removing diagnosed cases of TB from the public by either placing them in local African TB wards or, more frequently, since the number of beds for African TB cases fell far short of the number required, by referring them to the NAD for repatriation to their home districts. The total number of beds provided for "non-European" tubercular patients in South Africa in 1924 was 52. By 1933 that number had only increased to 191, despite a dramatic rise in TB cases. Not a single bed was added to this total until 1938.[31]

Even where space was available for African TB cases, it was often difficult for Africans to get treatment. The Public Health Act placed responsibility for treatment on the shoulders of the municipality within which an African worker resided, with the government reimbursing the municipality for half of the resulting expenses. This system led to frequent arguments between municipal authorities concerning who was responsible, since the municipal authorities in the area in which the African was diagnosed would frequently claim that the African's real home was elsewhere. As a result of these disputes treatment was delayed and many cases were never treated. Although the majority of these disputes involved African cases, similar obstacles existed for poor whites during this period.[32]

It is important to note that not all medical authorities ascribed to the physiological paradigm. Perhaps most significant in their dissent were a number of medical officers with extensive experience working among rural Africans. Peter Allan, for example, as noted earlier, conducted extensive TB surveys in the Transkei and Ciskei during the 1920s. He rejected the "virgin soil" theory and with it the view that Africans were physiologically susceptible to TB.[33] Allan was convinced that African susceptibility to TB was environmentally induced.[34]

The physiological paradigm in fact appears to have been most influential among medical authorities working in the urban and industrial centers of South Africa, where economic and social pressures urged the adoption of control measures designed to remove susceptible Africans from contact with healthy workers and white society and inhibited the adoption of effective environmental reform efforts. Where these pressures did not exist, the physiological paradigm had less influence and was even rejected.

Yet even in the urban and industrial centers, the high tide of physiological explanations was reached during the late 1930s as the rising toll of TB and rapidly deteriorating conditions of African urban life forced white medical authorities to recognize that holding actions and faith in the eventual physical adaptation of Africans were insufficient and that more direct action to improve the conditions under which Africans lived and worked had to be carried out. At the same time, as we will see in chapter 8, this change in perspective reflected a broader tidal shift in attitudes toward the status of Africans within white society and a growing, if temporary, acceptance of the permanence of the urban African. This shift in turn reflected transformations in the industrial development of South Africa during the 1930s and 1940s.

CHAPTER VIII

Industrial Expansion, Squatters, and the Second Tuberculosis Epidemic, 1938–1948

If efforts to control tuberculosis in South Africa during the 1920s and 1930s were an exercise in building social barriers against the rising tide of tubercular infection, the late 1930s and 1940s must be seen as a period in which these barriers were swept aside by a crashing new wave of disease. The tendency for urban authorities to deal with TB by applying exclusionary social control measures, rather than by dealing directly with the conditions under which Africans lived and worked, had left a legacy of overcrowding, malnutrition, and disease within the African townships, locations, and peri-urban slums surrounding the cities of the country. With the onset of World War II these conditions grew rapidly worse as thousands of African men, women, and children, the vast majority of whom were infected with TB, poured into the urban areas in search of both employment and escape from the growing impoverishment of the reserves. The result, predictably, was a second epidemic of tuberculosis. The mining industry, after years of declining TB morbidity, similarly faced a rising incidence of the disease among its African workforce in the 1940s. This rise, like the urban epidemic, resulted in large measure from the industry's failure to make more extensive improvements in living and working conditions during the 1920s and 1930s. When labor supply problems returned in the late 1930s and 1940s, dissolving the beneficial effects the former surplus labor supply had had on the incidence of TB, the health costs of the earlier failure to initiate effective industrial reforms were revealed.

TABLE 11

INCREASES IN URBAN TB MORTALITY RATES, 1938–1945

City	Deaths per 1,000		% Increase
	1938	*1945*	
Cape Town	7.0/1,000	14.0/1,000	100
Port Elizabeth	7.0/1,000	11.0/1,000	57
East London	4.5/1,000	7.0/1,000	55
Durban	2.2/1,000	6.0/1,000	172
Johannesburg	1.0/1,000	2.4/1,000	140
Mean	4.3/1,000	8.1/1,000	88

Everywhere, tuberculosis mortality rates rose dramatically after 1938. The average African mortality rate for the major urban centers of South Africa rose from roughly 4.3 per 1,000 to over 8 per 1,000 between 1938 and 1945. The reported rate increases for Africans in individual cities are shown in table 11. Though some of this increase was no doubt caused by the inability of municipal authorities to keep track of the large number of Africans, especially women and children, flooding the urban areas, the size of the increase and the testimonies of medical authorities confirm that the incidence of all forms of TB reached epidemic proportions during this period. The MOH of Cape Town in fact suggested that the position was even worse than it appeared since a substantial number of Africans who contracted the disease emigrated and thus were not counted in Cape Town figures.[1]

With the exception of Johannesburg, where again the influence of the mining industry and its repatriation policy skewed mortality rates downward for the city as a whole, the TB mortality rates in the 1940s were as high or higher than those recorded in the same cities at the turn of the century. Even on the mines there was a major increase in TB *incidence,* from roughly 3 per 1,000 in 1937 to 7 per 1,000 in 1942 and 1943, dropping to 6 per 1,000 in 1944.[2]

Although lack of data makes it difficult to measure changes in the incidence of TB in the rural areas during this period, there is some evidence that the TB situation deteriorated still further. Prevalence surveys conducted by B. A. Dormer's team in the rural areas of Natal in 1937 and again in 1948 indicate that a dramatic increase in TB occurred there as well, with the overall prevalence increasing from 250 per 100,000 to 800 per 100,000. In the Ciskei and Transkei, where TB rates were already high before the war, the rise may not have been so great, yet medical opinion at the time suggests that it was increasing.[3]

Surveys conducted in the early 1950s present additional evidence of the extent to which TB had established itself in the rural areas of South Africa. In the Transkei, a survey of 21,080 Africans living within a forty-mile radius of Umtata in 1953 and 1954, using both radiology and sputum tests, concluded that 2.3 percent of the population over five had active tuberculosis.[4] That equates to a prevalence of 2,300 per 100,000, which is considerably higher than the rough estimates made by Allan in the late 1920s. Other surveys discovered lower but nonetheless substantial prevalences throughout the rural areas of the country. Given the use of different testing and sampling procedures these surveys cannot be compared. There are also questions concerning the accuracy of x-rays alone as a diagnostic tool. There seems to be general agreement among TB specialists that x-rays alone tend to overestimate the number of active cases. In many instances, depending on the skill and experience of those reading the plates and the quality of the equipment, old cases or other lung problems may be diagnosed as active TB. Most of the studies, moreover, did not use statistical samples but depended on volunteers. The various factors that may have skewed such a sample cannot be determined, though it is possible that such skewing may have worked in both directions. All of this said, the surveys do give some impression of the TB situation in the rural areas of South Africa during the early

TABLE 12

PREVALENCE OF TB AMONG AFRICANS LIVING WITHIN
SELECTED RURAL AREAS IN THE 1950s

Area	Date Surveyed	Method	% Active TB
Western[5] and Northwest-ern Cape	1954	x-ray over 20 yrs	1.4
Western[6] Natal	1954	x-ray, all ages, Towns and Rural	1.1
Northern[7] and Eastern Transvaal	1953	x-ray, 3 yrs and above	.78
Orange Free State[8] and Northern Cape	1954	x-ray, over 5 yrs	.55 to 2.6

1950s. Medical authorities at the time accepted that the overall prevalence among Africans in the rural areas was roughly 1 percent, which is
a very high prevalence for a rural population.

The rising tide of tuberculosis among African workers and their
families created a public outrage among white voters against the government's failure to cope with the disease. Predictably, much of this outrage was stimulated less by concern over the suffering the disease was
inflicting on Africans than by the potential costs that African ill-health
might have for whites. This concern is accurately reflected in the following editorial from the Johannesburg *Sunday Times:*

> Tuberculosis is another scourge which, it is stated, is a very real danger to the
> European community. "Ample evidence is available" . . . "that lung tubercu-
> losis is rapidly increasing among the non-European population living in the
> locations and elsewhere away from the mines, and is likely to spread to the
> European population unless the advance of the disease is checked. . . . Unless
> we realize the necessity for these measures . . . two things will happen. The
> native population upon which we depend for labour, will become increas-
> ingly inefficient, and the risk of the spread of tubercular infection to the
> European population will be also increased."[9]

For medical authorities and government officials throughout South
Africa the rapidly increasing toll of black TB represented dramatic
proof of the failure of earlier efforts to curb the disease and, for many,
a clear sign that the theory upon which these efforts had been based
was flawed. The optimistic forecasts of Traill, Cummins, and others
that the problem of African TB would slowly resolve itself as Africans
acquired greater physiological resistance to the disease could not account for the "killing epidemic" that accompanied World War II. The
epidemic forced municipal medical officers to look for other explanations for African susceptibility to tuberculosis. They did not have to
look far.

Describing the set of events leading up to the epidemic, Dr. B. A.
Dormer, superintendent of Durban's King George V Jubilee Hospital
and government advisor on tuberculosis, wrote,

> The rural Bantu, most of them positive tuberculin reactors, poured by the
> hundreds of thousands into urban areas to seek work at a time when housing
> was at a standstill because the countries resources were mobilized for war. The
> result was a killing TB epidemic. The environmental stresses—malnutrition,
> crowding, and a lack of hygienic amenities—could not have been more classi-
> cally arranged to demonstrate that it is not racial susceptibility but these very
> stresses that cause a major epidemic.[10]

The same conclusions were reached by Dr. George Gale, chief health officer for the Union. Writing in 1948 he noted that,

> The principal cause of the high incidence of tuberculosis is the rapid industrialization of the non-European at a time when housing and nutrition are hopelessly inadequate. Overcrowding in grossly unhygienic slums favours the spread of infection, and chronic malnutrition provides the soil upon which infection flourishes.[11]

Although Dormer, Gale, and others were correct in identifying the general conditions contributing to the wartime TB epidemic, they failed to accurately diagnose its underlying causes. It was not simply wartime austerity or industrialization per se which created the epidemic. Nor was it either the system of migrant labor or rural poverty, though both contributed to it. The epidemic instead was ultimately the result of structural contradictions in the development of racial capitalism in South Africa.

The low-wage policy enforced by employers of African labor up through the depression was based on the existence of an African peasantry that could support the reproduction of labor. Yet the continued existence of this peasantry was undermined by other policies designed to restrict African access to land, labor, and capital in order to satisfy the often conflicting economic interests of white farmers, workers, and industrialists. As we saw in chapter 4, this contradiction had undermined the productive capacity of most independent black farmers in South Africa by the mid-1930s. The result was the creation of an African rural population who, far from supporting the reproduction of labor, had become dependent for their own survival on industrial or farm employment. The droughts and declining agricultural prices of the 1930s, combined with further marketing restrictions, narrowed the margin of subsistence to such a degree that many Africans simply gave up their struggle for independent survival on the land and sought employment on white farms or in the cities. Reports on conditions in the Transkei in the mid-1940s revealed that 25 percent of the families were landless, 20 percent of the arable land was unsuitable for cultivation, 44 percent of the families owned no cattle, and 20 percent of families owned five or less cattle. As a result half of all able-bodied men were away at any one time.[12] The growing proletarianization of farm labor and the increased exploitation of labor tenants during the 1930s, however, made this avenue of escape increasingly unattractive, adding additional pressure to the rural–urban movement of Africans.

A second contradiction emerged in the late 1930s as the country's economy began to climb out of the depression and secondary industries expanded, creating a fresh demand for industrial labor. The onset of World War II and the need to develop new industries to offset wartime shortages of manufactured imports served as a catalyst to this growth. The number of factories increased from 9,655 to 10,877 between 1936 and 1945 while the value of gross output of all factories and productive industries (excluding mining, agriculture, and extractive industries) increased 250 percent.[13] Manufacturing by 1943 had surpassed mining in its contribution to GNP. The new industries that emerged during this period greatly increased the demand for labor. This demand was further accentuated by the withdrawal of white workers who served in the war. To facilitate the industry's demand for labor the government loosened influx-control laws during the war, suspending them entirely between 1942 and 1943. Though there was considerable white opposition to this development, the Union government was generally sympathetic to the needs of the manufacturing industry it saw as the instrument for the economic revitalization of the country. The government also made some moves to accommodate the growing urban African workforce through the implementation of school meal plans, the establishment of pension plans for certain categories of African workers, and increased expenditure on African education. The government in addition continued to offer subeconomic (low-interest) loans to municipalities wishing to provide housing for their workers.

Yet the government's interests in fostering the growth of an African urban workforce did not go so far as to provide the funds necessary to insure the development of a healthy and prosperous African working class. Wartime restrictions on government's finances, combined with an unwillingness either to impose the taxes needed to provide African workers with basic social and economic amenities or to force industry to bear these costs, meant that the welfare of the African workers and families was left in the hands of municipal authorities. Yet, as seen in chapter 5, municipal councils represented the interests of white rate-payers who had fought all along for restrictions on African urban settlement. These rate-payers refused to allocate the funds needed to provide housing or to subsidize the low wages provided by industry so that Africans could cope with the high cost of food and other basic necessities. These costs, moreover, increased dramatically during the war.[14]

Although the government had provided loans at subeconomic rates since 1934 to municipalities wishing to construct low-income housing, municipal councils had been slow to take advantage of this offer. Local authorities continued to maintain that in spite of the government's offer to bear three-quarters of the cost of subeconomic housing, they could not afford to suffer the remaining one-quarter. The costs of building and providing the essential services were said to have increased so much that they exceeded the ability of the municipalities to pay.[15] The costs of course were high not simply because of the rising price of materials but because of the continued insistence of white trade unions that only white labor be employed to construct subeconomic housing.

The result of this impasse was a reenactment of the housing and nutritional crisis of the 1920s and 1930s in which no one was willing to bear the costs of creating an African industrial workforce. This time, however, the crisis was heightened by the magnitude of the African population involved. The African populations of the major industrial centers increased by an average of 60 percent between 1936 and 1946.[16]

In Johannesburg, where serious housing shortages existed prior to the war, the construction of new housing ground to a halt, with only 750 new dwellings built in 1941 and 1942 and none in 1943 and 1944. Yet the number of people needing housing mushroomed. The number of males alone working in the municipal area, excluding the mines, rose

TABLE 13

WAITING LIST FOR AFRICAN
HOUSING, JOHANNESBURG,
1937–1947

Year	Number on Waiting List
1937	11
1938	75
1939	143
1940	473
1941	4,524
1942	6,258
1943	7,047
1944	8,485
1945	12,474
1946	15,124
1947	16,195[17]

from 133,484 in December 1941 to 266,074 in February 1948.[18] Whereas up to 1937 there were vacancies in the municipal locations of Orlando and Western Native Townships, due largely to resistance on the part of Africans to the more controlled life of the municipal locations, from 1938 there was a growing waiting list.

To accommodate the rapidly increasing African population Johannesburg's City Council began in 1940 to issue permits that allowed renters to take in subtenants. This made any attempt to regulate the number of occupants per dwelling impossible and led to acute overcrowding. Cases of two or more families, and in one case five families, occupying a single room, were discovered by the chief native commissioner.[19] The overcrowding also affected the single-sex hostels. On March 8, 1948, the South African police raided the Wemmer Hostel and found in addition to the 2,789 legitimate tenants, 3,200 trespassers. Of these, 3,000 were Africans with bonafide employment in the city "who had no alternative accommodation available."[20]

The growing waiting lists by themselves do not reflect the enormity of the problem, for there was a growing army of squatters who did not bother to follow the bureaucratic rules established by the council and simply occupied whatever structures were available or created their own structures. The squatter movement began in 1944 with the movement of subtenants out of Orlando location into open land near the township, where they constructed shelters from sacking, scraps of wood, and corrugated iron. Many of these squatters were employed but earned wages that were not commensurate with the high rents charged by householders in the locations. The size of the squatter community mushroomed after the war, fueled by declining employment opportunities and the increased need of families to reduce living expenses. Although municipal authorities viewed the squatter camps as both a threat to their authority and to community health, the central government refused to take action since many of the squatters were employed in industry and squatting provided them with housing for which neither the government nor industry had to contribute. By 1948 there were an estimated 90,000 Africans living in squatter camps on the outskirts of Johannesburg.[21] The manager of the municipal Non-European Affairs Department claimed in 1948 that Johannesburg needed an additional 40,000 houses immediately. At the time the City Council had placed orders for only 11,000 houses and the present output was only 4 per day, or just under 1,500 per year. The impression of municipal officials in 1948 was that the present rate of constructing houses was probably not even keeping pace with the new influx.[22]

A survey of housing conditions in Orlando in 1948 found that half of all households were overcrowded according to minimum occupancy standards. The percentage of people living in overcrowded households was 66 percent. Overcrowding was most prevalent among children, with as many as 80 percent of children under fifteen living in over-crowded conditions.[23]

In the Cape Town area the housing crisis was said to be as bad or worse as in Johannesburg. Industrial and military demands for labor increased rapidly during the war necessitating an almost unrestricted admission of African workers after 1939. This influx contributed to the 130 percent increase in the official African population of Cape Town between 1936 and 1946. In the face of inadequate housing supplies in the established native locations and a slowdown in housing construction during the war, the large-scale influx of Africans led to both the growth of slum areas within the city and the emergence of extensive shantytown settlements on land owned by whites and coloreds in neighboring townships such as Windermere and on the Cape flats east of the municipal boundaries. Investigations into the slum areas within the city found as many as seven or eight Africans sleeping in a room. In no case was it found that a family occupied more than one room. Landlords taking advantage of the situation charged rents between fifteen and fifty shillings per month for these accommodations.[24]

In Windermere, increased demand for housing led to a similar subdivision of existing houses into rooms occupied by entire families. The exact number of Africans living in houses was unknown. When questioned, landlords claimed that this did not concern them. They simply made one person responsible for the dwelling and assumed that they would sublet rooms. On the Cape flats landlords sometimes constructed shacks and leased them to African families. In other cases Africans had to erect their own dwellings. Sanitation throughout this area was nonexistent, the residents using the dunes and bushes. For water, people dug holes, and water was consequently subject to gross pollution.[25] The quality of housing on the flats was so poor, it was suggested that simple V-type huts would be a material benefit to the lives of "those Natives at present forced to live in sack, reed, tin and other forms of shelter which admit rain."[26] Summarizing the situation in 1947, the superintendent of Langa township observed that,

At present there are 31,000 Natives of whom service contracts are registered in the Peninsula. 11,000 are housed in Langa, and another 5,000 obtain approved accommodation from their employers. The rest live mainly in dwellings that are unfit for habitation.[27]

In East London, Port Elizabeth, and Durban the housing situations were much the same. The municipal authorities in East London did virtually nothing to provide housing for African workers between 1928 and 1940, and by the end of the war the East and West Bank Locations were sprawling shantytowns with as many as 20 people per house.[28] Most of the 40,000 plus Africans who crowded into Durban between 1936 and 1946 found housing in the uncontrolled shanties of Cato Manor. In general, efforts to control overcrowding within municipal limits contributed to the creation or enlargement of existing peri-urban slums.[29] The desperate housing shortage in Port Elizabeth was attested to by the MOH who described the ends to which Korsten residents would go to acquire economical housing:

> During 1938 as Medical Officer I decided to confine slum elimination at Korsten to those areas which had been more seriously infected during the plague outbreak. It was soon discovered that persons occupying slums in the particular areas which were being dealt with, were rehoused in sub-economic houses, and with the set purpose of securing a new house as quickly as possible, slum dwellers from every part of the city crowded into these areas, not infrequently deliberately occupying plague infected houses, knowing that plague contacts were always offered new Council houses after being discharged from quarantine.[30]

At the same time massive overcrowding facilitated the spread of infection, malnutrition once again reduced the ability of infected Africans to resist the disease. A survey of African schoolchildren in Durban during the early 1940s identified 40 percent suffering from clinical signs of malnutrition. Dr. Neil McVicar, speaking on the basis of years of experience in working with Africans in the Ciskei, was appalled at the condition of African schoolchildren he saw in Johannesburg:

> It seems to me I have never before seen such a collection of miserable looking objects. One could only suppose that they were the victims of mass undernourishment.[31]

The Superintendent of the Edward VIII Hospital in Durban made clear the connection between malnutrition and disease.

> Nearly all Native patients, quite apart from the disease or injury for which they were admitted, were malnourished. One can safely say that about half

of them were grossly undernourished. . . . Symptoms of pallegra and similar diseases were quite frequent and in children, conditions such as nutritional oedema [kwashiorkor] were commonplace. . . . A fair description for most of our patients admitted for any disease or injury would begin with the phrase: "an undernourished Native with intestinal parasites."[32]

Some municipal authorities embarked on various feeding plans aimed particularly at children. Germiston, for example, established a program to ensure the retail distribution of milk at prices urban residents could afford. Yet milk was difficult to obtain at low contract prices, and after a year the daily amount of milk that was available per capita came to only a fifth of a pint.[33] Other plans for increasing the sale of fresh vegetables in urban areas and for providing food for schoolchildren were initiated on a limited scale in several urban locations. Overall, however, these efforts were limited by the same unwillingness of white rate-payers to bear the cost of supporting an African workforce which had prevented the construction of adequate housing supplies.

Such minimal efforts could not overcome the nutritional problems created by the low wages paid to most African workers and the high prices generated by war and postwar inflation. Official figures published by the Office of Census and Statistics showed that the cost of living rose from a base of 100 in 1938 to 104 at the beginning of 1941 and 161.1 by November of 1949. In Johannesburg the cost of necessary items of consumption increased between 20 and 50 percent during the first years of the war (mealie meal by 20 percent, rice by 50 percent, candles by 45 percent, wood by 50 percent, boermeal by 25 percent, paraffin by 25 percent, and coal by 50 percent).[34] A study in Cape Town found that the cost of living, for maintaining the bare minimum of health and decency, rose by 87 percent between 1938 and 1950. The cost of food alone had risen 75 percent. Although some of this increase was offset by wage hikes, African salary increases lagged far behind inflation. A study by the Non-European Bus-Services Commission found that the average income deficiency per month of African families was £3.0.5 in Johannesburg, £1.13.2 in other Reef towns, and £3.13.0 in Pretoria.[35] As the buying power of urban Africans declined they were forced to purchase food in smaller quantities, which meant that per amount they paid a higher price. This in turn further decreased their food consumption.[36]

The urban TB epidemic of the late 1930s and 1940s did not hit all Africans with equal force. The mortality rate of industrial workers was reported in the Johannesburg *Star* to be nearly three times that of domestic servants. This was attributed to the fact that domestic servants lived in less-crowded quarters and had access to better food, presumably in the form of handouts from their employers.[37] Given the poor conditions under which most domestic servants continued to live and evidence that during the 1930s domestic servants suffered higher case mortality rates than industrial workers (see chap. 5), this figure may tell us more about the appalling conditions suffered by industrial workers than about the lives of domestic servants. No doubt, however, the *Star*'s white readers would have endorsed the more optimistic view of domestic servitude embodied in the article's conclusions.

Evidence also suggests that people living within "native townships," where conditions were far from ideal, nonetheless suffered less from TB than those inhabiting the uncontrolled slum areas that sprang up around major urban centers. Looking at data from Cape Town, TB rates in Langa township are uniformly lower than those for "non-Langa" Africans. On one hand, the explanation for this difference may lie in the fact that Langa residents were more established and more likely to be employed. It would also appear that overcrowding and sanitation conditions in Langa were better than in the squatter camps located on the Cape flats or in Windermere. On the other hand, some of this difference may reflect better control of influx and thus a more accurate fix on the size of the population at risk in Langa.[38]

A comparison of black rates for Cape Town indicates that Africans suffered much greater losses to TB than did other blacks during this period. See graph 1, which gives the rates for all blacks in Cape Town. Graph 19 gives those for African men and women living outside of Langa.

Women and small children suffered the most overall. Part of this difference may again have been due to poorer demographic data on the numbers of women and children who were entering the rapidly expanding urban areas during this period. This is particularly true for women, for although a comparison of gender-specific TB mortality among Africans in Cape Town (outside of Langa) suggests that women had significantly higher rates than men, averaging 3 per 1,000 higher between 1938 and 1946, a comparison of the rates in 1936–1937 and 1946–1947, census years in which the denominators were presumably more accurate than during the intervening years, reveals a difference of 1 per 1,000. One cannot, however, discount the very real possibility that women having higher nutritional needs and fewer opportunities for employment may have done worse than men during this period of high inflation.

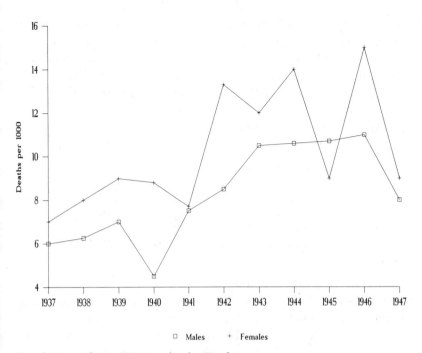

□ Males   + Females

Graph 19.   African TB Mortality by Gender
Cape Town (non-Langa), 1937–1947
Source: Cape Town, *Reports of the Medical Officer of Health,* 1937–1948.

In a similar fashion, the rates of black children under two years of age were both dramatically higher than those of the general black population and underwent a greater increase during the war years. This difference, moreover, is not reduced by a comparison of census year data. The TB mortality rate for children between one and two years increased nearly 200 percent, from 5.5 per 1,000 to 15.8 per 1,000 between 1936–1937 and 1946–1947. The rate for infants under one year increased by 166 percent from 3 to 8 per 1,000. During the same period the general rate increased by 50 percent from 4 to 6 per 1,000 (see graph 10).[39]

The higher susceptibility of young children may be related to the economic pressure experienced by black women within the urban areas. Severe economic conditions associated with high rates of inflation forced women to find employment in a range of informal or illegal occupations that required them to leave their children in the hands of others who were not always able to care for them properly. Infants who

would normally have been breastfed were placed on breastmilk substitutes. Given the difficulties of obtaining fresh milk, often this meant no
more than watered-down gruel made of maize meal. This food may
have filled their stomachs, but it lacked the necessary vitamins and
protein needed by growing infants. Commenting on this pattern, Dr.
A. B. Xuma, who would later become president of the African National
Congress (ANC), observed that the inability of mothers to nurse their
babies was due

> to the fact that many mothers have to walk long distances to do odd jobs in
> order to supplement their husbands' low wages. The babies under these
> circumstances are left in the care of children barely older than they for
> feeding and general care. . . . Many people cannot afford to buy the ap-
> proved baby foods for children on account of lack of money. The[y] often
> resort to home preparations which upset the child's digestion with often
> regrettable results.[40]

Such misfeeding contributed not only to gastroenteritis, but, for those
who survived it, there was the aftermath of malnutrition which provided fertile ground for a fatal case of primary progressive TB.

The rising tide of African TB was also fueled by the continued absence of adequate medical care. Although medical authorities recognized the importance of isolating TB cases in order to stem the spread of
infection, the number of beds provided for black TB cases continued to
fall far short of the number of cases identified. The Gluckman Commission estimated in 1944 that the accepted standard for accommodation
was one bed for every death per annum. On this basis there were officially 610 beds, located primarily in either special tuberculosis hospitals
or in infectious disease hospitals, for 750 white deaths yet only 1,850
such beds, for an estimated 13,000 black deaths, and this does not
include the thousands of black deaths never recorded. Quite a number
of other beds for blacks were scattered through the wards of mission
hospitals and did not allow for adequate isolation of infectious cases.[41]
In 1943 there were 325 beds in Durban for an estimated 4,500 black
cases of TB. Neither Addington Hospital nor King Edward VIII Hospital had special beds for tuberculosis patients, though it was said that
cases in their wards were awaiting transfer to a TB hospital. The only
hospitals designed to deal directly with black TB cases were King
George V and McCord Zulu Hospitals, and both gave preference to
early cases and had long waiting lists.[42] Until 1942 there were only 50
beds in the whole of the Transvaal for black TB cases and many cases in
Johannesburg had to be placed in the overcrowded wards of the Non-

European Hospital. Although efforts were made to expand the number of beds during the 1940s, these efforts were clearly a case of too little too late.

Even where beds were available, there was frequently a delay in gaining admission unless one could afford to pay for treatment. Given the nature of the disease and the class of people most affected by it, most patients could not afford treatment. These cases were, as noted in chapter 7, the responsibility of the municipality within which they became ill, with the state and provincial governments reimbursing the municipality for half the costs. As occurred before World War II, the financial burden this placed on municipal authorities caused them to question the residency of indigent cases and to try to place the responsibility for treatment on to other authorities. These efforts could delay treatment for weeks. The medical history of Zacharia Nzuza illustrates this experience. On April 18, 1946, the MOH of Johannesburg wrote to the secretary of public health,

> This Department is notified that the above-named [Zacharia Nzuza] is suffering from Pulmonary Tuberculosis. He was employed as a teacher at Newadi School, P. O. Deepdale, Natal, from 1940 to August 1945 when the onset of the disease occurred. He was admitted to McCord's Hospital in August 1945 and discharged in February 1946. He was admitted to the Non-European Hospital, Johannesburg, on 4th February, 1946. An application has now been made for his admission to Reinfontein Tuberculosis Hospital.

The MOH reported he had written to the city medical officer of Durban, asking him to accept responsibility for hospitalization and treatment since Nzuza was not from Johannesburg. The Durban MOH replied that the patient contracted his disease in Deepdale and therefore was the responsibility of the Union authorities. He suggested that the Johannesburg medical officer write to the deputy chief health officer in Durban who would "no doubt be glad to take up the matter on his behalf with the local authority at Deepdale." The case dragged on for months, during which Nzuza was again discharged from the Non-European Hospital. There is no record of the final resolution of the case, yet it is likely that he became a source of infection to others.[43]

Patients who could not afford to pay for treatment were dependent on local or state authorities to provide it for them. But these poor patients were often prevented from getting treatment early in their illness, or from being treated for nonpulmonary TB due to a restricting clause in the public health law that limited state—and therefore local—treatment to TB patients with "communicable" forms of the disease.

The effects of this restriction on the provision of medical treatment for Africans living in the Ciskei was described by a local white medical practitioner working at Glen Grey Mission Hospital.

> The present regulations, according to which the Government is responsible only for tubercular cases in the "communicable form," are sufficiently strangling all efforts to improve the situation materially. . . . More than once I have had to refuse to admit patients who offered every hope of cure. But they themselves could not pay anything. The Hospital's resources for free patients were already strained to the utmost and the Government's provision of 2/6d a day did not apply as the case was not yet one in a communicable form. All that is left for the unfortunate patient to do is to return to his extremely unsatisfactory surroundings, there to deteriorate further and further, and in due course after having possibly infected several members of his community, to return to the Hospital only to find that, although he is now eligible for the Government scheme, his hope of a permanent cure has dwindled away, if it has not gone altogether.[44]

Long delays in hospitalization often resulted in the death of patients whose lives might have been saved. Failure to isolate infectious cases, moreover, contributed to the further spread of the disease. One such case from Orlando was described by social researcher Jacqueline Eberhart in 1948.

> A single shelter with no front built on, contained twelve persons. The head of the household and his wife both had T.B. and had papers from the Public Health Department to say that they were awaiting a bed in hospital. They had two of their children living with them, one of whom had already been diagnosed as having T.B. Living with them, and all sleeping in the one shelter, were a nephew and his wife and children, a sister and a friend.[45]

Though hospitalization could not effect a "cure" in the absence of effective chemotherapeutic regimens, rest and a nutritious diet could and did cause remissions and reduce opportunities for the spread of infection. Yet, as the case of Nzuza also illustrates, remissions were often temporary. Even if a case was fortunate enough to receive medical care, tuberculosis patients often required considerable periods of rest and rehabilitation after their release from hospital. There were only a few places in sanatoria for Africans, so that most cases had to regain their health at home. For those with limited means such rehabilitation was often impossible, especially where the patient was also the family bread winner. The health of urban families was often seriously compromised by the illness of a household member who was the main source of income. Such families were doubly at risk of contracting the disease from the tubercular member. The Smit Committee in fact argued that it was among these families, whose members had been exposed to more than ordinary risks of tubercular infection, that there was special need for a liberal allowance of resistance-building foodstuffs and for hygienic housing and surroundings.[46] Yet there were no special programs for supporting the families of tubercular patients whether they were hospitalized or at home. One could apply for a maintenance grant but this carried with it certain risks, as indicated by the experience of an African woman from Krugersdorp whose husband had died of pneumonia leaving her the sole supporter of four children.

The woman had been born in Krugersdorp location and lived there all her life. After her husband's death she lived with a relative who was in the employ of the municipal parks department. During this period she contracted tuberculosis. She received treatment from a local clinic and her children were placed under observation as contacts. She regained sufficient health to do some work but evidently was unable to support her family, and on January 11, 1943, she applied for a maintenance grant from the Department of Social Welfare. During the department's investigation of the case it was discovered that the woman's family had originated from Zwartruggens. Upon receipt of this information the native commissioner, acting on regulations set forth by the department and the Union Department of Native Affairs stating that applicants for grants who have relatives in rural areas must be repatriated to these areas, promptly placed the woman and her family on a train with a rail warrant for that destination. As a result she was deprived of medical treatment for herself and her family and lost her job.[47]

The paper trail ends at this point preventing us from knowing what happened to this woman and her children, who according to the Krugersdorp health authorities represented but one of a number of cases lost through repatriation. Given general conditions in the reserves, however, and the experience of repatriated mine workers with TB noted in chapter 4, the odds are good that she would have died within two years. What is clear is that the only source of pauper relief available to African TB patients was in effect designed to transfer the cost of African ill-health onto the shoulders of rural relatives and off the shoulders of urban and state authorities. It is an example of the continued application of the Stallardist definition of the African as a person whose true home was not in the towns and cities of South Africa.

In general, lack of adequate medical treatment combined with the loss of family income resulting from illness caused many Africans to return to the rural areas to seek treatment from local herbalists and to find support from relatives. A few made it to local mission hospitals. By and large, however, they were either seen once and then disappeared or never sought western medical assistance. These returning victims of the urban-based TB epidemic represented new sources of infection in the rural areas of South Africa. In areas like the Ciskei and Transkei which had long been involved in migrant labor and where infection levels were already high, this additional influx may have had little impact. In areas where contact had been less intense prior to the war, however, such as Natal, the rapid buildup of secondary industries, resulting in generally increased levels of labor migration, led to an increase in the urban–rural transmission of TB. This increase in opportunities for transmission largely accounts for the substantial increase in TB prevalence that Dormer recorded in the rural areas of Natal immediately after the war (see above).

LABOR SHORTAGES AND TUBERCULOSIS ON THE MINES

During the mid-1930s, health authorities working on the mines looked at the record of falling TB incidence over the previous twenty years with some pride and confidence in their ability to control what had once been a significant source of morbidity and mortality. What they could not know was that they stood at the lowest point in an epidemiological curve that would from that point onward rise gradually over the next forty years, retracing most of the gains made in the previous twenty. Although the subsequent rise in TB incidence would occur more gradually than the previous decline, and there would be periods of remission when rates would fall back somewhat, the long-term trend from 1935 to 1985 was upward. By the mid-1970s, the incidence of TB on the mines stood at the same level at which it had been in 1919.

The reemergence of TB on the mines was something of an enigma for mine medical officers and managers during the 1930s and 1940s, and in fact remains so to this day. Working and living conditions on the mines, as well as medical services, continued to improve during the years following the depression, though World War II interrupted reform efforts. Improvements in diet and feeding meant that scurvy became less and less prevalent, while improvements in sanitation and, most importantly, the introduction of waterborne sewage after 1938, reduced the incidence of enteric fever and other parasitic infections. Notwithstanding these improvements, the incidence of TB rose during the war years and, following a respite during the early 1950s, rose again from 1953 onward.

Looking at the period from the mid-1930s through the 1940s it is clear that the initial resurgence of TB does not reflect any improvements in case finding. Instead it resulted in large measure from a reversal of the historical conditions that had played a major role in bringing down TB rates during the 1910s and 1920s. Central to these changing conditions was the economic recovery that began just before World War II. This recovery involved not only an expansion of secondary industries that attracted labor away from the mines but also a parallel growth in the mining industry itself, marked by the extension of existing mines and the development of new ones. This economic resurgence created a serious labor shortage. As early as 1934, the Chamber of Mines began making representations to the government for the removal of regulations that required mines to terminate a fixed number of workers at the end of their contracts in order to accommodate unemployed labor in the native reserve areas. The chamber argued that the mines could not find enough new workers to replace workers removed by these termination quotas. In addition they found that already engaged workers were leaving voluntarily at a faster rate than during the depression and that termination quotas were no longer required.[48]

By the late 1930s the mines were beginning to face a serious shortage of labor, and by 1941 competition for labor was causing a negative growth in the labor supply. Over the next seven years the total labor force declined by 92,509 workers, a 25 percent decrease. Part of this decline represented a planned retrenchment caused by a declining ability to acquire the stores necessary to maintain operations and by the loss of European miners to the military. The retrenchment nonetheless meant that the mines were operating at between 80 and 85 percent of their full labor capacity. Though this was compensated by some increases in operating efficiency, production in terms of tons milled nevertheless decreased by 11 percent.[49]

This labor shortage and resulting decline in production resulted in changes in the composition of the mine workforce that reversed some trends largely responsible for the earlier decline in TB incidence. The most important of these was the reintroduction of tropical labor.

Faced with the possibility of declining labor supplies within the areas from which they had traditionally drawn their labor, the Chamber of Mines began a campaign in the early 1930s designed to obtain permission from the government to reopen recruiting in the north. After considerable discussions, and assurances by the chamber that conditions at the mines had improved substantially and were no longer a threat to the health of tropical workers, the government responded positively but cautiously, agreeing in 1934 to allow the introduction of 2,000 tropical workers on an experimental basis.[50] The chamber's apparent success in lowering the incidence of TB on the mines was an important piece of evidence in these discussions.

The Chamber of Mines took extreme care to protect the new tropical workers so as to prevent a recurrence of the high mortality rates that had accompanied the earlier introduction of tropical workers. The workers were only allotted to mines with relatively good health records. Each tropical recruit in addition was provided with blankets, shorts, and a woolen jacket to protect them from the elements. They were housed in rooms containing no more than twenty workers, and all were inoculated against pneumonia three times at prescribed intervals with Lister's Community Autogenous Vaccine. And all tropical recruits underwent an extended period of acclimatization; any tropical recruit who appeared unfit was placed on surface work and not included in the experiment. The new recruits were, in short, treated with kid gloves.[51]

As a result of this special treatment the overall mortality rate for the experimental tropical workers from all diseases was kept to just under 6 per 1,000. Although this was roughly twice the rate for all other mineworkers, it represented a dramatic improvement over the rates among tropical workers prior to 1913, when mortalities hovered around 75 per 1,000. The rate for 1935–1936 for all tropical workers shot up to 16.27 per 1,000.[52] It was still a marked improvement, however, and the mining industry was able to convince the government that these rates were not unreasonable in a "newly industrialized" population, and that the great improvement over earlier tropical mortality rates reflected the major improvements that had taken place in the mining industry. As a consequence the ban on recruiting north of the twenty-second parallel was removed. The number of tropical workers on the Rand rose to 10,540 in 1937, 19,668 by 1939, and exceeded 40,000 by 1948, or roughly 15 percent of the total African workforce.[53] The use of tropical workers helped solve more than the labor shortage during the war. It also had advantages in terms of both the cost of recruitment and the ability of the mines to allot labor according to the needs of particular mines, since tropical recruits had no choice of where they worked.[54]

The relationship between the reintroduction of tropical workers and the rising incidence of TB at the mines was complex. New tropical workers initially had a somewhat higher incidence of TB than did non-tropical workers, and this may have had some effect on overall TB rates. Their rates were not so high, however, or their numbers so great as to have caused a major increase in overall TB incidence.[55]

Tropical workers, however, were susceptible to pneumococcal pneumonia despite the use of antipneumonial vaccine. Although this susceptibility did not increase their overall mortality rate, thanks largely to the introduction of sulfonamide therapy in 1938, it may have contributed to the increase in TB morbidity that occurred on the mines during this period.

The incidence of pneumonia among tropical workers rose steadily from 60 per 1,000 to 140 per 1,000, or by 133 percent, between 1939 and 1946, paralleling the increase in the number of tropical recruits on the mines and the rise in TB incidence. The reasons for the rising incidence of pneumonia were not immediately clear. David Ordman, in a paper presented to the Transvaal Mine Medical Officers Association meeting in 1949, explained the increase in terms of the susceptibility of tropical workers to new forms of bacterial respiratory flora, to which they were unaccustomed, and concluded that,

> as long as a "new" susceptible population is introduced into an established immunologically stabilized population, so long will there be an increase in the incidence of disease among them.[56]

Ordman's general hypothesis explained the high incidence of pneumonia among tropical workers, but it did not explain why the *incidence rate* among tropical workers increased as their numbers increased. Why did raising the number of tropical workers increase their vulnerability to pneumonia? One explanation is that as the mines increased their recruiting networks within tropical areas they drew on populations from more tropical areas who may have been more vulnerable to the climatic conditions of the Rand.

Of equal or perhaps greater importance, however, was the fact that having succeeded in convincing the government that tropical workers were relatively safe on the mines, the mines were under less pressure to maintain the strict health controls that had existed during the experimental years. Tropical workers were allotted to nearly all of the mines, regardless of their overall health record, and they were increasingly treated like all other workers. Because it was believed, moreover, that tropical workers had a high tolerance for heat and thus were more resistant to heat stroke, they were increasingly used in the deep-level mines, where conditions of work were often most severe and, as we have seen, most likely to produce the pattern of exposure and chill that contributed to pneumonia. It is important to note that these alterations in the conditions under which tropical workers were employed would not have been possible had it not been for the development of sulfonamide therapy, which kept the death rate of tropical workers down and thus did not raise the attention of government authorities. The role of "silver bullet" technologies in deflecting public attention from declining health conditions would occur again during the 1950s and 1960s when effective chemotherapeutic agents for TB itself were introduced in South Africa.

The rising incidence of pneumonia among tropical workers was paralleled by an increase in the incidence among nontropical workers. The incidence rate for all forms of pneumonia among nontropical workers increased from 20 to 30 per 1,000 between 1939 and 1946.[57] Given the size of the nontropical workforce this represented an increase of 2,300 cases per year. Although deteriorating working conditions, due to wartime restrictions on supplies and inflation, accounted for part of this increase, it is likely that a good deal of the increase was due to increased opportunities for infection created by the growing number of tropical cases on the mines.

Increased incidence of pneumonia on the mines contributed to the rising incidence of TB by reactivating tubercular lesions among infected African mineworkers. Thus mine medical officers observed that tubercular infections frequently followed bouts of pneumonia and influenza.[58] This relationship would have been more marked in mineworkers from highly infected areas of the Cape than for tropical workers who had lower TB *infection* rates. This may explain why tropical workers did not suffer high rates of TB despite their vulnerability to pneumonia. In short, the reintroduction of tropical workers in the face of growing labor shortages during the 1930s and 1940s increased the incidence of pneumonia at the mines, which in turn triggered preexisting TB infections and contributed to a rise in the incidence of this disease.

The labor shortage of the late 1930s and 1940s may also have contributed to a rising incidence of TB among African workers by forcing the mines to lower their fitness standards. Recurrent complaints about the poor quality of recruited labor during this period point toward the declining ability of the mines to recruit high-quality labor and to the inability of the resulting workforce to cope with the arduous conditions of mine labor. The industry's decision to cut back on its activities and reduce its African workforce after 1941 may have lessened the effects of this problem.

With alternative opportunities for employment available, the average duration of mine employment also declined, as did the percentage of old hands within the workforce. Both of these changes reversed patterns established in the late 1920s and may have had a negative impact on TB rates.

Along with the introduction of workers with reduced capacity to resist the arduous conditions of mine life, the incidence of TB in the mines like that in the major cities may also have been affected by the rising cost of living. The cost of feeding an African worker on the Rand rose from 4s 15d per day in 1936 to 7s 90d per day in 1945. In 1946 it jumped to 9s 79d per day. Part of this increase was due to drought years and poor maize harvests in 1942 and 1945. Faced with rising food costs and declining buying power, produced by a decline in gold production, a number of mines cut back on their rations. The fixed ration of 3.25 pounds of fresh meat per worker, for example, was from time to time reduced to 2.75 pounds of tinned stewed meat. There were also re-ported shortages of mealie meal. The supply of "Boermeal" (whole-wheat meal) was also erratic, and at times the bread rations had to be reduced from 6- to 4.5-ounce loaves. Since bread rations were fre-quently provided for workers before going on shift, this cutback re-duced an important source of energy during the shift.[59] Despite these reductions, food rations at the mines remained in excess of government regulations. They were, moreover, certainly superior to the rations of the 1910s and 1920s. As we saw in chapter 6, nonetheless, small alter-ations in diet could have significant effects in the overall health of workers involved in heavy labor.[60]

Such changed conditions of recruitment and diet did not result in a return to the high morbidity rates of the 1920s. Conditions in the mines, after all, had improved in significant ways since the early years of the century and were leading to a change in the etiology of the disease (see chap. 6). Yet, the fact that TB rates increased at all underscores both the extent to which conditions in the industry remained a threat to the health of African workers and the fact that earlier successes in bringing down the incidence of TB were based on historically specific conditions that were subject to change.

THE RISE OF ENVIRONMENTALISM AND
THE "MYTH OF THE HEALTHY RESERVE"

In 1948 B. A. Dormer published an article in the *South African Medical Journal* modestly titled "A Case of Tuberculosis." The article began innocently enough with a clinical presentation of the case history of a married African man, identified simply as "A. N.," who at age twenty-four was admitted to Springfield Hospital, where he died three weeks later. The man was found to be suffering from pulmonary TB, tuberculous enteritis, and possibly tuberculosis of the kidney, complicated by secondary syphilis, amebic dysentery, ascariasis, hookworm, and secondary anemia. After describing the clinical evidence, diagnosis, treatment, and postmortem findings, Dormer posed a question. What was the primary cause of death? He then proceeded to describe the man's "past history." The tale is of a young man brought up in an open-air, healthy rural environment who at age twenty-two came to Durban in search of work to pay his taxes. He obtained employment with a contractor which involved hard labor with a pick and shovel for nine hours a day. The article continued:

> After work he walked four miles to his lodging in Cato Manor, which lodging was a small room in a dirty tin shack, shared with four other men.
>
> He walked this distance to his work every morning so that, in addition to his manual labour he covered at least eight miles a day on his feet. His food in the city consisted of bread or mealie meal, and black tea with sugar. About once a month he managed to obtain about ½ lb. of meat offal . . .
>
> The water-supply to his lodging was from a stream polluted in every possible manner and sewage disposal was in a pit privy, which was used in the day time only. At night everyone defecated at random around the shack. It was probably at this time that the patient contracted amoebic dysentery. . . .
>
> After a few months of life in Durban, the patient met and liked a young native prostitute, and from her he contracted his syphillis.
>
> Sharing his rooms were four other men, one of whom died of tuberculosis about six months before the patient's admission to hospital. There is therefore no doubt as to the source of his tuberculosis.[61]

Expanding the scope of his initial diagnosis on the basis of this history, Dormer reasked the question, "What killed him?" and proceeded to provide what he termed a "social diagnosis."

> Surely not syphillis or tuberculosis, or amoebic dysentary. If he had continued to live in the country he would never have contracted any of these bacterial infections. The organisms and the disease patterns were just the

results of something far more potent. Industry, economic need, Western civilization—call it what you will, it is to-day's social system which was responsible for the death of our patient, as it is for a death rate from tuberculosis of 900 per 100,000 of industrial natives in South Africa to-day—perhaps the highest death rate in the world.[62]

Dormer's story of "A. N." represented an emotional example of a growing tendency among western-trained medical authorities in South Africa. He saw tuberculosis among Africans as a product of the adverse social and economic conditions under which they were forced to live within the rapidly expanding industrial economy of South Africa, and not as a product of racial susceptibility to the disease. Faced with the rising tide of TB during the late 1930s and 1940s, white medical authorities were forced to confront the failure of their earlier explanations for African susceptibility to TB. This led to a reassessment of the causes of TB among Africans and to the emergence of an explanation based on an environmental model that placed a much greater emphasis on the conditions of African life.

The environmentalism of the 1940s, like earlier etiologies, reflected and was part of a broader discourse on the status of Africans within South African society. It echoed the reformist language of the Fagan (Native Laws), Smit (Inter-departmental Committee on Social, Economic and Health Conditions), and Gluckman (National Health Services) Commission Reports, as well as to some degree that of the earlier Native Economic Commission, in accepting the permanence of African urban settlement and the need to develop social and economic policies that reflected this reality. Like these other initiatives, the new environmentalist discourse on African health coincided with the interests of manufacturing capital, which had the ear of the ruling United Party. These interests saw both the inevitability of African urbanization and the social and political dangers that uncontrolled settlement were creating. Yet, the new etiology of African TB also shared with these other products of liberal capitalism discordant themes that undercut the full force of its reformist language and represented an intellectual connection to the racial theories of the 1920s and 1930s. Like Fagan, Smit, and Gluckman, the new discourse on African TB recognized the reality of African urbanization without fully challenging the underlying political economy shaping this process.

The growing emphasis on housing, diet, and working conditions which punctuated discussions of African susceptibility to TB in the

1940s was not new to European medical circles in South Africa. In fact environmental issues had been raised as far back as the turn of the century. Part of the behavioral arguments during that period rested on the assumption that African susceptibility to TB resulted from their having been removed from one environment, that of their "primitive" rural homes, and placed in a "civilized" industrial environment to which they were unaccustomed. In addition, we have seen that European medical authorities, such as Neil McVicar, George Gale, and Peter Allan, who had substantial experience in working with Africans in rural areas of South Africa, were arguing that African susceptibility to TB was not inherent in their physiology but resulted from the harsh conditions under which they lived and worked in industrial areas. The same argument had also been made by a few urban medical officers like P. W. Laidler in East London. What changed in the late 1930s and 1940s was the extent to which these views came to be accepted within the mainstream of medical thought in urban as well as rural areas, becoming the dominant etiological paradigm. The dominance of the environmental model was in no small measure enhanced by the appointment of Gale as secretary for health and Allan as secretary for public health.

The shift to an environmental paradigm within the mainstream of western medical opinion can be seen in statements made by government medical authorities from the late 1930s onward. In a memo to the minister of health, for example, the secretary of health in 1938 stated,

> Nutrition and housing stand out prominently from this social background as factors favouring tuberculosis. . . . No single enterprise would do so much for the eradication of tuberculosis, and for the public welfare generally, as the provision of adequate dwellings for the poorer classes at rentals they can afford.[63]

Similarly a conference of municipal, provincial, and Union health authorities on tuberculosis in 1939 resolved that,

> This conference being conscious of the gravity of the tuberculosis situation in this country is of opinion . . . that the chief cause is to be found in the depressed social and economic conditions of large sections of the population resulting in undernourishment, overcrowding, and other factors promoting tuberculosis . . .[64]

The conference report also noted that "Underlying factors of the problem are largely social and economic, with a wage rate insufficient to enable poorer families to maintain a proper standard of nutrition." Both statements not only stressed the importance of environmental factors but, in their references to "poorer classes" and "large sections of the population," implicitly rejected the importance of racial differences in favor of social and economic ones. Although there was little doubt that most of the poor were blacks, the changing pathology of the disease and the realization that poor whites during the depression shared a susceptibility to TB led medical authorities to underplay the importance of race.

This rejection of racial susceptibility was made more explicit in a major article on TB by Drs. Dormer, Friedlander, and Wiles, who were centered at King George V Hospital for Tuberculosis in Durban.

> It is stated in all the books that primitive races are more susceptible and less resistant to tuberculosis than so-called civilized people. The disease in general tends to run a much more rapid course in primitive people, and this is ascribed to a racial susceptibility or a racial lack of resistance. We are loth [sic] to subscribe to this as in the South African Bantu in the Native reserves, there is the problem of the high rate of infection combined with the low rate of disease in the same areas to be explained away.[65]

Drawing on survey work in rural Natal, the article noted three types of TB that occurred among Africans in the reserves: (1) the delayed disease characteristic of the European; (2) the disseminated disease of all infants, European or Native; and (3) the progressive primary disease that occurred among "Natives who had returned from industry in the Towns." They concluded that "Race is not a factor per se" and that TB in the progressive form occurred primarily under conditions of physical stress and malnutrition associated with industrial employment.

The same point was made by members of an Expert Committee on TB chaired by Dr. Peter Allan which convened in Cape Town in 1939. After noting that the type of TB experienced by coloreds was similar to that of Europeans but that it may be profoundly modified by the conditions under which the colored people lived, the committee's report noted: "It is to be stated, however, that many poor Europeans living under bad environmental conditions revealed tuberculosis of an acute type."[66]

Although environmental explanations for African susceptibility to TB gained prominence in the late 1930s and 1940s, their influence was not felt in all medical circles. Such explanations were particularly popular among two groups of physicians: those who worked in the reserves, and those who worked in the rapidly expanding centers of manufacturing. The former group as noted above had had the opportunity to see the difference between the disease experience of Africans living within a rural setting, and of those who returned near death from the towns. For medical authorities working in the growing manufacturing centers, the rising toll of African tubercular deaths forced them to come to grips with the failure of earlier explanations and the role played by the appalling conditions under which Africans lived.

Such environmentalist arguments carried less weight among medical officers at the mines. Though published statements of mine medical officers recognize the importance of social and economic factors, they continued to stress the dominant importance of the African's lack of physiological resistance to disease. For example Dr. Frank Retief, chief medical officer for WNLA, concluded,

> In our opinion, as mentioned before, the native races are more susceptible to tuberculosis than the white ones and also have a low racial immunity to this disease. This is shown by their greater mortality and morbidity rates, greater severity, more extensive caseation, less reparative processes and more tendency to dissemination by lymph and blood stream. It would appear that in the native there is a comparative inability to develop acquired immunity, which in the European so markedly alters the course of the disease, and also the fate of reinfection lesions.[67]

Although Retief went on to acknowledge the importance of the "socioeconomic aspect," malnutrition and overcrowding, it is clear that here as elsewhere such concerns were of secondary importance, their relevance undercut by the overiding belief in the racial susceptibility of Africans.

The continued acceptance of racial etiologies among mine medical officers in the 1940s must be viewed within the context of the mines' continued and in fact growing dependence on migratory labor. As David Yudelman and Alan Jeeves note, the mines' heavy investment in establishing a northern recruiting system and the promise of unlimited tropical labor resources "made it more difficult for Chamber of Mines executives to consider seriously alternatives to its low wage labor policies based on maximum utilization of transitory, unskilled labour."[68] It must also be viewed within the context of the debate in wider government and public circles over the costs and benefits of migrant labor on both the migrants themselves and their families. This debate was central to the inquiries of the Fagan Commission.

In testimony before that commission, representatives of the Chamber of Mines presented the expert opinion of Sir Lyle Cummins, citing his 1946 study of colonial tuberculosis. The study concluded that tuberculosis among "native people" was not primarily the result of industrial conditions. It was rather the result of relatively isolated primitive people ("natives") being brought into sudden contact with older communities that are more tubercularized and more resistant. In such circumstances "It [was] the isolated people who run the greater risk of developing acute and fatal disease." Cummins, as seen in chapter 7, attributed this greater susceptibility of the "primitive people" to a "lack of that inherited power to respond to infection, so well exhibited by European races." The lesson of this experience was that

> the sudden settlement of large numbers of primitive people, highly susceptible and highly sensitive to tuberculosis infection, in closer and more sustained contact with European communities and living under industrial conditions, would lead to a greater exacerbation of acute tuberculosis amongst them.[69]

The chamber argued further, through its representative, Dr. Orenstein, that the establishment of a permanent workforce would heighten the risk of African workers developing silicosis and TB whereas retaining the current intermittent labor force reduced the risk of these diseases.[70]

The chamber's representative to the Mine Wages Commission argued at the same time that the African worker's "position as peasant farmer and stockholder" guaranteed the support of his family and assured him of a "prolonged holiday at home" between contracts.[71]

The mining industry had, in effect, resurrected the arguments based on a physiological explanation of African TB susceptibility that it had made before the 1914 TB Commission to argue anew against the elimination of migrant labor in favor of a more permanently settled workforce. Mine medical officers' support of this argument was no doubt influenced by their recent experience in combatting TB on the mines. During the 1940s they were, as we have seen, faced with a rising incidence of TB. Given the improvements in living and working conditions that they believed to have caused the earlier decline in the disease, this rise did not appear to be the product of environmental conditions. The inherent racial susceptibility of Africans was, therefore, an explanation that appeared empirically correct. For many mine medical officers, in short, racial susceptibility was not simply a convenient explanation that suited the needs of their employers.

Yet even among those who sought to stress the importance of environmental factors, one can hear elements of earlier paradigms. In reading the statements of those medical authorities who advocated environmental explanations, one must listen carefully to the language employed

and the images invoked. For in these images one can find certain intellectual links to earlier explanations going back to the beginning of the
century. In other words, the advocates of an environmental explanation
for African susceptibility to TB were presenting their arguments for a
new etiological paradigm within the idiom of earlier paradigms.

This continuity can be seen clearly in Dormer's 1948 article, "Tuberculosis in South Africa." In it Dormer, perhaps the foremost advocate of
the environmental paradigm, and who as the Union government's first
tuberculosis officer was influential in shaping the development of both
attitudes and policies toward African TB, wrote,

> In truly rural areas (some tribal reserves) the Bantu lives a pastoral existence
> of blissful ease. There is the social life of the Kraal, the sitting at ease in the
> sun, the Spring ploughing, the reaping, the celebration of the harvest, all the
> simple and comparatively slothful existence of the primitive . . .

> When the Bantu people go to live in the towns the picture changes rap-
> idly . . . the black man moves . . . from the 14th to the 20th Century in a
> matter of days. His environment is suddenly changed and he moves from a
> life of ease to heavy sustained physical work for eight hours a day, with the
> added effort of getting to and from work, often a walk of eight miles or more
> a day.

> The incidence of tuberculosis rises rapidly in such urban areas and the type of
> the disease is a soft exudative rapidly advancing lethal type of tuberculosis.[72]

The same line of argument was presented by Dr. Allan in the 1943
report of the secretary of public health:

> With increased industrial development, where the Native comes in contact
> with *new surroundings and mode of life, it is inevitable* that many will
> develop tuberculosis in an active form. (emphasis added)[73]

The theme is again seen in the following statement by Dr. F. J. Wiles of
Durban's King George V Tuberculosis Hospital.

> One of the reasons for the high mortality rate among Natives was the tremen-
> dous impact of hard industrial life on a people who were not prepared for it.
> In the reserves the men lived lives of ease and were not accustomed to hard
> physical work. Although they came in contact with the disease, their constitu-
> tions did not break down until a physical strain was placed upon them.[74]

Critics of the racial arguments of the 1920s and 1930s were fond of
citing the experience of American blacks as proof that it was not race
but urbanization that caused the high incidence of TB among Africans.
An example of this use of comparative history can be seen in the annual
report for 1939 of the MOH for Johannesburg:

> If it is claimed that all or most native tuberculosis is based on a racial suscepti-
> bility, then it must be remembered that as slaves, the negroes of U.S.A. lived a
> country life and knew not tuberculosis. It was the urbanization that followed
> freedom, dissipation and excess that was followed by tuberculosis.[75]

This dubious evocation of the healthfulness of plantation life compared
to the physical insults of urban society, reinforced the image of the
African's difficult transition to industrial society imbedded in the above
quotations.

A final example of this thinking, a brochure prepared by the National Association for the Prevention of Tuberculosis in 1948, included
the following discussion of the problem of TB among urban Africans:

> [T]he high incidence of the disease among Natives in the urban areas is
> largely due to their changed methods of living, being engaged in hard manual
> labor, living in large compounds or in slum shacks, and often inadequately
> fed.
>
> In rural areas evidence is scanty, but surveys show that there must be ample
> opportunity for infection in the Native reserves. Despite this, however, mor-
> tality is relatively low *when the Native lives under his natural conditions.*
> (emphasis added)[76]

These arguments echo statements made by white physicians as far back
as the eighteenth century when the relative absence of TB among Africans was attributed to the pastoral, open-air existence. During the early
years of this century, as we have seen, it was the Africans' "primitive"
life-style and their incomplete adjustment to the conditions of "civilized" life which were said to account for their susceptibility to TB.
During the 1920s and 1930s, this inexperience took on biological dimen-
sion. Yet there remained the idea that Africans in their own surroundings were healthier than when they tried to enter western civilization
and were exposed to bacterial flora to which they were unaccustomed.
The new environmental discourse contained within it two themes that
run through these earlier explanations. The first is what one might call
the "myth of the healthy reserve," the image of a bucolic rural life style
that contrasted sharply with the harsh world of industrial society. This
image, fostered by the mining industry throughout the century, was a
principle assumption underlying their arguments concerning the medical value of repatriating sick workers and, more generally, of employing
migrant workers who recuperated in the "restful" reserves between
their contracts on the mines.

Second, the new environmentalism shared with earlier paradigms an implicit tendency to blame Africans for their susceptibility to TB, namely, to blame the victim. Despite their emphasis on the environmental conditions under which Africans were forced to live—their condemnation of overcrowding and malnutrition—the environmental paradigm implied that the impact the harsh conditions of industrialized society had on the health of Africans was in some measure the result of their inexperience with these conditions. The implicit reverse of this argument was that whites, accustomed to industrial life, were less susceptible to these conditions. In short, the impact of the environmentalists' critique of the conditions of industrial life and their calls for social and economic reform were tempered by a continued tendency to define Africans as essentially different from whites and to see this difference as in some way responsible for African susceptibility to disease.

It must be said in qualification, that within the body of writings by environmentalists during this period one can find varying degrees of acceptance of this underlying tendency to blame the victim by romanticizing rural life. Whereas Dormer represented the general tendency, there were those with experience in rural areas, like Dr. George Gale and Sidney Kark, who were well aware of the conditions that existed there and were much less prone to adopt images of the "healthy reserve" and to attribute African susceptibility to TB to their inexperience with harsh living conditions. Commenting on the activities of the Polela Health Unit in Natal, Dr. Sidney Kark wrote,

> The influence of social economic factors is still felt in all spheres of the Unit's activities. One example of such an influence is the disintegration of family life by the withdrawal of large numbers of men to the towns with the inevitable spread of venereal disease. A further even more important influence is the rapid progress of soil erosion. The devastating process dwarfs all the Unit's efforts to encourage increased production of protective foodstuffs. Such are but two factors beyond the powers of a Health Unit to combat, no matter how clearly their detrimental influence on health may be realized.[77]

At the same time, Dr. Peter Allan, who also had extensive rural experience, did invoke the image of the healthy reserve. Though this may have resulted from his efforts to reject earlier notions of racial susceptibility by drawing attention to the different experiences of Africans in rural and urban surroundings, it nonetheless contributed to the tendency to blame the victim. In the same light it is interesting to speculate why Dormer, who had done extensive survey work in the rural areas of Natal, adopted a view of rural life so out of touch with the reality of rural existence described by Kark. Part of the reason may be that he did most of his work in Natal prior to World War II, when conditions were considerably better than in the Transkei and Ciskei or in Natal after the war. He may, however, have been caught in the same trap of logic as Allan. By trying to show how different the disease experience of Africans in rural areas was from that of Africans in urban areas, he may have overromanticized African rural life. Yet at the same time we must wonder whether the underlying view of Africans as fundamentally different from whites was not so pervasive in white society by the 1940s that these men, despite their good intentions, found it difficult to completely break from the this view?

Whatever the reason, the "myth of the healthy reserve" and the correlate that African ill-health was a product of their historical inexperience became intertwined with the language of environmental reform. In doing so it provided an intellectual justification for inaction. For those who opposed the stabilization of labor and the costs that this would entail, the logic of the argument that Africans were paying the price of industrialization was that these costs were somehow inevitable, and while the costs could be reduced they could not, given the Africans' inexperience, be eliminated. This line of argument was taken up strongly by representatives of the mining industry, invoking their earlier arguments about the "healthy reserves," as seen in the following statement by the chief medical officer for WNLA:

> This, then, is possibly the price the Bantu has to pay for the change from his traditional lazy tribal life and easy habits, from rural agricultural occupations to industrial labour with sustained physical effort: from living room to crowded compounds and locations where he has to adjust his hours, his mode of life and living conditions. No doubt the native who remains in his kraal or village, leading an easy life, surrounded by wine and women, or love and beer if you like, and no maladjustments, has less and milder tuberculosis than his compatriots who labour in the mines or in industry.[78]

The inevitability of health costs involved in the transition to an industrial life was also used by those who saw the linking of industrialization to increased TB rate among African workers as an attack on industrial development.

> With a view to the development of a socially healthy as well as physically healthy native industrial population, therefore, the right method of approach to the problem is not to proclaim to the natives that industrialization exposes them to the danger of tuberculosis but to teach them, encourage them and (when absolutely necessary) assist them to *adapt themselves to conditions of life in industrial centers. Some, inevitably, will fall by the way,* but it is as

grave an error to fail to see the wood for the trees as to fail to see the trees for the wood. (emphasis added)[79]

Ultimately the arguments about the health of the rural reserves and the health costs of the transition to industrial life would find a comfortable home during the 1950s and 1960s within the Nationalist Party's arguments for separate development and a return to Stallardist views of Africans as temporary sojourners in white industrial areas. The explanation reinforced beliefs in the moral correctness of racial segregation. For it implied that while the African was able to cope with TB in his rural setting, he was fundamentally unable to do so when he entered the European's world. In this way the environmentalists' discourse on the causes of African ill-health represented not only a link to the past but a bridge to future discussions, and though the intent of environmentalists may have been very different from that of their successors, their language reflected a common intellectual heritage and provided "apartheid medicine" with intellectual legitimacy. Put another way, by failing to effectively challenge the historical assumptions that underpinned the racist paradigms of their predecessors, the environmentalists provided the designers of Nationalist social policies with an intellectual justification for renewed efforts at sanitary segregation on a grand scale.

We must look finally at the impact environmentalists had on the development of policies for combatting TB. As in the case of their ideas, the environmentalists' policies failed to make a significant break with the past. This can be seen in both their recommendations and their actions. For example the 1939 Tuberculosis Conference, which, as already noted, resolved that the chief cause of TB could be found in the depressed social and economic conditions under which large sections of the population lived, made the following recommendations:

> (1) the provision of a greatly increased number of hospital beds for the treatment and isolation of patients, especially those of non-European races;
>
> (2) the institution of tuberculosis clinics in all centres with expert medical control and the necessary home-visiting and other staff;
>
> (3) adequate provision for the economic assistance of cases and contacts, including after-care, without which much of the benefit from the expenditure under the foregoing headings is likely to be lost.[80]

The proposed policies represented in essence a classic medical response— treating the disease, not the causes of ill-health the conference had identified. This is not to underplay the importance of such measures or to ignore the fact that access to adequate medical care was a major problem for Africans. It does, however, point to the failure of environmentalists to act directly on their convictions in making recommendations about the causes of African susceptibility to TB.

The disparity between recognition of environmental factors in the causation of the disease and the application of "medical solutions" for preventing it is also illustrated by the following discussion from the above-cited memorandum by the secretary of health in 1938. After stressing the desirability of providing better housing and diets for the poorer classes, the report proceeds to commend efforts to control TB in Cape Town:

> Cape Town is grappling with the tuberculosis problem. It has just decided to appoint a specialist tuberculosis officer and it is about to build a new clinic and a hospital providing additional beds.[81]

Similarly the Smit Committee's report on "The Social Health and Economic Conditions of Urban Natives," after decrying the effect of poverty on the ability of Africans to maintain good health, and particularly their inability to care for themselves through the acquisition of food, beds, or invalid appliances, limited its formal recommendations almost exclusively to improvements in medical care, that is, the provision of more beds and medical training for blacks.[82] Although the need for more hospital beds and medical personnel was real, the committee's recommendations clearly ducked the general economic problem in favor of a narrow medical response.

Men like Gale, Allan, and Dormer recognized the need to improve housing and nutrition and, during the 1940s, called for programs that would accomplish these ends.[83] Yet few programs were instituted. Most of the attention was devoted to the providing of more beds in order to isolate the diseased and thereby prevent the spread of infection. In addition, education and health weeks were organized to help instruct Africans about the dangers of tubercular infection,[84] a policy in keeping with the underlying image of the inexperienced African but hardly with the call for environmental reform. The mid- and late-1930s also saw an increase in efforts to train African medical personnel which had got underway in the 1920s. Plans were also devised to establish reserves for "tuberculous natives" in the rural areas. These would allow Africans to live within a "kraal environment" under regular medical supervision, including education on hygiene, and with subsidized food provided, yet separated from other rural Africans. The tuberculous reserves were viewed as a way of dealing with the problem of repatriated African workers infecting their kin and neighbors in a cost-efficient manner that placed no burden on urban health budgets.[85]

A few local programs were developed to provide food for school-children. Municipalities, in addition, were encouraged to take advantage of the low-income housing loans offered by the government under the 1934 Slum Clearance Act.[86] Yet no national policies were developed for dealing with either housing or nutrition (A state-aided feeding program had been initiated under the Department of Welfare in 1935, but it did not include Africans). And local authorities, for reasons discussed in chapter 5, were loathe to take on the cost of such programs, especially during the war when the costs of food and building materials skyrocketed.

By 1945, however, white public hysteria over the growing TB epidemic among Africans and its threat to both labor supply and their own health caused the government to initiate a nationwide attack on tuberculosis. Numerous articles on TB and the dangers it posed to whites and their supply of domestic servants and workers appeared in the major newspapers of the country during the mid-1940s. An article by George Heard, for example, appeared in *The Cape Times* of June 1, 1941, under the banner headline, "State Must Take Control of TB Menace: Grave Threat to Nation." It began, "First of all our humanitarian instincts should tell us that we cannot abandon these unfortunate people to their fate." The article then goes on to quote an unnamed Durban health authority as stating,

> If we are not swayed by this first consideration, there are two others which we simply cannot elude. The first is that this disease is rapidly exhausting our available reservoir of native labour in South Africa. And the second is that the health of European South Africa is at stake. There is no colour bar in disease.

Predictably, the primary instruments of the attack were conceived in narrow medical terms. They included the appointment of a tuberculosis division within the Department of Public Health directed by Dr. Dormer, the assumption by the Union government of 100 percent of medical costs for TB patients, the allocation of funds for constructing tuberculosis hospitals and clinics, and the training of more nursing staff. The minister of health noted that, "In the National Campaign . . . there were not only questions of hospitals and early detection and isolation, but the important one of preventing it occurring at all." This he went on to explain meant, "The people must be educated."[87]

That men like Gale and Dormer did not push harder for broader social reform during this period but instead concentrated on developing medical initiatives is not perhaps surprising. These men, after all, were physicians not social planners. However much they recognized that housing and nutritional conditions were undermining any effort to combat TB, they were committed to their profession and to doing whatever they could to help. Like many progressive medical professionals in South Africa today, they were faced with a difficult choice between accepting the futility of health reform without political and economic reform and doing nothing, or trying to work within the existing system to help as best they could. In the end, they chose the latter course.

The failure of medical authorities concerned about the underlying economic causes of tuberculosis to direct more energy to removing those causes was not unique but represented much of the reformist efforts of the 1940s. The Gluckman Commission's report was clear about the underlying causes of ill-health in South Africa, stating, "Unless there are vast improvements made in the nutrition, housing and health education of the people, the mere provision of more 'doctoring' will not lead to any real improvement in the public health." Yet despite this rhetoric, the commission's proposals—although revolutionary in terms of their emphasis on quality preventive and curative primary health care, and in fact progressive by even the standard of postwar England—contained few recommendations about the provision of housing or food. More fundamentally, they said little about the exploitative wage structure that underlay the inability of large segments of the population to adequately house and feed themselves.

The Fagan Commission on Native Laws, while recognizing the need for making provisions for the stabilization of urban labor, similarly waffled on the question of administrative responsibility for housing Africans. In the end they suggested that the government should perhaps consider viewing housing as a national problem and take responsibility for providing it but expressed the hope that Africans would be able to solve the problem themselves: "We look forward to a time when the increasing productivity of Native labour may lessen and ultimately remove the need for sub-economic adjustments."[88]

The limits of reform, and the failure of those who recognized the underlying causes of poverty and ill-health to address these causes directly, is hardly surprising. Reformism in South Africa during the 1940s occurred within a particular political and economic environment created by the massive buildup of urban populations in response to expanding industrial development and deteriorating rural conditions. This buildup, together with the failure of both industry and state to provide the basic necessities of life for African workers and their families, created an explosive environment marked by strikes, boycotts, and squatters' movements. For the United party, reform was a means of coping with this environment. As Cedric de Beer suggests, the elements of the United party that were toying with reform did not have any major changes in mind. "They were rather looking for ways to insure social stability and to protect an economic system that had changed so rapidly that it was threatening to tear itself apart."[89] It is therefore not surprising that dominant classes in the state were not, as Shula Marks and Neil Andersson point out, prepared to sustain the welfare costs involved in such enterprises as a national health service or to act on the more wide-reaching proposals of the Smit Commission. Much less were they willing to question the very political and economic foundations upon which the state was established, the political and economic exploitation of black labor.[90] Whether the majority of white medical professionals were willing to go further than the state, although debatable, is perhaps irrelevant. Any action designed to combat the underlying economic and political causes of TB required resources that could only be accumulated through the actions of the state. Industry would remain unwilling to pay for the cost of adequately housing and feeding its employees without direct coercion by the state. Municipalities could ill afford to provide these amenities, even assuming the goodwill of its white rate-payers, without massive subsidies by the state. The state, in turn, could not provide these subsidies without taxing either industry, white rate-payers, or both. Given the alignment of class interests within the United party and the nature of the electorate, it is hardly surprising that the state chose to do neither.

With the election of the Nationalist party in 1948, the state would take more direct action to solve the social and economic crisis that had stimulated the reformist activities of the 1940s. In doing so, however, the Nationalist government followed a very different blueprint for reform, one directly opposed to accommodating African urban settlement and which resurrected the wall-building efforts of an earlier generation of medical and civic leaders.

CHAPTER IX

Tuberculosis and Apartheid: The Great Disappearing Act, 1948–1980

The victory of the Nationalist party in 1948 brought to power a government whose political agenda was markedly different from that of its predecessor. The Nationalists represented a constellation of interest groups who were diametrically opposed to the pattern of social and economic development that had shaped South African society over the previous twenty years. They rejected out of hand the view of the Fagan and Smit Commissions that the development of a permanent urbanized African population was both inevitable and essential for the economic development of the country. In its place they reasserted the Stallardist doctrine that the African's natural place was in the reserves and that African workers were only temporary sojourners whose presence in the urban areas was dictated by the needs of the white populace. If the 1940s had broken down the social barriers established during the previous three decades to segregate Africans from the industrial centers of the country, the 1950s, 1960s, and 1970s were marked by renewed efforts to rebuild these walls on an unprecedented scale.

The Nationalist era has been marked by dramatic changes in the epidemiology of tuberculosis in South Africa. Beginning in 1952, urban mortality rates for all races began to fall sharply. This decline was brought about by the introduction of effective antitubercular drugs, the most important of which was isoniazid (INH). These drugs saved the lives of thousands of TB cases who might otherwise have died. At the same time, however, the incidence of African cases, as measured by

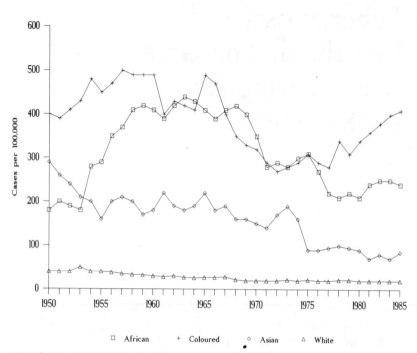

Graph 20.   TB Notification Rates, RSA, 1950–1985

Source: SAMJ (March 21, 1979): 463; and H. G. V. Kustner, "Tuberculosis Notifications: An Update," *South African Journal of Science* 82 (July 1986): 386.

official notifications, increased with equal force—from 200 per 100,000 in 1952 to nearly 450 per 100,000—by the mid-1960s. This was followed by a sharp drop in TB notifications during the late 1960s, declining to just under 300 per 100,000 in 1970. The incidence increased somewhat again in the early 1970s before continuing its downward trend until 1980, when it began to move upward again.

Notification rates are difficult to interpret for a variety of reasons. They are particularly sensitive to changes in case-finding methods and may have only a limited relationship to the actual incidence of the disease in a particular population. Health officials in South Africa, in fact, have attributed the sharp rise in TB notifications during the 1950s and early 1960s to increased case-finding efforts. As the current head of SANTA (South African National Tuberculosis Association) notes in an article on the history of TB in southern Africa,

> Looking back at the TB control programme of this country, it seems that this sharp increase in notifications which eventually reached a peak of nearly 400/100,000 in the late 1950s and early sixties is possibly due in part to the

fact that under the able guidance of the late Dr. B. A. Dormer and Dr. F. J. Wiles a number of 70 mm mobile x-ray units commenced operating in 1947. They roamed far and wide throughout South Africa and SWA, and many thousands of subjects were screened annually until mass x-ray surveys fell into disfavour some 10 years later. Inevitably, many new cases were diagnosed during these surveys.[1]

In addition, the mining industry greatly expanded the use of x-ray examinations as part of its preemployment, periodic, and termination physicals for African mineworkers during the late 1950s and early 1960s. Following the introduction of effective chemotherapy in the early 1950s, notifications may also have been increased by the growing confidence of Africans in the ability of western medical treatment to cure TB and thus their willingness to come forward for treatment.

Although white medical authorities in South Africa were generally skeptical about the relationship between the rise in notifications and actual increases in the incidence of TB during the 1950s and 1960s, they were quite willing to accept that the general decline in TB notifications after 1965 reflected the relative success of their TB control programs combined with improved living conditions. Some, moreover, have argued that other indicators, particularly the "risk of infection" rate that appears to have decreased significantly since 1950, reinforce the conclusion that the actual incidence of TB has declined.[2]

A closer look at the history of TB control efforts and of the changing political economy of South Africa under the Nationalist government, however, causes one to question the accuracy of both official interpretations—skepticism toward the rise in TB notifications during the 1950s and 1960s versus faith in such statistics later when the data supported more optimistic conclusions. The present chapter suggests that the earlier rise in TB notifications, although clearly influenced by increased case-finding efforts, also reflected a real increase in TB incidence. Conversely, the decline in TB notifications after 1965 may have been more apparent than real.

We will argue first in this chapter, that the social and economic conditions under which Africans lived in the urban areas of South Africa improved little during the 1950s and 1960s and in fact deteriorated significantly after 1965, when official TB notifications began to decline. Rural conditions, moreover, took a sharp downturn after 1955. There was therefore little or no amelioration of the underlying causes of tuberculosis among Africans over the whole period from 1948 to 1985. If anything the situation grew more grim. This record suggests that underlying patterns of social and economic development in South Africa may have contributed to a real rise in TB incidence between 1950 and 1960. The record also challenges the assumption that the fall in TB notifications after 1965 was due to improved African living conditions. Second, we will argue that efforts to control TB through the use of chemotherapy and BCG vaccinations have been only marginally successful in curing active cases and preventing the further spread of the disease. In fact, TB control efforts may have contributed to a real rise in the incidence of TB during the 1950s and early 1960s. Thus, neither efforts at environmental reform or at curing the sick is likely to have had a positive impact on the incidence of the disease.

Finally, we argue in this chapter that the apparent decline in TB incidence since 1965 has been largely an optical illusion, part of what has been referred to as South Africa's "great disappearing act": the mass removal of millions of urban and rural Africans to the already over-crowded reserves, alternatively labeled "bantustans," "homelands," and "national states." The incidence of the disease has in effect not so much been diminished as been displaced, moved from the urban and industrial centers of the country to the rural dumping grounds to which the Nationalists have relegated an ever-growing portion of the country's impoverished African population. The Nationalists have thus continued a long tradition of dealing with TB through the application of exclusionary social controls, only they have done so on a much grander and more tragic scale.

PUBLIC HEALTH VERSUS
SOCIAL ENGINEERING

The Nationalist victory did not lead to a sudden turnaround in the ideas of white medical authorities about the causes and prevention of TB among Africans. The need for environmental reform so strongly pushed by men like Dormer and Gale during the 1940s continued to be recognized. Yet, the availability of an effective form of chemotherapy combined with both the economic and political costs of environmental reform efforts, and the Nationalists' commitment to reversing the process of African urbanization rather than adapting conditions to accommodate it, encouraged state and local medical authorities to emphasize curative measures in their campaign against TB. The view of most medical officers during the 1950s and 1960s was reflected in the following remarks by the Cape Divisional Council MOH to a TB conference in 1957.

In any general plan for combating tuberculosis two factors are always prominent, namely (1) housing and overcrowding and (2) undernourishment. But
whilst these factors are very important and not to be overlooked, they must
be regarded as belonging to a long-term policy, over which we have limited
control and which must not be considered in any *short-term campaign*.[3]

Despite this downplaying of environmental concerns, the Nationalist government recognized the need to resolve the massive housing
crisis that existed in the urban areas. They in fact accomplished a good
deal more in this area than the United party had, despite its rhetoric.
The actions taken by the Nationalists, however, were carried out
within the context of their wider plan for separate development and
represented a return to the exclusionary social policies of the 1920s
and 1930s. Housing policies were designed to transfer Africans into
peripheral housing estates and hostels located at first on the borders of
white cities and towns and then, from the mid-1960s, within neighboring "bantustans" outside the borders of "white" South Africa. As
before, this form of social engineering did little to resolve the problems
of African housing or eliminate the overcrowding that underlay the
country's TB epidemic. Although short-term gains were achieved in
housing Africans, in the long run, the Nationalists' housing policies
simply shifted the housing problem beyond the eyes of white voters
and, more importantly, in terms of disease notifications, outside the
purview of health statisticians.

The Nationalist initiatives in housing during the early 1950s reflected
their realization that apartheid could not be established overnight. The
country's economy depended on the continued growth of manufacturing, which in turn required an adequate supply of African labor.
Though they might talk about turning back the clock on African urbanization, they realized that for the foreseeable future a substantial number of African workers would remain on a more or less permanent basis
within the urban centers of the country. Yet they were also conscious of
the political dangers involved in maintaining the status quo. Their white
working-class and farming constituents were vociferous in calling for
more stringent controls over the flow of Africans into the urban areas,
the elimination of inroads Africans had made during the war into formerly white-only occupations, and the redirection of African labor back
toward white farming areas. At the same time, the slumlike conditions
under which the majority of Africans were living was seen as both a
threat to the health of the white community and as a breeding ground
for African political radicalism.

The Nationalists responded to these various concerns by tightening up influx controls and trying to solve the country's housing crisis in a manner that preserved, or reestablished, the dominance of white interests within the urban areas and insured the removal of unemployed "superfluous" Africans. As the secretary of native affairs, W. H. M. Eiselen, observed in 1951, "Only by the provision of adequate shelter in properly planned Native townships can full control over urban Natives be regained, because only then will it be possible to eliminate the surplus Natives who do not seek or find an honest living in the cities."[4] In both of these areas they made progress during the early 1950s; however, neither the control of African urban settlement nor the elimination of the housing problem was fully accomplished.

Some immediate gains were made in influx control through the tightening up of existing administration. The Johannesburg municipality for instance refused entry to 14,587 Africans between July 1, 1948, and June 30, 1949, and "endorsed out" (removed) a further 10,439 who were unable to find work. Over the next three years a series of Native Laws Amendment Acts were passed establishing labor bureaus to direct and control the flow of labor into "prescribed areas" and to generally limit the ability of Africans to move freely to and within urban areas. The 1952 act required the registration of incoming jobseekers with the labor bureaus and instituted the "72-hour" law reducing the time an unemployed worker could seek employment on his own from fourteen days to seventy-two hours. Control of population movements was further enhanced by the replacement of passes with a more uniform system of reference books for everyone over age sixteen, including women. The passes had to be endorsed by the labor bureau and contained information about the holder's current employment.[5]

Despite these efforts, Africans continued to enter the cities illegally. The total African population of Johannesburg rose from an estimated 455,000 in June 1948 to 516,600 in June 1953. Though some of this rise was caused by the postwar expansion of the mining industry,[6] the nonmine population probably increased by roughly 50,000. It must be remembered that this increase occurred during a period of economic recession within the manufacturing sector of the economy, so most of these entrants joined the city's growing ranks of unemployed or partially employed workers. Overall the period between 1950 and 1960 saw a net increase of some 307,000 Africans in metropolitan areas, and 49,000 into towns.[7]

This continued influx contributed to the existing housing crisis and hampered Nationalist attempts to solve it. Despite concerted efforts to increase the supply of urban housing, the shortfall in supply mounted steadily through the mid-1950s.[8] The Nationalists nonetheless were able to provide the groundwork for future efforts during this period.

Underlying the Nationalists' plans for rehousing Africans was the principal of segregation. Although the various Urban Areas and Slum Clearance Acts had provided a legal basis for creating segregated housing, they did not go far enough nor provide the state with sufficiently broad authority to remove Africans and other "non-whites" from areas that were predominantly white or that the government chose to make white. It was in this context that the government pushed through the Group Areas Act in 1950. Under this act, urban areas were required to be segregated and any "non-white" living in an area proscribed as white would have to move to the areas designated for their race. This act was followed by the Illegal Squatters Act in 1951, which allowed the state to "endorse out" of an urban area any person living in an illegal squatters camp. The new laws did not, however, relieve municipal authorities of the obligation to provide alternative housing for displaced residents. Implementation of the acts therefore required a massive increase in the construction of black housing.[9]

To achieve this goal the Nationalist government took steps to facilitate the construction of new housing. First they succeeded in coercing industry into accepting some responsibility for providing housing for their workers. The passage of the Native Services Levy Act in 1953 made it mandatory for employers in eighteen major urban centers to contribute on a per-worker basis to a Service Levy Account that would be used for providing water, sanitation, lighting, and road services both inside and outside native locations, villages, or hostels. It was estimated that the annual levy would be about £1,750,000, of which employers would contribute about £450,000.[10]

The Nationalists also were able to pass the Native Building Workers Act in 1951. The act provided for the training of African labor to be used in the construction of African housing and thus partially removed the color bar that had kept the cost of housing artificially high. Although critics of the bill perceived that it clearly delineated the spheres within which Africans could be trained and employed as building workers, and thus further defined the job color bar in construction, it did pave the way for substantial savings to be made in the construction of African housing.[11]

Finally, the Nationalists instituted the "site and service" plan. Site

and service involved the supplying of a building site within an established location or "native village" which could be rented for a monthly
fee. The sites would be provided with services by the local authority
from funds supplied by the Native Services Levy Act. Renters were
obliged to construct a dwelling on the site with their own resources,
though some loans were available. The "site and service" plan was the
brainchild of the Native Affairs Department, which took an increasing
role in the provision of African housing. It was seen as a way of increasing more rapidly the pool of available housing and thus of speeding the
elimination of slum areas. Site and service projects, in principle, were an
emergency measure designed to supplement the slower and more expensive process of providing African housing.[12]

The "site and service" approach, however, clearly became a replacement for low-cost housing during the 1950s and early 1960s. Figures
for houses built and revenue spent on "economic" (market-rate) and
"subeconomic" (subsidized) housing after 1948 show that while economic housing increased dramatically from 1952–1953, subeconomic
housing decreased sharply. In short the state's commitment to providing
housing was directed primarily at market-rate housing, out of reach of
the majority of African workers. Site and service was thus a means of
cutting the losses incurred by local authorities and the state in constructing subsidized housing by placing the cost of housing squarely on the
shoulders of the average African worker and his family.

TABLE 14

PROVISION OF AFRICAN HOUSING BY LOCAL
AUTHORITIES, 1948–1957[13]

| Year | Funds (in pounds) | | No. of Houses | |
	Economic	Subeconomic	Economic	Subeconomic
1948–1949	72,934	1,765,486	1	3,310
1949–1950	103,541	1,158,174	348	7,407
1950–1951	741,867	2,161,728	1,019	3,383
1951–1952	313,446	1,449,147	958	3,395
1952–1953	789,324	1,841,343	1,770	6,592
1953–1954	1,683,907	1,886,465	3,360	5,667
1954–1955	2,446,064	669,465	8,252	3,446
1955–1956	4,301,748	209,982	12,977	1,735
1956–1957	2,847,287	26,789	15,364	555 (10 months)

The government's desire to shift the focus of housing development toward site and service projects was also revealed by its dealings with individual municipalities. Port Elizabeth, for example, was one of the first communities to take advantage of the Native Building Workers Act and employ teams of African workers in the construction of African housing. By 1954, 7,500 new houses had been constructed in New Brighton at relatively low cost through this means. The minister of native affairs, however, refused to provide additional subeconomic loans to the municipal council, insisting that they should instead implement site and service plans.[14]

The government in 1958 suspended further provision of subeconomic loans for African housing. The government argued that reductions in the cost of construction had reduced the cost of market-rate housing to a level the majority of African workers could afford and that there was consequently much less need for subsidized rents. That this was simply untrue was made abundantly clear by the growing list of households in arrears with their rent during the late 1950s and 1960s. In Pretoria 10,000 renters were in arrears by 1957, while 70 percent of the renters in Port Elizabeth were judged to be similarly delinquent that same year. Fifteen thousand renters in Soweto were in arrears by the end of 1961.[15] Those unable to pay their rent were prosecuted and fined unless they could prove real hardship. Many of those fined could not afford to pay both the fine and their rent and so chose to spend thirty days in jail in lieu of the fine. This option, however, often meant that they lost their jobs.

Although the government continued to rent existing subeconomic housing at below-market rates, eligibility requirements prevented Africans earning more than R30 a month from gaining access to this low-cost housing. The R30 requirement remained fixed from 1954 to 1968. Yet during this period the average worker's wage grew significantly. This meant that a decreasing percentage of African workers were eligible for low-cost housing. It did not mean, however, that the percentage of African workers needing low-cost housing also decreased. In fact the reverse was true. For, as will be discussed below, the rise in wages was less than the rise in the cost of living during this period.[16]

Through the use of site and service projects, the government by 1960 succeeded in removing Africans from many of the urban slum areas that had arisen during the war. In Johannesburg, the last of the squatter camps had been cleared and efforts were underway to house Africans living in other areas that had been proclaimed "white areas." In addition, of course, African freehold areas such as the Western Townships—

Sophiatown, Martindale, and Newclare—and parts of Alexandra were transformed into whites-only suburbs and the African inhabitants removed to the peripheral African housing estates. By 1960, 33,000 of 35,000 site and service properties had been occupied and the South African Institute for Race Relations (SAIRR) estimated that the shortfall in housing was only 1,600 houses, down from 20,000 in 1957. In Durban some 80,000 Africans were removed from Indian-owned tenements in the city center in 1961.[17]

Yet, the site and service plan did not solve the African housing problem. It led in many cases to the construction of housing that was substandard from a health viewpoint. This was because potential homeowners, even with the use of African labor, could not afford to construct adequate shelters. In addition, as was the case at the turn of the century when a similar approach was used in the construction of the first "native locations," insecurity of tenure and lack of property ownership, limited to a thirty-year leasehold, deterred people from making large investments in housing. The services provided for these schemes were also inadequate to the needs of the population living within them. In order to expedite the development of site and service and avoid the delay involved in providing waterborne sewage systems, the Department of Native Affairs opted for the provision of bucket sewage disposal systems, seen as a temporary expedient but known to be detrimental to health.[18] The City Council of Johannesburg objected to this decision but capitulated under the threat of losing access to government housing funds.[19] The lack of sanitation accounts in part for increases in gastroenteritis and typhoid reported in these areas.[20]

The government recognized that site and service housing was substandard but saw it as a temporary measure. These houses, it was argued, would eventually be replaced by ones constructed from regular housing budgets. This, however, turned out to be wishful thinking, as shown by the continued existence today of houses originally built during the 1950s. Moreover, little control was exercised over the numbers of Africans living in site and service houses, with subletting and overcrowding common. A 1957 article in *Drum* reported that certain site and service developments were little better than some of the squalid camps from which the people had been removed.[21]

In East London, for example, municipal authorities exercised little control over the number of people living in privately constructed housing. By 1955 privately owned houses in the East and West locations outside the city had an average of nearly twenty persons per house.

Continued pressure for housing despite influx control allowed the owners of private location housing to make profits by subletting rooms. As a
result of this profit incentive, private landlords tended to build on more
and more rooms, either as lean-tos or separately. Usually the additions
were progressively worse built and worse cared for. Some of the add-on
rooms were "no more than dark, crazy, leaking little sheds." Sanitation
facilities remained inadequate, and early-morning lines of people waiting to relieve themselves were a daily sight in the location. Some residents preferred the simpler method of "thowing their slops out of the
house."[22]

In the face of the rapidly deteriorating conditions within the site and
service areas, a number of municipalities began constructing "half-
houses" consisting of two rooms—a living room and a kitchen—on sites
originally designed for four rooms. The plan was introduced to "prevent the site and service schemes from degenerating into a slum shanty."
Occupants were permitted to construct temporary shacks on the back of
these half-houses, but the houses were to be brought up to standard by
the owner or the local authorities within five years.[23] In many cases this
restriction was ignored and the irregular construction remained for
years.

Poor services, lack of security, and the cost of building in the site and
service projects made them unpopular among Africans and many such
sites went undeveloped until the late 1950s. At that time a slowdown in
the construction of subeconomic housing together with an acceleration
of forced removals from "white" areas increased the demand for site
and service housing. Local authorities nonetheless were forced to renew
the construction of low-cost African housing in the early 1960s to prevent the growth of new slum areas in the site and service zones.

In addition to the poor conditions that developed in many site and
service areas, there remained large congeries of ill-housed Africans
within many municipalities. In Cape Town, where municipal officials
refused to cooperate with the Nationalists in implementing the Group
Areas Act, removals from congested areas such as Windermere and
Retreat were delayed and work on new housing at Nyanga did not
begin until 1959. Similarly, in Durban there remained some 55,000
Africans living in squalid conditions in the emergency camp of Cato
Manor, and it was estimated that the city needed another 15,000 houses
and 20,000 hostel beds to meet its current housing needs.[24]

Everywhere the situation grew worse during the 1960s. The so-
called apartheid boom created by a massive influx of foreign capital

and the growth of manufacturing, generated a rapidly expanding demand for African labor. At the same time deteriorating conditions in the reserves (see below) continued to produce a flood of jobseekers and families who were no longer able to survive in the countryside. The demand for African housing as a result accelerated. The list of families awaiting housing in Johannesburg grew to 18,000 in 1961 and continued to range between 13,000 and 17,000 over the next decade. A report by the city engineer and manager of non-European affairs in Johannesburg predicted in 1967 that a new African city, more than a quarter of the size of Soweto, which then contained over 500,000 official residents, would have to be built to accommodate the increase in African population between 1967 and 1980. This proved to be a major underestimate.[25]

The situation was even grimmer in the Durban area. Despite the settlement of some 90,000 Africans in the newly constructed township of KwaMashu, the Department of Bantu Affairs estimated in 1965 that there were 38,000 squatters in the Port Natal area and stated that if they were evicted they would simply move to other shack settlements. The shortfall in housing was estimated to be 10,000. By 1968 the estimated number of squatters in the Port Natal area had risen to 150,000.[26]

In Cape Town despite a decrease in the number of contract workers, the African population continued to grow. By 1967 the housing shortage was so severe that the City Council began permitting employers to house their workers in temporary prefabricated barracks within the African locations. Thirteen of these were built in Langa. Each consisted of one large room without partitions measuring seventy feet by thirty feet and housed forty men. They had no cement floors, no ceilings or cupboards for clothes or the storage of food, and lacked adequate ablution facilities. Yet even this did not absorb the growing army of illegal entrants who continued to squat on the Cape flats.[27]

In Port Elizabeth, the Ford Motor Company provided temporary housing for some of its employees in dwellings fashioned out of packing crates in the mid-1950s. These were intended to have a maximum life of five years. Yet thirty years later they were still standing in a part of New Brighton that was called KwaFord. The municipal council announced plans to deal with the acute overcrowding that existed in the "Red Location" area of New Brighton in 1966. Yet action on the project was delayed by discussions of where to get the money, what form the new housing should take, and what to do with the people in the meantime. Eighteen years later the council was still debating these questions.[28]

The housing crisis deepened during the mid-1960s following the announcement of the Nationalists' intention to halt the development of African urban townships in favor of housing Africans in so-called homeland townships located in neighboring bantustans. The effects of this shift in policy, designed to move the African housing problem beyond the "borders" of South Africa, are evident in the number of houses built for Africans in Johannesburg from the late 1950s onward. The construction of new housing peaked in 1957 at 15,000 new units. By 1961–1962 the number was reduced to 3,336 units, and from 1963 to 1970 the average number of houses built annually was 1,231.[29] In East London, all new construction of housing in the municipal townships was halted in 1965 in the face of the government's plan to develop a "homeland township" at Mdantsane, located eleven miles outside the city in the Ciskei. By March of 1965, 1,200 families had been moved to the new location.

In 1968 the government ceased funding the construction of African family housing within the municipal townships and began directing all housing funds toward the construction of "homeland townships" or barracks-like unisex hostels. At the same time, the government began moving African families from the municipal townships to the newly constructed homeland townships. Although implementation of this policy was delayed due to the resistance of local authorities, "homeland townships" with names like Garankuwa, Mdantsane, Kabokweni, and Mphophomeni received an estimated 670,000 Africans removed from municipal areas between 1968 and 1980.[30] The movement did not go smoothly as removals outpaced the creation of housing and conditions in some of the new townships were marked by extensive overcrowding. The government's drive to clear out East London, for example, combined with the removal of Africans from the western Cape led to massive overcrowding in Mdantsane. Already 40,000 people by 1967 had been officially settled in the new township with an average of 6 persons occupying each dwelling. Yet estimates of the de facto population ranged from 80,000 to 100,000 people, giving an average occupancy ratio of 12 or more per dwelling.[31]

Conditions in the municipal locations also grew worse following the government's decision to cease the funding of African housing in them. Delays in the creation of alternative housing in the homeland townships often created a lag between the decision to move people out of the municipal townships and the ability to do so. During this period the municipal populations expanded, and yet no new housing was being provided for them. The situation in Soweto was particularly acute during this period. The government rejected a move to make the township a homeland on the grounds that it would not accept the permanent presence of so large an African community in close proximity to Johannesburg. Since this prevented the allocation of building funds, it led to a near stoppage of construction. By 1970 there were an estimated 67,000 people waiting for housing who had to crowd in with other families.[32] The situation grew intolerable by mid-decade and was an important contributing factor in the urban revolt of 1976. Construction in Kwa-Mashu, outside Durban, similarly came to a standstill following the government's decision to cease the construction of municipal housing and the development of Umlazi Village located on Native Trust Lands.[33]

Although municipal authorities were concerned about the conditions that existed in the newly developed African townships, their concern was subordinated to the overriding goal of cleaning out Africans from white areas and establishing a pattern of rigid segregated housing. The various housing and slum acts of the 1960s and 1970s, like those of the 1930s, continued to exempt African townships from the purview of the law, permitting municipal authorities to turn a blind eye to conditions that could not have been tolerated if the law had been applied with equal force in all urban areas.[34]

The urban revolt of 1976 and 1977 forced both the state and capital to reexamine the whole question of African urban settlement as well as the underlying principle that African workers and their families were merely temporary sojourners in the white urban areas. This led to the reform policies of the late 1970s and early 1980s, embedded in the Reikert and Weihahn Commissions and in the work of the Urban Foundation. These policies were designed to accommodate the development of a stable African working class, a privileged population of "insiders" within the urban areas of the country. This development was viewed as an essential step in the government's efforts to revitalize the country's economy. Throughout much of the 1970s it had been mired in a recession caused not only by fluctuations in the wider world economy but also by the limited size of South Africa's domestic market and the inefficiency of industrial production. Both these factors were products of industry's dependence on unskilled low-wage black labor. The development of a more stable and skilled African workforce was seen as a means of eliminating these handicaps.

Central to the reform efforts was the rethinking of the housing question. As Peter Wilkinson has shown, the central principle of the new housing policy that emerged in the early 1980s was the withdrawal of the state from the role as primary provider of African housing and the development of a free market for African housing based on private sector involvement in its financing and construction. In effect, only Africans who could afford to buy housing at market rates would be able to obtain housing. This reversion to a modern form of a site and service plan was stimulated by two concerns. One was the enormous cost involved in providing for the housing needs of urban Africans, estimated in 1982 to be R1,700 million. The second was a desire to use the ability to acquire "an approved accommodation" as a method for controlling the growth of the African urban population. Put simply, those who could not afford to buy houses would be ineligible for permanent residence rights. Supply and demand rather than overt political action would separate the haves from the have nots.[35]

To encourage African participation in the new site and service plan the Nationalists increased leasehold rights to ninety-nine years. They also acquired the assistance of the building industry and building societies to provide the financial and institutional structures needed for implementing the new free-market housing policy. Despite these efforts, the self-help strategy of the 1980s was no more popular with urban African residents than the site and service schemes of the 1950s and 1960s. By March of 1982 only 1,721 leases had been registered under the plan. A major reason for this was the cost involved in building a house as compared to renting from one of the Administration Boards. As the Viljoen Report concluded, the relative cheapness of existing Administrative Board housing was "counter-productive to homeownership and leasehold and the system cries out for review." The free market would, in short, not operate as long as there were cheaper alternatives. To remedy this situation, the state decided to sell off its housing stock. This "sale of the century" begun in July 1983 was designed to foster private ownership by providing houses for a bargain price and by eliminating the alternative of renting. The bargain price, however, was still too expensive for most African renters and, by the end of 1983, only 1,400 of the 238,000 houses put up for sale had been purchased. In reaction to this slow response the state increased the rents of residents living in the for-sale properties in an effort to pressure them to convert their rent to purchase. This effort was a significant contributing factor to the urban protests of 1985–1986.[36]

The urban reform strategy of the 1970s, in short, did nothing to resolve the urban housing crisis. To the contrary it led to a virtual cessation of housing construction. Meanwhile the flood of African men and women seeking employment in the urban areas continued to grow. Transformations in the nature of industrial production involving increased technological capacities, however, reduced employment opportunities for Africans and greatly increased black unemployment. African townships as a result became home to a growing army of unemployed. Unable to buy or rent housing at market prices, the urban poor engaged in a range of housing strategies, including subletting and living in makeshift accommodations such as sheds and kitchens, all of which contributed to overcrowding. In Soweto, the housing shortage in 1984 was as bad as it had been in the early 1950s, with 25,000 families on the housing waiting list. David Webster in 1982 noted that,

> Many families live in overcrowded conditions, with houses designed to contain nuclear families often sheltering two or three. There has been a mushrooming of illegal and unofficial houses, in the form of backyard shacks, in which about 23,000 families are estimated to be living; some of the destitute are even reduced to living in car hulks in a scrapyard.[37]

The locations in Port Elizabeth became massively overcrowded in a similar manner. By 1984 it was estimated that 120,000 people needed housing; yet there was a shortfall of 20,000 houses. Some decrease did occur in the number of people living in squatter shacks following the passage of the 1976 Prevention of Squatting Act. The housing situation, however, remained a crisis.[38] The occupancy rates for the major black locations in Port Elizabeth in 1983 as shown in table 15.

TABLE 15

OVERCROWDING IN THE BLACK LOCATIONS OF PORT
ELIZABETH, 1983[39]

Location	Number of Housing Units	Est. Population	Persons per House
New Brighton	8,041	67,634	8.4
Kwazakele	11,652	100,028	8.6
Zwide	7,063	79,800	11.3
Soweto Veeplaas	8,471	90,000	10.6
Walmer	377	2,955	7.8

A sampling in Port Elizabeth of 2 percent of households found that 40 percent of families shared accommodations with another family and that in over 10 percent more than three families shared the house.[40] The shortage of location housing in Port Elizabeth as elsewhere led to the growth of "crossroads-style" squatter camps. One such camp was called Soweto Veeplaas. It was started in 1975 by people escaping the overcrowded conditions in the old townships. Some of the early settlers hoped to be rehoused more rapidly as squatters than lodgers. By 1984, population estimates ranged from 80,000 to 120,000. The area was not only excessively overcrowded but also lacked sanitation facilities.

> Until recently there were only 36 stand-pipes for the entire area; there are now 145, equivalent to approximately 60 shacks or 600 people per tap. Originally sewerage was disposed of by pit latrines, but because of the clay soil they tended to collapse and overflow in wet weather. A bucket system is now provided but, according to residents, they still need pit latrines because the collection is inadequate, frequently resulting in "overflow and random dumping of sewerage."[41]

Although the average income of the occupants of Soweto Veeplaas was the lowest of all the black locations, it also contained some of the highest paid workers, people who had jobs at Ford and General Motors but who could not find housing.

To conclude, the housing policy enacted by the Nationalists achieved part of their political goals. It did lead to the removal of African housing from white urban areas. It did not, however, defuse the potential for political unrest, as visibly shown by the uprisings of the mid-1970s and 1980s. Nor did it do much to improve the health conditions under which Africans lived in the urban areas of South Africa. From a tuberculosis viewpoint, African urban housing continued to provide a fertile breeding ground for the spread of infection. The residents of the new townships located miles from places of employment were forced, moreover, to travel long distances on public transport, which was always overcrowded and exposed the commuting workers to the risk of airborne infection.[42] Finally, increased transportation and housing costs, which reduced family budgets and contributed to malnutrition, together with longer workdays imposed on commuters who had to leave home at 3 or 4 A.M. to reach their place of employment by 8:30, reduced the ability of infected workers to resist their infections.[43] Thus it seems highly unlikely that the Nationalists' housing efforts could have contributed to a declining incidence of TB among urban residents after 1965. To the contrary, they seem ideally suited to foster the spread of the disease. What it achieved was a progressive relocation of this problem outside the official municipal areas of the country.

FOOD PROGRAMS AND THE
REPRODUCTION OF MALNUTRITION

The 1950s and 1960s saw numerous attempts to improve the nutritional status of Africans. Although the Nationalists eliminated government food programs developed by the Smuts government during the war, a wide range of local food programs, supported by government food subsidies, were introduced or extended during the Nationalist period. Yet these programs, like efforts at housing, need to be viewed against the background of the Nationalists' commitment to a vision of the African worker as a member of a functioning rural-based society that supported the worker's family. This anachronistic view legitimated the continued payment of subsubsistence wages to the mass of African workers. Although wages increased during the 1960s and then again in the 1970s, particularly in manufacturing, so did the cost of living, leaving most African workers little better off. Low wages undermined all efforts to improve African nutrition. The minister of health claimed that African malnutrition was a product of their ignorance of proper eating habits,[44] but the simple truth in the vast majority of malnutrition cases was that the families involved could not afford to purchase an adequate diet. A survey conducted in Nqutu in Kwazulu found that 62 percent of the mothers of malnourished children knew what was necessary for a balanced diet for their children but could not afford it.[45] Rather than attack the problem at its roots, which would have been both politically and economically unacceptable, government and voluntary agencies attempted to ameliorate the situation through food and subsidy programs that did little more than keep the chronically malnourished from starving.

Individual local authorities initiated school food programs to supplement the diets of African schoolchildren. For example in 1955–1956 the Johannesburg African Children's Feeding Scheme provided food for 12,000 schoolchildren. By 1962 the Johannesburg City Council was spending R60,000 a year on providing free powdered milk to African children. In addition, distribution centers were established in certain locations to provide reduced-price food for children. The number of milk distribution depots in African townships increased and a number of voluntary agencies became involved in additional child feeding programs. The privately funded Operation Hunger played a similar role in staving off starvation in the rural areas of the country.

For its part, the state initiated a program for subsidizing the costs incurred by local authorities in the distribution of free milk. Despite the potential health benefits of this program, many local authorities declined to incur the additional charge to their budgets and, by the late 1960s, only a quarter of the eligible local authorities were participating in the program. The government also increased its subsidies for other basic foods, including butter, wheat, maize, and bread, but not including high-quality protective foods such as meat and fresh fruits and vegetables. Some of these increases were motivated less by a concern for nutrition than by the state's inability to market the large food surpluses generated by their farm subsidy programs. In 1961, for example, the government increased the subsidy on cheese by 5 cents a pound and butter by 1¼ cents a pound in order "to bring them in reach of more people." The action, however, followed the partial closure of British markets to South African exports of butter and cheese and the creation of a massive surplus of these products. Surplus stores of butter rose from 28,000 tons at the end of 1960 to 40,000 tons at the end of 1961.[46]

Although food programs may have saved a number of lives, they failed to address the root causes of African malnutrition, the continued exploitation of African labor. Throughout the period, African wages lagged behind the cost of living. In 1954 the minimum cost of living for an average African family of five in Johannesburg was estimated to be £23 10s 4d per month. This represented a 32 percent increase over the same figure for 1950. The average family income in 1954 was £15 18s 4d per month, an increase of only 24 percent since 1950. The average deficit in 1954 was £7 11s 5d. It was estimated that 69 percent of African families earned less than the minimum cost of living, often referred to as the poverty datum line (PDL). In terms of nutrition, the cost of an adequate diet for the average African family in Johannesburg, calculated on the basis of the minimum diet required for maintaining good health, was £14 18s 4d per month or the equivalent of 94 percent of the average monthly income in 1954![47] Clearly many families were eating less than adequate diets.

Despite wage increases the situation grew no better during the 1960s. Although wages rose by 14 percent between 1962 and 1967, the number of families living below the PDL remained nearly the same as in 1952, 68 percent. It was estimated by 1971 that between 68 and 71 percent of Soweto households earned less than R60 per month, while the PDL was calculated to be R67. The situation in other major urban areas was essentially the same.[48]

Part of the reason why wages failed to keep up with the cost of living was, as noted above, that the relocation of Africans to "townships" contributed in many cases to increased housing and transportation costs while at the same time it reduced opportunities of informal employment. As the SAIRR noted in 1962, "The majority of urban Africans cannot afford to pay the rents and the necessary transport costs unless they spend much less on food than the minimum now considered to be necessary for health."[49]

If low wages were a primary cause of malnutrition among urban Africans, restrictions on trader's licenses for Africans in white areas were an additional factor. Such restrictions made it more difficult for African workers to obtain adequate food during the work day. Of particular note in this respect was the City of Johannesburg's attack on the African "coffee cart" trade.

> A few years ago there were some 1500 African owned coffee carts operating in the industrial and commercial areas of Johannesburg. They provided a well-nigh essential service in selling hot drinks and food to African workers who had left home without any breakfast and travelled long distances to work, and also served snacks at lunch time.[50]

The municipal authorities objected to these carts on the basis that many of them were unhygienic and, during 1961, they removed 900 of them. In their place they encouraged employers to establish canteens and planned to erect well-constructed refreshment kiosks with proper facilities to replace the coffee carts. This plan was vetoed, however, by the minister of Bantu administration and development on the grounds that Africans should not be allowed to trade outside their own areas.

Against this background of growing poverty and controls, a few food programs and subsidies made very little difference. In 1962, when kwashiorkor became a notifiable disease in South Africa, the minister of health acknowledged that in the vicinity of Cape Town there were no less than 22,000 children suffering from the disease. In the following year, the MOH of the Cape Divisional Council estimated that the true incidence of kwashiorkor for African children was 10 per 1,000 and that for every child suffering from the disease there were 30 to 40 with more or less severe protein deficiency. In Soweto, where 100 African children died every year of kwashiorkor, 900 malnourished children were admitted and another 2,000 were treated as outpatients at the Baragwanath Hospital.[51] In 1964 there were 66,701 officially reported cases of kwashiorkor in all of South Africa. The notification rate among white children was 0 per 100,000 while that among Africans was 112 per 100,000.[52] In 1968 the ministry of health removed kwashiorkor from the list of notifiable diseases because "notification was far too time-consuming, the figures were too inaccurate and a general idea of the prevalence of kwashiorkor had been gained." The last point was certainly true. But what was not said was that the "general idea" revealed such a disparity in incidence that notifications had become an embarrassment.[53] It should be noted that malnutrition was not limited to children. A survey of unskilled workers in Pretoria in 1962 found 70 to 80 percent suffering from dietary deficiency in one form or another.[54]

The urban reform movement of the late 1970s and early 1980s went some way toward narrowing the gap between wages and cost of living. The needs of manufacturing capital to expand their markets contributed to a movement to increase African wages, bringing for the first time an increase in wages above the PDL for many African workers. By 1981, for example, the average monthly wage in New Brighton's Kwazakele and Zwide locations outside of Port Elizabeth was R226, while the PDL was estimated to be R205.[55] Yet wages were still low. The PDL, it must be remembered, is a measurement of bare subsistence that will not sustain health over a long period. In addition, the benefits of this wage increase were not shared by all workers. Looking again at Port Elizabeth, a quarter of the houses sampled in its three "native" locations had incomes of less that R120. The average income of residents in the Soweto Veeplaas squatter camp, moreover, was only R185.37.[56]

Average wage levels also do not reveal that a large portion of potential workers were unemployed and that the reform measures that raised some wages led to an overall retrenchment in industrial employment. David Webster estimates that in Soweto, with its population conservatively estimated at 1.6 million, there was a shortfall of 400,000 jobs in 1984.[57] In Port Elizabeth, estimates of the unemployment rate in the early 1980s ranged from 25 to 50 percent.[58] In 1977 it was estimated that 22 percent of the African labor force nationwide was unemployed as compared to 18.3 percent in 1960. The University of Pretoria estimates that the ranks of the unemployed have grown by 14,000 every month since then.[59] It is important to note that average unemployment rates disguise considerable geographical and social differentiation. Thus Simkins notes that among the nonmigrant population of the major urban areas, unemployment was 13 percent for men and 22 percent for women in 1981.[60] By contrast, The Surplus People Project estimated that in the relocation townships of the Cape and Natal the unemployment rate was 17 percent for males and 36 percent for women.[61] The Quail Commission, appointed by the Ciskei "government," concluded that one-third of the Ciskei's urban population was unemployed.[62]

Thus despite increases in wages, many urban families still had difficulty making ends meet and malnutrition continued to be a problem during the 1970s and 1980s. Though improvements in nutritional status were reported in Soweto and Cape Town in the late 1970s and early 1980s, pockets of urban malnutrition often associated with unemployment or low wages remained. A nutrition survey in Port Elizabeth, for example, showed that 10.6 percent of school-aged children were below the third percentile by weight-for-age. In the squatter camp, however, where the average wage was below the poverty datum line and unemployment was high, 42.2 percent of the sample fell below the third percentile.[63] In Mdantsane, similarly, which as we have seen began as a so-called homeland township for East London but has become a dumping ground for Africans removed from the Western Cape, three-fourths of the children were undersized for their age in 1980.[64] As we will see later, the association of malnutrition with illegal squatter camps and "homeland townships" is part of a broader pattern of development in South Africa by which the burden of ill-health has been transferred beyond the official jurisdiction of white South Africa.

Aside from generalized malnutrition, specific nutritional deficiencies also occurred with some frequency in the urban areas. A 1977 Durban survey found that the incidence of scurvy among Africans was 3 per 1,000. This suggests a high incidence of subscorbutic conditions, which lower resistance to tuberculosis. There was also an increasing incidence of pellegra among male migrants in the towns, caused by vitamin B deficiency.[65]

Although malnutrition among urban Africans remains largely a product of poverty, it has in recent years been exacerbated by the marketing strategies of the major suppliers of maize meal to urban consumers. Milling companies such as the Premier Group have launched major advertising campaigns to encourage African consumers to purchase superrefined maize meal, which is both more expensive and significantly less nutritious than unrefined maize meal. The milling companies claim African consumers prefer the taste of the superrefined meal, its ease of preparation, and the fact that it lasts longer. Yet despite these claimed natural advantages, the milling companies spend millions of rands to promote superrefined meal, suggesting that comparative advantage alone does not account for African consumption of the product. These advertisements present an image of vitality and strength, using the Kaiser Chiefs soccer team as a symbol for the product.[66] The millers also use more subtle and insidious methods to promote superrefined meal, including the practice of providing superrefined meal in small sacks while limiting the sale of unrefined meal to large 200-kilogram sacks. This practice forces the poor urban African who frequently lacks the money to purchase maize meal in bulk to purchase the superrefined meal.

The reasons for this promotion of superrefined meal clearly lie in the profitability of the product. The profits come not so much from the higher cost of superrefined meal but from the fact that the milling companies are able to maximize their profits by using the germ and bran removed in the refining process to produce animal feeds. Premier Group, for example, controls half of the dry animal-food market. They also own Sunnyside Chickens, which uses the byproducts of maize milling to feed their birds,[67] and Epic Oils, which uses the oil from maize germ. In short, the refining of maize meal for human consumption fuels a wide range of vertically integrated industries at the expense of the African consumer's health.[68]

The variety of food and subsidy programs organized by the state, local authorities, and private voluntary agencies must, in the end, be seen as contributing to the reproduction of malnutrition among Africans. For all their good intentions, and for all the lives they may have saved, food programs such as Operation Hunger have simply kept the problem of malnutrition under control. They have done little to prevent malnutrition from occurring but, instead, have kept it from growing to a point where it would lead to wholesale starvation. Such programs at the same time have provided the impression, both domestically and internationally, that something is being done for the poor. In this sense they have contributed to the maintenance of the status quo. In the end, moreover, the provision of food provides a form of social control and creates dependence on the state and capital. Having eliminated all other forms of entitlements, the poor have been left reliant on the benefice of the very forces that have constructed their poverty.[69] For example Premier Milling, which grossed R947 million in 1980, donated R500,000 to the Urban Foundation and built 228 soup kitchens in Soweto in order to combat the very malnutrition to which its maize-meal production and marketing practices contributed; and a volunteer food van covered with the logos of Cape Town Industries, which barely pays its workers subsistence wages, distributes food to African preschool children in Crossroads. It is ironies such as these which epitomize the fundamental contradiction that has characterized efforts to feed the poor in South Africa since the 1950s.

APARTHEID AND RURAL POVERTY

If conditions in the urban centers of South Africa grew rapidly more distressing for the majority of Africans under Nationalist control between 1950 and 1980, they became disastrous for those confined to the rural reserves/bantustans. The conditions there were already alarming by 1955 when the Tomlinson Commission reported that the reserves were so overcrowded that "300,000 families or more than 1½ million persons, will have to abandon Bantu agriculture, in order to give those who remain, the opportunity of making a living out of the land without resorting to periodic spells of work elsewhere."[70] Soil erosion and declining productivity were reported everywhere, though not all rural families were impoverished and, according to Charles Simkins, total agricultural production remained stable and supplied a constant proportion of subsistence needs up till 1955.[71]

Between 1950 and 1970, however, the population of the homelands increased from approximately 3.4 million to over 7.3 million. Roughly 2 million of this increase represented people forced to move from rural and urban "black spots" in order to establish separate development. This led to a rapid increase in population density. During this period the average population density increased from 60 to 110 persons per square mile. Predictably agricultural production declined dramatically, figures for the late 1960s representing only two-thirds of the 1955 level. Few families were able to subsist on what they produced from farming and the vast majority depended on some form of wage income to meet their subsistence needs. A survey of 757 households conducted in ten locations in the Umtata, Tsolo, and Kentani Districts in 1974 found that 467 households or 61.6 percent were never able to produce enough to subsist or to reproduce themselves and were, in consequence, largely dependent upon wage labor for survival. Thirty percent or 165 households could feed themselves in good years but were basically dependent upon the sale of labor. Household incomes, overall, including earnings from agricultural production, pensions, and wages in the bantustans, were considerably lower than the incomes of urban families and often failed to meet subsistence needs. The above survey found that 50 percent of households had annual per capita incomes of less than R25, while 85 percent had less than R55, which was below the average monthly PDL for urban areas. Out of 3,760 people surveyed, 233 or 6 percent were wholly destitute, that is earned less than R5 per annum. There were only 33 households with incomes above R600. These households were made up primarily of salaried teachers, preachers, and bantustan authorities appointed by the white government.[72]

The population growth produced a growing number of families who could no longer subsist on the land available to them in the reserves. The number of such families was increased further by "betterment schemes" started in the 1940s, but greatly expanded in the 1950s and 1960s, in an effort to fight erosion and increase agricultural production. Although these programs had some success in curtailing environmental damage, they did so in a way that favored "the haves at the expense of the have-nots." Under the betterment schemes, those with enough land qualified for rehabilitation, whereas those without arable allotments were removed to "closer settlements."[73] In these sprawling rural slums located in what were often out-of-the-way wastelands, this growing rural underclass was joined by the thousands of former labor tenants, urban residents, and residents of "black spots"[74] who, as noted above, had been forcefully relocated to their appropriate "national homeland." A large portion of these removals were women and children.[75]

Prior to 1970 conditions in most of these closer settlement areas were appalling. Located in remote areas, most settlements were seldom seen by outsiders. In many cases no preparations were made for the thousands of people dumped by the government trucks. At Mondlo, located 28 kilometers south of Vryheid in Natal, people were provided with tents and three days' rations. Sanitation and water supplies were inadequate and mortality rates, especially among young children, were horrific. The story was repeated at Dimbaza in the eastern Cape, Morsgat in the western Transvaal, and Sahlumbe in Natal. Only after these conditions were publicized in books like Cosmas Desmond's *The Discarded People* and later in the film, *Last Grave at Dimbaza,* did the authorities begin to make improvements in the conditions.[76]

Public outcry forced the government to provide more facilities within the closer settlements, yet removals continued during the 1970s and the population of the homelands increased from 7.3 to 11 million. The reverse side of the government's efforts to create a stable urban population of skilled African workers, after 1976, was an attempt to force unskilled workers and their families to settle only in the rural reserves. So called "homelands" like KaNgwane, QwaQwa, and KwaNdebele which mushroomed during this period became little more than vast dormitory communities, with no internal resources and few opportunities for local employment. The population of KwaNdebele grew from 50,000 in 1975 to 250,000 in 1981. QwaQwa's population grew from 24,000 to between 200,000 and 300,000 over this same period. Land available to farm on was nonexistent. At Bothashoek in Lebowa there were 160 morgen (approximately 330 acres) of land made available for 3,600 families. In the Ciskei as a whole only 6 percent of Ciskeians now live on plots large enough to provide basic subsistence. The Nqutu District in KwaZulu that, according to Tomlinson, could support 13,000 people in subsistence agriculture in the mid-1950s, had a population of 200,000 by 1979.[77] Residents of the "homelands," now totally dependent on finding work within white South Africa, were no longer allowed to reside there except in unisex hostels or as daily commuters. Overall, 71 percent of the workers in the closer settlements in 1984 were migrants who either commuted daily to work over distances of sixty to seventy miles, spending most of their "leisure" time on buses or trains, or lived in hostels visiting their families when they could afford the bus or train fare. Life for the families left behind was difficult, dependent on incomes that were both inadequate and unreliable, and meant living in often squalid conditions. Sanitation in many of these areas remained rudimentary at best and contributed to high rates of typhoid and diarrheal diseases. Typhoid rates in Venda, Gazankulu, and KaNgwane in 1980 were six times higher than the country as a whole, and African rates overall have risen steadily since 1973.[78] KaNgwane, with less than 1 percent of the country's population, reported 20 percent of the country's cases of typhoid in 1980.[79]

In the late 1970s, the infant mortality rate among migrant families living in the bantustans (227 per 1,000) was nearly three times as high as among nonmigrant insiders living in the metropolitan areas (82 per 1,000)—a figure that again vividly illustrates the process of transferring the health costs of racial capitalism beyond the borders of white South Africa. As bad as this situation was, and is, the plight of those families who do not have access to outside employment is even worse. The infant mortality rate among these families was 282 per 1,000.[80] The number of such families remains very large as some estimate unemployment in the "homelands" to be in the order of 40 percent.[81]

Charles Simkins has recently argued that, in aggregate terms, there has been an improvement in "homeland" household incomes between 1960 and 1980. Whether or not this is the case has been hotly debated.[82] Yet even if it is true, two facts need to be kept in mind. First, even with this increase, 80 percent of the households still live below the urban-based PDL. This compares with 99 percent in 1960 and 85 percent in the late 1960s,[83] representing an improvement, but hardly one of great significance. Second, the aggregate improvement has not been universal. Specifically the income of the lower 30 percent of households has declined, either relatively or absolutely. The number of households totally without income has trebled since 1960, with a full 13 percent now having no cash income. Although Simkins prefers to view the improvement in the upper 70 percent as an indicator of the future trend, developments in the political economy of South Africa since 1980 lead one to suspect that the number of destitute people at the bottom is likely to increase as employment opportunities within both the homelands and South Africa continue to grow at a slower rate than the population. Without a radical restructuring of the economy, and particularly the redistribution of land, there seems little likelihood that Simkins' optimistic forecast that the percentage of homeland Africans living under the PDL will be reduced to 50 percent by 2000 will occur.

The above picture of social and economic development in both the urban and rural areas of South Africa between 1950 and 1980 leads to two conclusions. First, the rise in African TB notifications between 1953 and 1963 was not simply the product of better case finding. The conditions of poverty, overcrowding, and malnutrition continued to operate and provide a catalyst for TB. Second, the apparent decline in TB notifications between 1965 and 1980 does not reflect an improvement in overall health conditions. Although some sections of the African population benefited from increased wages during the late 1970s and there has been a growing stratification between African insiders and outsiders in terms of their health and welfare, conditions for the vast majority of both urban and rural Africans have not improved to a degree that would account for the sharp decline in TB notifications or the decline in risk of infection that have occurred since the mid-1960s. Declines in TB notifications must therefore reflect either better medical care or a statistical illusion. Both possibilities will be examined below.

APARTHEID MEDICINE AND THE
CONTINUED RISE OF TB

TB control efforts in South Africa since the 1950s have been impressive in terms of the scale of the attack mounted by both governmental and private voluntary organizations. Government expenditures for TB control increased steadily and by the early 1980s amounted to R50 million a year. In terms of their effectiveness, however, these efforts have fallen far short of their goal. Although South Africa is not alone in this respect, there are specific conditions within South Africa which have contributed to this failure. These conditions, like those that shaped housing and nutrition policies, have resulted from the subordination of public health to the overriding political and economic designs of the Nationalist government and from the failure of the state to place any constraints on capital's exploitation of labor.

Armed for the first time with a "silver bullet," in the form of streptomycin (SM) and isoniazid (INH), South African medical authorities launched an all-out attack on TB during the 1950s. Mass x-ray surveys were carried out in both urban and rural areas to identify existing cases, hospital accommodations were increased, and educational campaigns were developed. Chemotherapy brought a sharp decline in TB mortality during the early 1950s and created an expectation among medical authorities that TB would soon be brought under control. The optimism of many health authorities over the eventual outcome of the campaign was expressed clearly by a speaker to the national Tuberculosis Conference of 1957:

> I have a conviction, which I feel sure must be shared by many of us, that we have reached the stage when we are in a position to group ourselves to plan our El Alamein, and may look forward with hope and enthusiasm to driving back the enemy and, within the foreseeable future, to bringing this enemy under control.[84]

For some, however, optimism was tempered by the realization that, despite declining death rates, efforts to control TB through curative methods were not achieving their desired goals and were in fact producing a growing backlog of uncured cases. This realism was reflected in the observations of the MOH of Cape Town to the same conference.

> The most disturbing feature in Cape Town is the accumulation of persons without permanent cure. More people are contracting the disease, especially children: far fewer people are dying from it. Despite the regular removal of healed cases, the Tuberculosis Register increases yearly. . . . In these circumstances it seems inevitable that the accumulation of chronic cases, already considerable, may grow to form a mass of contagion, increasingly unmanageable with the present facilities.[85]

The MOH was observing what has since become a common experience of TB control programs in Africa and elsewhere. Chemotherapy provided medical authorities with the ability to cure TB victims and thus lower mortality rates. Not all cases were being identified, however. Many that were identified, moreover, were for one reason or another being treated only partially.

Chemotherapy requires lengthy treatment and there is a constant problem of cases being lost to treatment. To be effective in reducing the infected population, therefore, a TB control program has to be highly efficient in keeping track of people under treatment and in following up cases who are lost to treatment. These activities need to be coordinated and are difficult to organize and sustain where, as in the case of most of Africa, resources and manpower are limited. As a result many cases are only partially cured. This allows them to survive but often in a chronic infectious state. Such cases increase the pool of infection within the community beyond what it would have been had they died. To make matters worse, failure to completely cure TB cases leads to the development of drug-resistant strains of TB bacillus, which further undermines the ability of health officials to combat the disease and contributes to the growing number of uncured cases. For all these reasons the actual incidence of TB, and not simply notification rates, often increases following the introduction of effective chemotherapeutic measures.

Although South Africa has had more resources than most countries to spend on TB control and therefore should have been more successful in reducing the pool of infectious cases, this does not appear to have occurred. The reasons for this failure can be traced to specific patterns of development associated with the construction of apartheid.

If one compares the accumulation of black cases on TB registers with the accumulation of white cases, it is immediately apparent that the two differ not simply in the number of cases recorded but in the pattern of case accumulation. TB registers include all reported cases that have not been cured. The rate at which the number of cases on a register increases, therefore, reflects both the rate at which new cases are identified and the rate at which they are cured. A continual accumulation of cases indicates that new cases are being identified faster than existing cases are being cured. In South Africa black TB registers reveal this type of steady accumulation of cases between 1950 and 1960. White TB registers, by contrast, show an initial increase in cases followed by a leveling off and eventual decline by 1960. Since both black and white populations were subject to active case-finding efforts during this period, the difference in the pattern of accumulation reflects the fact that white cases, on the one hand, were being cured at a rate that equaled and then exceeded the rate at which new cases were being identified. New black cases of TB, on the other hand, were accumulating faster than existing services could handle them. This difference in cure rates in turn reflected disparities in access to health services.[86]

Measuring medical services simply by the number of beds available for TB cases, an inadequate measure but one which health authorities were fond of using, the difference in treatment availability is clear. Taking 1957 as an example, the incidence of reported cases among whites was approximately 45 per 100,000. This translated into approximately 1,350 new cases a year. The accommodations available for these cases in the same year were 1,230 beds. By contrast, the notification rate for Africans in that year was 400 per 100,000, or approximately 40,000 new cases. The number of beds available for all blacks in TB institutions nationwide in 1957 was 14,410. In effect there were nearly three times as many black cases per available bed as there were white cases per bed.

The Nationalist government in fact made considerable efforts to increase the number of beds available for blacks, nearly tripling them between 1952 and 1957. These efforts, like those in the 1940s, appear to have been stimulated as much by white voter concern for preventing the spread of TB infection into the white population as from any desire to improve health facilities for blacks. This concern was no doubt heightened by newspaper articles, such as the following, which highlighted the danger posed by the black TB cases.

> Results of miniature X-rays carried out by Santa's mobile unit show that at least one in every 100 of our domestic servants are carriers of this dreaded disease—coughing billions of TB germs into our children's faces and over our food. . . . It is shocking to learn that nearly 5000 men, women and children are walking about our city now suffering from TB but receiving no treatment.[87]

Despite such white anxiety and government efforts to increase hospital accommodations for blacks, a massive backlog of cases who could not find beds remained.

The situation was in fact worse than it appeared. To begin with, African TB patients frequently required longer stays in hospitals than whites because their disease tended to be more acute in nature. For example in Durban, in 1954, whites averaged 6.2 months per stay while Africans averaged 12 months. By 1958 the figures for both groups had been reduced by improvements in the effectiveness of treatment, yet the differential remained, with the average white stay being 3.6 months and the average African stay 5.4 months.[88] This meant the turnover of pa-tients was much faster for whites than for Africans, making the dispar-ity in number of beds available for each group even greater.

Second, many TB beds were in TB centers or settlements which had been established from public donations and a small grant from the government by the South African National Tuberculosis Association (SANTA), a private voluntary organization. These settlements were spe-cifically set up to cope with ambulatory and convalescent patients whose disease was of a mild form. They did not treat the more acute cases so often found in the urban areas among Africans. As the medical superintendent of Nessie Knight Hospital in the Transkei wrote, the settlement idea took "no cognizance of the vast majority of Native sufferers who are quite unsuitable for admission to SANTA settlements and whose only hope is accommodation in proper hospitals where they must stay in bed for varying lengthy periods."[89] The lack of hospital accommodation for advanced cases prevented many Africans from gain-ing any treatment until they had infected others. The problem was cited in a parliamentary debate in 1955 by Mr. Lee-Warden.

> I wish to draw the attention of this House to the appalling conditions that exist as regards African T.B. sufferers for whom there is no accommodation in hospitals. . . . The position was brought to my notice when an African asked me if it would be possible to remove a sufferer from his house. On inspection I found that living in a one room hovel that was unfit for human habitation, there was a man, his wife, and three children and this consumptive African, and from investigations which I subsequently made, it was discovered that this particular African was in a very advanced state of T.B. and that there are thousands of others in and around Cape Town who cannot be accommodated in hospitals. I was told that if this particular case had been less serious, his name could have been put on a waiting list and that possibly within six months he might be able to get into a hospital, but as he was an advanced case, there was absolutely no accommodation whatsoever.[90]

He went on to note that he had subsequently learned that the man's wife and two of the three children had since contracted the disease. The government was in fact contributing to this problem by depending on SANTA to solve the bed problem, rather than by spending money on more hospitals.

Lack of hospital accommodations forced the government to begin treating discovered cases on an out-patient basis rather than waiting for accommodations to become available. To ensure that a complete cure was achieved all TB patients were supposed to receive a government ration while under treatment,[91] and patients who missed treatment were to be followed up by a trained health visitor. Patients who were too ill to attend clinics were to be treated in their homes until they were well enough to collect their own treatment. Finally, because out-patient treatment prevented patient isolation and increased the likelihood that a patient would infect others, it was recognized that out-patient treatment required intensive contact tracing.

For a number of reasons out-patient treatment programs have been largely a failure in South Africa. To begin with, even with out-patient treatment, acute cases still needed to begin treatment within a hospital setting and there were simply not enough beds to treat them.[92] Second, local health authorities were overtaxed by the large numbers of cases who needed treatment, and it was impossible to visit, much less keep track of, all the cases on the books. Contact tracing was often inefficient or nonexistent. Finally, not all municipalities were willing to bear the cost of providing rations for TB patients receiving treatment despite the government's offer to cover seven-eighths of this cost.

Some municipalities were clearly more efficient and spent more money than others on TB work. For example, whereas Durban had 2,000 beds for TB cases and eighteen full-time TB officers in 1955, Johannesburg, with twice the population, had only 300 beds and one TB officer.[93] Yet even Durban did not initially participate in the government's ration scheme.[94] In the absence of adequate health facilities or manpower to supervise treatment, responsibility for insuring that patients received treatment until cure was achieved was left up to the patients themselves. For a variety of reasons this often resulted in patients failing to complete their full course of chemotherapy. Recommended treatment with INH and PAS was for twelve months, though it was believed in the mining industry that a cure could be obtained in milder cases in six to nine months in at least 50 percent of the cases.[95] Many patients, however, felt considerably improved after two to three months and if not supervised began missing treatments. Patients who failed to complete their treatments were labled "defaulters." This term implied that it was the patient who was at fault, and white medical authorities often attributed treatment failure to the African's ignorance or "native mentality." Yet in South Africa completion of treatment was discouraged by a range of factors. Some of these are common to all out-patient TB treatment programs; others are peculiar to the South African political and economic environment of the 1950s, 1960s, and 1970s.

Lack of financial resources was perhaps the primary reason why a

high percentage of blacks did not complete their treatments. Most Africans who contracted and were diagnosed as having TB lost their jobs.
Only a few enlightened employers permitted infected workers to continue working while they received treatment. From the start, therefore,
TB patients and their families were faced with financial crisis. Although
African TB patients were eligible for disability grants, the amounts
provided were both less than that provided white patients and inadequate for the needs of African families with no other source of income.
In 1965 the disability grant was R3.50 per month plus R1.25 per child.
No support was available for spouses. A family of four would thus
receive R6 per month. In the same year, the poverty datum line for a
family of four in Johannesburg was roughly R53. A white tuberculosis
patient, by contrast, received R31 for himself plus R16 for his wife and
R9 per child, which for a family of four came to R56 per month.[96] Not
only were disability grants inadequate, they were administered in a way
that discouraged many black workers from obtaining them. The Nationalist's policy of separate development, which denied the vast majority of
urban workers permanent residence rights within the cities, together
with a prohibition on paying pensions or disability grants outside the
area in which a worker lawfully and permanently resided, meant that
the majority of disabled black workers had to leave the place in which
they had been employed and return to a rural bantustan in order to
obtain these inadequate support payments. For many workers not born
in an urban area but who had worked there on a continuous basis for a
number of years, such a move would eliminate their chance of obtaining
urban residence status under section 10(1)b of the Urban Areas Act. In
addition the chances of obtaining treatment for the disease were, as will
be shown below, severely reduced within the rural areas. For both
reasons, African TB patients were understandably reluctant to collect
the small disability grant available to them.

Lacking alternatives, many black breadwinners chose to seek new
employment as soon as they felt well enough to work, which was
frequently long before they were "cured." This often meant looking
for a new job since their old employer would be aware of their condition and refuse to employ them. While looking for work—and if fortunate enough to find a new job, while working—it was difficult for a
patient to continue his or her treatment. Visiting clinics during working hours was difficult and few clinics operated evenings or Sundays to
accommodate employed patients, since TB patients were by definition
unemployed.[97]

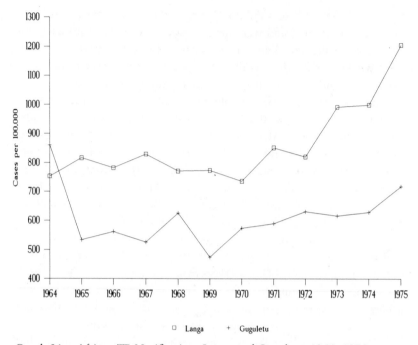

Graph 21.   African TB Notifications Langa and Guguletu, 1964–1975
Source: Cape Town, *Reports of the Medical Officer of Health,* 1964–1975.

Prospects for TB patients varied a good deal. In Durban for example, Dormer was successful in convincing some employers to allow patients who were in treatment but no longer infectious to return to employment. Yet in 1964 a survey of 169 firms found that only 38 provided treatment facilities on the premises so that the worker would not have to lose wages while getting treatment.[98] In Cape Town evening clinics were held during the first week of every month at the central chest clinic located at Chapel Street. This was said to benefit the patient who returned to work and almost to guarantee against relapse. For the black worker in Guguletu or Langa townships, however, getting to the Chapel Street clinic often represented an expense that discouraged attendance. There were no evening clinic hours at the Langa or Guguletu clinics during the 1960s.[99]

Those who were unemployed had an additional incentive for quickly seeking employment. For the Native Laws Amendment Act required Africans residing in the urban areas to possess an employment contract. Failure to do so placed a TB patient at risk of being repatriated. Prior to

1960 there was no provision for exempting African tuberculotics from this rule and, as Dr. A. Strating of the Transvaal Peri-Urban Health Board stated, this often caused them to fall foul of the law.

> Native patients in urban areas receiving home treatment were often arrested by the police on their way to clinics because they were not in possession of a service contract. These Natives often spent several weeks in jail.[100]

Strating proposed that local authorities prepare a special form stating that the bearer was a tuberculotic and not capable of carrying a service contract. This system, however, placed such cases in a Catch-22 dilemma. For while the attachment of such a document to a patient's identity papers might save him from being arrested or facing repatriation, it would also effectively prevent him from obtaining employment.

The combination of financial constraints and discriminatory legislation created obstacles for all Africans seeking treatment, but migrant workers were at greatest risk of defaulting. Lacking a network of support within the urban areas and being ineligible for the payment of urban disability grants, migrants often had to return to the bantustans. The relationship between labor migrancy and treatment is reflected in statistics from Cape Town (graph 22), which indicate the percentage of first attenders at TB clinics who were lost to treatment because they were either untraceable or had "disencamped." Comparing clinics in Cape Town, Guguletu, and Langa, it can be seen that for the ten years between 1965 and 1975, Langa, which had a high percentage of male migrant workers, most of whom lived in unisex hostels, also had the highest percentage of untraceable or disencamped patients. Guguletu, a more permanent black community, had the next highest and Cape Town, which included white and coloreds as well as Africans, had the lowest.[101]

Getting treatment clearly became more difficult during the 1960s as the Nationalists became serious about enforcing the Group Areas Act as well as about tightening up influx control. The MOH of Port Elizabeth claimed that as a result of removals under the Group Areas Act patients were forced to move away from clinics to which they had been going for treatment. This often led to their being lost to treatment.[102] In Cape Town, John Western found that coloreds who had been removed from Mowbray were on average 5.29 kilometers further from the nearest hospital than they had been before relocation.[103] The removal of coloreds beyond Althone during the mid-1960s resulted in a decline in colored TB notifications and an increase in percentage of clinic first

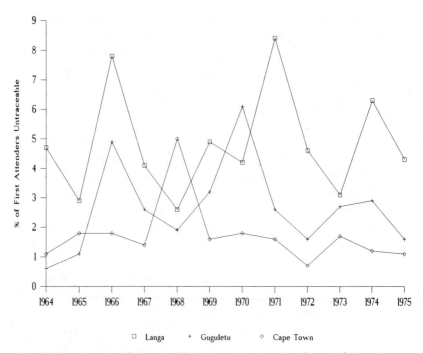

Graph 22.   Percent of Untraceable Patients, Langa, Guguletu, and Cape Town
Source: Cape Town, *Reports of the Medical Officer of Health,* 1964–1975.

attenders lost to treatment from 1964.[104] The sharp rise in untraceables in Cape Town in 1968 may well reflect the impact of removals from District Six on clinic attendance. A survey of TB patients living in an African residential area of Cape Town found that 50 percent of those interviewed had difficulty getting treatment. Distance from the clinic was noted as an important problem.[105] The MOH for Durban also noted that the removal of blacks from Cato Manor to KwaMashu during the 1960s led to cases being lost to treatment.[106] In more extreme cases, patients attending urban clinics were removed to rural resettlement camps with the same effect. The creation of bantustans caused a further reshuffling of people within the rural areas as people were relocated in their "appropriate" ethnic area. This had a similar negative impact on treatment and follow-up.[107]

Additional problems were created by the state's efforts to transform the bantustans into self-governing national states, each with its own health service, during the 1970s and early 1980s. There are currently no less than seventeen separate authorities responsible for health in South

Africa, with minimal coordination among them. This fragmentation has further increased the likelihood of patient "default." As members of a medical team working in the Gazankulu "homeland" located in the eastern Transvaal noted in 1984,

> Homeland borders and structures limit us and fragment services. Just over half of our patients come from Lebowa [a neighboring "homeland"]; but we may not follow them up at home, visit their families or organize SAC [supervised ambulatory care] for them. We also cannot trace contacts or defaulters, or do case finding in Lebowa.[108]

In theory a process existed for following up on cases lost in this way. It was highly inefficient, however, and in practice never worked.[109]

Fragmentation also resulted in the use of different drug regimens by neighboring health authorities. Thus, a patient from Lebowa who began one regimen in a hospital in Gazankulu, would find another set of drugs being supplied by local health authorities when he or she returned home to complete his or her ambulatory care. This change inhibited the patient's recovery and could contribute to drug resistance.[110]

The problem of coordinating treatment was even greater for Africans living on white farms. A large proportion of TB patients showing up at Gazankulu Hospital came from white farm areas. Similarly health authorities in Bophuthatswana claimed in 1984 that many of the most severe cases of TB came from the neighboring white farms. In this situation, not only did local health workers lack the authority to follow up and supervise the treatment of farm workers who came to them for help, but there were no local authorities to take up these responsibilities within the white farming areas.[111]

In short, although patient defaulting from ambulatory treatment programs has been a common problem of tuberculosis control programs in Africa, the inequitable distribution of health and social services in South Africa—combined with the pattern of racial segregation and control enforced by the Nationalist government and the fragmentation of local health services—exacerbated these problems, decreasing the likelihood that black cases would be effectively cured and increasing the number of half-cured chronic cases who were sources of infection to others.

The medical team at Gazankulu estimated that in 1980 and 1981 only 38.7 percent of their admitted patients completed enough treatment. In 1981 the figure was 44.1 percent. Using shorter regimens and full supervision they were able to increase this to 84 and 86 percent in 1982 and 1983 respectively. This was viewed as exceptional and required a commitment of manpower and resources which were both far in excess of those employed by the average rural health service and in all likelihood not sustainable in Gazankulu, given its limited health budget.[112]

The director of the South African Tuberculosis Research Institute (TBRI) optimistically claimed that medical authorities had treated more than half a million people between 1972 and 1982 and probably rendered 90 percent of them noninfectious. Though this figure may be accurate, rendering a patient noninfectious is not the same as curing him or her. Most cases in fact are rendered noninfectious after only a few weeks of treatment. If treatment is stopped at this point, however, or before a cure is achieved, the patient has a good chance of relapsing and becoming infectious once again. The Brown Commission of Inquiry into Health Services estimated in 1986 that nationwide only 25 percent of out-patients were effectively treated.[113] In addition relapse rates have been very high. In 1980 it was estimated that 38 percent of all hospital TB patients represented relapse cases.[114] This finding led the current head of SANTA to conclude that the treatment program "has to a considerable degree been a failure."[115]

Figures for treatment failure disguise a wide divergence between urban and rural health services, and it is clear that once a patient was relegated to a rural area his or her chances of receiving a full course of treatment declined sharply. A comparative study of treatment in several therapeutic settings found that the percentage of patients receiving 75 percent of their treatments ranged from 50 percent for Cape Town clinics to 25 percent for clinics in the Ciskei.[116] Similarly a follow-up study of fifty cases referred to local clinics for therapy in Natal found that referrals to urban clinics had a compliance rate of 68 percent whereas only 28 percent of referrals to rural clinics completed their treatment.[117] Not all urban clinics had high compliance rates, however. A follow-up survey, of patients receiving treatment in Soweto in 1978, found that only 21 percent received 80 percent or more of their prescribed treatments.[118]

It should be noted that the low rates of treatment success recorded for rural areas are roughly similar to those recorded in neighboring countries. Yet it must also be recognized that these countries lack the resources available in South Africa. More importantly, it is only in South Africa that people who cannot find jobs, as well as the families of many of those who do, have been forcefully removed to rural areas where their chances of getting treatment are greatly reduced.

The inability of patients to complete their treatment meant not only that the number of chronic "half-cured half-ill" cases continued to climb but also that the number of patients who developed resistance to INH increased, further complicating efforts at TB control. As the MOH of Cape Town told the 1957 Conference on TB,

> We find that many chronic cases finally develop resistance to S.M. and I.N.H. following irregular intake. The frequent finding that progressive improvement in new cases of I.N.H. and P.A.S. comes to a sudden stop after 6 to 8 weeks strongly suggests the emergence of resistance.[119]

In the long run, moreover, the recurrent development of patient resistance led to the development of INH- and SM-resistant strains of tubercle bacilli. By 1978, 10 percent of blacks under treatment for the first time in Pretoria were resistant to INH. In 1986 it was estimated that primary INH resistance was 15 percent nationwide whereas acquired resistance (resistance in previously treated patients) had increased to 50 percent in many of the rural areas surveyed.[120] In other African countries with well-established TB treatment services, by contrast, the figure for primary resistance is generally about 8 percent.[121] Resistance to other drugs has also been reported. Primary resistance to rifampicin for example is 1.2 percent while secondary resistance occurs in 5.6 percent of old cases.[122]

The mining industry evidently played a significant role in the development of drug resistance as it has in the wider history of the disease in South Africa. Mine medical officers, like other health authorities, began employing antitubercular drugs to treat African mineworkers in the late 1940s. This led to a marked decrease in TB mortality on the mines. Yet prior to the 1980s few if any African workers received a complete course of treatment. The vast majority were treated for a couple of weeks within the individual mine hospitals before being sent to the WNLA hospital for examination by the Silicosis Bureau for possible compensation. The examination process could take several weeks during which the patients would continue to receive treatment. Once the compensation went through, however, and assuming the infected workers were fit to travel, they were repatriated. As a result the majority of African workers with TB received chemotherapy for between two weeks and two months. A few received treatment for as long as three months. Although many of these cases became sputum negative as a result of this treatment, they had a good chance, without further treatment, of breaking down again in the reserves to which they returned.[123] Even if they were somehow fortunate enough to be picked up by local health authorities, which evidently was infrequent despite efforts to notify rural health authorities, their chances of receiving a complete treatment were slim.

In cases where workers were repatriated to "local authority" areas, towns such as Umtata or Grahamstown or any of the white farming areas, as opposed to magisterial areas (which included most of the bantustans), the local authorities were often unwilling to take the financial responsibility for treatment, maintaining that the TB was not discovered in their area and, in most cases, that the worker had been away for more than six months. Playing on the mines' own claims about the thoroughness of their preemployment examinations, moreover, local health authorities argued this proved that any African employed by the mines was ipso facto free of TB before he left their area of jurisdiction and responsibility.[124] In some cases the Department of Health took direct responsibility for treating these cases, yet this often produced delays in treatment since the normal process of form filling and correspondence, required before treatment could be provided, could take months.[125] In the meantime patients often became sicker and often sought alternative therapies. The chief medical advisor for TEBA (The Employment Bureau of Africa, successor to the NRC), the central recruiting organization for the mining industry, found that 95 percent of the workers repatriated with TB did not seek further treatment at the place to which they were sent home.[126] All in all, the system of repatriation of partially treated TB cases, in the absence of an efficient system of care in the rural areas, could not have been better designed to invite the development of both secondary and primary resistance as further obstacles to the fight against TB.

Certain medical men on the mines were highly cognizant of this problem and tried to inaugurate a more effective system of treatment. The chief medical advisor for TEBA obtained the Chamber of Mine's permission in the mid-1950s to hold back any African workers who would accept six to nine months of treatment. During this period the worker would be fed and housed but not paid. The experiment failed because he could not convince any of the patients to remain at the mines that long for treatment. At the time he attributed this refusal to their primitive mentality.

> I have spoken to many of them. They don't care two hoots. If you say "you will die if you go home," it does not mean a thing. They are prepared to die at home. If you say to them, "Think about your children, you are going to infect them"—all the reasons that would keep a European in hospital, they

just laugh at. If the wife gets it, he has got two more; if those get it, it is bad luck.[127]

This sentiment, shared by other mine medical officers, was used as a primary justification for not providing more long-term treatment. The mining industry also continued to argue that quick repatriation was beneficial to the health of the African worker, thus perpetuating the "myth of the healthy reserve." In a letter to the government secretary of Swaziland, the general manager of the Native Recruiting Corporation stated in 1952, "The policy of repatriation has been stated by good authority to have a beneficial effect on the course of the disease, in that the open-air life of the rural native is the condition of choice."[128] Thus, while the discovery of effective medical treatments for TB short-circuited debates in South Africa over the causes of African susceptibility to TB, some of the same arguments were now being employed to explain why Africans were not provided with effective health care.

As TEBA's medical advisor came to learn later when he traced repatriated mineworkers to see how many received treatment after repatriation, his view of the "native's primitive mentality" failed to appreciate that the mineworker was very often the primary breadwinner for a family who was heavily dependent on his employment. The mineworker who refused treatment was indeed thinking of his wife and children when he refused to remain at the mines for treatment, for he knew that without his income the chances of his family escaping TB, or one of a vast number of other diseases and conditions affecting rural Africans, were small indeed. His only hope was to get home and get back to work as fast as possible. Thus when asked why they did not seek treatment on returning to their homes, the miners replied, "Who will feed my family while I am in the hospital?"[129]

If the Chamber of Mines had been truly concerned about the health of the mineworker with TB, they could have solved the problem of treatment refusal by providing the workers under treatment with sick pay. This was in fact done at the DeBeers Diamond Mines. Workers diagnosed with TB at the DeBeers mines were transferred to the Public Health Hospital. While they underwent treatment they received approximately half their pay. This continued until the patient's disease was quiescent, at which time they were given employment in a sheltered position. With this system DeBeers officials claimed to have been very successful in getting African workers to accept treatment.[130] The absence of such benefits on the gold mines meant that hospital treatment

represented a loss of income and a delay in the payment of compensation. It is therefore not surprising that the average African worker on
the gold mines who contracted TB opted for repatriation.

In the late 1970s the Chamber of Mines embarked on a more extensive program for treating TB cases at the mines, agreeing to pay full
underground wages for black workers who were forced to work aboveground while receiving treatment. This policy accompanied a broader
reorganization of the mines' African labor force, involving the internalization of labor recruitment and the development of a smaller, more
skilled and permanent workforce. These changes, discussed later in the
epilogue, increased the chamber's interest in retaining experienced workers and thus in treating to cure workers who became ill. In 1985 the law
preventing mineworkers who had contracted TB from ever working
again in dust-laden occupations was withdrawn, allowing the reemploy-
ment of cured cases in their former jobs. Today the mining industry
claims to be treating until cured nearly all identified TB cases.[131]

In the meantime, however, a great deal of damage was certainly
done. Although there is no way of measuring the impact the repatriation
of 1,200 partially treated cases a year had on the development of drug
resistance in the reserves, it no doubt played a role. Conversely, the
generally low success rate of all medical services treating Africans identified with TB means the mines were only one player in a large cast of
actors contributing to drug resistance in South Africa. Yet it must also
be noted that the mines' role in the dissemination of drug resistance was
geographically more extensive since a large portion of its labor force
came from outside South Africa prior to 1976.

Although the prospects of cure for blacks discovered through various
case-finding methods was not good, it is clear that many cases simply
were not discovered until they were dead or near death. For example,
although notification rates for Johannesburg in the early 1950s hovered
around 200 per 100,000, an x-ray survey of domestic workers concluded that 1 percent or 1,000 per 100,000 had TB. It was estimated
there were 5,000 cases of undetected TB in Johannesburg in 1955.[132]
Similarly the MOH for Cape Town noted that

> It is astonishing that so many persons with advanced disease, particularly
> men, can remain unknown, at least to official agencies by avoiding the case-
> catching net—however wide the mesh—until abject illness or some catastro-
> phe brings them to the notice of the clinics.[133]

If the situation was bad in the urban areas, it was impossible in the rural
reserves. Only a small portion of the estimated 25,000 cases of active

TB in the Transkei were actually seen and treated. This situation, more-over, became increasingly worse after 1960, as we shall see.

Health authorities in South Africa did not restrict their control ef-forts to curative measures but also engaged in preventive work. Given the limits placed by South Africa's political economy on major struc-tural changes that would alleviate the conditions giving rise to the dis-ease, however, preventive work in practice meant medical intervention in the form of BCG campaigns. As with their curative efforts, attempts to prevent the early onset of TB among children through vaccination were only partially effective.

The objective of BCG (Bacillus Calmette Guerin) vaccination is to reduce the incidence of childhood tuberculosis and in particular of se-vere forms such as tuberculosis meningitis. Worldwide, the use of BCG in third-world countries has led to mixed results. In fact the level of protection afforded by BCG in well-conducted trials has ranged from none to 80 percent. Numerous factors have contributed to poor protec-tion levels, including low potency of vaccines, sensitization of non-tuberculous mycosensitizing bacteria, the "host" status of the vacci-nated population, and the fact that heavy or repeated infection may overwhelm immunity derived from BCG.[134] In South Africa, where BCG campaigns began in the early 1960s, the effects of these various factors are difficult to sort out. A study in Pretoria of children who were household contacts of known adult TB cases found that in children under four years of age the risk of developing TB was eight times greater among children without BCG than among those who had received the vaccination. For children five and older, however, there was virtually no difference, suggesting that the protection afforded by BCG may not be very long lasting.[135] It is clear, moreover, that high levels of malnutri-tion among young black children in the country, combined with over-crowding in an environment in which TB is endemic, can contribute to the "overwhelming of protection." A study of TB meningitis in Cape Town in 1979–1981 revealed that 45 percent of the children who devel-oped the disease had had BCG.[136]

In addition, the distribution of BCG coverage, like that of health services in general, has been highly uneven. In the rural areas where children are increasingly at greatest risk, only a small percentage of chil-dren had been vaccinated prior to 1970.[137] In 1972 only 1.5 percent of children in the Transkei had BCG scars.[138] BCG coverage was also lim-ited in the many peri-urban slums and squatters' camps that surrounded the major cities of the country.[139] Both the limited coverage and the relative ineffectiveness of BCG in the face of malnutrition and widespread opportunities for infection suggest that BCG campaigns made little dent in the overall incidence of TB among Africans prior to 1975.

The 1970s saw a significant increase in the use of BCG. A random survey of 418 preschool children in rural Ciskei in 1984 found that 68.7 percent had been vaccinated according to medical records. For children under one year the figure was 87.5 percent, where as for five-year-olds the percentage was only 39.2 percent.[140] This increase in coverage may account for the declining percentage of African children under fifteen among notified cases between 1971 and 1984.[141] This decline, however, could also be explained by the pattern of population removals described below.

In conclusion, it should be obvious to any but the most chauvinistic medical authorities that TB control in South Africa through the use of modern medical treatments has not achieved the optimistic goals set in the 1950s and 1960s. It should be equally apparent, moreover, that much of this failure is due to the government's overriding concern for separate development, preventing the creation of an efficient system of health care, as well as to the continued existence of living and working conditions that prevent blacks from maintaining good health. Given these realities it is highly unlikely that the decline in African TB notifications after the mid-1960s reflects achievements in either preventive or curative health care. What then accounts for this decline?

THE GREAT DISAPPEARING ACT

Notification rates, as observed earlier, give a distorted picture of the true incidence and distribution of TB in South Africa. The rise in TB notifications in the 1950s and early 1960s was clearly affected by mass surveys and an overall increase in case-finding efforts. So too the decline in TB notifications after 1963 has been shaped by factors that are in part independent of the actual epidemiology of the disease. There can be little doubt that a slowdown in case-finding efforts is partly responsible for the downturn in notifications.

By the late 1950s medical authorities had ceased large-scale surveying of various rural and urban populations since the number of discovered cases far exceeded the capacity of existing medical facilities to treat them. This probably had more impact on rural than urban notifications, for local municipal health authorities continued screening urban workers for TB throughout the 1970s. In some municipalities there was in fact an increase in the use of x-rays for detecting TB among jobseekers during the 1960s. In Cape Town the mass x-raying of migrant workers in Langa began in 1967. By 1971, 27 percent of black cases were discovered by this method. Although this led to a brief rise in Cape Town's notification rate in 1968, the rate dropped in the following years.[142] The rise in 1968 reflected the fact that many of the workers who were screened had been in Cape Town for six months and thus by definition were the financial responsibility of the municipality. After 1968 this backlog was removed and the cases identified were primarily new jobseekers who had not lived in the city for the requisite six months and thus were not the responsibility of the municipality. As such they were not included in its notification rates.[143]

In the rural areas, passive case finding, involving the identification of cases who turned up at clinics with limited follow-up of the contacts of cases identified, remained the only basis for notifications after 1960. Although passive case finding currently produces the highest yield of cases, it does not provide an accurate picture of the true incidence of the disease since an estimated 31 percent of all TB cases are asymptomatic or at least unaware of the significance of their symptoms and thus do not go for treatment of them.[144] Thomas and Myrdal found that none of the African TB patients they surveyed in the Cape Town area were aware of the significance of their symptoms.[145] The number of doctors involved overall in tuberculosis work has progressively decreased in South Africa since 1960 and, according to one observer, the medical manpower situation is now critical.[146] The decline in physician involvement in TB control may well reflect the movement toward privitization of health services in South Africa. TB work has always been the purview of central state health departments, and as these were cut back, so too were TB services.

Yet the decrease in case finding is not the only reason why notification rates declined. A second factor has been the mass removals of millions of black South Africans from both urban and rural areas to the bantustans and their exclusion from South Africa's official health statistics following their transformation into residents of "national states" in the mid-1970s. This process has removed particularly susceptible segments of the black population from the urban areas of the country, where record keeping and medical surveillance are most efficient, to rural areas where they are much poorer. It is not a coincidence that the period of most intense relocation, from the early 1960s to 1970, was also the period during which the most dramatic drop occurred in TB notifications nationwide.

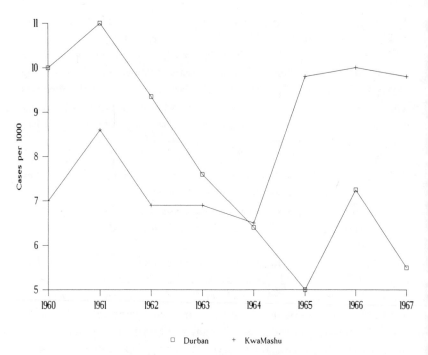

Graph 23.   African TB Notifications, Durban vs. KwaMashu, 1960–1967
Source: Durban, *Report of the City Medical Officer of Health,* 1967.

The process of removals and their impact on urban notifications can be clearly seen in the case of Durban. The building of KwaMashu began in 1957 and removals from Cato Manor got underway in 1958. By 1960 there were 35,000 blacks living in the new municipal location. In 1961 the TB notification rate for KwaMashu was 8.5 per 1,000 while that for blacks living within the rest of Durban was 11 per 1,000. As following graph 23 shows, these rates were gradually reversed as more blacks were removed from Cato Manor, and other areas officially defined as slums, to KwaMashu. By 1967 when Cato Manor was finally cleared, KwaMashu had a notification rate of 9.7 per 1,000 while the rate for blacks in the rest of Durban was reduced to 5.6 per 1,000. Clearly the disease burden had been shifted to the new location, which despite its better housing remained a hotbed of TB.

In April of 1977, the disappearing act was completed when Kwa-Mashu became part of the national state of Kwazulu. With the stroke of a pen, the black population of Durban declined from 240,341 to 97,023 and the 1,525 cases on the TB register were removed from Durban's statistical records. The notification rate for black TB cases declined from 3.80 to 3.23 per 1,000. The crude death rate dropped from 8.88 per 1,000 to 6.97 per 1,000, and the black infant mortality rate (IMR) dropped from 62.15 per 1,000 in 1977 to 52.63 per 1,000 in 1978 (the impact of the removal on the IMR being delayed because IMR measures deaths during the first year of life).[147] A similar pattern can be seen in the notification rates for coloreds in Cape Town following their removal to beyond Althone in 1964.

The Nationalists' resettlement policy also involved the removal of urban blacks to rural areas. Simkins has estimated that, overall, the period between 1960 and 1970 saw a net decline in the African population of major metropolitan areas of 65,700 males and 129,000 females. In addition there was a net decline of 94,000 women from the towns. The actual number of men, women, and children who were removed to achieve this net decline was of course considerably larger given increases due to births and the continued influx of new workers. These removals, like the creation of "relocation townships," contributed to the decline in black TB notification rates.[148]

To understand the impact of these removals on notification rates one has to recognize that the Nationalists did not remove a representative sample of urban residents. Removals were instead aimed at the unemployed or underemployed segment of the population. This meant not only unemployed workers but also women, children, and old people who did not have section 10 rights and who were deemed to be economically "inactive." By targeting these groups, resettlement had the effect of removing people who were the most marginalized and consequently the most vulnerable to TB. If one compares age-specific TB notification rates for blacks during the 1960s and early 1970s[149] with the pattern of removals from metropolitan centers and towns during the 1960s,[150] the effect of removals on overall TB rates becomes clear. (graphs 24, 25)

Removals during the 1960s led in effect to decreases in high-risk groups. Specifically it removed children ages fourteen and under, with a weighted average notification rate of 280 per 100,000, and adults over thirty, with an average notification rate of nearly 450 per 100,000. The population that increased, by contrast, males and females between fifteen and twenty-nine, had an average notification rate of roughly 200 per 100,000. Thus relocations led to the removal of those segments of the urban African population with high notification rates. At the same time the continued reliance of rural families on urban employment combined with the strict enforcement of influx control laws led to net

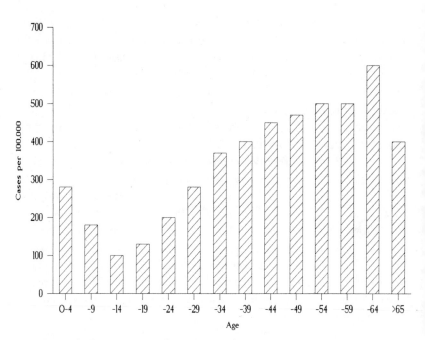

Graph 24.   African TB Notification Rates by Age, 1970
Source: SAMJ (March 21, 1979): 466.

increases in the number of blacks with relatively low notification rates. The relocations, therefore, almost certainly reduced the overall notification rates in the urban areas.

Conversely, the population of the bantustans gained high-risk groups and lost those with low notification rates. In principle this should have led to an increase in notification rates in these areas, so that overall black TB rates in South Africa would have been unaffected. In reality, however, the poor quality of health services in the rural areas has led to the underreporting of rural cases so that the impact of this transfer, as well as of the deteriorating conditions in the bantustans, has been muted. This is revealed by a comparison of notification rates with prevalence rates as determined by several rural TB surveys. In 1974 a TB survey of Kwazulu estimated that the prevalence of active cases of TB was 804 per 100,000 while the notification rate was 177 per 100,000.[151] In other words, 22 percent of the estimated number of cases were notified. Similarly only 11 percent of the estimated number of cases existing in the Transkei were notified in 1973. In 1977 just over 6 percent of the estimated number of cases were notified. By contrast, roughly 30 percent of the estimated

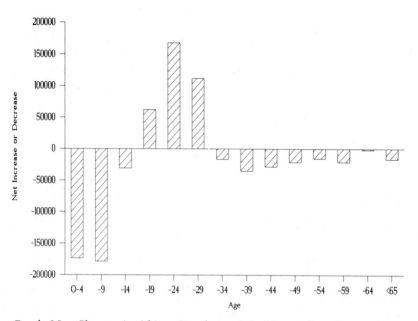

Graph 25.   Changes in African Population S.A. Metropolitan Areas, 1960–1970

Source: C. Simkins, *Four Essays on the Past, Present, and Future of the Distribution of the African Population of South Africa* (Cape Town: SALDRU, University of Cape Town, 1983).

number of total cases within the Republic were reported in 1979.[152] Within some urban areas such as Soweto, Davyton outside Johannesburg, and Atteridge outside Pretoria, moreover, it is estimated that all or nearly all of the estimated annual production of cases are identified.[153] In effect the removal of cases to the bantustans led not only to a reduction in overall TB notifications in the major urban areas but to their virtual disappearance from health statistics.

Despite this underreporting of cases, TB notification rates in the Transkei are nearly twice that for blacks within the "legal borders" of the Republic: 500 versus 250 per 100,000. Similarly, as W. Shasha points out, if one examines the distribution of TB in Natal in 1976,

It is striking that there is a "TB axis" that starts from the district of Nongoma and runs straight southward (west of Durban) toward Harding. This area has two "prongs" that point to the west. The upper prong covers Msinga district while the lower one covers the small bit of Transkei that is within Natal. The present national state of Kwazulu coincides almost exactly within the high risk TB area delineated above.[154]

While the overall risk of infection for blacks in the Republic was 2.2 percent in 1982, the rate for the Transkei and Ciskei was 4.5 percent.

South African government authorities began their final move in the great TB disappearing act in 1976 with the granting of "independence" to the Transkei and the removal of the region's estimated 90,000 cases of TB and its 500 per 100,000 notification rate from the South African statistical area. The TB notification rate for Africans in South Africa in 1976 was 280 per 100,000. In 1977, with the Transkei excluded, the rate dropped to 225 or by nearly 20 percent. As one observer noted, "Logically one could continue this trend and eliminate TB altogether from South Africa with a few flourishes of a statistical pen."[155] That the drop was not larger given the high prevalence of TB in the Transkei strongly suggests that TB notifications in the rest of the country were rising. Similarly, it is likely that the rise in notifications in 1979 would have been greater had Bophuthatswana not been removed from the South African statistical area.

All in all, a close examination of black TB rates in South Africa during the Nationalist era leads to two conclusions. First, the rising notification rate from 1950 to 1965 was not simply an optical illusion produced by better case finding. Living conditions and the partial effectiveness of TB control efforts produced a growing backlog of partially cured infectious cases that contributed to an increased spread of infection. Second, the subsequent decline in TB rates after 1965 cannot be attributed either to improvements in living and working conditions, which in some cases grew worse, or to better medical care. It was instead largely the product of reduced case finding efforts and demographic shifts related to the Nationalists' efforts to implement grand apartheid. These efforts reduced TB notification by removing particularly susceptible subsections of the urban and rural black population beyond the statistical boundaries of "white" South Africa.

Epilogue: The Present and Future of Tuberculosis in South Africa

> The well-being of one section of the community, whatever its colour, is of necessity dependent upon the well-being of all other sections, whatever their colour . . .
>
> We have now reached the stage where "development along their own lines" would produce merely a black reservoir of tuberculosis, venereal disease, and typhus, which from time to time would overflow.[1]
>
> —P. W. Laidler, MOH, East London, 1938

A central argument of this study has been that TB control measures in South Africa from the beginning of this century up to the present time have involved the application of exclusionary policies designed to keep the disease out of the social and economic centers of white society. Despite shifts in medical ideas concerning the causes and prevention of TB among blacks; developments in the area of treatment, including the use of chemotherapy and BCG; and occasional efforts to provide blacks with better housing and diets, South African local and state authorities have relied primarily on legislative instruments to deal with the problem of TB among blacks. Using a long list of public health acts, urban areas acts, influx control laws, slum clearance acts, housing legislation, group areas acts and, ultimately, acts establishing bantustans as "independent national states" beyond the boundaries of white South Africa, South African authorities have methodically removed the health problems of blacks from the purview of white society. Similarly, although the mining industry made significant improvements in the conditions under which blacks live and work while at the mines, their primary weapon against TB has until recently been preemployment medical exams and the repatriation of miners who develop the disease.

These exclusionary policies have always been justified on the basis that they provided blacks with better opportunities for acquiring a decent place to live within their own social and cultural milieu, or in the case of repatriated workers, as providing those who became ill with a chance for recovery in the alledgedly "healthy environment of the reserves." In both cases exclusionary controls have been presented as beneficial to the health and well-being of blacks. In reality, however, these measures have contributed to the production of squalid peri-urban slums and impoverished rural bantustans which are home to an ever-growing population of diseased and malnourished men, women, and children whose lives depend on access to employment within white South Africa.

The cumulative effect of these exclusionary policies in combination with the failure to address the underlying social and economic causes of TB has, as we have seen, been the creation of an expanding reservoir of TB among South Africa's black populations. Although African notifications nationwide declined in 1985, after rising in the early 1980s, there seems little reason to accept that this reflects anything more than a reduction in surveillance. The mass surveying of factory workers in Cape Town, for example, has decreased steadily since 1976. Mass x-rays do not produce a large percentage of the new cases found each year in South Africa. Nor are they, on a strict accounting basis, cost efficient. Yet it is clear that the elimination of this surveillance tool without any effective alternative has resulted in the build up of unnotified cases within factories where screening was formerly carried out. This led a member of the Industrial Health Research Group at the University of Cape Town to observe,

> It seems to me that the phasing out of mass X-ray screening, without their replacement by a regular system of other checks, of proven effectiveness for the local situation, leads inevitably to the danger that instead of combating TB we combat notifications.[2]

The recent decline in notifications was almost certainly also caused by the almost continual pattern of unrest and violence that dominated township life from 1984 to 1986 and disrupted health services. In the Cape Town area, for example, the number of persons x-rayed in Langa declined by 10.4 percent from 1984 to 1985 while screenings at Chapel

Street declined by 31.3 percent. BCG vaccinations also declined by 17 percent for blacks and by 19.3 percent for coloreds. Total attendance at TB clinics was down by 12.5 percent. This decline reflected the damaging or closing of some clinics and perhaps also the reluctance of patients to attend clinics for fear of their personal safety.[3] Prior to July of 1986, when influx controls were relaxed, the "illegal" status of a growing number of African residents in the major urban areas of the country, and particularly of women and children in the western Cape, discouraged people with TB and other diseases from attending government clinics and hospitals for fear of being sent back to the bantustans. In addition Myers notes that workers who suspected the presence of a chest problem avoided screening in a context of recession, high unemployment, and the employer practice of dismissing workers with TB.[4] Many cases therefore have gone unreported.

In this regard, it may be significant that the notification rates for coloreds have been increasing steadily since 1975. Nationwide, coloreds now have significantly higher notification rates than Africans, whereas from 1960 to 1975 the rates of both groups were more or less equal (see graph twenty).[5] The disparity between rising colored rates and declining African rates does not appear to have any relationship to differences in known etiological factors.[6] Africans and coloreds suffer from many of the same social and economic disabilities, with Africans being generally more disadvantaged. It may instead be another reflection of the general underreporting of African cases exacerbated by the "great disappearing act" of the late 1970s and the disruption of medical services described above. The fact that African TB notifications have continued to rise in the Western Cape, where despite recent disruptions, surveillance measures are recognized as being the most efficient also suggests that the decline in national figures reflects underreporting.

The same factors that cause one to question the reliability of recent notification figures, also lead one to suspect that the actual incidence of TB may in fact be increasing. To begin with, cutbacks in medical services not only reduced surveillance measures but also possibilities for treatment. The number of beds available for TB patients nationwide, for example, has declined since the mid-1970s from 22,000 to 11,600. In Cape Town, the City Council reduced the number of TB beds by 1,000 between 1976 and 1980, increasing the ratio of beds to new patients to 1/25. This reduction reflected economic cutbacks combined with the belief that the introduction of short-term therapy using rifampicin had reduced the need for beds. Yet rifampicin has proven to be too expensive for many local health authorities. The Transvaal Health Department, for example, ceased using the drug for financial reasons in 1980, and today very few bantustan medical services employ the drug for similar reasons. The decline in hospitalization has increased the likelihood of patient default since compliance among out-patients is significantly worse than among hospitalized patients. This in turn is likely to have increased the number of infectious cases in the community.[7] Similarly the disruption of township clinics over the last two years curtailed treatment and follow-up services as well as notifications and thus contributed to treatment failures. It is therefore not surprising to learn that there has been an increase nationwide in treatment failures and drug-resistant relapsed or chronic cases.[8] These patterns make it unlikely that the actual incidence of TB is declining, and even if there has been a real decline in the last few years, it is unlikely to be sustained.

The Tuberculosis Research Institute of the state's Medical Research Council has concluded nonetheless that the TB situation among blacks has improved steadily since the mid-1950s. They base this conclusion on data collected in a series of prevalence studies carried out over the past three decades. Between 1972 and 1985 alone the TBRI conducted fifteen surveys involving over 40,000 persons. These studies have at various times included tuberculin testing to determine infection rates and the use of x-rays and bacteriological examinations to estimate the prevalence of actual TB cases. By comparing the results of these surveys over time, it is argued, one can identify a clear downward trend in both infection and prevalence rates.

The sheer magnitude of the accumulated data would appear to lend credence to the TBRI's conclusion. Yet drawing epidemiological conclusions from longitudinal comparisons of prevalence data is not an easy task. There are numerous methodological problems inherent in the use of such data which have to be looked at carefully before the data can be interpreted. It is not at all clear that in making their optimistic assessment, TBRI researchers have taken these issues into account.

Let us look first at their claims concerning the decline in annual risk of infection. Risk of infection is an index for estimating the rate of attack of TB within a given community. It is calculated from data derived from tuberculin surveys of young children. The rate, given as a percent, indicates the chances of a child being infected with TB during one year. Thus a 6 percent risk of infection would indicate that a child has 6 chances in 100 of being infected. The risk of infection also provides an indirect indicator of the prevalence of infectious cases in a community. According to the director of the TBRI, the annual risk of infection among Africans dropped by 5 to 8 percent per year from the mid-1950s up to 1977.[9] Yet an examination of the studies upon which this conclusion is based raises serious questions about the reliability of this estimate. The surveys carried out in the 1950s, in fact, are in no way comparable with those conducted in the 1970s. Rabie and Wiles working in the Transkei in the mid-1950s, for example, surveyed children between the ages of five and nine. They used ten units of PPD tuberculin to test for positivity and employed a criteria of positivity of 6 mm. The study did not test for the presence of other mycobacteria and thus a number of the children who tested positive may have been nonspecific reactors (false positives).[10] By comparison, the surveys conducted in the Transkei by the Tuberculosis Research Group in 1972 and by the TBRI in 1977[11] tested children ages four and under, employed only two units PPD tuberculin, and used a higher criteria of positivity—10 mm. They also screened for the presence of nontubercular mycobacteria, thereby reducing the number of false-positive reactions. As a result of these differences, the Rabie and Wiles survey would have produced a higher prevalence of infection than the 1972 and 1977 surveys, even if all three surveys had been testing the exact same population at the same moment in time. The incompatibility of the two sets of data make it impossible to draw any meaningful conclusions about changing risk of infection between the mid-1950s and the 1970s.

The TBRI claims that there has been a further drop in risk of infection among Africans of roughly 6 to 8 percent per year since 1977. This conclusion is based on a comparison of surveys conducted during two periods, 1972–1978 and 1979–1985.[12] This data is difficult to interpret for three reasons. First, the figures presented are based on pooled data taken from different areas over several years. They are not based on carefully controlled studies of specific populations at different points in time. Second, it must be remembered that by the early 1980s a large majority of the children in the areas being surveyed had been vaccinated with BCG. In the Ciskei, as noted in chapter 9, nearly 70 percent of the children surveyed had BCG scars. As Derek Yach notes, the interpretation of infection rates can be obscured in the presence of high BCG rates.[13] High levels of BCG coverage, in fact, generally reduce the value of risk-of-infection data as an instrument for measuring the rate at which TB is attacking a community.

The significance of the TBRI's findings regarding declining risk of infection since 1977 may also be limited by the occurrence of false-negative reactions. As E. U. Rosen notes,

> The high frequency of false-negative results on skin testing in developing countries is well known. This is due to a combination of several factors. Apart from poor technique in administering the test, incorrect storage and inactive testing material, false-negative results arise from conditions which lead to depression of the cellular arm of the immune response.

She goes on to observe that,

> Cell-mediated immunity may be depressed in children after clinical measles, measles immunization, or other viral infections, in the presence of overwhelming tuberculosis infection and also with protein energy malnutrition. The latter is often due not to poor diet alone but to the latter together with recurrent bacterial and viral infections. In addition some children remain intrinsically tuberculin negative whether they are infected or not. All these situations are common in developing countries.[14]

The combination of protein energy malnutrition (PEM) with recurrent viral and bacterial infections certainly occurs with great frequency among African children in South Africa. The question we need to ask in evaluating the reliability of the TBRI's claims of declining risk of infection, is whether or not these conditions grew worse between 1977 and 1985 and thus whether the percentage of false negatives may have increased over this period. It is of course very difficult to answer this question with any precision in the absence of reliable epidemiological data on the incidence of various viral and bacterial infections. We do know, however, that the early 1980s were marked by recurrent drought and human deprivation throughout much of southern Africa. The period was also marked by recession and growing African unemployment within both the urban and rural areas of the country. One can easily imagine that the incidence of PEM and related infections increased in association with these conditions and that this is likely to have increased the incidence of false-negative tuberculin reactions. If so the declining risk-of-infection index may in fact reflect a general worsening of health conditions rather than an improvement.

Obviously one can only speculate about the effects of such factors on risk-of-infection estimates. It cannot, for example, be proven that false negatives were more frequent in later periods than during earlier periods. But neither can it be disproved. At the very least these problems throw into question conclusions about current trends in TB prevalence based solely on risk-of-infection data. Thus, S. Grzybowski, in a paper presented to the 1982 MEDUNSA Conference on TB in the 1980s, warned that as an index of TB prevalence, risk of infection "is good but in many countries must be somewhat imprecise, and should if possible, be supplemented by reliable data on the incidence and prevalence of morbidity and mortality from tuberculosis."[15]

This brings us to the TBRI's conclusions regarding the decline in the prevalence of active TB cases. In a paper presented at the first TBRI symposium in 1985, TBRI researchers, P. B. Fourie and Karin Knoetze observed that "In Transkei, for example, the prevalence of bacteriological disease in persons older than 14 years was 2.4 percent in 1982. This rate is more than 50 percent lower than it was ten years earlier."[16] In assessing the reliability of this statement it must first be noted that it misrepresents the existing data on TB prevalence in the Transkei. Fourie and Knoetze were evidently referring to the 1972 TB survey of the Transkei conducted by the South African TB Study Group. Yet this study did not employ bacteriological examinations. They based their prevalence assessment instead on radiographic findings. They concluded, moreover, that the poor quality of the films and their great variability made it difficult to make an exact estimate of prevalence. They nonetheless provided a rough estimate of 8 percent.

It is well recognized that prevalence estimates based on radiographic evidence alone tend to significantly overestimate the actual prevalence of the disease and that bacteriological examinations are much more reliable. The 1972 study is therefore not comparable with the 1982 study. It may, however, be comparable to the earlier study by Rabie and Wiles which used similar methods. If so then there would appear to have been a major increase in the prevalence of TB in the Transkei between the mid-1950s—when Rabie and Wiles estimated TB prevalence to be 2.3 percent—and 1972. One wonders why this comparison is never mentioned by TBRI researchers when they are making claims about the downward trend in TB since the mid-1950s.

The only earlier study of TB prevalence in the Transkei comparable to the 1982 study was conducted by Fourie et al. in 1977. This study estimated the prevalence of bacteriological disease in persons over fourteen to be 4.3 percent on culture. If this estimate was correct, then the 50 percent drop to which Fourie and Knoetze refer occurred in only five years, a remarkable achievement.[17]

The first question one needs to ask in evaluating this conclusion is simply: Is it conceivable that the prevalence of TB in the Transkei could have been reduced by 50 percent in a period of five years, given the conditions that exist in the Transkei, and if so, how was it achieved? Kleeberg has suggested that massive coverage with BCG, improved living standards, particularly in the towns, and twenty to thirty years of case finding and chemotherapy have played a major role in limiting the spread of TB in South Africa.[18] Could these factors explain the fall in TB prevalence in the Transkei claimed by TBRI researchers.

Let us look first at the role of BCG. Though BCG may have played some role in reducing the overall prevalence of TB among blacks in South Africa after 1975 it could not have had much, if any, impact on the drop in TB prevalence referred to here, for the simple reason that, as noted in chapter 9, BCG coverage in the Transkei prior to 1972 was negligible and only began to expand in the mid-1970s. Since the prevalence figures reported by Fourie and Knoetze are for persons fourteen and over, it is highly unlikely that any of the persons tested in either 1977 or 1982 would have received BCG. To the extent that children vaccinated after 1972 were protected and did not develop TB and therefore did not infect older people, a fairly rare occurrence in any case, the BCG campaign may have had some impact on the prevalence of TB among those fourteen and over in the Transkei. But the impact would have been small at best and, given the questionable efficacy of BCG in South Africa, it may have had no effect at all.

Whether living conditions in the Transkei improved between the 1960s and the 1980s is hotly debated, as noted in chapter 9. At best it would seem there was some improvement in households at the upper end of the socioeconomic spectrum and a real deterioration at the bottom end. How this affected the prevalence of TB is difficult to say. There seems to be a fairly wide consensus, however, that the situation deteriorated in the 1980s as a result of the recession and droughts mentioned above. It in fact seems unlikely that improved conditions could account for much of a decline in TB prevalence between 1977 and 1982.

Finally, what effect has chemotherapy and case finding had? Probably none. With inefficient case finding and contact follow-up, and a cure rate of between 25 and 35 percent, it is mathematically impossible to reduce the overall prevalence of TB by these means alone in a population in which the disease is widespread. If one assumes that each infective case results in only one other case among the tubercular person's contacts, a conservative estimate given conditions in the Transkei, then one has to cure at least 50 percent of the reported cases just to stay even. When one realizes that only a small portion of the total pool of new infective cases is identified each year, it quickly becomes apparent that a TB control program needs to cure at least 75 percent of its notified cases in order to make a dent in the overall prevalence of the disease.

Overall it seems highly unlikely that the actual prevalence of TB in the Transkei declined by 50 percent between 1977 and 1982. One therefore has to presume that one or both of the TBRI's surveys failed to accurately assess the actual prevalence of the disease or that there are problems of comparability between the two studies similar to those noted above for tuberculin surveys.

There is therefore considerable room for skepticism about the TBRI's opitimistic view of recent trends in tuberculosis among blacks in South Africa. It may well be that some improvement has occurred in some urban areas of the country over the last ten years as a result of the combined use of BCG and chemotherapy.[19] Yet even if we accept that this is true, a sizable reservoir of infective TB cases remains among those Africans and colored populations that have been increasingly marginalized and moved beyond the social and political borders of white South Africa. A prevalence of 2,400 per 100,000 in the Transkei, although an improvement over 4,300 per 100,000, would still be appalling.

There is evidence, moreover, that this reservoir of infection is now overflowing its "legal" boundaries. It is flooding back into the urban areas along with the thousands of black men and women who are trying to escape the abject poverty of the bantustans in order to benefit even temporarily from the marginally better opportunities that exist within South Africa, even if this effort to better their lives results in arrest and imprisonment. In the late 1970s, as the current economic downturn began, Jan Lange and Sheena Duncan estimated that an illegal worker from the Ciskei who worked nine months in Peitermaritzburg and then spent three months in prison would increase his living standard by 702.7 percent. A person from Lebowa who worked six months in Johannesburg and spent six months in prison would improve his standard of living by 170 percent, and a person from Bophuthatswana who worked for only three months and spent six months in prison would benefit from a 28.5 percent increase in standard of living.[20] Economic pressures have thus encouraged tens of thousands of African men and women to flock to major urban centers of the country defying influx control laws.

The state has recently responded to these developments by initiating a new urbanization strategy, outlined in 1985 in the President's Council report, *An Urbanization Strategy for the Republic of South Africa,* and symbolized by the removal of pass laws in July of 1986. The new strategy rejects earlier efforts to keep the rural poor, the so-called outsiders, out of the urban centers of the country and acknowledges the interconnected nature of South Africa's political economy through the creation of regional economic zones incorporating both rural and urban areas. Although the strategy accepts the inevitable flow of Africans to the urban centers, it envisions a process of state-controlled urbanization facilitated by the operation of free-market forces. The state in effect will permit the urban influx of tens of thousands of bantustan residents but will not take responsibility for their welfare. Where they live and work will depend on their skills and what they can afford. The strategy projects the emergence of an internally stratified urban black population living in circumstances ranging from squatter camps to well-designed middle-class housing estates constructed by private capital rather than the state.[21]

The new strategy clearly reflects the interests of industrial capital, and not just international pressure for reform. The owners of industry saw the insider/outsider policies, initiated following the recommendations of the Reikert Commission in the late 1970s, as having increased the cost of black labor.[22] They thus pushed for a relaxation of influx control which would allow urban labor to be exposed to the competition of surplus labor from the bantustans. The new strategy permits this to occur while relieving the state of the responsibility of providing for the collective consumption of the new urban proletariat and lumpenproletariat.

The whole scenario is reminiscent of the 1940s when the Smuts government stopped enforcing influx control laws in order to meet the labor requirements of industrial capital. As in the 1940s, the state has abrogated its responsibility for the social welfare of the rapidly expanding urban population. Also like the 1940s, the new initiative has been catastrophic from the viewpoint of housing and social services. Officially, there were 914,000 squatters residing in the Johannesburg area in mid-1988. Unofficial estimates, however, ran as high as 1.5 million. In Cape Town, the congerie of squalid squatter communities known collectively as Crossroads mushroomed from 30,000 in 1980 to nearly 200,000 in 1987.[23] Durban's KwaMashu, now officially part of Kwa-Zulu, is rapidly becoming an uncontrolled squatter community. Nationwide it is estimated there are currently 3.5 million squatters in urban and suburban areas.[24]

There can be little doubt that this movement of unemployed, often malnourished, migrants coming from areas with extremely high prevalences of TB was a primary cause of the rising TB notification rates of the early 1980s and, in all probability, continues to generate an ever-growing reservoir of infection within African urban and peri-urban areas, particularly in the Cape Town area. Statistically, however, it is difficult to assess the impact of these developments on the incidence of TB. Although cases occurring among these new urban squatters fall within the official statistical boundaries of South Africa, they remain largely invisible as a result of the state's refusal to provide for the welfare needs of those who cannot afford to pay. There are few if any health services available to the poorest of the poor. Far from lending encouragement to those who view TB as a disease on the run, these trends seem to indicate that we are on the verge of a major upsurge in TB in the major urban centers of South Africa.

Though South African authorities may lament the disease burden this influx has thrust on the country's urban communities, there has never been a clearer case of the "chickens coming home to roost." In effect the municipal authorities, who for decades pushed the sick beyond the city limits and thereby sowed the seeds of TB infection in the surrounding black peri-urban and rural areas, are now having to reap the harvest of TB cases their exclusionary policies have produced. We are thus currently witnessing a replay of the processes that contributed to upsurges in urban black TB mortality during the 1930s and 1940s.

Perhaps the clearest evidence of the costs of having for decades driven TB "underground" is the recent rise in TB incidence among African mineworkers on the Rand. Following World War II, the incidence of TB on the mines first declined and then began to rise again between 1952 and 1960, with a particularly sharp upward trend between 1957 and 1960 (see graph 16). This rise reflected in part changes in diagnostic criteria and improvements in case-finding methods.

During the early 1950s the board that certified cases of silicosis and TB plus silicosis for compensation (but not simple TB) changed chairmanship. Over the previous twenty years there had been a series of chairmen who applied increasingly strict criteria to the certification of these diseases. This contributed to a progressive decline in certifications. The appointment of a new chairman in the early 1950s led to a return to earlier levels of certification. Commenting on the impact that one particularly conservative chairman had had on certifications and the effect of his removal, a witness to the Commission of Inquiry on the relationship of silicosis to TB in 1954 commented,

> We might have arrived at the position, had this gentleman been chairman for another three or four years, where it might have been 15 or 20 average per annum. It might have arrived at this position where it could be stated, on available data, that silicosis and tuberculosis, as such, had completely dis-

appeared—that it was non-existent. Instead of doing that, you have this sudden increase in certifications, since we took up this matter through the Mines
Department, and got a little bit of reorganization.[25]

A second factor in the rise of TB notifications in the early 1950s was
a change in the criterion used for diagnosing the disease. Prior to 1953
evidence of pleural effusions in the absence of other chest abnormalities
or a positive sputum was not accepted as proof of TB. A study of pleural
effusion cases, however, revealed that at least 40 percent were irrefut-
ably TB. This led to a loosening of the criterion and to an increase in TB
notifications.[26]

Beginning in the late 1950s the mines increased their use of x-ray
machines in the examination of recruits. Although novices diagnosed as
having TB were rejected and not included in calculating miners' TB
rates, x-ray exams turned up cases in men who had previously worked
on the mines. If they had worked on the mines in the previous six
months, they were considered the responsibility of the mines and were
included in the mines' statistics.[27]

During the early 1960s the mines also began using x-rays for examining all mineworkers who had worked for nine months and in termination physicals. This practice inevitably led to the discovery of more TB
cases and to an increase in the incidence of the disease. The effects of
this increase dissipated by the mid-1960s as the backlog of previously
undiscovered cases was eliminated and the introduction of new cases
was reduced. Incidence rates leveled off at between 3 and 4 per 1,000
between 1965 and 1975.

It should be noted that increased surveillance did not eliminate the
presence of active undiagnosed cases of TB on the mines. A random
sample of 1,503 mineworkers during the mid-1960s uncovered 7 (4.66
per 1,000) previously undiagnosed cases of bacteriologically positive
TB.[28] At the same time a sample of 1,841 "new employees" found 20
cases of TB not picked up by the screening process. Twelve of these 20
cases were diagnosed from x-rays taken at the time of their employment
but not properly read. Ten cases had passed through x-ray examinations at both the recruiting depot and the mine property. In short,
although the x-raying of mineworkers increased the number of cases
discovered on the mines, it did not completely eliminate the introduction of cases.[29]

Better case finding may not explain all the increase in TB incidence
during the 1960s and early 1970s. Underground conditions in the mines

grew worse during this period as the depth of mineworking increased. During the 1960s the number of persons working in areas in which the temperature was above the heatstroke level, defined as a wet-bulb temperature of 28.9 C (84 F), increased from 48,000 to 80,000, or by 60 percent. Though this evidently did not lead to a "dramatic increase" in heatstroke cases, a result of acclimatization procedures developed by the Applied Physiology Laboratory of the SAIMR,[30] it certainly increased the stress involved in mine work and may well have contributed to the reactivation process in workers previously infected with TB.

Beginning in 1976 the incidence of TB on the mines began to climb, jumping from roughly 4 per 1,000 to over 10 per 1,000 by 1978. Since then it has been fluctuating between 8 and 10 per 1,000. The reasons for this sharp rise are complex, yet like earlier fluctuations they are clearly related to changes in the composition of the black labor force and specifically to the policy of internalization that was initiated in the mid-1970s in the face of growing concern about the security of foreign sources of labor and changes in the wider South African economy.

As Yudelman and Jeeves[31] have recently noted, the Chamber of Mines considered increasing the use of labor from areas within South Africa at various points during the 1960s, primarily in response to concerns by the government about the industry's dependence on foreign labor and the need to develop more fully local labor resources.

The idea, however, had been rejected as unworkable given the mines' continued need to reduce labor costs and claimed inability to pay wages that could compete with manufacturing for local labor.

The sudden rise in gold prices in 1974 undercut some of these arguments and resulted in an increase in wages. The rise in the gold price, moreover, permitted the mines to invest in labor-saving technology. This in turn encouraged the development of a smaller more skilled black workforce. These developments were paralleled by two events that shook the chamber's confidence in the dependability of foreign labor sources. The first was the withdrawal of 120,000 Malawian workers, following a plane crash that killed 74 returning Malawaian miners. This was followed by the drastic decline in Mozambican labor following Mozambique's independence in 1975. The number of Mozambique workers declined from 114,385 in January 1976 to 48,565 by December of that year.[32]

Paralleling the withdrawal of foreign labor and restructuring of the mining process, the South African economy began to show the signs of a deepening recession, which, as noted in chapter 9, was deep-seated and structural. African unemployment increased steadily, creating for the first time in over two decades a demand among local African workers for employment within the mining industry.

In response to these developments the mines moved to restructure their workforce. They reduced their reliance on foreign sources of labor while lowering the total number of black workers involved in mine labor through the creation of a more stabilized and skilled body of African workers who were increasingly viewed as more or less permanent employees of the industry.

The combination of labor stabilization and internalization significantly altered the structure of the workforce. Specifically, the proportion of workers from South African recruitment areas increased from 32 percent of the total workforce in 1974 to 58 percent by 1983. Tropical labor, conversely, dropped from 23 percent of the total workforce in 1973 to 11 percent in 1974, following the withdrawal of Malawi workers, and to 3 percent in 1983. Mozambique workers dropped from 27 percent of the total workforce in 1974 to 10 percent in 1983.[33] Second, the average age of the workforce increased as did the average length of employment at the mines. All of these factors may have contributed to a rising incidence of TB.

As noted in chapter 6, the changing etiology of TB in the mines reduced the susceptibility of tropical and Mozambican workers to TB. Following World War II, TB morbidity among mineworkers was increasingly related to the degree of TB infectivity in the areas from which labor was drawn, with workers coming from the most infected areas having the highest TB morbidity rates. Mozambicans and tropicals coming from areas of relatively low infectivity were thus less at risk of developing TB than African workers from the more highly infected areas of South Africa and the neighboring BLS countries (Botswana, Lesotho, and Swaziland). A follow-up study of new recruits in the mid-1960s found that those coming from nontropical areas had a TB incidence of 22.4 per 1,000 while those from tropical areas had a rate of 4.3 per 1,000. Among existing workers the difference was 6.9 per 1,000 among nontropical workers and 2.9 per 1,000 among tropical workers. The specific relationships between infection rates and TB morbidity in this study are indicated in table 16.[34]

The data in table 16 suggest that differences in infection rates played a role in determining the relative risk of contracting TB experienced by workers from different recruiting areas. At the same time, the fact that the differences in infection rates are not as great as the differences in

TABLE 16
TB INFECTION AND MORBIDITY RATES OF AFRICAN
MINE RECRUITS BY TERRITORY OF ORIGIN

Territory of Origin	Incidence per 1,000	Average Percentage Tuberculin Positive
Transkei	10.1	98.6
Swaziland	9.2	92.5
Botswana	8.6	90.5
Lesotho	5.6	85.2
Republic of South Africa	4.5	97.4
Northern Mozambique	3.3	85.4
Zambia	3.1	84.6
Malawi	2.1	75.2

incidence rates suggests that other factors may have been at work in determining the relative risk of developing TB on the mines. One such factor may have been differences in the overall health of workers coming from these regions. Thus it is possible that the overall health of tropical workers was better than that of workers coming from areas that had served as labor reserves for longer periods of time. In other words, the labor reserve economy may have had a long-term debilitating effect on the overall health of labor supplies.

It is alternatively possible that the low degree of differentiation between infection rates disguises significant differences in degrees of reaction to tuberculin and that given the higher incidence of nonspecific mycobacteria in tropical areas the figures for the tropical workers contain a high percentage of relatively low-grade reactions (Heaf grades I and II) that are not due to tubercular infection. There may have been, in other words, a relatively high number of false positives among the tropical workers. The study, unfortunately, neither controlled for the presence of nonspecific reactions nor compared levels of reactions with territorial origin. It did, however, note that the workers with Heaf III and IV reactions had a much higher incidence of TB than workers with Heaf I and II reactions.[35] Thus if the tropical workers did have predominantly lower-grade reactions, it would account for their relatively high infection rates and yet low incidence rates.

Finally, the fact that "Republic of South Africa" workers had very high infection rates but moderate morbidity rates would seem to contradict the correlation between infection levels and incidence rates. Without knowing more about sample sizes and the specific territorial origins of these recruits it is difficult to provide an explanation for this anomaly. If these recruits came from the northern Transvaal or from low-lying coastal areas in the southeast of the country, their tuberculin reactions may also have been artificially high due to the presence of nonspecific mycobacteria. Alternatively, a number of other factors, such as the age of this contingent, their length of service, overall health, or subjection to better screening prior to recruitment, could have reduced their incidence rate. None of these factors, however, can be identified from the data provided in the study.

Despite this apparent anomaly, it remains clear that workers coming from tropical areas experienced lower levels of TB morbidity on the mines than workers coming from nontropical areas. When this difference is compared with changes that occurred in the territorial distribution of mine labor between 1973 and 1977, noted above, the impact of these changes is immediately apparent. The percentage of high-risk workers increased while that of low-risk workers decreased. Conversely, it is possible that the increased use of tropical labor from the 1940s to the 1970s may have had a suppressing effect on the incidence of TB on the mines, obscuring the health costs of increasingly oppressive underground working conditions during the 1960s.

Martiny has suggested that labor stabilization also may have had an adverse effect on TB rates on the mines by increasing the average age of the mine workforce.[36] Although no figures are available on the changing age composition of the mine workforce, the increased mining experience of the workforce and the drastic reduction in the number of novices employed in the mining industry suggested that the average age of African mineworkers has increased. The above study revealed the relationship between age and TB morbidity shown in table 17.

The average age of the workers in this study, however, was between twenty-seven and twenty-eight years. If we assume this was typical of the industry, the average age of the workforce would need to have increased by some ten years to have had any substantial impact on TB morbidity.

Martiny has also suggested that an increase in the length of time the average worker spends on the mines has contributed to the rising incidence of TB.[37] The average contract length increased from 4.5 to 13.5 months. This increase not only raised the average worker's exposure to conditions which encouraged the reactivation of TB, but also increased

TABLE 17

AGE-SPECIFIC MORBIDITY FOR TB, NEW MINE
EMPLOYEES

Age	Incidence per 1,000 New Employees	Incidence per 1,000 Existing Workers
Under 17	0	0
18–20	7.5	2.9
21–25	8.6	2.5
26–30	8.4	4.4
31–35	4.3	6.1
36–40	26.3	10.4
41–45	36.4	15.5
46–50	34.3	13.0
51–55	41.7	23.0
over 55	0	.5

the likelihood he would have his disease diagnosed, given improvements in TB surveillance efforts.

Readers familiar with past criticisms of the mining industry's use of migrant labor may find it ironic that the mines are now being criticized for trying to stabilize their labor force. It is, however, important to recognize that the negative impact that labor stabilization has had on TB rates among black mineworkers has been mediated by the effects of labor internalization. In other words, the impact that increased age and work experience have on TB morbidity are greatly heightened by the fact that a larger proportion of the workforce now comes from highly infected areas and carries with it the seeds of TB infection. The high infection rates of workers from internal source areas in turn is the result of decades of insensitivity on the part of mine managers and other users of black labor to the conditions that existed in these areas (other than to monitor the effect these conditions had on labor supplies) and their application of social control policies that methodically transferred the health costs of industrial production to the rural African populations through the repatriation of sick and injured workers. These costs are now being placed squarely on the shoulders of the mining industry. Second, one must also recognize that the mines' internalization and stabilization policies do not represent a rejection of the basic premise that mineworkers are migrant workers. The mines remain unwilling to bear the cost of creating a permanently settled workforce in which black miners, like white miners, are permitted to live with their wives and children within the industrial centers of the country. Stabilization in fact represents an intensification of worker exposure to the adverse conditions of mine work without any significant change in the terms of employment or an increase in the industry's financial responsibility for the welfare of the worker or his family. Although mine wages have increased, they remain low in relation to those of white workers and even in comparison with those of black workers in other industries. More important, they fail to meet the consumption needs of the majority of workers and their families.

Although the increase in TB incidence on the mines appears related to changes in the composition of the labor force, it is also noteworthy that health reports from the Rand Mines Ltd. indicate that within the group of workers defined as being other than tropical or Mozambican, and thus those workers with the highest risk of developing TB, there has been a steady rise in TB incidence since 1977. On one hand, this increase may be related to increasing age or length of exposure. On the other hand, it may reflect an increase in the proportion of this group's coming from resettlement areas where the prevalence of TB is extremely high. It may also, of course, indicate the worsening of conditions in either the mines or the areas from which this domestic labor was drawn during the late 1970s and early 1980s.

Medical authorities working in the mining industry, although initially alarmed at the rising incidence of TB among its black workforce, appear to have adopted a somewhat fatalistic acceptance of the conditions of mine work and the effects of labor stabilization, having responded by developing more efficient ways of treating the inevitable toll of TB cases these changed conditions are producing. Improvements in treatment have in the mining industry's view reduced concern about the rising incidence of TB.

> From a practical point of view, the increased incidence is very minor and will not present a problem to the industry which has agreed on common curative treatment regimes, with re-employment for all tuberculotics who develop tuberculosis on the mines. It is also expected that in the very near future, cured tuberculotics will be allowed to return to their previous occupations for which they have been trained.

> Tuberculosis amongst mineworkers need therefore no longer pose the threat of the past when they lost jobs and had to go home with inadequate compensation. By curing them at work and re-employing them, a new era has dawned for dealing with tuberculosis in the mining industry.[38]

sion closely linked to the country's changing political economy. High
TB mortality rates associated with the early growth of industry at the
beginning of the century encouraged local medical and governmental
authorities to apply exclusionary social controls that pushed those most
at risk of disease beyond the boundaries of white society. This policy
served a series of economic and social interests within white South
Africa but did little to reduce the burden of disease. In the absence of
more profound improvements in the social and economic conditions
under which the majority of blacks lived, and in fact a significant deterioration in the conditions of rural Africans, a reservoir of infection and
disease grew within the rural and peri-urban areas of the country. This
pool overflowed its banks in the late 1930s and 1940s as the country
once again expanded its industrial capacity and lowered the barriers to
African urban settlement in response to the particular needs of manufacturing capital. Yet neither the city fathers, nor rate-payers, nor the
owners of industry, nor the state was willing to take responsibility for
the welfare of these workers despite a great deal of talk about the need
for urban reform. In the near absence of efforts to accommodate this
urban influx, African workers and their families, many of whom had
been previously infected with TB, entered a world of low wages and
overcrowded slums that was antithetical to the maintenance of good
health. Predictably this resulted in a major new wave of urban TB.

In the wake of this epidemic, and outcries from the same rate-payers
who refused to contribute to the welfare of black workers, exclusionary
policies were once again employed under the banner of apartheid. The
obvious futility of reapplying the ineffective control efforts of an earlier
generation of civic leaders was, however, obscured by the introduction
of control programs based on the use of newly developed antitubercular
drugs and BCG vaccinations. In the face of exclusionary policies and
ongoing patterns of discrimination, unfortunately, chemotherapy and
BCG had little hope of significantly reducing the overall prevalence of
the disease. These measures may in fact have contributed to the long-
term expansion of TB in South Africa by deflecting attention away from
the need for social and economic reform, so widely recognized during
the 1940s. Thus, the reservoir of infection beyond the borders of white
South Africa continued to grow, at least through the early 1970s, and in
all likelihood up to the present.

Now it would appear we are once again seeing the inevitable break-
down of the barriers constructed to keep out disease. A new resurgence
of TB is surfacing in the urban areas of the country as thousands of

workers and their families attempt to escape the poverty of the bantu-stans. Once again, industrial capital and the state have combined to lay the groundwork for a major upsurge in urban-based TB. The question that remains is whether the state and/or local authorities will also once again apply their time-honored policies of exclusion to solve this growing problem, perhaps in conjunction with new promises about the virtues of chemoprophylaxis. Or will they at long last recognize the futility of this policy and begin to deal with the underlying causes of TB? The current push by conservative whites for stronger segregation and stiffer laws aimed at controlling the spread of illegal squatter communities would seem to indicate that a 1950s-like exercise in wall building is in the offing. If this course is chosen, the next generation of South African leaders, whatever their political or racial complexion, is likely to face an even greater epidemic of the "white plague."

Notes

PREFACE

1. P. B. Fourie, G. S. Townshend, and H. H. Kleeberg, "The Importance of Tuberculosis," Proceedings of the First TBRI Symposium, August 8–9, 1985, reported in *South African Journal of Science* 82 (July 1986): 386.

2. Thus the director of the TBRI observed in 1982 that "Proof that one can control TB without general uplift of the people and change in their socio-economic situation is everywhere . . ." H. H. Kleeberg, "The Dynamics of Tuberculosis in South Africa and the Impact of the Control Programme," *SAMJ*, special issue (November 17, 1982): 23.

3. WHO, *Apartheid and Health* (Geneva: WHO, 1982); Cecil De Beer, *The South African Disease* (Trenton, N.J.: African World Press, 1986).

4. Constance Hays, "Shelter to Aid Homeless Men Who Have TB," *New York Times*, October 4, 1988, pp. B1, 4.

5. Shula Marks, "Women's Health in South Africa," in Marcia Wright, Zena Stein, and Jean Scandlyn, eds., *Women's Health and Apartheid*, proceedings of the Third Workshop of the Project on Poverty, Health, and the State in Southern Africa, Columbia University, May 13–15, 1988, p. 8.

INTRODUCTION

1. Rene and Jean Dubos, *The White Plague* (Boston: Little, Brown and Company, 1953), p. 10.

2. E. R. N. Grigg, "The Arcana of Tuberculosis," *The American Review of Tuberculosis and Pulmonary Diseases*, pt. 3, 78 (1958): 426–446.

3. Dubos, *The White Plague*, pp. 185–196.

4. Thomas McKeown, *The Modern Rise of Population* (London: Edward Arnold, 1976).

5. Dubos suggests that it takes approximately 100 years ". . . in a fairly closed community to weed out the human strains most susceptible to the disease" (Dubos, *The White Plague*, p. 264).

6. The relative importance of these two factors has been greatly debated in western medical circles and, as we will see, was a central focus of disagreement among medical authorities in South Africa. The popularity of different positions reflected changes in the wider political and economic setting within which the debate occurred as much as advancements in medical knowledge.

7. Grigg, "The Arcana of Tuberculosis," 445.

8. Dubos, *The White Plague*, pp. 185–197.

9. This pattern can also be seen in U.S. cities after 1850, though the differences between blacks and other immigrant white communities is not so great as in the South African cases. The difference between white and African workers in South Africa has, moreover, continued to persist and has in fact increased over the last fifty years.

10. See chap. 8. It may be argued of course that it is too early to assert that the western pattern is not being repeated in Africa. The average length of a TB wave from early rise to decline in Europe and America was roughly 200 years. In many African countries we are still in the early or middle stages of such a long-term curve. It must be remembered, however, that the fall in TB mortality in Europe and America was generated in part by improvements in living and working conditions and that these in turn reflected the convergence of political and economic interests in support of health reform. There is little sign that such a convergence is occurring in South Africa, or that it is likely to occur under the current system of racial capitalism.

11. See for example, WHO, *Apartheid and Health* (Geneva: WHO, 1982); University of Cape Town, Medical School, *Consumption in the Land of Plenty—TB in South Africa* (Cape Town: University of Cape Town Press, 1982).

12. There is a considerable debate about the causes of the eighteenth-century rise in population. Thomas McKeown (*The Modern Rise of Population*) for example, argues that it was caused by declining mortality brought on largely by improvements in agricultural production and nutrition. This argument, as noted below, conflicts with dietary data. Others have argued that the increase was caused at least in part by changing marriage and fertility patterns that were a response to the collapse of peasant strategies for insuring the social reproduction of the household in the face of increasing proletarianization. (See E. A. Wrigley, "The Growth of Population in Eighteenth Century England: A Conundrum Resolved," *Past and Present* 98, for an attempt to evaluate the impact that different factors may have had on population growth.) I wish to thank Professor Howard Malchow for his comments concerning this complex period of English history.

13. Anthony Wohl, *Endangered Lives* (London: Methuen, 1983), p. 3.

14. Dorothy George notes how the poor laws encouraged parishes to attempt as far as possible "to thrust all who might become a burden on the rates on to some other parish." *England in Transition* (New York: Penguin Books, 1965), p. 137.

15. Dubos, *The White Plague*, p. 207.

16. See Wohl, *Endangered Lives.*

17. The effect of different levels of population stability on the rate of adjustment to local infectious diseases has been clearly demonstrated by Philip Curtin in his discussion of the epidemiology of the Atlantic Slave Trade. Curtin argues that the cheapness of slaves fostered a labor system that reproduced itself through the replacement of deceased slaves rather than by providing for the local reproduction of labor. This, he argues, greatly retarded the seasoning process. Curtin, "The Epidemiology of the Atlantic Slave Trade," *Political Science Quarterly* 83 (1968): 190–216. There was some variability in this pattern. Of particular note were a large number of Irish laborers who, in effect, acted as a reserve army, contracted for short periods to provide extra labor at peak production times and to break strikes in factories. Although comparative TB mortality data for different segments of labor are unavailable, one would expect to find the development of TB resistance among Irish laborers, operating in this migrant labor system, would have taken longer than among more permanently settled segments of the industrial workforce. In this respect the experience of Irish workers may have been similar to that of African migrant workers in South Africa described below.

18. Gareth Steadman Jones, *Languages of Class* (Cambridge: Cambridge University Press, 1983), p. 30, discusses John Foster's *Class Struggle and the Industrial Revolution.*

19. For example, Jones, *Languages of Class,* p. 73, observes in reference to the reform measures of the Peel government, "it is difficult there to separate the effect of Chartist Activity from the direct pressure of manufacturers."

20. The 1832 Reform Act may have been less critical from a health viewpoint that the 1835 Municipal Government Act, which provided for local elective governments under a franchise that was more democratic than the national franchise.

21. Steadman Jones, *Languages of Class,* p. 38.

22. K. J. Fielding, ed., *Speeches of Charles Dickens,* p. 128, cited in Wohl, *Endangered Lives,* p. 6.

23. In England, as in South Africa, the language of health reform was not simply about health. There was a metaphoric association of disease with the "dangerous classes," and middle-class reformers were not simply concerned with cholera infection but also with "the infection of Chartism and political radicalism in general" (personal communication, Howard Malchow).

24. Poor Law Administration in fact tightened up and became more repressive during the 1860s and 1870s.

25. Thomas McKeown and C. R. Lowe, *An Introduction to Social Medicine* (Oxford: Blackwell, 1974), p. 237, cited in David Sanders, *The Struggle for Health* (London: Macmillan, 1985), p. 49.

26. Wohl, *Endangered Lives,* pp. 285–328.

27. McKeown, *The Modern Rise of Population,* pp. 128–142.

28. Wohl, *Endangered Lives,* p. 48–58.

29. For more extended discussion of this process see: Shula Marks and Richard Rathbone, ed., *Industrialization and Social Change in South Africa* (London: Longmans, 1982); Colin Bundy, *The Rise and Fall of the South African Peasantry*

(Berkeley, Los Angeles, London: University of California Press, 1979); William Beinart, *The Political Economy of Pondoland* (Cambridge: Cambridge University Press, 1982); Alan Jeeves, *Migrant Labour in South African's Mining Economy* (Kingston: McGill-Queens University Press, 1985).

30. For a discussion of this problem see T. Keegan, "The Sharecropping Economy: African Class Formation and the 1913 Land Act in the Highveld Maize Belt," in B. Bozzoli, ed, *Town and Countryside in the Transvaal* (Johannesburg: Ravan Press, 1983), pp. 108–127.

31. F. A. Johnstone, *Class, Race, and Gold* (London: Routledge & Kegan Paul, 1976); Francis Wilson, *Labour in the South African Gold Mines* (Cambridge: Cambridge University Press, 1972).

32. The history of this response has been described by Bundy, Beinart, Keegan, and others cited above. In addition, see Jonathan Crush, *The Struggle for Swazi Labour* (Kingston: McGill-Queens University Press, 1987); and C. Bundy and W. Beinart, "State Intervention and Rural Resistance: The Transkei, 1900–1965," in M. Klein, ed., *Peasants in Africa* (Beverly Hills and London: Sage Publications, 1980).

33. Although the 1913 Land Act resulted in an increase in the supply of industrial labor and was a major instrument in the process of primitive accumulation in South Africa, this effect should not obscure the mining industry's efforts to insure that land alienation was not more extensive as large-scale farming interests advocated.

34. See chap. 4. Infection does not of course necessitate the development of clinical TB. Whether one progresses from infection to active symptoms depends on a range of physiological and environmental factors, the most important of which are nutrition, other forms of physical stress, and the existence of concurrent infections.

35. See chap. 2.

36. S. Marks and N. Andersson, "The State, Class and the Allocation of Health Resources," *Social Science and Medicine,* Special Issue on the Political Economy of Health in Africa and Latin America, 28 (1989): 515–530; and Elaine Katz, "White Workers' Grievances and the Industrial Color Bar," *South African Journal of Economics* 42 (1974): 127–156, for discussions of early white workers' struggles over health issues.

37. Charles van Onselen, *Studies in the Social and Economic History of the Witwatersrand, 1886–1914,* vol. 1, *New Babylon* (London: Longmans, 1982), pp. 1–23.

38. For early descriptions of the health problems facing white workers see G. Burke and P. Richardson, "The Profits of Death: A Comparative Study of Miner's Phthisis in Cornwall and the Transvaal," *JSAS* 4, 2 (1978): 147–171; Elaine Katz, "White Workers' Grievances and the Industrial Color Bar."

39. S. Marks and S. Trapido, "Lord Milner and the South African State," *History Workshop* 8 (1979): 50–80.

40. See Johnstone, *Class, Race, and Gold;* R. H. Davies, *Capital, State and White Labor in South Africa, 1900–1960* (Brighton: Harvester Press, 1979), for discussions of the development of the color bar in South Africa's gold-mining industry.

41. Symbolic of the role of the state in implementing a pattern of labor stratification was its provision of housing for white workers in newly constructed working-class suburbs around Johannesburg during the first decade of this century, in order to prevent white workers from living in close proximity to Africans and other blacks in boarding houses and slum tenements. Van Onselen, *Studies in the Social and Economic History*, 1: 29–31.

42. Marks and Andersson, "The State, Class and the Allocation of Health Resources"; and Katz, "White Workers' Grievances and the Industrial Color Bar."

43. See Jeeves, *Migrant Labour in South Africa's Mining Economy*, for a discussion of the development of this system.

44. Maynard Swanson, " 'The Sanitation Syndrome': Bubonic Plague and Urban Native Policy in the Cape Colony, 1900–1909," *JAH* 18 (1977): 387–410.

45. M. Wilson and L. Thompson, *The Oxford History of South Africa*, vol. 2 (New York: Oxford University Press, 1971), p. 453.

46. See S. Marks and Neal Andersson, "Industrialization, Rural Health and the 1944 Health Services Commission in South Africa," in S. Feierman and J. Janzen, eds., *The Social Basis of Health and Healing in Africa*, forthcoming, for a discussion of the relationship between deteriorating labor supplies and health reform.

47. A. W. Stadler, "Birds in the Cornfields: Squatters Movements in Johannesburg, 1944–1947," in B. Bozzoli, ed., *Labour, Townships and Protest* (Johannesburg: Ravan Press, 1979), pp. 19–48.

48. See Marks and Andersson, "Industrialization, Rural Health," and Cecil de Beer, *The South African Disease* (Trenton, N.J.: African World Press, 1986), for discussions of the failure of health reforms during the 1940s.

49. J. Saul and S. Gelb, *The Crisis in South Africa* (New York: The Monthly Review Press, 1981).

50. Included among this growing literature are: L. Doyal, *The Political Economy of Health* (London: Pluto Press, 1979); V. Navarro, *Medicine Under Capitalism* (New York: Prodist, 1976); R. Elling, "Industrialization and Occupational Health in Underdeveloped Countries," *International Journal of Health Services* 7 (1977): 209–235; M. Segall, "The Politics of Primary Health Care," *IDS Bulletin* 14 (1983): 27–37; R. Packard, "Industrial Production, Health and Disease in Sub-Saharan Africa," *Social Science and Medicine*, Special Issue on the Political Economy of Health, 28 (1989): 475–496; Merideth Turshen, *The Political Ecology of Disease in Tanzania* (New Brunswick, N.J.: Rutgers University Press, 1984); Helge Kjekshus, *Ecology Control and Economic Development in East Africa* (Berkeley, Los Angeles, London: University of California Press, 1977).

51. John Ford, *The Role of Trypanosomiasis in African Ecology* (Oxford: Clarendon Press, 1971).

52. R. M. Packard, "Maize, Cattle, and Mosquitoes: The Political Economy of Malaria Epidemics in Colonial Swaziland," *JAH* 25 (1984): 189–212; and "Agricultural Development, Migrant Labor and the Resurgence of Malaria in Swaziland," *Social Science and Medicine* 22, 8 (1986): 861–867.

53. Shula Marks and Neal Andersson, "Epidemics and Social Control in Twentieth Century South Africa," *Bulletin of the Society of the Social History of Medicine* 34 (1984).

54. Mark Dawson, "Small Pox in Kenya, 1880–1920," *Social Science and Medicine* 13, B (1979): 245–250.

55. More recently, the rising tide of TB on the mines and the realization of the mining industry that this rise is related to the industry's heavier dependence on local labor sourcing areas where the TB infection has become widespread, the result of years of repatriating sick workers, has encouraged the mining industry to take a more concerned attitude toward the effects of repatriation and to begin treating all TB cases until cure at the mines. See Epilogue.

1. PREINDUSTRIAL SOUTH AFRICA: A VIRGIN SOIL FOR TUBERCULOSIS?

1. Neil McVicar, "Tuberculosis among South African Natives," *South African Medical Record* 6, 13 (1908): 204.

2. TBRC, *Tuberculosis in South African Natives with Special Reference to the Disease among Mine Labourers on the Witwatersrand* (Johannesburg: South African Institute for Medical Research, Publication No. 30, 1932).

3. An example of this can be found in T. F. B. Collins, "The History of Southern Africa's First Tuberculosis Epidemic," *SAMJ* 62 (Nov. 13, 1982): 780–788.

4. See for example, David Webster, "Capital, Class and Consumption: A Social History of Tuberculosis in South Africa," in University of Cape Town, Medical Students Council, *Consumption in the Land of Plenty,* conference papers (Cape Town, 1982), p. 34; Cedric De Beer, *The South African Disease* (Trenton, N.J.: African World Press, 1986), p. 3. Also my own earlier article, "Industrialization, Rural Poverty and Tuberculosis in Southern Africa, 1850–1960," in S. Feiermen and J. Janzen, eds., *The Social Basis of Health and Healing in Africa* (Berkeley, Los Angeles, London: University of California Press, forthcoming).

5. McVicar, "Tuberculosis among South African Natives," p. 173.

6. Ibid., p. 199.

7. Ibid.

8. CMA, TBRC, Gemmill Private Files, File 7a, 8th Progress Report of Dr. Peter Allan, 1928.

9. William H. McNeill, *Plagues and Peoples* (New York: Doubleday, 1976), p. 156.

10. For other infectious diseases, like measles or small pox, this longer experience may have been limited by the absence of sufficiently large concentration of population prior to the nineteenth century. For TB, however, this was not required for the maintenance of infection within the population.

11. Jeff Guy, *The Destruction of the Zulu Kingdom* (London: Longmans, 1982).

12. U.G. 34–14, *Report of the Tuberculosis Commission* (Cape Town: Government Printers, 1914), p. 110.

13. McNeill, *Plagues and Peoples*, p. 54.

14. T. F. B. Collins, "The History of Southern Africa's First Tuberculosis epidemic," *SAMJ* 62 (Nov. 13, 1982): 780–788.

15. Rene and Jean Dubos, *The White Plague* (Boston: Little, Brown and Company, 1953), p. 205.

16. Ibid., pp. 194–195.

17. Ibid., p. 195.

18. A. Borrel, "Pneumonie et tuberculose chez les troupe noires," *Annales Inst. Pasteur* 24 (1920): 105–148.

19. L. Cummins, *International Journal of Public Health* 1 (1920): 83–95.

20. Charles Wilcocks, *Aspects of Medical Investigation in Africa* (London: Oxford University Press, 1962).

21. CMA, TBRC, Gemmill Private File 7a, 8th Progress Report of Dr. Peter Allan, 1928.

22. Charles Rosenberg, *The Cholera Years* (Chicago: University of Chicago Press, 1962), p. 5.

2. URBAN GROWTH, "CONSUMPTION," AND THE "DRESSED NATIVE"

1. David Welsh, "The Growth of Towns," in M. Wilson and L. Thompson, eds., *The Oxford History of South Africa* (New York: Oxford University Press, 1971), 2: 179.

2. Shula Marks, personal communication.

3. Cape of Good Hope, "Report of the Medical Officer of Health on the Public Health, 1904–5," p. 114.

4. U.G. 34–14, *Report of the Tuberculosis Commission* (Cape Town: Government Printers, 1914), p. 107.

5. Cape of Good Hope, *Report of the Medical Officer of Health for the Colony on the Public Health, 1906* (Cape Town: Government Printers, 1907), p. xxxi.

6. P. W. Laidler and M. Gelfand, *South African Medical History*, p. 318.

7. Laidler and Gelfand, *South African Medical History*, p. 380.

8. U.G., *Report of the TB Commission, 1914*, p. 28.

9. Although early biographers assumed that Rhodes was a tuberculotic and that he came to the Cape for health reasons, medical evidence collected by his most recent biographer contradicts this conclusion. Robert Rotberg. *The Founder* (London: Oxford University Press, 1988).

10. Ramsbottom, F. "The Threatened Conquest of South Africa by Bacillus Tuberculosis," *Transvaal Medical Journal* 1, 2 (August 1907): 10. The particular threat that indigent immigrant consumptives represented eventually led the South African Medical Congress to recommend that such persons should be refused entry at the ports. This recommendation was amended by the TB Commission in 1912 to read that all consumptive immigrants must possess sufficient means to support themselves during the period covered by their entry permits and to deposit £20 with the immigration officer to cover the cost of possible deportation or any other cost incurred by the government on their behalf. Union

of South Africa, *Tuberculosis Commission: First Report Dealing with the Question of the Admission of Tuberculosis Immigrants into the Union* (Cape Town: Government Printers, 1912), p. 3.

11. Dr. Neville Wood in an article in the *Practitioner,* cited in *SAMR* 11 (1913).

12. U.G., *Report of the Tuberculosis Commission, 1914,* p. 36.

13. W. Russell, "An Analysis of the Consumptive Cases Admitted into Kimberley Hospital," *SAMR* 4, 14 (1906): 214.

14. U.G., *Report of the Tuberculosis Commission, 1914,* p. 28.

15. Annual report, Dr. B. J. Guillemard, district surgeon, Aliwal North, in Cape of Good Hope—Cape of Good Hope, *Report of the Medical Officer of Health for the Colony on the Public Health* (Cape Town: Government Printers, 1897), p. 17.

16. Cape of Good Hope, *Report of the Medical Officer of Health for the Colony on the Public Health, 1906,* p. 2.

17. Ibid.

18. TAD, SNA 305, George Birch, "Memorandum on the Spread of Tuberculosis" for secretary of native affairs, 8/11/05; commenting on the fact that 20 percent of the cases seen in Addington Hospital were Jews, one physician noted that "All these Jews were of the poorer classes and had come to this country with the disease upon them. *SAMR* 4, 14: 213; Dubos, *The White Plague,* pp. 96, 195.

19. C. Van Onselen, *Studies in the Social and Economic History of the Witwatersrand, 1886–1914,* vol. 1, *New Babylon* (London: Longmans, 1982), pp. 73–74.

20. M. S. Evans, *Black and White in South East Africa* (London, 1911), pp. 296–297, cited in Welsh, "The Growth of Towns," p. 172.

21. Maynard Swanson, "The Sanitation Syndrome," *JAH* 18 (1977): 400.

22. MOH Johannesburg, testimony to Insanitary Area Commission, 1902, cited in *Annual Report of the MOH Johannesburg, 1916–1919,* p. 38.

23. *Annual Report of the Medical Officer for Health,* Johannesburg, 1904. Similarly, there were 112 whites living in the predominantly African East Bank location of East London in 1912; East London, *Report of the Medical Officer of Health, 1931,* p. 112.

24. Van Onselen, *New Babylon,* p. 27.

25. Ibid., p. 39

26. CMA, TBRC, Municipal and Territorial Investigations, file 24, James Irvine-Smith, director of Abbatoir and Livestock Market Department, Johannesburg, "The Prevalence and Suppression of Tuberculosis amongst the Live Stock of South Africa," paper presented to The Royal Sanitary Institute Congress at Johannesburg, March 1913.

27. U.G., *Report of the Tuberculosis Commission, 1914,* p. 218.

28. Ibid.

29. Ibid., p. 219.

30. Ibid., pp. 221–224.

31. TAD 199/A4082, "Memo of Points Brought Forward by the Delegates of the Witwatersrand Dairy Farmers Association," June 15, 1911.

32. TAD 199/A4082, Provincial Secretary to Acting Secretary for Agriculture, June 26, 1911.

33. TAD 199/A4082, Acting Principal Veterinary Surgeon to Acting Secretary for Agriculture, January 31, 1911.

34. TAD 199/A4082, memo from Acting Minister of Agriculture to Acting Secretary of Agriculture, July 29, 1911.

35. CMA, TBRC, "Municipal and Territorial Investigations," file 24, James Irvine-Smith, "The Prevalence and Suppression of Tuberculosis amongst the Live Stock of South Africa."

36. TBRC, *Tuberculosis among South African Natives* (Johannesburg: South African Institute for Medical Research, Publication No. 30, 1932), p. 423.

37. In 1939, the Department of Agriculture with the support of the Department of Public Health developed a national control plan that involved the segregation of reactors from nonreactors and the gradual disposing of reacting animals while raising up a new herd from the nonreacting portion. This method was considerably less costly than the previous slaughter method and spread the farmers' losses over a number of years. It therefore won the cooperation of the dairymen. Unfortunately, the outbreak of the war delayed implementation of the scheme. Following the war, the plan was delayed still further by the absence of needed manpower. It was estimated in 1947 that the prevalence of bovine tuberculosis in the dairy cattle of South Africa was between 30 and 40 percent. Gillies de Kock, "Bovine Tuberculosis in Its Relationship to Pure Milk Supply," *PTMMOA* 27, 294 (1947): 14–15.

38. CMA, Department of Mines, Departmental Committee of Inquiry into the Incidence of Tuberculosis on the Mines, Record of Proceedings, 1954, Testimony of Dr. Scott-Millar, MOH, Johannesburg, p. 1092.

39. de Kock, "Bovine Tuberculosis . . . ," p. 15.

40. Ibid., p. 13.

41. CMA, Department of Mines, Departmental Committee of Inquiry into the Incidence of Tuberculosis on the Mines, Record of Proceedings, 1954, Testimony of Dr. Scott-Millar, MOH, Johannesburg, p. 1092.

42. TAD, GES 645/7042, Dr. George Turner, Medical Officer of Health for the Transvaal to The Assistant Colonial Secretary, April 24, 1906.

43. TAD, SNA 303/3940, 1905.

44. I wish to thank Dr. Shula Marks for this observation. My own data indicate that mission Christian communities were a major focus of TB morbidity and mortality during the early years of this century. The association of western dress with disease and high rates of TB among mission Christian Africans contains a certain irony, for as Jean Comaroff has noted, Protestant missionaries in the nineteenth century associated the acquisition of European dress with improved health. Jean Comaroff, "The Diseased Heart of Africa: Medicine, Colonialism and the Black Body," in M. Lock and S. Linden Savin, eds., *Analysis in Medical Anthropology,* forthcoming.

45. Cape of Good Hope, *Report of the Medical Officer of Health for the Colony on the Public Health, 1906,* p. xxxvi; "Report on South African Medical Congress, Peitermaritzburg, 1905," in *Annual Report MOH, Johannesburg, 1906,* p. 25.

46. CMA, T19 1912–1913, Tuberculosis Commission, Testimony of Dr. T. E. Water.

47. Cape of Good Hope, *Report of the Medical Officer of Health for the Colony on the Public Health, 1906*, p. xxxvii.

48. The aberrant nature of this opinion was indicated in a summary of medical opinion prepared for the secretary of native affairs by George E. Birch in 1905. The opinion of Dr. Gregory, medical officer for health for the Cape Colony, that Africans had a constitutional predisposition to tuberculosis, was prefaced by the statement that he "is apparently a disciple of the NeoDarwinian theory of evolution by Natural Selection." TAD, SNA 303/3940.

49. Neil McVicar, "Tuberculosis among South African Natives," sec. 3, *SAMR* 6, 13 (1908): p. 207.

50. U.G., *Report of the Tuberculosis Commission, 1914*, pp. 25–27.

51. This attitude may have been reinforced by early work on the question of black susceptibility to TB in America. Frederick L. Hoffman in 1896 published a study entitled, *Race Traits and Tendencies of the American Negro*. In it he argued that emancipation had allowed Africans to fall into immoral living habits, and that the result was a decline in their vital capacity and a corresponding increase in their susceptibility to consumption. Marion Torchia, "Tuberculosis among American Negroes: Medical Research on a Racial Disease, 1830–1950," *Journal of the History of Medicine and Allied Sciences* 32 (1977): 261–262. Although South African medical authorities stress the possibility of improvement through education and experience, Hoffman took a more fatalistic view that improvement would only come through generations of natural selection.

52. GNLB 164 481/14.

53. McVicar, "TB amongst the Coloured Population of South Africa," *SAMR* 8 (1910): 44.

54. Cape of Good Hope, *Report of the Medical Officer of Health for the Colony on the Public Health, 1906*, p. xxxiii.

55. U.G., *Report of the Tuberculosis Commission, 1914*, p. 129n; see also Cape of Good Hope, *Report of the Medical Officer of Health for the Colony on the Public Health, 1904–5*, p. lxxxi.

56. Ibid., 1906, p. xxxii.

57. Maynard Swanson, "The Sanitation Syndrome," p. 401.

58. U.G., *Report of the Tuberculosis Commission, 1914*, p. 129.

59. Ibid., p. 126.

60. Swanson, "Sanitation Syndrome," p. 403–404.

61. U.G., *Report of the Tuberculosis Commission, 1914*, p. 126.

62. Ibid., p. 129.

63. Ibid., p. 127.

64. Ibid., p. 138.

65. Ibid., p. 134.

66. Ibid., p. 134.

67. Ibid., p. 133.

68. Data on diarrheal disease drawn from Johannesburg, *Reports of the Medical Officer of Health, 1913–14 to 1920s*.

69. U.G., *Report of the Tuberculosis Commission, 1914*, p. 131.

70. In response to this problem, the Municipal Council voted £200 for a two-room cottage on the outskirts of the location for the accommodation of persons suffering from TB. Although the TB commission found this to be a commendable effort, it must be noted that the cost of the facility equaled only a quarter of the year's profits from native revenues. Redistributing the year's surplus revenue in the form of better housing and sanitation might not have eliminated the need for a better health facility, but it most certainly would have had a greater impact on the long-term development of TB among location inhabitants than the token addition of an isolation facility.

71. U.G., *Report of the Tuberculosis Commission, 1914*, pp. 130–140.

72. Francis Wilson and Dominique Perrot, eds., *Outlook on a Century: South Africa 1870–1970* (Lovedale, South Africa: Lovedale Press, 1973), p. 361.

73. David Webster, "The Political Economy of Food Production and Nutrition in Southern Africa in Historical Perspective," *Critical Health* (Nov. 1981): 8–11. Sonya Jones, *A Study of Swazi Nutrition* (Durban: Institute for Social Research, 1963), p. 66.

74. U.G., *Report of the Tuberculosis Commission, 1914*, p. 130; P. Bonner, "The Transvaal Native Congress, 1917–1920: The Radicalization of the African Petty Bourgeoisie on the Rand," in S. Marks and R. Rathbone, eds., *Industrialization and Social Change in South Africa* (London: Longmans, 1982), p. 284.

75. Rene Dubos, "The Host in Tuberculosis," *Acta Tuberculosea* 37 (1959): 46.

76. D. P. Marais, "The Prevention of Consumption," *SAMR* 10 (1912): 42.

77. Maynard Swanson, "The Sanitation Syndrome," pp. 401–402.

78. Dr. D. C. Rees, medical officer, Port Elizabeth, in Cape of Good Hope, *Report of the Medical Officer of Health for the Colony on the Public Health, 1907*, p. 31.

79. I wish to thank Professor Joyce Kirk for information on the early social history of Port Elizabeth.

80. Maynard Swanson, "The Sanitation Syndrome," pp. 402–404.

81. U.G. *Report of the Tuberculosis Commission, 1914*, p. 144.

82. E. R. N. Grigg, "The Arcana of Tuberculosis," *The American Review of Tuberculosis and Pulmonary Diseases* 78, 2 (1958): 167.

83. Personal communication, Shula Marks.

84. Cape of Good Hope, *Report of the Medical Officer of Health for the Colony on the Public Health, 1904–5* (Cape Town: 1906), p. lxxiv.

85. GES 598 178/13B, Report of the City Engineer for Port Elizabeth, Re. Water Supply, 1929.

86. U.G., *Report of the Tuberculosis Commission, 1914*, p. 144.

87. This does not necessarily mean that it did not play a role in the changing epidemiology of TB. There unfortunately are no notification rates available for this period and thus it is impossible to know if TB morbidity, as opposed to TB mortality, was affected by the changing size of the population. Although mortality and morbidity tend to move in similar directions during the early stages of a TB epidemic, momentary improvements in certain economic and social condi-

tions may lead to a decline in the case mortality rate and thus of mortality while TB incidence continues to rise.

88. U.G., *Report of the Tuberculosis Commission, 1914*, pp. 144–145.

89. Annual reports of the medical officer for health, Johannesburg, 1906–1914.

3. BLACK MINEWORKERS AND THE PRODUCTION OF TUBERCULOSIS

1. The following discussion of mining conditions focuses on the gold and diamond mines of South Africa. Other types of mining existed, the most important of which was coal mining. Conditions in the coal mines, particularly in Natal were appalling, even in comparison with those of the Rand at the beginning of the century. The rations and housing conditions were often much worse. Reporting on the housing conditions, the 1914 TB Commission reported:

> As a general rule the quarters are bad; on some collieries they are extremely bad. In nearly all cases the rooms have mud floors, and there are no bunks, so that the inmates lie on the floor, which in the majority of cases was extremely filthy, and littered with dirty kit, old sacking and debris of food and merwe . . . (U.G., *Report of the Tuberculosis Commission, 1914*, p. 184)

The average ration for African workers was 2.5 to 3 pounds of mealie meal per week and 2 pounds of raw meat once a week or every other week. No vegetables, fruit, or other foods were provided. The commission concluded that this was extremely inadequate and accounted for the 10 to 15 percent absentee rate. The total attrition (deaths plus repatriations) from TB among Indian workers, who received better rations than the African workers, ranged from 15 per 1,000 to an incredible 32 per 1,000 per year between 1908 and 1910.

2. Dr. Orenstein, "Discussion of Tuberculosis," *PTMMOA* 7, 4 (1927): 5.

3. For discussions of the economics of labor in the South African gold mines, see: Francis Wilson, *Labour in the South African Gold Mines* (Cambridge: Cambridge University Press, 1972); Frederick Johnstone, *Class, Race, and Gold* (London: RKP, 1976); R. Davies, *Capital, State and White Labour in South Africa, 1900–1960* (Brighton, 1979); H. Wolpe, "Capitalism and Cheap Labour Power: From Segregation to Apartheid," *Economy and Society* 1, 4, (1972); Peter Richardson and Jean Jacques Van-Helten, "Labour in the South African Gold Mining Industry," in S. Marks and R. Rathbone, eds., *Industrialization and Social Change in South Africa* (London: Longmans, 1982), pp. 77–98.

4. The Transvaal, *Report of the Coloured Labour Compound Commission* (Pretoria: Government Printers, 1905), p. 33.

5. J. Grant Millar, "A Native Aspect of the Native Labour Question," *SAMR* 7 (1909): 163.

6. GNLB 164, 481/14, Chairman, Miner's Phthisis Prevention Committee, to President, Chamber of Mines, February 20, 1914.

7. BRA, H. Eckstein and Co., vol. 244, File 98, "Health of the Natives," W. H. Brodie to the Secretary, WNLA, Nov. 8, 1904.

8. Dr. Brodie reported performing an autopsy on a man who had dropped

dead on his way from the WNLA compound to the Nourse deep mine. He found that "The stomach was crammed to overdistension with undigested mealie meal and fish . . . ," BRA, H. Eckstein and Co., vol. 244, File 98, "Health of the Natives," W. H. Brodie to the Secretary, WNLA, Nov. 8, 1904.

9. The Transvaal, *Report of the Coloured Labour Compound Commission*, p. 70.

10. BRA, H. Eckstein and Co., vol. 244, File 98, "Health of the Natives," Brodie to the Secretary, WNLA, Nov. 22, 1904.

11. Ibid., file 107, "Health of the Natives," W. H. Brodie, Report to Chamber of Mines, April 12, 1903.

12. Ibid., W. H. Brodie to the Secretary, WNLA, Nov. 8, 1904.

13. Ibid., W. H. Brodie to the Secretary, WNLA, July 7, 1904.

14. Alan Jeeves, *Migrant Labour in South Africa's Mining Economy* (Kingston: Queens-McGill University Press, 1985), pp. 57–58.

15. Ibid., pp. 76–82.

16. CMA, T19, TB commission, 1912–1913, Testimony of B. G. Brock, May 1, 1912. The cursory nature of such exams no doubt accounts in large measure for the following episode reported by Brock:

> There was a boy employed by Simmer and Jack; he entered the hospital on the 7th of September with pneumonia, and he was repatriated on 30th September on account of "disability after pneumonia and possibly phthisis supervening." He was registered and passed by GLB on 23 October for Simmer and Jack and rejected by the MMO and repatriated again on the 5th of November.

17. Ibid.

18. Ibid.

19. CMA, TBRC corr. (j) 1928, file 17; Dr. Mavrogodato, "Tuberculosis Prevalence Rates among the Native Miners on the Witwatersrand Gold Mines, 1916–1927," typescript, p. 25. This high incidence during the first months of work may also reflect to some degree the presence of Africans with no prior exposure to TB and a hereditary susceptibility to the disease within the ranks of new recruits.

20. G. Burke and P. Richardson, "The Profits of Death: A Comparative Study of Miner's Phthisis in Cornwall and the Transvaal," *JSAS* 4, 2 (1978): 152.

21. BRA, H. Eckstein and Co., Committee of Medical Officers, Report on the Mortality of Natives on the Mines of the Witwatersrand to the Commission on Native Affairs, 1903, vol. 244, file 107H, "Health of the Natives."

22. Although the numbers tested, particularly in the case of Nyasaland and Mozambique, were small in relation to the population at risk, they are large enough for the differences to reach statistical significance.

23. U.G., *Report of the Tuberculosis Commission, 1914*, pp. 113–114.

24. L. G. Irvine, A. Mavrogodato, and H. Pirow, *A Review of the History of Silicosis on the Witwatersrand Goldfields* (Johannesburg: International Silicosis Conference, 1930), p. 183. See chap. 6 for further discussion of humidity problem on mines.

25. Rob Turrell, "Kimberley Model Compounds," *JAH* 25, 1 (1984): 63–64.

26. U.G., *Report of the Tuberculosis Commission, 1914*, p. 151.

27. Ibid., p. 169.

28. Ibid., p. 168.

29. Ibid., p. 175.

30. Turrell, "Kimberley Model Compounds," p. 65.

31. See chap. 3 n. 3 for citations.

32. The Transvaal, *Report of the Coloured Labour Compound Commission*, pp. v–vi.

33. Ibid., pp. xv–xviii.

34. BRA, H. Eckstein and Co., vol 135, file 107H, S. Evans to L. Reyersbach, Aug. 15, 1904. Turner was clearly viewed as being antagonistic to the interests of the mining industry at this time. It is therefore interesting to note that he subsequently was employed as chief medical advisor for WNLA and by 1912, when he was named as a member of the Union Government's TB commission, he had become a major defender of the mining industry's interests.

35. The Transvaal, *Report of the Coloured Labour Compound Commission*, p. iv.

36. Ibid., p. xi.

37. Even Turner, while recognizing the problem created by the close proximity of men in the compounds, maintained certain ideas that were based on a theory of contagion. Thus in his testimony to the Coloured Labour Compound Commission he argued that the susceptibility to phthisis increased with the crowding and foulness of the air. Quoting Pakes, he noted that not only did proximity facilitate the spread of the disease but, "there is reason to believe that the bacilli acquire a more virulent infective power in the foul atmosphere of our crowded rooms and damp houses, than they originally possessed on leaving the lungs of a phthsical person." CMA N9 Compound Commission, 1904, "Response to Report by George Turner, MOH, Transvaal."

38. A. P. Cartwright, *Doctors on the Mines* (Cape Town: Purnell, 1971), p. 21.

39. BRA, H. Eckstein and Co., vol. 244, file 107H, "Health of the Natives," memorandum from the Chamber of Mines, September 3, 1903.

40. Jeeves, *Migrant Labour in South Africa's Mining Economy*, p. 231.

41. The TB commission attributed this difference to the more experienced nature of the workers in these older compounds. A study done at the Premier Diamond Mines, however, compared hospital admissions from two compounds, one built according to government regulations with excessive ventilation, the other built without regard to ventilation requirements. The hospital admissions in the former were 100 percent higher than in the latter. CMA, Health Conditions, Tropical Natives, 1911–1912, proceedings of a meeting between Secretary of NAD and representatives of the Transvaal Chamber of Mines, p. 33. See also, The Transvaal, *Report of the Coloured Labour Compound Commission*, p. x.

42. Rob Turrell, "Kimberly, Labour and Compounds, 1877–1888," in S. Marks and R. Rathbone, eds., *Industrialization and Social Change in South Africa* (London: Longmans, 1982), pp. 62–64.

43. It is unclear what other factors may have affected the mineworkers

choice in this matter, or whether the superintendent was simply trying to blame the workers for the nutritional problems they experienced. U.G., *Report of the Tuberculosis Commission, 1914*, p. 151.

44. BRA, H. Eckstein and Co., vol. 244, file 107H, "Health of the Natives," G. A. Turner to Transvaal Chamber of Mines, June 24, 1905.

45. U.G., *Report of the Tuberculosis Commission, 1914*, p. 164.

46. U.G., 37–14, *Report of the Native Grievances Inquiry, 1913–14* (Cape Town: Government Printers, 1914), p. 17.

47. CMA, Low Grade Ore Commission, 1930–1931, exhibits 112–186, Correspondence of Mckenzie to Gemmill, July 3, 1923.

48. Jeeves, *Migrant Labour in South Africa's Mining Economy*, p. 22.

49. U.G., *Report of the Tuberculosis Commission, 1914*, p. 212. It is unclear how common this practice was. The incidents were reported to the commission by mine managers and may have been a means of explaining nutritional problems in a way that deflected attention away from the mine's own cost-cutting practices.

50. Cartwright, *Doctors on the Mines*, p. 17.

51. BRA, H. Eckstein and Co., vol. 244, file 107H, "Health of the Natives," report of Irvine and McCauley to Chamber of Mines, 1903.

52. TAD, SNA 188 3159/03, Resident Magistrate Winburg to Colonial Secretary Bloemfontein, November 11, 1903. Similar reports were made by district surgeons in the Cape Province. Cape of Good Hope, *Reports of the Medical Officer of Health for the Colony on the Public Health, 1907* (Cape Town: 1908).

53. TAD, SNA 45 1481/02, proceedings at an inquest dealing with the death of Matabo Ramapiai, held by Mr. J. A. Ashburnham, Resident Magistrate at Bloemfontein, on July 14, 1902.

54. Transvaal Colony, *Final Report of the Mining Regulations Commission* (hereinafter *FRMRC*) (Pretoria: 1910), p. 71.

55. Cartwright, *Doctors on the Mines*, p. 33.

56. *FRMRC*, p. 74.

57. G. A. Turner, "Anchylostomiasis in South Africa," *Transvaal Medical Journal* (September 8, 1908): 34–39.

58. *FRMRC*, p. 71.

59. *Report of the Tuberculosis Commission*, p. 271.

60. Elain Katz, "Silicosis on the South African Gold Mines," in Francis Wilson and Gill Westcott, *Economics of Health in South Africa*, vol. 2. (Johannesburg: Ravan Press, 1980), p. 202.

61. Jeeves, *Migrant Labour in South Africa's Mining Economy*, p. 23.

62. *Report of the Tuberculosis Commission*, p. 205.

63. Burke and Richardson, "The Profits of Death," p. 152.

64. BRA, H. Eckstein and Co., vol. 244, file 98, "Health of the Miners," H. Warrington Smyth, Secretary of Mines Department, to Secretary of the Transvaal Chamber of Mines, June 1, 1906.

65. BRA, H. Eckstein and Co., vol. 258, File 154 M, "Miner's Phthisis," T. J. Britten to President and Executive Members of the Chamber of Mines, June 18, 1906.

66. U.G., *Report of the Tuberculosis Commission, 1914*, p. 210.

67. Jeeves, *Migrant Labour in South Africa's Mining Economy*, p. 24.

68. U.G., *Report of the Tuberculosis Commission, 1914*, p. 209.

69. CMA N21, "Coloured Labourer's Health," second meeting of "Committee Appointed to Inquire Whether Change Houses Are Necessary on the Mines," January 23, 1907.

70. CMA N21, "Committee Appointed to Inquire Whether Change Houses . . . ," p. 6.

71. BRA, Rand Mines Ltd. Annual Report, Department of Sanitation, 1916, 1917.

72. Similar adjustments should be made for the 1916 and 1917 figures provided above. The raw data is not available, however, to make these calculations.

73. U.G., *Report of the Tuberculosis Commission, 1914*, p. 207.

4. MIGRANT LABOR AND THE RURAL EXPANSION OF TUBERCULOSIS

1. Reported in *SAMR* 5, 10 (1907): 311.

2. Grant J. Millar, "On the Spread and Prevention of Tuberculosis Disease in Pondoland, South Africa," *The British Medical Journal* (Sept. 24, 1908): 380.

3. TBRC, *Tuberculosis in South African Natives, with Special Reference to the Native Workers on the Witwatersrand* (Johannesburg: South African Institute for Medical Research, Publication No. 30, 1932).

4. TBRC, *Tuberculosis in South African Natives*, p. 223.

5. Ibid., pp. 241–242.

6. Ibid., p. 242.

7. Department of Native Affairs, *Report of the Native Laws Commission* (Fagan Commission), 1946–1948 (Pretoria: Government Printers, 1948), p. 38.

8. Reported in *SAMR* 5, 10 (1907): 311.

9. A. J. Orenstein, "Discussion on Tuberculosis," *PTMMOA* 5, 7 (January 1926): 3–4.

10. This argument was clearly stated in the Chamber of Mine's response to suggestions that workers would be better off living with their families at the mines. See chap. 6 for a fuller discussion of the use of this argument to support a system of migrant labor.

11. TBRC, *Tuberculosis in South African Natives*, p. 240.

12. Cited in W. Watkins-Pitchford, "The Industrial Diseases of South Africa," *SAMR* 12, 3 (1914): 49.

13. U.G. 34–14, *Report of the Tuberculosis Commission, 1914* (Cape Town: Government Printers, 1914), p. 197.

14. Colin McCord, "Persistent and Increasing High Risk of Tuberculosis after Work in the South African Gold Mines," unpublished paper, 1988.

15. Neil McVicar, "Tuberculosis among South African Natives," *SAMR* 6, 11 (Cape Town, 1908): 167.

16. Ibid., p. 166.

17. Cape of Good Hope, *Report of the Medical Officer of Health on the Public Health, 1904–1905*, p. 58.

18. McVicar, "Tuberculosis among South African Natives," p. 167.

19. There were, however, exceptions to this pattern. At the Illovo Sugar Estates a survey in 1922 uncovered 15 cases in a workforce of 600. This works out to a prevalence of 25 per 1,000. All of the cases were said to have previously worked on the Rand, though this may have been intended to distract attention from the poor living and working conditions found in sugar estates.

20. U.G. 18–24, *Report of the Tuberculosis Survey of the Union of South Africa* (Cape Town: Government Printers, 1924), pp. 18–19; *PTMMOA* 2, 4 (August 1922): 4.

21. TBRC, *Tuberculosis in South African Natives,* p. 41.

22. This is a particularly low rate given the presence of nontubercular mycobacterium in Mozambique; G. D. Maynard, "The Relative Importance of Infection and Heredity in the Spread of Tuberculosis," in U.G., *Report of the Tuberculosis Commission, 1914,* pp. 340–341.

23. TBRC, *Tuberculosis in South African Natives,* p. 220.

24. SNA, H. W. Dyke, PHO, Basutoland, memorandum on the Incidence of Tuberculosis in Basutoland and the Necessity for Hospital Treatment of Tubercular Patients, Maseru, Aug. 25, 1936.

25. I. Schapera, *Migrant Labour and Tribal Life* (New York: Oxford University Press, 1947), p. 176.

26. U.G., *Report of the Tuberculosis Commission, 1914,* p. 107.

27. One must of course keep in mind the possibility that this attribution reflected concerns about the mines' impact on local labor supplies as much as the actual distribution of cases.

28. Cited in Schapera, *Migrant Labour and Tribal Life,* p. 176.

29. Patrick Harries, "Kinship, Ideology and the Nature of Pre-colonial Labour Migration: Labour Migration from the Delagoa Bay Hinterland to South Africa up to 1895," in S. Marks and R. Rathbone, eds., *Industrialization and Social Change in South Africa* (London: Longmans, 1982), p. 144.

30. Jeeves notes that according to the Mozambique Convention of 1909, Mozambican mineworkers were permitted to engage for a maximum initial contract of twelve months with a possible six months' extension. In actual practice, most Mozambique miners stayed at least eighteen months at the mines. Alan Jeeves, *Migrant Labour in South Africa's Mining Economy* (Kingston: McGill-Queens University Press, 1985), p. 220.

31. Grant J. Millar, "On the Spread and Prevention of Tuberculosis Disease in Pondoland, South Africa," *The British Medical Journal* (Sept. 24, 1908): 381.

32. The spread of tuberculosis among rural dwellers in the Transkei and Ciskei as well as Basutoland may also have occurred as a result of their staying in overcrowded town locations en route to white farms during periods of peak labor demand. Thus the district surgeon of Lady Grey, located on the Transkei border, reported that, "At certain seasons of the year, too, is overcrowding more prevalent amongst the Natives than others, especially just before shearing and dipping occurs at the farms in the districts. At these times natives passing through Lady Grey from Hershel (in the Ciskei) or Basutoland arrange to spend the night at the hut of a friend in the location. At such times, as many as

eighteen persons have slept in one small hut." Dr. A. W. Dalgardo, in Cape of Good Hope, *Report of the MOH on the Public Health*, 1897 (Cape Town: 1898).

33. Henry Slater, "The Changing Pattern of Economic Relationships in Rural Natal, 1838–1914," in Shula Marks and Anthony Atmore, eds., *Economy and Society in Industrial South Africa* (London: Longmans, 1980), p. 161.

34. U.G., *Report of the Tuberculosis Commission, 1914*, pp. 103–104.

35. SNA, Swaziland Protectorate, Annual Medical and Sanitation Report, 1931, RCS 22/32.

36. TBRC, *Tuberculosis in South African Natives*, p. 41.

37. E. R. N. Grigg, "The Arcana of Tuberculosis," *American Review of Tuberculosis and Respiratory Diseases* 78, 2 (1958): 160.

38. See for example, PTMMOA 2, 4 (August 1922): 3–4; Peter Allan, *Report of Tuberculosis Survey*, p. 21.

39. U.G. 18–24, *Report of the Tuberculosis Survey*, p. 19.

40. Colin Bundy, *The Rise and Fall of the South African Peasantry* (Berkeley, Los Angeles, London: University of California Press, 1979); William Beinart, *The Political Economy of Pondoland* (Cambridge: Cambridge University Press, 1982); Colin Murray, *Families Divided* (Cambridge: Cambridge University Press, 1981).

41. William Beinart, *The Political Economy of Pondoland*, p. 22; J. Crush, *The Struggle for Swazi Labour, 1890–1920* (Kingston: McGill-Queens University Press, 1987), p. 16; P. Delius, *The Land Belongs to Us* (London: Heinemann, 1983), p. 74.

42. F. W. Fox and D. Back, *A Preliminary Survey of the Agricultural and Nutritional Problems of the Ciskei and Transkei Territories*, 1938, Chamber of Mines Library, Johannesburg, p. 106.

43. C. W. De Kiewiet, *A History of South Africa: Social and Economic* (London: Oxford University Press, 1957), p. 200.

44. Fox and Back, *A Preliminary Survey*, p. 32.

45. U.G. 22–32, *Report of the Native Economic Commission* (Pretoria: Government Printers, 1932), p. 40.

46. R. M. Packard, "Maize, Cattle, and Mosquitoes: The Political Economy of Malaria Epidemics in Colonial Swaziland," *JAH* 25 (1984): 192.

47. The African population in the rural areas of South Africa increased by 22 percent (absentees not included) between 1921 and 1936. RSA, Bureau of Statistics, *Urban and Rural Populations of South Africa, 1904–1960* (Pretoria: Government Printers, 1968).

48. Fox and Back, *A Preliminary Survey*, p. 44–45.

49. Ibid., p. 44.

50. U.G. 61/1955, *Summary of the Report of the Commission for the Socio-economic Development of the Bantu Areas within the Union of South Africa* (Tomlinson Commission Report) (Pretoria: Government Printers, 1955), p. 78.

51. F. W. Fox, "Diet and Life in South Africa," *SAMJ* (Jan. 11, 1936): 29.

52. Beinart, *The Political Economy of Pondoland, 1860–1930*, p. 48.

53. Fox and Back, *A Preliminary Survey*, p. 47.

54. C. Simkins, "Agricultural Production in the African Reserves," *JSAS* 7 (1981): 256–283.

55. Beinart, *The Political Economy of Pondoland*, pp. 99–100, 175.

56. See Packard, "Maize, Cattle, and Mosquitoes . . . ," for a detailed history of the impact of the depression on the health and welfare of Swazi households during the early 1930s.

57. Beinart, *The Political Economy of Pondoland*, p. 52.

58. Fox and Back, *A Preliminary Survey*, p. 187.

59. The report, moreover, did not hide the investigators' view that the mines' labor recruitment low-wage policies were a contributing cause to these conditions. This may explain why the report was suppressed by the Chamber of Mines and only released under pressure from the government in 1943. "Fox and Back Report Released," *The Guardian*, October 14, 1943.

60. Fox and Back, *A Preliminary Survey*, p. 23.

61. Ibid., table c.

62. E. Joki, "A Labour Manpower Survey of the Transkeian Territories," typescript, 1943, SAIRR file 38.6.2, University of Witwatersrand, p. 6.

63. Fox and Back, *A Preliminary Survey*, p. 195.

64. U.G., *Native Economic Commission*, p. 183.

65. Monica Hunter, *Reaction to Conquest* (London: Oxford University Press, 1936), pp. 68–69.

66. SNA, RSC 33/33, Swaziland Annual Medical Report, 1932.

67. Fox and Back, *A Preliminary Survey*, p. 195.

68. Ibid., p. 205.

69. Ibid., p. 124. The importance of such noncultivated foods for the maintenance of health and their declining availability in the face of expanding agricultural production has been recently studied in Nigeria by Nina Etkin and Paul Ross, "Food as Medicine and Medicine as Food: An Adaptive Framework for the Interpretation of Plant Utilization among the Hausa of Northern Nigeria," *Social Science and Medicine* 16 (1982): 1559–1573; "Malaria, Medicine, and Meals: Plant Use and Its Impact on Disease," in L. Romanucci et al., *The Anthropology of Medicine* (New York: Praeger, 1983), pp. 231–259.

70. Fox and Back, *Preliminary Survey*, p. 132.

71. F. W. Fox, "Diet and Health in South Africa," *SAMJ* (January 11, 1936): 29.

72. For a general discussion of these measures see, F. Wilson, "Farming, 1866–1966," in M. Wilson and L. Thompson, eds., *Oxford History of South Africa*, vol. 2 (Oxford: Oxford University Press, 1971), pp. 136–152.

73. CMA, file 85, 1938, "Native Labour—Diet Nutrition," E. Thompson, District Superintendent NRC, Umtata, to W. Gemmill, April 14, 1938.

74. CMA, file 85, 1938, "Native Labour—Diet Nutrition," L. D. Crowther, Transkeian Territories European Civic Association, memorandum on Maize Control Proposals, February 28, 1938.

75. Quoted in Fox and Back, *A Preliminary Survey*, p. 180.

76. CMA, file 85, 1938, "Native Labour—Diet Nutrition," F. W. Fox to A. J. Orenstein, July 4, 1938.

77. Packard, "Maize, Cattle, and Mosquitoes," p. 198.

78. Fox and Back, *A Preliminary Survey*, p. 182.

79. See chap. 6 for a fuller discussion of mine recruitment policies during the depression.

80. Fox and Back, *A Preliminary Survey*, p. 58.

81. TBRC, *Tuberculosis in South African Natives*, pp. 199–207.

82. Ibid., p. 209.

83. Ibid., p. 208.

84. Ibid., p. 221.

85. Ibid., pp. 242–243.

86. Ibid., p. 203.

87. Fox and Back, *A Preliminary Survey*, p. 215; A. B. Xuma, "The Social and Economic Aspects of Native Health," typescript, 1939, SAIRR, A. B. Xuma Papers, n. 16, p. 8.

88. B. A. Dormer, J. Friedlander, and F. J. Wiles, "A South African Team Looks at Tuberculosis," *PTMMOA* 23, 257 (1943): 78.

89. TAD, GES 999 401/176, 1937, Dormer, "The Use of Native Health Assistants for Survey Work in the Reserves," unpublished report, p. 2.

90. Personal communication, Shula Marks.

91. U.G. 28/1948, *Report of the Native Laws Commission* (Fagan Commission) (Pretoria: Government Printers, 1948), p. 8.

92. WHO, *Apartheid and Health* (Geneva: WHO, 1982), p. 203.

93. See Tim Keegan, "The Sharecropping Economy: African Class Formation and the Native Land Act of 1913 in the Highland Maize Belt," in Marks and Rathbone, eds., *Industrialization and Social Change in South Africa* (London: Longmans, 1982), pp. 195–211.

94. Helen Bradsford, " 'A Taste of Freedom,' Capitalist Development and Response to the ICU in the Transvaal Countryside," in B. Bozzoli, *Town and Countryside in the Transvaal* (Johannesburg: Raven Press, 1983), pp. 128–150.

95. U.G., *Report of the Native Economic Commission*, p. 56.

96. CMA, file 90a, Native Labor Misc. (1), 1938, "Desertions and Recoveries among Natives Employed on the Gold Mines."

97. U.G., *Report of the Native Farm Labour Committee, 1937–1939* (Pretoria: Government Printers, 1939), p. 46.

98. Ibid., p. 47.

99. Ibid., p. 47.

100. Shula Marks and Neil Anderson, "Industrialization, Rural Change and the 1944 Health Commission in South Africa," in S. Feierman and J. Janzen, *The Social Basis of Health and Healing in Africa* (Berkeley, Los Angeles, London: University of California Press), forthcoming. It should be noted, however, that the chamber continued to reject the idea that TB was an industrial health problem and that they were responsible for its spread into the rural areas. Thus in 1936, the chamber's Gold Producers' Committee rejected the suggestion that they should contribute £15,000 to £20,000 to the cost of constructing a TB hospital in the Ciskei. CMA, "Native Labour—Miscellaneous (1)," 1936, Technical Advisor, Acting General Manager to Secretary for Public Health, October 16, 1936.

101. This phenomenon continues today with rural health services reporting that their worst TB cases come off the farms. See chap. 9.

102. Personal communication, Shula Marks.

5. SLUMYARDS AND THE RISING TIDE OF TUBERCULOSIS

1. A. Proctor, "Class Struggle, Segregation and the City: A History of Sophiatown, 1905–1940," in B. Bozzoli, ed., *Labour, Townships and Protest* (Johannesburg: Ravan Press, 1979).

2. P. Bonner, "The Transvaal Native Congress, 1917–1920," in Shula Marks and Richard Rathbone, eds., *Industrialization and Social Change in South Africa* (London: Longmans, 1982), p. 272.

3. Shula Marks and Richard Rathbone, eds., *Industrialization and Social Change in South Africa*, p. 12.

4. U.G. 28–1948, *Report of the Native Laws Commission* (Pretoria: Government Printers, 1948), p. 6.

5. RSA, Bureau of Statistics, *Urban and Rural Populations of South Africa, 1904–1960* (Pretoria: Government Printers, 1968).

6. Johannesburg, *Report of the Medical Officer of Health* for the years 1914–1919.

7. On an annualized basis these rates would have been 1,476 per 100,000 for positive reactors and 694 per 100,000 for negative reactors. Of the 471 recorded cases of TB in this study, 95 occurred in negative reactors, 376 in positive reactors. Of the 95 tuberculin negative cases, 23 (23.2 percent) were military, whereas only 18 (4.7 percent) of the tuberculin-positive cases were military. TBRC, *Tuberculosis in South African Natives*, (Johannesburg: South African Institute for Medical Research, Publication No. 30, 1932), pp. 97–102.

8. Cape Town, *Report of the Medical Officer of Health*, for the years 1921–1936.

9. E. R. N. Grigg, "The Arcana of Tuberculosis," *American Review of Tuberculosis and Respiratory Diseases* 78, 2 (1958): 167.

10. Proctor, "Class Struggle, Segregation and the City," p. 53.

11. Bonner, "The Transvaal Native Congress," p. 284.

12. Influenza may also have adversely affected TB rates by incapacitating household wage earners and restricting or eliminating their ability to provide their families with food during the epidemic. The MOH for Cape Town noted that even in households that were not normally indigent, occupants were actually starving through there being no person sufficiently well to buy or supply food. Cape Town, *Report of the Medical Officer of Health, for the Year Ending 30 June 1919*, appendix 8, pp. xxii–xix.

13. Proctor, "Class Struggle and Segregation," p. 65.

14. Ibid., p. 56–59.

15. Ibid., p. 59–61.

16. Ibid., p. 59.

17. Eddie Koch, " 'Without Visible Means of Subsistence': Slumyard Cul-

ture in Johannesburg, 1918–1940," in B. Bozzoli, ed., *Town and Countryside in the Transvaal* (Johannesburg: Ravan Press, 1983), p. 154.

18. Proctor, "Class Struggle and Segregation," pp. 63–64.

19. See ibid.; and E. Helleman, *Rooiyard: A Sociological Survey of an Urban Native Slum* (Cape Town: Oxford University Press, 1948).

20. U.G., *Report of the Inter-departmental Committee on the Social, Health and Economic Conditions of Urban Natives* (hereinafter Smit Committee) (Pretoria: Government Printers, 1942), pp. 15–16; Monica Hunter, *Reaction to Conquest* (London: Oxford University Press, 1961), p. 445, notes that municipal housing in East London locations was built with white labor and that the cost of this housing set the standard for rents in privately owned houses.

21. A similar pattern occurred in Port Elizabeth, where in 1934 it was reported that accommodations for 200 single Africans remained empty. TAD, GES 598 175/13B, "Sanitation—Port Elizabeth."

22. Proctor, "Class Struggle and Segregation," p. 63.

23. Ibid., p. 66.

24. U. G., *Report of the Commission of Inquiry into the Disturbances of 30 August 1947, at the Moroka Emergency Camp.* (Pretoria: Government Printers, 1948), pp. 18–19.

25. U.G., *Report of the Native Economic Commission, 1930–1932* (Pretoria: Government Printers, 1932), p. 68.

26. GES 598 175/13A, Port Elizabeth, *Report of the Medical Officer of Health,* for the year ending June 30, 1928, p. 3.

27. GES 598 175/13 B, *Report on Housing and Sanitary Conditions at Korsten, Port Elizabeth,* January 27, 1933.

28. GES 818 593/13, Joint Council of Europeans and Natives, *Report on the Housing of Natives in Durban and the Peri-Durban Areas,* 1930, pp. 3–4.

29. Hunter, *Reaction to Conquest,* p. 446.

30. East London, *Report of the Medical Officer of Health,* for the year ending June 30, 1931, p. 62.

31. Ibid., p. 115.

32. Ibid.

33. Ibid., p. 118.

34. Ibid., p. 119.

35. Johannesburg, *Reports of the Medical Officer of Health,* 1920–1934.

36. Cape Town, *Reports of the Medical Officer of Health,* 1921–1936.

37. Smit Committee, p. 15.

38. GES 598 175/13B, memorandum of Meeting between the Port Elizabeth Council and the Secretary for Health on July 16, 1934.

39. Smit Committee, p. 8.

40. East London, *Report of the Medical Officer of Health,* 1931, p. 112.

41. R. Phillips, *Bantu in the City* (Lovedale, S.A.: Lovedale Press, 1938), p. 34.

42. U.G., 22–32, *Native Economic Commission,* p. 208.

43. Hellmann, *Rooiyard,* p. 27.

44. SAIRR, AD 843 63.4.4, statement by Sen. Reinholt-Jones, Sept. 23,

1938. This price differential was itself an example of the negative impact of urban removals on African health.

45. Phillips, *Bantu in the City*, p. 120.

46. F. W. Fox, Diet in the Urban Locations as Indicated by the Survey, appendix 1, in NAD, *Survey of African Income and Expenditures in 987 Families* (Pretoria: Government Printers, 1942), p. 32.

47. Three of the budgets collected by Phillips were discarded because they did not contain data on the amounts spent on individual food items. Eighteen of the budgets were from the families of mine clerks who received some of their food from the mines. A separate analysis of the mine-clerk budgets and the non-mine-clerk budgets did not reveal a significant difference in the purchasing patterns of the two groups.

48. Phillips, *Bantu in the City*, p. 120.

49. SAIRR, AD 843, 63.4.4, Reinhalt-Jones, September 23, 1938.

50. East London, *Report of the Medical Officer*, 1931, p. 99.

51. SAIRR, AD 843, 9-185, "Milk Depot at Germiston Location."

52. Ibid.

53. Fox and Back, *A Preliminary Survey of the Agricultural and Nutritional Problems of the Ciskei and Transkei*, 1938, appendix 2, annexure 3.

54. Ibid., appendix 2, annexure 2, report of F. Rodseth, Inspector of Urban Locations.

55. East London, *Report of the Medical Officer*, 1931, p. 99.

56. Ibid., p. 121.

57. See U.G., *Report of the Commission Appointed to Enquire into the Causes of, and Occurrences at, the Native Disturbances of Port Elizabeth on the 23rd October 1920, and the General Economic Conditions as They Affect the Native and Coloured Population.* (Cape Town: Government Printers, 1921).

58. Jacklyn Cock, *Maids and Madams* (Johannesburg: Ravan, 1980).

59. Because of the 1919 customs agreement between South Africa and the neighboring protectorates of Swaziland, Basutoland, and Bechuanaland, which prohibited the participant governments from imposing impediments to the free flow of goods and services, these restrictions were often imposed under the guise of protecting South African herds from the importation of cattle diseases. For example, Swazi cattle producers during the 1920s and 1930s were required to sell their herds at one of two "quarantine markets" established at Durban and Johannesburg. This prevented these producers from taking advantage of the free market and allowed the South African government to impose, in effect, a quota on beef imports. Other methods were used to deal with imports from Rhodesia. See R. M. Packard, "The Political Economy of Malaria Epidemics in Colonial Swaziland," *JAH* 25 (1984): 119–200; I. R. Phimister, "Meat Monopolies: Beef Cattle in Southern Rhodesia, 1890–1938," *JAH* 19, 3 (1978): 391–414.

60. Dan O'Meara, *Volkskapitalisme* (Johannesburg: Ravan Press, 1983), p. 36.

61. "Mealie Control Scheme," editorial, August 1929, in Francis Wilson and Dominique Perrot, eds., *Outlook on a Century: South Africa 1870–1970* (Lovedale, S.A., Lovedale Press, 1973), p. 414.

62. Phillips, *Bantu in the City*, p. 38.

63. East London, *Report of the Medical Officer*, 1931, p. 99.

64. SAIRR, AD 843, 63.4.4, September 23, 1938.

65. Charles van Onselen, *Studies in the Social and Economic History of the Witwatersrand, 1886–1914*, vol. 2, *New Babylon* (London: Longmans, 1982), pp. 44–102.

66. Hellmann, *Rooiyard*, pp. 41–43.

67. U.G., *Report of the Native Farm Labour Committee* (Pretoria: Government Printers, 1939), p. 50.

68. U.G. 22–32, *Native Economic Commission*, p. 110.

69. Ibid., p. 109.

6. LABOR SUPPLIES AND TUBERCULOSIS ON THE WITWATERSRAND

1. Numerous communications from the NAD to the Chamber of Mines stress the need for the chamber to improve working conditions, especially for tropical miners, in the three years immediately prior to the closing of mine recruitment north of twenty-two north latitude. The following passage from a letter addressed to the Chairman of the Chamber of Mines from Henry Burton, Minister of Native Affairs, June 12, 1911 (CMA N 14/1911, "Native Mortality"), emphasizes the seriousness of the situation: "I have discussed this subject of the heavy mortality of tropical Natives with my colleagues, who are in agreement with me that unless a decided improvement can be affected at an early date the Government will have no alternative to the measure of entirely prohibiting the introduction of tropical natives."

2. Suggested reforms and failure of compliance are recorded in the CMA, "Health Conditions—Tropical Natives, 1911–1912," reports of the Special Committee re Health of Tropical Natives, organized by WNLA, A. Jeeves, *Migrant Labour in South Africa's Mining Economy, 1890–1920* (Kingston, McGill-Queens University Press, 1985), pp. 323–233.

3. Jeeves, *Migrant Labour in South Africa's Mining Economy*, pp. 230–235. Some tropicals workers made their way into South Africa illegally, crossing the border into the Transvaal where they were picked up by local recruiters. This practice continued after the ban so that tropical workers remained on the mines though they were not recorded in the official statistics.

4. A. P. Cartwright, *Doctors on the Mines* (Cape Town: Purnell, 1971), p. 30.

5. Jeeves, *Migrant Labour in South Africa's Gold Mining Economy*, pp. 232–234.

6. As Cartwright notes, Evans had a "fly phobia" and was convinced that all forms of infection were spread by the housefly. "Thus he convinced himself that pneumonia was caused by the unwholesome activities of flies and that Gorgas' success in reducing the mortality from this disease among the Negroes working on the Canal was due to the destruction of flies and the fly-proofing of the men's huts. In this he was wrong." Cartwright, *Doctors on the Mines*, p. 29.

7. TBRC, *Tuberculosis in South African Natives*, publication of the South Africa Institute for Medical Research, No. 30 (Johannesburg, 1932), p. 49.

8. Cartwright, *Doctors on the Mines*, pp. 34–35.

9. Ibid., p. 36.

10. CMA, Low Grade Ore Comm. Native Labour Shortage, file 11, 1931. Acting General Manager, Crown Mines to Frank Raleigh, Chairman, Crown Mines Ltd., July 11, 1930.

11. CMA, file 11, 1931, Low Grade Ore Commission, Native Labor Shortage, C. S. McClean, Manager, West Rand Consolidated Mines, "Memo on effects of labor shortage."

12. CMA, file 11, 1931, Low Grade Ore Commission, Native Labor Shortage, memorandum on the Subject of Native Labor Shortages on the Witwatersrand, G. M. Co. Ltd., Dec. 3, 1930.

13. CMA, file 11, 1931, Low Grade Ore Commission, Native Labor Shortage, C. S. McClean, Manager, West Rand Consolidated Mines, "Memo on effects of labor shortage."

14. TAD, GNLB, 386 33/44, E. H. Culver, Asst. Health Officer for the Union, to the Acting Secretary for Public Health, May 15, 1931.

15. TAD, GNLB 386 33/44, Dr. Culver, Investigations into Health Conditions on the Mines, 1931.

16. TBRC, *Tuberculosis in South African Natives*, p. 342; TAD, GNLB 386 33/4, Mine Inspection of the Simmer and Jack Mine, Oct. 22, 1930.

17. TAD, GNLB 386 33/4, E. H. Thorton to Manager, Simmer and Jack Mine, May 30, 1930, "In view of the company's financial position this Department will not press for the erection of a new compound as recommended by Dr. Culver. Some steps must be taken, however, to relieve overcrowding."

18. TBRC, *Tuberculosis in South African Natives*, 1932, p. 269. Records from the Rand Mines Ltd. Group collected by Orenstein indicate a close correspondence between variations in the incidence rates of TB and influenza.

19. Figures based on data for individual mines from: CMA, TBRC, file 19, Corr(L), 1929–1931, Transvaal Chamber of Mines, "Native Tuberculosis 12 Months July 1929 to June 1930—Gold Mines."

20. BRA, CM/RM, Health Department Report, 1936.

21. CMA, 22/1931, Low Grade Ores Commission, E. H. Thorton, "Employment of Tropical Natives on Mines," Jan. 19, 1931.

22. CMA, 22/1931, Low Grade Ores Commission, E. H. Thorton to the Chairman, Low Grade Ore Commission, Jan. 19, 1931, p. 4.

23. CMA, 22/1931, Low Grade Ores Commission, E. H. Thorton to the Chairman, Low Grade Ore Commission, Jan. 19, 1931. Thorton in fact implied that scurvy cases were being deliberately misdiagnosed in order to avoid blame for providing inadequate health supervision. Under examination by Gemmill at the commission hearing, he was unable to substantiate that specific allegation. CMA, 22/1931, Low Grade Ore Commission, Tropical Natives, Extracts of Evidence (corresponding to pp. 2,528 to 2,556), p. 10.

24. TAD, GNLB 347 66/23, H. T. H. Butt, Senior Medical Officer, to Acting General Manager, Randfontein Estates Gold Mining Company, January 11, 1927.

25. TAD, GNLB 293 191/18, Orenstein to Manager, Rand Mines Ltd., December 31, 1919.

26. TAD, GNLB 347 66/23, H. T. H. Butt, Senior Medical Officer, to Acting General Manager, Randfontein Estates Gold Mining Company, January 11, 1927.

27. Reported in CMA, Low Grade Ore Commission, 1931, Exhibits 112–186. E. H. Thorton, "Employment of Tropical Natives on the Mines."

28. F. W. Fox, "Scurvy on the Witwatersrand Gold Mines: A Consideration of Some Statistical Data," *PTMMOA* 19, 216 (1940): 301.

29. CMA, 22/1931, Low Grade Ore Commission, "Extract of Statement of Evidence by Sir Edward Thorton."

30. BRA, CM/RM, Sanitation Department Report, 1926.

31. CMA, 22/1931, Low Grade Ores Commission, E. H Thorton to the Chairman, Low Grade Ore Commission, Jan. 19, 1931.

32. TAD, GNLB 33/44, Investigation into Health Conditions on the Mines, Dr. Culver's Report, 1931.

33. TAD, GNLB 386 33/44, Scurvy on the Witwatersrand Mines, Culver to C. J. Sweeny, June 6, 1931.

34. TBRC, *Tuberculosis in South African Natives,* pp. 71, 271.

35. CMA, TBRC, Corr. (L) 1929–1931, file 19.

36. TBRC, *Tuberculosis in South African Natives,* p. 71.

37. Ibid., p. 73.

38. Ibid., p. 272.

39. Ibid., pp. 73–74.

40. CMA, TBRC, Corr.(K) 1928–1929, file 18. Memorandum by A. J. Orenstein on Mines and Works Machinery Regulations: "The Use of Water for Dust Prevention."

41. CMA, TBRC, Excessive use of water, file 31, Lister, Chairman of TBRC, to Gemmill, Chairman, Chamber of Mines, June 24, 1929.

42. L. G. Irvine, A. Mavrogodato, H. Pirow, *A Review of the History of Silicosis on the Witwatersrand Goldfields,* International Silicosis Conference (Geneva: International Labor Office, 1930), p. 183.

43. CMA, TBRC, Corr.(K) 1928–1929, file 18. Memorandum by A. J. Orenstein on Mines and Works Machinery Regulations: The Use of Water for Dust Prevention.

44. CMA, TBRC, Excessive use of water, file 31, General Manager, Chamber of Mines, to Chairman, TBRC, June 12, 1929.

45. TBRC, *Tuberculosis in South African Natives,* pp. 343–344.

46. CMA, TBRC, Report—Drafting of, file 28. Gemmill to Sir Lyle Cummins, October 16, 1929: "A central sanitary committee on the lines you suggest would involve the impossible position that members of that committee would have certain rights of supervision and interference in the internal affairs of mines with which they are entirely unconnected"; TBRC, W. Gemmill, Private Files, "Report of the sub-Committee of the TMMOA on Tuberculosis among mine Natives, 1923," rejects the idea of central examination procedure, p. 2.

47. In 1915 Orenstein proposed that "native miners" be issued better clothing, especially in the deep mines, to reduce chill when coming out of the over-

heated environment of the mines to the much cooler temperatures on the surface. Both recommendations met with resistance by mine managers because of the additional cost they represented. In the case of clothing, some mines began issuing tunics to their African workers, taking the cost out of their wages. But the policy did not become generally accepted until 1935, when the Gold Producers Committee finally agreed to issue free tunics as part of their campaign to convince the NAD and Department of Health that the mines were safe for tropical labor (see chap. 8); BRA, Rand Mines Ltd. Annual Report of Department of Sanitation, 1915, 1935.

48. CMA, TBRC, W. Gemmill, Private File 7a, "Report of the Sub-Committee of the Transvaal Mine Medical Officers Association on Tuberculosis among Mine Natives," 1921.

49. CMA, TBRC, file 17, Corr.(J) 1928, Mavrogodato, "Tuberculosis Prevalance Rates among the Native Miners on the Witwatersrand Gold Mines, 1916 to 1927," pp. 25–26.

50. L. F. Dangerfield, "Pulmonary TB in South Africa and the Problem of Native Mine Labor," PTMMOA 22, 249 (1942): 174.

51. PTMMOA 1, 8 (1921): 6.

52. "Discussion on Tuberculosis," PTMMOA 5, 2 (1925).

53. CMA, Cooke, report to the General Manager NRC on Rejection of Recruited and Voluntary Natives after Their Arrival in Johannesburg, June 6, 1933, p. 7.

54. "Discussion on Tuberculosis," PTMMOA 5, 2 (1925): 2.

55. Dr. A. Frew, "A Standard of Fitness for Natives on the Mines," PTMMOA 1, 8 (1921): 4.

56. TAD, GNLB, 164, 481/14, Medical Officer, NAD, to Director of Native Labor, April 19, 1915; CMA, TBRC, Corr. 1926, file 12, Acting Director of Native Labor to the General Manager, Transvaal Chamber of Mines, June 14, 1926.

57. "Discussion of TB Detection and Prevention during Work Period," PTMMOA 5, 5 (1925); 3.

58. TAD, GNLB, 347 66/23, H. T. H. Butt to Acting General Manager, Randfontein Estates GM. Co. (W), Ltd., January 11, 1927.

59. PTMMOA 2, 4 (August 1922): 8.

60. "Discussion of Detection of Tuberculosis by Weighing," in PTMMOA 5, 5 (1925): 4–8.

61. TBRC, Tuberculosis in South African Natives, p. 110.

62. CMA, TBRC, General Corr. 1926, file 10, "Report of Questionnaire . . . Issued to All Mine Medical Officers," July 23, 1925.

63. TAD, GNLB 259 429/16, "Miner's Phthisis Act," Director of Native Labor, Oct. 2, 1918.

64. TAD, GNLB, 259 427/16, NAD, Roodepoort to the Director of Native Labor, May 19, 1920; Statement of Evidence by Director of Native Labor re Miner's Phthisis Act of 1919.

65. TAD, GNLB 259 247/16, Department of Native Affairs, memorandum on Miner's Phthisis Act, 40/1919.

66. The failure of termination physicals to detect TB may have been further

complicated by the fact that any African worker who was certified as having TB
would have his passport endorsed preventing him from ever being employed
again on the mines. There is some evidence that mineworkers who suspected
that they might have the disease would send substitutes forward for their examination in order to avoid being identified and debarred from future employment.
The cost of this ruse was potentially the loss of compensation. However, most
workers were unwilling to run the risk of never being employed on the mines
again in order to obtain the small amount of compensation paid to African
mineworkers suffering TB. The trade-off was made more unpopular because,
under the various Miner's Phthisis Acts, many cases of TB without silicosis were
not compensatable. (TAD, GNLB 258, 427/16, Inspector, Native Affairs Department to Director of Native Labor, April 22, 1925).

67. TAD, GNLB, 259 427/16, Department of Native Affairs, memorandum
on Miner's Phthisis Act, 40/1919, pp. 2–3.

68. An early draft of the Miner's Phthisis Act of 1925 included a requirement that all African workers be stethoscopically examined every three months.
The Mine Medical Officers' Association, recognizing the impossibility of this
measure within the confines of conditions on the mines, objected that this
requirement was unnecessary and that the present system of weighing was
efficient in detecting TB (*PTMMOA* 4, 2 (1924): 3). The requirement was
subsequently dropped.

69. CMA, Gold Producers Committee, Health Conditions, 1940, file 41, C.
Drummond, Secretary for Chamber of Mines to Secretary, Gold Producers
Committee, July 1, 1940.

70. CMA, TBRC, Corr. 1926, file 11, Mavrogadato and Pringle to Chairman, Medical Committee on Tuberculosis, April 27, 1926.

71. Dr. A. Frew, "A Standard of Fitness for Mine Natives," *PTMMOA* 1, 8
(1921): 5.

72. CMA, TBRC, file 8, General Corr. 1925, Minutes of Meeting of TBRC,
June 30, 1925.

73. *PTMMOA* (January 8, 1938): 33.

74. These figures are for the Central Mining—Rand Mines Group and in
most years are somewhat lower than those for the industry as a whole.

75. U.G. 34-14, *Report of the Tuberculosis Commission* (Cape Town: Government Printers, 1914), p. 205.

76. CMA, Acting General Manager, Crown Mines, to Chairman, Crown
Mines, July 11, 1930, "Low Grade Ores Commission—Native Labour Shortage," file 11, 1931.

77. CMA, file 80, 1935, "Native Labour—Committee of Inquiry, Report of
Departmental Committee . . . upon certain questions relating to Native Labour
in Zululand, the Transkeian Territories and the Ciskei," p. 4.

78. CMA, Cooke, report to the General Manager NRC on Rejection of
Recruited and Voluntary Natives after Their Arrival in Johannesburg, June 6,
1933, p. 2.

79. TBRC, *Tuberculosis in South African Natives,* p. 63.

80. CMA, file 68, Gemmill, "Native Labour Supply," July 12, 1932.

81. CMA, file 68, 1932, Native Labour Supply, H. M. Taberer, Native

Labor Advisor, memorandum to the General Manager (NRC) on the Repatriation of Time-Expired BSA Natives, February 25, 1932; A. V. Lange, General Manager, City Deep Ltd., to the Consulting Engineer, City Deep Ltd., February 19, 1932; General Manager, the Central Mining and Investment Corporation, Ltd., to Chairman, Technical Advisory Committee, Chamber of Mines, March 1, 1932.

82. CMA, file 68, 1932, Native Labour Supply, the General Manager, Chamber of Mines, to Acting Director of Native Labor, March 2, 1932.

83. TBRC, *Tuberculosis in South African Natives*, p. 350.

84. Ibid., pp. 347–348.

85. Ibid., p. 350.

86. See discussion of causes of this variability in *PTMMOA* 2, 2 (1922): 3.

87. CMA, TB N14, "Native Mortality," G. D. Maynard, "Report Re Mortality Amongst Natives Employed on Mines and Works in the Labor Area of the Transvaal," 1911.

88. CMA, file 68, Native Labour Supply, 1932, W. Gemmill, Memo on Native Labor Supply, July 12, 1932; David Yudelman and Alan Jeeves, "New Labour Frontiers for Old: Black Migrants to the South African Gold Mines, 1920–1985," *JSAS* 13, 1 (1986): 123.

89. TBRC, *Tuberculosis in South African Natives*, pp. 146–147.

90. In addition, there is some evidence that labor shortages in general may have adversely affected TB rates, by reducing the amount of money that the mines were willing to spend on supplies including food. Figures from West Rand Property Mines presented by the mine manager to the Low Grade Ore Commission in 1931 indicate that, "a 34 percent reduction in the labor supply would produce a 34 percent reduction in wages but a 44 percent reduction in stores and purchase power." In other words the percentage reduction in stores would be greater than the percentage loss of labor. CMA, file 11, 1931, Low Grade Ores Commission, memorandum on Effects of Native Labor Shortage.

91. Novice workers from these areas would also be at risk, though they are less likely to be strongly positive than older workers.

92. CMA, file 86, Native Labour Supply, 1936, W. Gemmill, "Native Labour Supply," May 14, 1936, p. 3.

93. CMA, file 86, "Native Labour Supply," 1936, Gemmill, General Manager, Chamber of Mines, Memorandum on Native Labor Supply, May 14, 1936.

94. It should also be noted that because AVS workers were not subject to nine-month contracts, mine managers were more willing to take risks in hiring marginal AVS workers for whom they had only a limited liability. Thus AVS workers potentially provided the mines with more flexibility in terms of the standards they applied to new workers. This flexibility was not very significant as long as there was a labor surplus, for the mines were in a position to be particular about who they employed. When labor shortages emerged in subsequent years, however, the flexibility of the AVS system allowed the mines to adjust their standards quickly. CMA, Cooke, report to the General Manger NRC on Rejection of Recruited and Voluntary Natives after Their Arrival in Johannesburg, June 6, 1933, p. 13.

7. SEGREGATION AND RACIAL SUSCEPTIBILITY: THE IDEOLOGICAL FOUNDATOINS OF TUBERCULOSIS CONTROL

1. Maynard Swanson, " 'The Sanitation Syndrome': Bubonic Plague and Urban Native Policy in the Cape Colony," *JAH* 18 (1977): 387–410.

2. See Saul Dubow, "Race, Civilisation and Culture: The Elaboration of Segregationist Discourse in the Inter-War Years," in S. Marks and S. Trapido, eds., *The Politics of Race, Class and Nationalism in Twentieth Century South Africa* (London: Longmans, 1987), pp. 71–94, for a further discussion of the changing discourse on race in South Africa.

3. G. D. Maynard, "The Relative Importance of Infection and Heredity in the Spread of Tuberculosis," *Transvaal Medical Journal* 8, 3 (1912): 58–81.

4. For examples of the debate that Maynard's paper sparked see *The South African Medical Record* 8: 74–82; 10: 387–393, 405–407; 11: 316–323, 381–382, 407–408. The debate was occasionally impassioned and led opponents of Maynard's hereditary arguments to go to extraordinary lengths to challenge his claims regarding the unimportant role of infection in the spread of TB. For example, Dr. I. Stusser, district surgeon for Oudtshoorn, in a letter to the editor of the *SAMR* (10 [1912]: 406) observed,

> Again it is well-known that Jewish rabbis have infected the infantile penis after circumcision, when the method of stopping haemorrhage by suction was adopted in prehistoric days. A case recorded of a woman sitting on a chamber utensil into which her consumptive husband expectorated. The chamber utensil broke, she cut herself, and the wound came in contact with tuberculous sputa. She shortly developed a tuberculous ulcer at the cite of the wound.

5. D. Traill, "The Cause of the Declining Death-rate from Tuberculosis," *SAMR* 11 (1913): 241.

6. G. E. Bushnell, *A Study in the Epidemiology of Tuberculosis* (New York: William Wood and Company, 1920).

7. E. L. Opie, "Widespread Tuberculous Infection of Healthy Individuals and Its Significance," *Bulletin of the New York Tuberculosis Health Association* 5 (1924): 1–2.

8. A. Borrel, "Pneumonie et tuberculose chez les troupes noires," *Annales de l'Institut Pasteur* 34 (1920): 105–148.

9. S. L. Cummins, "Virgin Soil—and After: A Working Conception of Tuberculosis in Children, Adolescents and Aborigines," *British Medical Journal* 2 (1929): 39–41.

10. Peter Richardson and J. J. van Helten, "Labour in the South African Gold Mining Industry," in S. Marks and R. Rathbone, eds., *Industrialization and Social Change in South Africa* (London: Longmans, 1982), pp. 89–90.

11. U.G. 34-14, *Report of the Tuberculosis Commission* (Cape Town: Government Printers, 1914), p. 203.

12. W. Gorgas, *Recommendation as to Sanitation Concerning Employees on the Mines on the Rand* (Johannesburg: Argus Printing and Publishing Company, 1914).

13. U.G., *Report of Tuberculosis Commission*, p. 212.

14. Ibid., p. 101.

15. It could of course be argued that the high mortality rates from TB encouraged mine owners to increase their use of migrant labor. Historically, however, it would appear that the labor crisis that led to an increased reliance on migrant labor preceded the shift to a physiological paradigm, which supported its use. Nonetheless, once the physiological model was accepted as the paramount cause of African susceptibility to TB, it took on a life of its own and may have encouraged the expansion of the use of migrant labor. In short, as long as the physiological paradigm suited the needs of the mining industry, it was accepted by the mine owners and mine medical officers as a valid explanation and not simply as a convenient tactical instrument.

16. U.G., *Report of Tuberculosis Commission*, p. 101.

17. A. P. Cartwright, *Doctors on the Mines* (Cape Town: Purnell, 1971), p. 38.

18. In a letter to the editor of the *SAMR* (Sept. 12, 1924, p. 312), Dr. Gregory described the rear guard efforts of Drs. Turner and Porter to prevent his criticisms from being published without a rejoinder: "Even after the final Report had been agreed to, and the Commissioners finally dispersed, the two Johannesburg members took possession of the draft and refused to give it up for presentation to the Government until certain clauses prepared subsequently by themselves, championing the existing system of mine health control, with which they are both identified, were introduced, thereby converting what had been until then an unanimous Report into one which myself and Mr. Jameson could not sign in its entirety."

19. Kuhn writes, "I would argue . . . that in these matters neither proof nor error is at issue. The transfer of allegiance from paradigm to paradigm is a conversion experience that cannot be forced." Thomas Kuhn, *The Structure of Scientific Revolutions* (Chicago: University of Chicago Press, 1970), p. 151.

20. Cartwright, *Doctors on the Mines*, pp. 36–38.

21. Dr. Watkins-Pitchford noted at a Mine Medical Officers Association meeting in 1922 (*PTMMOA* 2, 4 [1922]: 11),

I have a native discharge certificate here, issued to natives after working underground 180 shifts or more, and it states therein that natives returning within four months are entitled to a bonus. If he returns within four months I think he ought to be fined for daring to come within that time.

22. CMA, Tuberculosis Research Committee, file 8, General Corr., Minutes of Meeting, June 30, 1925.

23. Reported in *PTMMOA* 7, 4 (Sept. 1927).

24. TBRC, *Tuberculosis in South African Natives*, p. 252.

25. Kuhn, *The Structure of Scientific Revolutions*, p. 24.

26. J. A. Mitchell, "The Problem of Tuberculosis in South Africa," *SAMR* 19 (1921): 228.

27. SNA, High Commissioner for South Africa to I. H. Thomas, MP. Dominions Office, Sept. 5, 1932, RCS 34/32 Annual Report of MOH, Swaziland.

28. D. P. Marais, "Some Changing Viewpoints Regarding Tuberculosis," *SAMJ* (1933): 457.

29. B. A. Dormer, "Tuberculosis in South Africa," *British Journal of Tuberculosis* 50, 1 (1956): 52–60.

30. Dr. Strachan, quoted in report on Fourteenth South African Medical Congress, *SAMR* 11 (1913): 9.

31. CMA, Health—Tuberculosis, 1957. J. J. DuPre Le Roux, Secretary for Health, TB Conference, Johannesburg, Dec. 2–4, 1957, p. 3.

32. TAD, GES 997 401/173, E. H. Thorton, Secretary for Public Health, to Provincial Secretaries, Cape Town, Bloemfontein, Peitermaritzburg, and Pretoria, Feb. 21, 1934.

33. CMA, Gemmill, Private Files, 7a. Peter Allan, 8th Progress Report, 1928.

34. CMA, TBRC, Dr. Peter Allan, Quarterly Reports, file 26, 1928.

8. INDUSTRIAL EXPANSION, SQUATTERS, AND THE SECOND TUBERCULOSIS EPIDEMIC

1. Cape Town, annual report of the MOH, 1945, p. 42.

2. These figures are for the industry as a whole. In the mines of the Central Mining–Rand Mines Ltd. group, presented in graph 16, the rise was less dramatic. CMA, Sil-TB Dept. CTE. 1954 (1), minutes of the Meeting of the Sub-Committee of Group Medical Officers, Oct. 1, 1954.

3. The medical officer for the native battalion at Umtata, on the basis of an examination of military recruits in 1942, estimated that "not more than 1% of the male native 'walking' population between the ages of 15 and 50 in the Transkei may be assumed to suffer from active pulmonary tuberculosis." SAIRR Archives, 38.6.2, Dr. E. Joki, "A Manpower Survey of the Transkeian Territories," p. 10.

4. F. J. Wiles, and C. J. Rabie, "Tuberculosis in the Transkei," *SAMJ* 29 (1955): 866.

5. Oslo, L. W., *SAMJ* 30 (1956): 613.

6. L. W. Oslo, "Tuberculosis in Natal," *SAMJ* (July 1956): 641.

7. J. Schneider, "Tuberculin Testing and Mass Miniature X-Ray Survey of the Northern and Eastern Transvaal," *SAMJ* 28 (1954): 689.

8. H. Dubovsky, "A Mass Miniature X-Ray and Tuberculin Survey in the Orange Free State and Northern Cape," *SAMJ* (October 1955): 992.

9. "Grim Disease Position," *Sunday Times*, Johannesburg, August 14, 1939.

10. B. A. Dormer, "Tuberculosis in South Africa," *British Journal of Medicine* 50, 1 (1956): 53.

11. SAIRR Archives, University of the Witwatersrand, AD 1715, 9.5.96, G. W. Gale, "Health Services in the Union," typescript, 1948.

12. Roger J. Southall, *South Africa's Transkei* (New York: Monthly Review Press, 1983), pp. 85–87.

13. U.G. 28–1948, *Report of the Native Laws Commission* (Pretoria: Government Printers, 1948), p. 18. Hereinafter referred to as the Fagan Commission.

14. A. Proctor, "Class Struggle, Segregation and the City: A History of Sophiatown, 1905–1940," in B. Bozzoli, ed., *Labour, Townships and Protest* (Johannesburg: Ravan, 1979).

15. GES 1,000 401/19L, Director of Housing to the Secretary for Public Health, May 4, 1947.

16. RSA, Bureau of Statistics, *Urban and Rural Populations of South Africa, 1904–1960* (Pretoria: Government Printers, 1968).

17. *Report of the Commission of Inquiry into the Disturbances of 30 August 1947, at Moroka, Johannesburg* (Pretoria: Government Printers, 1948), p. 20.

18. Ibid., p. 93.

19. Ibid., pp. 20–22.

20. Ibid., p. 99.

21. See A. W. Stadler, "Birds in the Cornfields: Squatters Movements in Johannesburg, 1944–1947," in B. Bozzoli, ed., *Labour Townships and Protest* (Johannesburg: Ravan, 1979), for a discussion of the squatters' movement and of the conflicting economic and political interests that gave rise to the squatter problem.

22. *Report of the Commission of Inquiry into the Disturbances at Moroka,* p. 92.

23. Jacqueline Eberhart, *A Survey of Family Conditions with Special Reference to Housing Needs, Orlando Township, Johannesburg* (Johannesburg: Non-European Affairs Department, 1949), 131.

24. GES 560 113/13B, "Report of Inspection of Conditions of Natives in the Cape Peninsula," 1943.

25. GES 877 894/13, P. G. Caudwell, "Report on Sanitation and Housing in Cape Town," 1941, pp. 8–18.

26. GES 560 113/13B, "Report of Inspection of Conditions of Natives in the Cape Peninsula," 1943.

27. Fagan Commission, p. 18.

28. Philip and Iona Mayer, *Townsmen in the Making* (Cape Town: Oxford University Press, 1974), p. 45.

29. Fagan Commission, p. 5.

30. Report of the MOH, Port Elizabeth, for the year ending June 30, 1939, p. 47.

31. U.G., *Report of the Inter-departmental Committee on the Social, Health and Economic Conditions of Urban Natives* (Pretoria: Government Printers, 1942), p. 5. Hereinafter referred to as the Smit Committee Report.

32. Smit Committee Report, p. 5.

33. Ibid., p. 6.

34. A. W. Stadler, "Birds in the Cornfields," p. 21.

35. SAIRR, AD 1715, 9-1-4, evidence submitted to the commission considering the feeding of school children, p. 8.

36. Smit Committee Report, p. 6.

37. "1000 Union Natives in Each 100,000 Die from Tuberculosis," *The Star,* November 18, 1948.

38. Annual reports of the MOH, Cape Town, 1940–1941 to 1944–1945.
39. Ibid.
40. A. B. Xuma, "The Changes . . . Taking Place in Health . . . ," typescript (n.d.—1936?), p. 6, Xuma Papers, SAIRR Archives, n. 16.8.
41. U.G. 30-1944, *Report of the National Health Services Commission, 1942–1944* (Pretoria: Government Printers, 1944), pp. 76–77. Hereinafter, the Gluckman Commission.
42. *The Natal Daily News,* April 10, 1943.
43. GES 957 93/17, MOH Johannesburg to Secretary of Public Health, April 18, 1946.
44. SNA, 141/42, E. Fullois to Senator R. Jones, February 25, 1942.
45. Jacqueline Eberhart, *A Survey of Family Conditions with Special Reference to Housing Needs, Orlando Township, Johannesburg* (Johannesburg: Non-European Affairs Department, 1949), p. 72.
46. Smit Committee Report, p. 11.
47. GES 1,000 401/17J, Organizing Secretary, South African National Council for Child Welfare to the Secretary, Department of Social Welfare, December 24, 1943, and January 25, 1944.
48. CMA, "Native Labour Supply," file 88, 1934, A. L. Barrett, Director of Native Labour, to General Manager, Transvaal Chamber of Mines, August 8, 1934.
49. See various letters between Chamber of Mines and Department of Native Affairs, CMA, "Native Labour Supply," file 88, 1934.
50. CMA, file 88, 1933, "Native Labour—Tropicals," Secretary to the Prime Minister to the President, Chamber of Mines, October 21, 1933.
51. CMA, W. Gemmill, memorandum for Health Advisory Committee: Employment of Tropical Natives, October 27, 1933, file 88, 1933; A. J. Orenstein, "Draft of Statement for Consideration of the Gold Producers Committee," June 24, 1935, file 90, "Native Labour—Tropicals," 1935.
52. CMA, Gemmill to Senior Provincial Commissioner, Northern Rhodesia, November 11, 1937, file 89, "Native Labour—Tropicals," 1939.
53. David Yudelman and Alan Jeeves, "New Labour Frontiers for Old: Black Migrants to the South African Gold Mines, 1920–1985," *JSAS* 13, 1 (1986): 124.
54. CMA, memorandum by W. Gemmill to Members of the Gold Producers Committee, April 30, 1945, file 101, 1945, "Native Labour—Tropical."
55. CMA, A. J. Orenstein, "Draft of Statement for Consideration of the Gold Producers Committee," June 24, 1935, file 90, "Native Labour—Tropicals," 1935.
56. David Ordman, "The Incidence and Control of Pneumonia in the Native Labourers of the Witwatersrand Goldfields with Special Reference to the Tropical Natives," *PTMMOA* 29 (1949): 79.
57. Ibid., p. 79.
58. L. F. Dangerfield, "Pulmonary Tuberculosis in South Africa and the Problem of the Native Mine Labourer," *PTMMOA* 22 (1943): 173.
59. CM/RM Health Department Reports, 1936–1946.
60. A study conducted on one group of mines between 1938 and 1940

found that workers who were provided with a more nutritious diet than that normally provided to African workers in the industry had significantly lower overall morbidity rates; L. S. Williams, "The Food and Feeding of Mine Native Labourers," *PTMMOA* 22 (1941): 8.

61. B. A. Dormer, "A Case of Tuberculosis," *SAMJ* (Feb. 14, 1948): 84–85.

62. Ibid., p. 85.

63. TAD, GES 998, 401/17E, "TB and the Public Health Act," memo to the Minister of Health from the Secretary of Public Health," February 23, 1938.

64. TAD, GES 998 401/17E, Report on Tuberculosis Conference, Cape Town, February 6–7, 1939.

65. B. A. Dormer, J. Friedlander, and F. J. Wiles, "A South African Team Looks at Tuberculosis," *PTMMOA* 23 (1943): 75–76.

66. TAD, GES 998 401/E, Report on Meeting of Expert Committee on Tuberculosis, Cape Town, January 23, 1939.

67. Frank Retief, "Random Notes and Observations on Tuberculosis," *PTMMOA* 27 (1947): 27.

68. Yudelman and Jeeves, "New Labour Frontiers for Old," p. 112.

69. U.G., *Report of the Native Laws Commission*, p. 36.

70. Ibid., pp. 36–37.

71. Colin Bundy, *The Rise and Fall of the South African Peasantry* (Berkeley, Los Angeles, London: University of California Press, 1979), p. 225.

72. B. A. Dormer, "Tuberculosis in South Africa," *PTMMOA* 27 (1948): 65.

73. Cited in U.G., *Report of the National Health Services Commission*, p. 94.

74. Reported in "TB Threat to Labour Reserves," *Natal Mercury*, August 9, 1945.

75. Johannesburg, *Report of the Medical Officer of Health* for the year ending June 30, 1939, p. 11.

76. Quoted in *Rand Daily Mail*, November 19, 1948.

77. Frank Retief, "Random Notes and Observations on Tuberculosis," *PTMMOA* 27 (1947): 25.

78. SAIRR, AD 1715, 9.6.97, "Health: Kark to Editor," *Race Relations* (Johannesburg), October 28, 1942.

79. "Industry and 'T.B.,' " *The Cape Times*, July 5, 1945.

80. TAD, GES 998 401/17E, Report on Tuberculosis Conference, Cape Town, February 6–7, 1939, p. 3.

81. TAD, GES 998, 401/17E, "TB and the Public Health Act," memo to the Minister of Health from the Secretary of Health," February 23, 1938.

82. Smit Committee Report, pp. 7–10.

83. See for example, TAD, GES 1000, 401/17J, Meeting of the Council of Public Health, January 12–13, 1943.

84. Dr. Peter Allan, quoted in Johannesburg *Star*, September 8, 1941.

85. TAD, GES 999, 401/176, B. A. Dormer, "A Scheme for the Control of Tuberculous Natives in Natal," 1939.

86. TAD, GES 998, 401/176, "TB and the Public Health Act," memo to the Minister of Health from the Secretary of Health," February 23, 1928.

87. "Tuberculosis Campaign," *The Star*, October 25, 1945.

88. U.G., *Report of the Native Laws Commission*, p. 50.

89. Cedric De Beer, *The South African Disease* (Trenton: African World Press, 1986), p. 23.

90. S. Marks and N. Andersson, "Industrialization, Rural Change and the 1944 Health Services Commission," in S. Feierman and J. Janzen, eds., *The Social Basis of Health and Healing in Africa* (Berkeley, Los Angeles, London: University of California Press, forthcoming).

9. TUBERCULOSIS AND APARTHEID: THE
GREAT DISAPPEARING ACT

1. T. B. F. Collins, "The History of Southern Africa's First Tuberculosis Epidemic," *SAMJ* 62 (1982): 785.

2. E. Glatthaar, "Tuberculosis Control in South Africa," *SAMJ*, Special Issue (Nov. 1982): 37; P. B. Fourie and Karin Knoetze, "Tuberculosis Prevalence and the Risk of Infection in South Africa," proceedings of the First Tuberculosis Research Institute Symposium, Pretoria, August 8–9, 1985.

3. CMA, "Health—Tuberculosis," 1957; J. P. De Villiers, "The Tuberculosis Problem in South Africa in the Light of Recent Advances," paper prepared for the Tuberculosis Conference, Johannesburg, December 2–4, 1957, p. 1.

4. Covering Minute to U.G. 61-1951, *Report of the Department of Native Affairs for the Years 1949–50* (Pretoria: Government Printers, 1951), pp. i–ii, cited in Peter Wilkinson, "The Sale of the Century? A Critical Review of Recent Developments in African Housing Policy in South Africa," Carnegie Conference Paper No. 160 (Cape Town, 1984), p. 10.

5. Michael Savage, "Pass Laws and the Disorganization and Reorganization of the African Population in South Africa," Carnegie Conference Paper No. 281 (Cape Town, 1984), p. 23.

6. The total mine force only grew by 30,000, and the number included within the Johannesburg statistics would have been only a small portion of that total.

7. Michael Savage, "Pass Laws and the Disorganization and Reorganization of the African Population in South Africa," p. 23.

8. Orlando had an official population of 60,000 in 1951. A sample survey by the Manager of Non-European Affairs indicated, however, that the de facto population was 90,000; CMA, Sil, TB Cte-5, 1954, Dr. Scott-Miller, MOH Johannesburg, evidence to Commission of Inquiry into Tuberculosis, vol. 5, p. 1084. Similarly, Cato Manor grew from 17,000 inhabitants, with an average house occupancy rate of 5.6 persons per house in 1944, to 60,000 people, with an occupancy rate of 10 per house; Durban, *Report of the City Medical Officer*, 1964, appendix C, p. 108.

9. Peter Wilkinson, "Providing 'Adequate Shelter': The South African State and the Resolution of the African Urban Crisis, 1948–1954," in D. C. Hindson, ed., *Working Papers in Southern African Studies*, vol. 3 (Johannesburg: Ravan Press, 1983), pp. 65–90.

10. Ibid., p. 80.

11. Ibid., p. 74.

12. Ibid., p. 78.

13. CMA, Health Tuberculosis, 1957, Comments by Dr. J. J. DuPre Le Roux, Secretary for Health, to TB Conference, Johannesburg, December 2–4, 1957, p. 21.

14. SAIRR, *Survey of Race Relations,* 1953–1954, p. 95.

15. Ibid., 1961, p. 160.

16. Ibid., 1962, p. 151.

17. Laurine Platzky and Cherryl Walker, *The Surplus People: Forced Removals in South Africa* (Johannesburg: Ravan Press, 1985), p. 100.

18. See Chap. 5.

19. Wilkinson, "Providing 'Adequate Shelter,' " p. 83.

20. Gastroenteritis deaths among infants per 1,000 live births rose from 22 per 1,000 in 1946 to over 40 per 1,000 in 1956 and 1957 among blacks in Cape Town; Cape Town, *Report of the Medical Officer of Health,* 1975, p. 56. In Durban's emergency site and service program in Cato Manor, typhoid became a major concern in the mid-1950s with over 200 cases a year being reported in a population of approximately 70,000 or roughly 285 per 100,000; Durban, *Report of the City Medical Officer,* 1964, appendix C, p. 109.

21. SAIRR, *Survey of Race Relations,* 1956–1957, p. 128.

22. P. and I. Mayer, *Tribesmen or Townsmen* (Cape Town: Oxford University Press, 1974), p. 46.

23. SAIRR, *Survey of Race Relations,* 1955–1956, p. 253.

24. Ibid., 1959–1960, p. 166.

25. Ibid., 1967, p. 179.

26. Ibid., 1969, p. 177.

27. Cape Town, *Report of the Medical Officer for Health,* 1967.

28. Caroline White, "Poverty in Port Elizabeth," Carnegie Conference Paper No. 21, Cape Town (1984), p. 5.

29. SAIRR, *Survey of Race Relations,* 1970, p. 197.

30. Platzky and Walker, *The Surplus People,* p. 118.

31. SAIRR, *Survey of Race Relations,* 1967, p. 178.

32. Ibid., 1970, p. 197.

33. Durban, *Reports of the City Medical Officer of Health* for the years 1970 to 1975.

34. Christiane Elias, "A Housing Study: Legislation and the Control of Urban African Accommodation," Carnegie Conference Paper No. 157, Cape Town (1984), p. 36.

35. Peter Wilkinson, "The Sale of the Century: A Critical Review of Recent Developments in African Housing Policy in South Africa," Carnegie Conference Paper No. 160, Cape Town (1984), pp. 16–18.

36. Wilkinson, "Sale of the Century," pp. 22–27.

37. David Webster, "The Reproduction of Labor Power and the Struggle for Survival in Soweto," Carnegie Conference Paper No. 20, Cape Town (1984), p. 1.

38. White, "Poverty in Port Elizabeth," pp. 4–5.

39. Stewart Fisher, "Measles and Poverty in Port Elizabeth," Carnegie Conference Paper No. 172 (Cape Town, 1984), p. 8.

40. J. Erwee, "Consumer Behavior and Shopping Patterns of Black Households in Port Elizabeth: A Reappraisal," U.P.E., 1982, cited in White, "Poverty in Port Elizabeth," p. 9.

41. White, "Poverty in Port Elizabeth," p. 10.

42. SAIRR, *Survey of Race Relations, 1956–1957*, p. 128.

43. For example, it was estimated that many Africans removed from the Western Native Townships to the new housing estate being built at Moroka experienced a significant increase in rent. In the WNT rents had ranged from R1.72 to R6.25. In Moroka the minimum rent was R5.50. Transport costs also rose from R1.20 to R2.20; SAIRR, *Survey of Race Relations*, 1961, p. 159. Residents of Mdantsane had to bear additional costs ranging from R2.80 to R8.95 per month depending on where they were employed; SAIRR, *Survey of Race Relations*, 1965, p. 193.

44. Minister of Health, Hansard Debates, March 8, 1963, col. 2415.

45. Cedric De Beer, *The South African Disease* (Trenton, N.J.: Africa World Press, 1986), p. 71.

46. SAIRR, *Survey of Race Relations*, 1961, p. 263.

47. SAIRR, *Survey of Race Relations, 1953–1954*, p. 32.

48. Data drawn from SAIRR, *Survey of Race Relations, 1952–1971*. In Cape Town, where wages were higher, it was estimated that 40 percent of African families and 32 percent of coloreds lived below the poverty datum line in 1957 (SAIRR, *Survey of Race Relations, 1956–1957*, p. 171). The situation was evidently worse in Port Elizabeth where it was estimated that 70 percent of African residents could not afford to pay their rent. By 1967, the average African household income was R59.16 per month, whereas the PDL was estimated to be 63.89. In the same year it was estimated that 70 percent of the households in Durban lived below the PDL (SAIRR, *Survey of Race Relations*, 1967, p. 105).

49. Ibid., 1962, p. 72.

50. Ibid., 1961, p. 261.

51. Ibid., 1962, p. 201.

52. Ibid., 1964, p. 309.

53. "Malnutrition—Why Is It No Longer Notifiable?" *Critical Health* (1982): 58–60.

54. SAIRR, *Survey of Race Relations*, 1962, p. 203.

55. Fisher, "Measles and Poverty in Port Elizabeth," pp. 8–9.

56. Ibid., p. 9.

57. Webster, "The Reproduction of Labor Power . . . in Soweto," p. 2.

58. White, "Poverty in Port Elizabeth," p. 4.

59. Webster, "The Reproduction of Labor Power . . . in Soweto," p. 2.

60. Charles Simkins, *The Demographic Demand for Labour and Institutional Context of African Unemployment in South Africa, 1960–1980* (Cape Town: SALDRU, 1981).

61. Platzky and Walker, *The Surplus People*, p. 359.

62. De Beer, *The South African Disease*, p. 53.

63. Fisher, "Measles and Poverty in Port Elizabeth," p. 8.

64. WHO, *Apartheid and Health* (Geneva: WHO, 1982), p. 143.

65. Ibid., p. 146.

66. "The Refinement of the Exploitation of Maize," *Critical Health*, 1982, pp. 36–38.

67. As one commentator noted in reference to the advertising slogan of Kentucky Fried Chicken, a popular fast-food franchise among Africans in South Africa, "Of course they taste finger lickin' good, they eat better than you"; Lesley Lawson, "Of course, he's finger lickin' good—he eats better than you," *Afrika* 4 (December 1980).

68. "The Refinement of the Exploitation of Maize," p. 37.

69. Ben Wisner, "Commodity Relations and Nutrition Under Apartheid: A Note on South Africa," in R. Packard, B. Wisner, and T. Bossert, eds., *The Political Economy of Health and Disease in Africa and Latin America*, special issue of *Social Science and Medicine*, 28 (1989): 441–446.

70. U.G. 61/1955, *Summary of the Report of the Commission for the Socio-economic Development of the Bantu Areas within the Union of South Africa* (Tomlinson Commission) (Pretoria: Government Printers, 1955), p. 145.

71. C. Simkins, "Agricultural Production in the African Reserves," *JSAS* 7 (1981): 256–283.

72. Roger Southall, *South Africa's Transkei* (New York: Monthly Review Press, 1983), pp. 219–220.

73. Colin Bundy, *The Rise and Fall of the South African Peasantry* (Berkeley, Los Angeles, London: University of California Press, 1978), p. 228.

74. These former freehold areas had been purchased earlier in the century by African families. They were surrounded by white farms whose owners often coveted the land they occupied. The Nationalist government viewed them as contradictory to the tenets of apartheid.

75. Between 1960 and 1970, the number of African children under the age of fourteen residing in metropolitan areas, towns, and nonreserve rural areas declined by 673,900, while the same age group in the "homelands" increased by 540,400. Similarly the number of African women residing outside the homelands decreased by 626,500, while the number of women within the homelands increased by the same number. Overall the percentage of women living in the bantustans increased from 44 percent in 1960 to 54 percent in 1970. C. Simkins, "Four Essays on the Past, Present and Possible Future of the Distribution of the African Population of South Africa," (Cape Town: SALDRU, University of Cape Town Press, 1983), chap. 2.

76. Platzky and Walker, *The Surplus People*, pp. 344–345.

77. De Beer, *The South African Disease*, p. 52.

78. WHO, *Apartheid and Health*, p. 126; Crispin Olver, "Poverty, Health and Health Care in South Africa," Carnegie Conference Paper No. 166 (Cape Town, 1984), citing South African statistics, 1982, published by Central Statistic Services, Pretoria.

79. De Beer, *The South African Disease*, p. 52.

80. WHO, *Apartheid and Health*, p. 110.

81. W. Sasha, "Control of Tuberculosis in the Homelands" in University of Cape Town Medical Students Council, *Consumption in the Land of Plenty,* conference papers (Cape Town, 1982), p. 107.

82. Charles Simkins, "Household Structure and Poverty among Black People," Carnegie Conference Paper No. 7 (Cape Town, 1984).

83. Southall, *South Africa's Transkei,* pp. 219–220.

84. CMA, Health Tuberculosis, 1957: J. P De Villiers, "The Tuberculosis Problem in South Africa in Light of Recent Advances," paper presented to the TB Conference, Johannesburg, December 2–4, 1957, p. 1.

85. CMA, Health Tuberculosis, 1957: Tuberculosis Conference, Report from the Conference, pp. 1–2.

86. In a study conducted in the western Cape, Yach and Bell found that the percentage of patients completing their treatment were 73.2 for blacks, 86.6 for coloreds, and 95.6 for whites. They note that these figures are falsely high because information about defaulters is not readily available in compliance surveys. The relative difference, however, between the rates of subgroups remains valid; D. Yach and John Bell, "Tuberculosis Patient Compliance in the Western Cape," unpublished paper, 1986, p. 8.

87. "Apathy Is Allowing TB to Kill at Random, Says Expert," Johannesburg *Star,* Nov. 14, 1955.

88. Durban, *Report of the City Medical Officer of Health,* 1958.

89. "Doctor Says SANTA Is Unwittingly Hindering Fight Against TB," Johannesburg *Star,* Nov. 19, 1956.

90. Hansard, 5, 1642–1643, February 24, 1955, "First Report of S.C. on Railways and Harbours."

91. Johannesburg *Star,* May 25, 1955.

92. CMA, Health Tuberculosis, 1957, Comments by Dr. J. J. DuPre Le Roux, Secretary for Health, to TB Conference, Johannesburg, December 2–4, 1957, p. 10.

93. Johannesburg *Star,* Nov. 2, 1955, Feb. 14, 1956.

94. Durban, *Report of the City Medical Officer of Health,* 1958.

95. CMA, "Silicosis—TB Dept.," CTE, 1954, testimony by Dr. Martiny, WNLA, p. 1184.

96. Port Elizabeth, *Report of the Medical Officer of Health,* 1965.

97. In the 1960s clinic hours in Durban were 9 A.M. to 3 P.M., Durban, *City MOH,* 1964, p. 25. This remains a problem today. L. Thomson, "State Policy with Regard to TB Control," in University of Cape Town, Medical Students Council, *Consumption in the Land of Plenty,* conference papers (Cape Town, 1982): 127.

98. Durban, *Report of the City Medical Officer of Health,* 1964, p. 25.

99. Cape Town, *Report of the Medical Officer of Health,* 1961, p. 57.

100. "40 in Every 100 Native Children Have TB," Johannesburg *Star,* May 4, 1955.

101. Cape Town, *Report of the Medical Officer of Health,* 1965–1975.

102. Port Elizabeth, *Report of the Medical Officer of Health,* 1965.

103. John Western, *Outcast Cape Town* (Minneapolis: University of Minnesota Press, 1981), p. 225.

104. Cape Town, *Report of the Medical Officer of Health*, 1964, p. 53, and reports for 1965–1975.

105. Elizabeth M. Thompson and Susan Myrdal, "Tuberculosis—The Patient's Perspective," *SAMJ* 70 (1986): 265.

106. Durban, *Report of the City Medical Officer of Health*, 1965.

107. S. Dubow, "Consumption and Underconsumption: The Effects of Population Resettlement on the Spread of Tuberculosis," in University of Cape Town, Medical Students Council, *Consumption in the Land of Plenty*, p. 119. Eric Buch et al., "Can Good Tuberculosis Care Be Provided in the Face of Poverty?" Carnegie Conference Paper No. 198 (Cape Town, 1984).

108. Buch et al., "Can Good Tuberculosis Care . . . ," p. 17.

109. The system was described as follows:

> If a patient from the area of Lebowa a few kilometers from our hospital defaults, we should report it to our head office in Giyani. They inform Lebowa's head office at Chuniespoort, who inform the superintendent of Masana (the nearest Lebowa hospital). He asks his public health nurse to follow up the patient. She then travels 40 km to our doorstep, to tell the patient to come back to Tintswalo. (Buch et al., "Can Good Tuberculosis Care . . . ," p. 17)

110. Buch et al., "Can Good Tuberculosis Care . . . ," p. 18.

111. Ibid., p. 13; Annual Report of the Health Department, Bophuthatswana, 1984, p. 29.

112. Buch et al., "Can Good Tuberculosis Care . . . ," p. 15.

113. RSA., *Eighth Interim Report of the Commission of Inquiry into Health Services: Interim Report on Hospitals and State Health Services* (Pretoria: Government Printers, 1986), p. 97.

114. E. Glatthaar, "Where Have We Gone Wrong—A Look at the Future?" in University of Cape Town, Medical Council, *Consumption in the Land of Plenty*, p. 13.

115. T. F. B. Collins, "Applied Epidemiology and Logic in Tuberculosis Control," *SAMJ* 59 (1981): 569.

116. E. T. Thomson and S. Myrdal, "The Implementation of Tuberculosis Policy in Three Areas in South Africa," *SAMJ* 70 (1986): 262.

117. J. R. Yeats, "Attendance Compliance for Short Course Chemotherapy at Clinics in Estcourt and Surroundings," *SAMJ* 70 (1986): 265.

118. L. D. Saunders et al., "An Evaluation of the Management of TB Patients in Soweto," paper presented to Conference on Tuberculosis in the Eighties, Pretoria, 1982.

119. CMA, Health Tuberculosis, 1957: Tuberculosis Conference, Report from Conference, p. 4.

120. P. B. Fourie and Karin Knoetze, "Tuberculosis Prevalence and Risk of Infection in Southern Africa," proceedings of the First Tuberculosis Research Institute Symposium, Pretoria, August 8–9, 1985, published in *South African Journal of Science* 82 (1986): 387.

121. D. H. Shennam, "Changes in Problems of Tuberculosis Control in Africa Between the Sixties and Eighties," paper presented to Conference on Tuberculosis in the Eighties, Pretoria, 1982, p. 3.

122. H. H. Kleeberg, "TB Bacteriology and the Laboratory Situation," pro-

ceedings of the First Tuberculosis Research Institute Symposium, Pretoria, August 8–9, 1985, published in *South African Journal of Science* 82 (1986): 394. Kleeberg also suggests that the rate of resistance to INH has declined since the 1960s. This is disputed by Fourie and Knoetze, cited above. There has been considerable regional variations in drug resistance levels in South Africa. C. Byrnes and G. J. Coetzee reported at the same symposium that resistance levels in the western Cape, an area noted for having the most efficient medical services, were considerably lower than the national average.

123. CMA, "Silicosis—TB Dept." CTE, 1954, testimony by Dr. Van Rensburg, Department of Health, p. 494.

124. Ibid.

125. TCM, "Silicosis—Natives, General," 1959, statement by Dr. Van Rensburg, minutes of meeting held at Office of the Native Chief Commissioner, Johannesburg, on January 21, 1955, p. 1.

126. Neil White, "TB as an Occupational Disease," in University of Cape Town, Medical Students Council, *Consumption in the Land of Plenty*, p. 84.

127. CMA, "Silicosis—TB Dept.," CTE-5, 1954, p. 1,185.

128. SNA, 3021m, June 10, 1952.

129. Neil White, "TB as an Occupational Disease," p. 84.

130. CMA, "Silicosis—TB Dept.," 1954, testimony of Mr. Stewart, DeBeers Mining, to the Department of Mines Inquiry into the Incidence of Tuberculosis on the Mines, 8: 479–480.

131. O. Martiny, "Attitudes to TB in the Mining Industry," in University of Cape Town, Medical Students Council, *Consumption in the Land of Plenty*, pp. 94–95; personal communication, July 2, 1985.

132. "Apathy Is Allowing TB to Kill at Random, Says Expert," Johannesburg *Star*, November 14, 1955.

133. CMA, Health Tuberculosis, 1957: Tuberculosis Conference, Report from Conference, pp. 1–2.

134. S. R. Benatar, "Tuberculosis—An Overview," in University of Cape Town, Medical Students Council, *Consumption in the Land of Plenty*, p. 8.

135. L. Coetzee and P. B. Fourie, "Efficacy of BCG Vaccination," proceedings of the First TBRI Symposium, August 8–9, 1985, published in *South African Journal of Science* 82 (1986): 388.

136. J. Denny, "Epidemiology of Tuberculous Meningitis in the Western Cape, 1979–1981," Carnegie Conference Paper, no. 175 (Cape Town, 1984).

137. In Kwazulu, a recent study suggested that only a small percentage (18.4%) of preschool children had been vaccinated. H. Coovadia, "BCG in South Africa," University of Cape Town, Medical Students Council, *Consumption in the Land of Plenty*, p. 54. This figure is based on the appearance of BCG scars. Coovadia notes that BCG does not always leave scars but concludes that the percentage vaccinated is still unacceptably low.

138. W. Sasha, "Control of TB in the Homelands," in University of Cape Town, Medical Students Council, *Consumption in the Land of Plenty*, p. 109.

139. Personal communication, Ivor Toms, Director, University of Cape Town Community Health Clinic, Crossroads.

140. L. Coetzee and P. B. Fourie, "Efficacy of BCG Vaccination," p. 391.

141. H. C. V. Kustner, "Tuberculosis Notifications: An Update." paper presented to First TBRI Symposium, August 8 and 9, 1985, published in *South African Journal of Science* 82 (1986): 387.

142. Cape Town, *Report of the Medical Officer of Health,* 1968–1971.

143. The Medical Officer of Cape Town described the city's policy as follows:

It must be noted that Table A omits a large group of Bantu and others who are found to be suffering from pulmonary tuberculosis within six months of their arrival in Cape Town, and are therefore not classified as the responsibility of the City Council of Cape Town. (*Report of the Medical Officer of Health,* 1962, p. 53)

144. J. R. Seager, "Is Active Case-finding an Effective TB Control Measure?" Proceedings of the First TBRI Symposium, Pretoria, August 8–9, 1985, reported in *South African Journal of Science* 82 (July 1982): 389.

145. Thomas and Myrdal, "Tuberculosis—The Patient's Perspective," reported in *South African Journal of Science* 82 (July 1982): 264.

146. Benatar, "Tuberculosis—An Overview," p. 9.

147. Durban, *Report of the City Medical Officer of Health,* 1967–1978.

148. Simkins, *Four Essays,* 1983.

149. *SAMJ* (Mar. 21, 1979): 446.

150. Simkins, *Four Essays,* chap. 2.

151. G. Arabin et al., "First Tuberculosis Prevalence Survey in KwaZulu," *Tubercle* 61 (1980): 71–79.

152. Shasha, "Control of Tuberculosis in the Homelands," pp. 112–115.

153. Kleeberg, "The Dynamics of Tuberculosis," p. 23.

154. Sasha, "Control of Tuberculosis in the Homelands," p. 107.

155. Coovadia, "BCG in South Africa," p. 54.

EPILOGUE: THE PRESENT AND FUTURE OF TUBERCULOSIS IN SOUTH AFRICA

1. P. W. Laidler, "The Unholy Triad: Tuberculosis, Venereal Disease, and Malnutrition," *SAMJ* (Sept. 24, 1938): 658, 665.

2. J. Cornell, "TB: Implications for Working People," University of Cape Town, Medical Students Council, *Consumption in the Land of Plenty,* conference papers, Cape Town, 1982, p. 104.

3. Derek Yach, "Tuberculosis in the Western Cape Health Region of South Africa," *Social Science and Medicine* (1986).

4. J. Myers, "Tuberculosis Screening in Industry," *SAMJ* 30 (Aug. 30, 1986): 251.

5. In the western Cape a virtual epidemic of TB is occurring among coloreds with an offical incidence of 628 per 100,000 in 1986. P. B. Fourie and Karin Knoetze, "Tuberculosis Prevalence and the Risk of Infection in Southern Africa," paper presented to Symposium on Infections in Developing Countries, Johannesburg, Aug. 29–Sept. 1, 1988.

6. Derek Yach, personal communication.

7. Derek Yach, "Tuberculosis in the Western Cape Health Region," *Soc. Sci. Med.* (1986).

8. P. B. Fourie and K. Knoetze, "Tuberculosis Prevalence and Risk of Infection in Southern Africa," proceedings of the First Tuberculosis Research Institute Symposium, Pretoria, August 8–9, 1986, published in *South African Journal of Science* 82 (1986): 387. A study of relapse cases at Cazibe Hospital in the Transkei, for example, reported an increase in the proportion of treated patients relapsing, with a corresponding increase in patients harboring drug-resistant bacilli. D. H. Shennan and H. Maarsingh, "Attacks and Relapses of Sputum-Positive Tuberculosis at Cazibe Hospital, Transkei, Over the 7 years 1978–1984," proceedings of the First Tuberculosis Research Institute Symposium, Pretoria, August 8–9, 1986, published in *South African Journal of Science* 82 (1986): 388.

9. H. H. Kleeberg, "The Dynamics of Tuberculosis in South Africa and the Impact of the Control Programme," *SAMJ*, special issue (November 17, 1982): 22.

10. Although some of the other studies conducted during the 1950s (see chapter 8) screened children four years of age and under, all of the other techniques and criteria were the same as those employed by Wiles and Rabie. F. J. Wiles and C. J. Rabie, "Tuberculosis in the Transkei," *SAMJ* (July, 1956): 641.

11. South African Tuberculosis Study Group, "Tuberculosis in the Transkei," *SAMJ* 48 (1974): 149; P. B. Fourie, et al., "Follow-Up Tuberculosis Prevalence Study of Transkei," *Tubercle* 61 (1980): 71–79.

12. By comparison the rate for coloreds has declined by only 2 percent per year, less than the population growth rate, meaning that the pool of infection is in fact expanding in this population.

13. Yach, "Tuberculosis in the Western Cape Health Region," p. 4.

14. E. U. Rosen, "The Problems of Diagnosis and Treatment of Childhood Pulmonary Tuberculosis in Developing Countries," *SAMJ*, special issue (Nov. 17, 1982): 26–27.

15. S. Grzybowski, "The Value and Limitations of the Tuberculin Test," *SAMJ* special issue (Nov. 17, 1982): 21.

16. Fourie and Knoetze, "Tuberculosis Prevalence and Risk of Infection," p. 387.

17. South African Tuberculosis Study Group, "Tuberculosis in the Transkei," pp. 149–161.

18. H. H. Kleeberg, "The Dynamics of Tuberculosis," p. 22.

19. H. C. V. Küstner, "Tuberculosis Notifications: An Update," paper presented to First TBRI Symposium, August 8 and 9, 1985, published in *South African Journal of Science* 82 (1986): 387.

20. Jan Lange and Sheena Duncan, *South African Labour Bulletin* 5, 4 (1978): 72.

21. Mike Morris and Vishnu Padayachee, "State Reform Policy in South Africa," paper presented at the Canadian Studies Association Meeting, Kingston, Ontario, May 11–14, 1988.

22. Describing the impact of the Reikert reforms on the cost of labor, Hindson notes,

With the decline of subsistence production, costs of living in the rural areas had increased. Migrants often faced higher subsistence costs than their urban counterparts;

housing had to be duplicated, transport was over greater distances and food and other commodities in the rural areas was more expensive. With pressure from unions, employers faced demands for higher wages to cover the full costs of reproduction of migrant labor. Migrant labor, once a source of cheap labor power, now imposed an added burden on profitability. (D. Hindson, *Pass Controls and the Urban African Proletariat* [Johannesburg: Ravan Press, 1987], pp. 82–83)

23. Personal communication, Dr. Ivan Tors, physician working in Crossroads Clinic.

24. John D. Battersby, "Pretoria's Pass Law Dies, but Spirit Lives," *New York Times*, June 27, 1988, p. A9.

25. CMA, "Silicosis—TB Dept.," CTE, Departmental Committee of Inquiry into the Incidence of Tuberculosis on Mines, 1954, 3: 104.

26. Ibid., 1: 26.

27. It is perhaps worth noting that x-rays had been used on a limited basis for examining recruits as far back as the 1930s and were used for examining recruits with more than five years' experience on the mines during the early 1950s. They were not employed on a universal basis, however, until 1958, at which time the mines entered a sustained period of surplus labor. The use of mass x-ray screening prior to then had been rejected by mine managers because it was not viewed as cost efficient. CMA, "TB Dept.," CTE-4, testimony of A. J. Orenstein, p. 915.

28. J. D. G. Laing, "Tuberculosis in the Mining Industry," *PMMOA*, 48 (1968): 10.

29. Laing, "Tuberculosis in the Mining Industry," p. 13.

30. G. C. Hinds, "The Contribution of Medicine to Gold Production," *PMMOA* (March 24, 1971): 50.

31. D. Yudelman and A. Jeeves, "New Labour Frontiers for Old: Black Migrants to the South African Gold Mines, 1920–1985," *JSAS* 13, 1 (1986): 112–121.

32. Yudelman and Jeeves note ("New Labour Frontiers for Old," p. 117) that restrictions placed on the exportation of labor by the Frelimo government in 1975 appear to have been more the result of the implementation of new administrative procedures than of a policy of withdrawal. All the same it caused a nervous mining industry to begin phasing out Mozambique workers. Dr. O. Martiny suggested that the initial rise in incidence in 1976 was due to the extreme shortage of labor created by these withdrawals and the fact that the mines were "Scraping the bottom of the barrel" in their efforts to find replacements for the loss in Mozambique and Malawi labor (personal communication, April 1982).

33. Yudelman and Jeeves, "New Labour Frontiers," p. 220.

34. Laing, "Tuberculosis in the Mining Industry," p. 10.

35. Ibid.

36. O. Martiny, "Attitudes to TB in the Mining Industry," in University of Cape Town, Medical Council, *Consumption in the Land of Plenty*, conference papers, Cape Town, 1982, p. 93.

37. Ibid., pp. 93–94.

38. Ibid., p. 94.

39. The last possibility is raised by a description of the means by which neotizide, a drug similar to INH, was administered on a trial basis by Dr. P. Smit, Chief Medical Officer, Gold Fields of South Africa, and reported in the Proceedings of the Mine Medical Association in 1968. In the study the whole population of five mines totaling 41,000 workers were given the drug for a year. They were given a "guesstimate" dose of 100 milligrams a day. It was a guesstimate because the method of administration was by adding the drug to Marewu and kaffir beer, a standard part of the miners' diet. Smit reported a 10 percent reduction in the previous rate of TB among Gold Fields employees and was given permission to expand the study to other mines. The question this raises of course is whether drugs diluted in this way do not encourage the development of drug-resistant strains of the TB bacillus, which may eventually spread to the wider population. Neil White, "TB as an Occupational Illness," in University of Cape Town, Medical Students Council, *Consumption in the Land of Plenty,* p. 85.

Select Bibliography

MANUSCRIPT SOURCES

Barlow Rand Archives, Sandton (BRA)
    Archives of H. Eckstein and Company, 1890–1910
Central Archives Depot, Pretoria (CAD)
    GES: Secretary of Health, 1909–1953
    NA: Native Affairs Department, 1910–1920
    GG: Governor General, 1910–1948
Chamber of Mines Archives, Johannesburg (CMA)
    Department of Mines Inquiry into the Incidence of Tuberculosis on the
        Mines Files, 1954
    Health Conditions—Tropical Natives Files, 1911–1913
    Low Grade Ore Commission Files, 1931
    Miner's Phthisis Commission Files, 1903–1919
    Native Labour Files, 1902–1955
    Native Labour—Tropicals Files, 1932–1945
    Tuberculosis Research Committee Files, 1926–1932
South African Institute of Race Relations Archives, University of Witwaters-
    rand, Johannesburg (SAIRR)
    A.B. Xuma Papers
    Henry Gluckman Papers
Swaziland National Archives, Lobamba (SNA)
    RCS: British Colonial Correspondence, 1909–1968
    MH: Ministry of Health, 1969–1982
Transvaal Archives Depot, Pretoria (TAD)
    GNLB: Government Native Labour Bureau, 1909–1935
    SNA: Secretary of Native Affairs, 1900–1910
Zimbabwe National Archives, Harare (ZNA)

OFFICIAL PUBLICATIONS

Cape of Good Hope. *Reports of the Medical Officer of Health for the Colony on the Public Health,* 1896–1909.

Cape Town. *Reports of the Medical Officer of Health,* 1910–1980.

Durban. *Reports of the City Medical Officer of Health,* 1920 to 1985.

East London. *Reports of the Medical Officer of Health,* 1915–1980.

Johannesburg. *Reports of the Medical Officer of Health,* 1910–1985.

Johannesburg, Non-European and Native Affairs Department. *Survey of Reef and Pretoria Locations.* Johannesburg: Radford Addington Ltd., 1942.

NAD. *Survey of African Income and Expenditures in 987 Families.* Pretoria, 1942.

Port Elizabeth. *Reports of the Medical Officer of Health,* 1910–1985.

RSA, Bureau of Statistics. *Urban and Rural Populations of South Africa, 1904– 1960.* Pretoria, 1968.

Swaziland. *Annual Health and Sanitation Reports,* 1921–1968.

The Transvaal. *Report of the Coloured Labour Compound Commission.* Pretoria, 1905.

The Transvaal. *Report of the Contagious Diseases amongst Natives Commission.* Pretoria: Government Printing and Stationary Office, 1907.

The Transvaal. *Final Report of the Mining Regulations Commission.* Pretoria: Government Printers, 1910.

U.G., 42-12. *Tuberculosis Commission: First Report Dealing with the Question of the Admission of Tuberculosis Immigrants into the Union.* Cape Town: Government Printers, 1912.

U.G., 34-14. *Report of the Tuberculosis Commission.* Cape Town: Government Printers, 1914.

U.G., 37-14. *Report of the Native Grievances Inquiry, 1913–1914.* Cape Town: Government Printers, 1914.

U.G. *Miner's Phthisis Commission Reports,* 1914–1931.

U.G., S.C. 3-19. *Report of the Select Committee on the Public Health Bill, 1919.* Cape Town: Government Printers, 1919.

U.G. *Report of the Commission Appointed . . . Disturbances of Port Elizabeth on 23 October 1920.* Cape Town: Government Printers, 1921.

U.G., 18-24. *Report of the Tuberculosis Survey of the Union of South Africa.* Cape Town: Government Printers, 1924.

U.G., 47-25. *Report of the Cost of Living Committee, 1925.* Cape Town: Government Printers, 1925.

U.G., 22-32. *Report of the Native Economic Commission.* Pretoria: Government Printers, 1932.

U.G. *Report of the Native Farm Labour Committee, 1937–1939.* Pretoria: Government Printers, 1939.

U.G. *Report of the Inter-departmental Committee on the Social, Health and Economic Conditions of Urban Natives (Smit Committee).* Pretoria: Government Printers, 1942.

U.G., 30-1944. *Report of the National Health Services Commission (Gluckman Commission), 1942–1944.* Pretoria: Government Printers, 1944.

U.G., *Report of the Commission of Inquiry into the Disturbances of 30 August 1947, at the Moroka Emergency Camp*. Pretoria: Government Printers, 1948.

U.G., 28-1948. *Report of the Native Laws Commission (Fagan Commission), 1946–1948*. Pretoria: Government Printers, 1948.

U.G., 61/1955. *Summary of the Report of the Commission for the Socio-economic Development of the Bantu Areas within the Union of South Africa (Tomlinson Commission Report)*. Pretoria: Government Printers, 1955.

RSA. *Eighth Interim Report of the Commission of Inquiry into Health Services: Interim Report on Hospitals and State Health Services*. Pretoria: Government Printers, 1986.

CONTEMPORARY SOURCES

Arabin, G., et al. "First Tuberculosis Prevalence Survey in KwaZulu." *Tubercle* 61 (1980): 71–79.

Borrel, A. "Pneumonie et tuberculose chez les troupe noires." *Annales de l'Inst. Pasteur* 24 (1920): 105–148.

Burney, P., and Shahyar, S. "Tuberculosis in the Transkei." In Francis Wilson and Gill Westcott, eds., *Economics of Health in South Africa*. Vol. 2 Johannesburg: Ravan Press, 1980.

Bushnell, G. E. *A Study in the Epidemiology of Tuberculosis*. New York: William Wood and Company, 1920.

Coetzee, L., and Fourie, P. B. "Efficacy of BCG Vaccination." Proceedings of the First Tuberculosis Research Institute Symposium, Pretoria, August 8–9, 1986. Published in *South African Journal of Science* 82 (1986): 391.

Collins, T. F. B. "Applied Epidemiology and Logic in Tuberculosis Control." *South African Medical Journal (SAMJ)*: 566–569.

Cummins, S. L. "Virgin Soil—and After: A Working Conception of Tuberculosis in Children, Adolescents and Aborigines." *British Medical Journal* 2 (1929): 39–41.

Dangerfield, L. F. "Pulmonary TB in South Africa and the Problem of Native Mine Labor." *Proceedings of the Transvaal Mine Medical Officers Association (PTMMOA)* 22, 249 (1942): 171–175.

De Kock G. "Bovine Tuberculosis in Its Relationship to Pure Milk Supply." *PTMMOA* 27, 294 (1947): 14–15.

Dormer, B. A. "Tuberculosis in South Africa." *British Journal of Tuberculosis* 50, 1 (1956): 52–60.

———. "A Case of Tuberculosis." *SAMJ* (Feb. 14, 1948): 82–88.

———, Friedlander, J., and Wiles, F. J. "A South African Team Looks at Tuberculosis." *PTMMOA* 23, 257 (1943): 71–114.

Eberhart. J. *A Survey of Family Conditions with Special Reference to Housing Needs, Orlando Township, Johannesburg*. Johannesburg: Non-European Affairs Department, 1949.

Fine, E. H., and Smit, P. B. "The Prevalence of Pulmonary Tuberculosis in the Durban Clothing Industry," *SAMJ* 29, 23 (1955): 539–543.

Fox, F. W. "Diet and Life in South Africa." *SAMJ* (Jan. 11, 1936): 29.

————. "Scurvy on the Witwatersrand Gold Mines: A Consideration of Some Statistical Data." *PTMMOA* 19, 216 (1940): 301–304.

————, and Back, D. *A Preliminary Survey of the Agricultural and Nutritional Problems of the Ciskei and Transkei Territories.* Johannesburg: Chamber of Mines, 1938.

Frew, A. "Tuberculosis among Mine Natives." *Transvaal Medical Journal* 6 (1910): 63–64.

————. "A Standard of Fitness for Natives on the Mines." *PTMMOA* 1, 8 (1921): 4–6.

Fourie, P. B., et al. "Follow-Up Tuberculosis Prevalence Survey of Transkei." *Tubercle* 61, 2 (1980): 71–79.

————, and Knoetze, K. "Tuberculosis Prevalence and Risk of Infection in Southern Africa." Proceedings of the First Tuberculosis Research Institute Symposium, Pretoria, August 8–9, 1985. Published in *South African Journal of Science* 82 (1986): 387.

Gale, G.W. "The Prevention of Tuberculosis in the Union with Special Reference to Urbanized Natives." *SAMJ* 23, (1943): 321–323.

Glatthaar, E. "Tuberculosis Control in South Africa." *SAMJ,* Special Issue (Nov. 1982): 31–36.

————, et al. "The Significance of the Tuberculosis Infection Risk and Its Application to Pretoria." *SAMJ* (April 22, 1978): 615–619.

Gorgas, W. *Recommendations as to Sanitation Concerning Employees on the Mines on the Rand.* Johannesburg: Argus Printing and Publishing Company, 1914.

Hellemann, E. *Rooiyard: A Sociological Survey of an Urban Native Slum.* Cape Town: Oxford University Press, 1948.

Irvine, L. G., Mavrogodato, A., Prirow, H. *A Review of the History of Silicosis on the Witwatersrand Goldfields.* Johannesburg: International Silicosis Conference, 1930.

Kleeberg, H. H. "The Dynamics of Tuberculosis in South Africa and the Impact of the Control Program." *SAMJ,* Special Issue (Nov. 17, 1982): 22–23.

————. "TB Bacteriology and the Laboratory Situation." Proceedings of the First Tuberculosis Research Institute Symposium, Pretoria, August 8–9, 1986. Published in *South African Journal of Science* 82 (1986): 394.

Kustner, H. G. "Trends in Four Communicable Diseases." *SAMJ,* 55, 12 (1979): 460–473.

Laidler, P. W. "The Unholy Triad: Tuberculosis, Venereal Disease, Malnutrition." *SAMJ* (Sept. 24, 1938): 658–666.

Laing, J. D. G. "Tuberculosis in the Mining Industry." *Proceedings of the Mine Medical Officers Association,* 48 (1968): 8–18.

McVicar, Neil. "Tuberculosis among South African Natives." *South African Medical Record (SAMR)* 6 (1908): 161–176, 181–185, 197–208, 213–222, 229–235.

Marais, D. P. "The Infectivity of Tuberculosis." *SAMR* 9 (1913): 9–16.

————. "The Coordination of Effort in Tuberculosis Control in South Africa." *SAMJ* (Nov. 14, 1976): 736–743.

Martiny, O. "A TB Programme for South Africa: The Mines and Voluntary Agencies." *Proceedings of the Mine Medical Officers Association* 49 (1970): 162–169.

Maynard, G. D. "The Relative Importance of Infection and Heredity in the Spread of Tuberculosis." *Transvaal Medical Journal* 8, 3 (1912): 58–81.

Millar, J. G. "A Native Aspect of the Native Labour Question." *SAMR* 7 (1909): 163–165.

———. "On the Spread and Prevention of Tuberculosis Disease in Pondoland, South Africa." *The British Medical Journal* (Sept. 24, 1908): 380–382.

Mitchell, J. A. "The Problem of Tuberculosis in South Africa." *SAMR* 19 (1921): 226–230.

Myers, J. "Tuberculosis Screening in Industry." *SAMJ* 30 (1986): 251.

Opie, E. L. "Widespread Tuberculous Infection of Healthy Individuals and Its Significance." *Bulletin of the New York Tuberculosis Health Association* 5 (1924): 1–2.

Ordman, D. "The Incidence and Control of Pneumonia in the Native Labourers of the Witwatersrand Goldfields with Special Reference to the Tropical Natives." *PTMMOA* 29 (1949): 75–83.

Orenstein, A. J. "Compound Sanitation." *SAMR* 21, 6 (1923): 122–133.

Pakes, W. "Tuberculosis in the Transvaal." *Transvaal Medical Journal* 1, 7 (1906): 219–220.

Ramsbottom, F. "The Threatened Conquest of South Africa by Bacillus Tuberculosis." *Transvaal Medical Journal* 1, 2 (1905): 7–12.

Retief, F. "Random Notes and Observations on Tuberculosis." *PTMMOA* 27 (1947): 26–27.

Rosen, E. U. "The Problems of Diagnosis and Treatment of Childhood Pulmonary Tuberculosis in Developing Countries." *SAMJ*, Special Issue (Nov. 1982): 26–27.

Russell, W. "An Analysis of the Consumptive Cases Admitted into Kimberley Hospital." *SAMR* 4, 14 (1906): 213–215.

Seager, J. R. "Is Active Case-finding an Effective TB Control Measure?" Proceedings of the First Tuberculosis Research Institute Symposium, Pretoria, August 8–9, 1985. Published in *South African Journal of Science* 82 (1986): 389.

South African Institute of Race Relations, *Survey of Race Relations,* Johannesburg, for the years 1950–1985.

South African Tuberculosis Study Group. "Tuberculosis in the Transkei." *SAMJ* 48 (1974): 149–161.

Thompson, E. M., and Myrdal, S. "Tuberculosis—The Patient's Perspective." *SAMJ* 70 (1986): 263–264.

———. "The Implementation of Tuberculosis Policy in Three Areas in South Africa." *SAMJ* 70 (1986): 258–262.

Traill, D. "The Cause of the Declining Death-rate from Tuberculosis." *SAMR* 11 (1913): 339–344.

Turner, G. A. "Anchylostomisis in South Africa." *Transvaal Medical Journal* (Sept. 8, 1908): 34–39.

Tuberculosis Research Committee. *Tuberculosis in South African Natives with Special Reference to the Disease among Mine Labourers on the Witwatersrand.* Johannesburg: South African Institute for Medical Research, Publication No. 30, 1932.

Watkins-Pitchford, W. "The Industrial Diseases of South Africa." *SAMR* 12, 3 (1914): 45–50.

Welsh, R. H. "The Problem of the Examination of Labour Recruits in the Transkeian Territories." *SAMR* 20, 17 (1922): 323–325.

Wiles, F. J., and Rabies, C. J. "Tuberculin and X-Ray Surveys in the Transkei." *SAMJ* 29 (1955): 866–868.

Yeats, J. R. "Attendance Compliance for Short Course Chemotherapy at Clinics in Estcourt and Surroundings." *SAMJ* 70 (1986): 265–266.

SECONDARY SOURCES

Beinart, W. *The Political Economy of Pondoland.* Cambridge: Cambridge University Press, 1982.

Bonner, P. "The Transvaal Native Congress, 1917–1920." In S. Marks and R. Rathbone, eds., *Industrialization and Social Change in South Africa.* London: Longmans, 1982, 270–313.

Bradsford, H. " 'A Taste of Freedom,' Capitalist Development and Response to the ICU in the Transvaal Countryside." In B. Bozzoli, ed., *Town and Countryside in the Transvaal.* Johannesburg: Raven Press, 1983.

Bundy, C. *The Rise and Fall of the South African Peasantry.* Berkeley, Los Angeles, London: University of California Press, 1979.

Burke, G., and Richardson, P. "The Profits of Death: A Comparative Study of Miner's Phthisis in Cornwall and the Transvaal." *Journal of Southern African Studies (JSAS)* 4, 2 (1978): 147–171.

Burrows, E. H. *A History of Medicine in South Africa Up to the End of the Nineteenth Century.* Cape Town: A. A. Balkema, 1958.

Cartwright, A. P. *Doctors on the Mines: A History of the Mine Medical Officers' Association of South Africa.* Cape Town: Purnell, 1971.

Cock, J. *Maids and Madams.* Johannesburg: Ravan Press, 1980.

Collins, T. F. B. "The History of Southern Africa's First Tuberculosis Epidemic." *SAMJ* 62 (1982): 780–788.

Comstock, G. M. "Frost Revisited: The Modern Epidemiology of Tuberculosis." *American Journal of Epidemiology* 101, 5 (1975): 363–382.

Crush, J. *The Struggle for Swazi Labour 1890–1920.* Kingston: McGill-Queens University Press, 1987.

Curtin, P. "The Epidemiology of the Atlantic Slave Trade." *Political Science Quarterly* 83 (1968): 190–216.

Davies, R. H. *Capital, State and White Labor in South Africa, 1900–1960.* Brighton: Harvester Press, 1979.

Dawson, M. "Small Pox in Kenya, 1880–1920." *Social Science and Medicine* 13 B (1979): 245–250.

De Beer, C. *The South African Disease.* Trenton, N.J.: African World Press, 1986.

Doyal, L. *The Political Economy of Health*. London, Pluto Press, 1979.

Dubos, R., and Dubos, J. *The White Plaque*. Boston: Little, Brown and Company, 1953.

Dubow, S. "Race, Civilisation and Culture: The Elaboration of Segregationist Discourse in the Inter-War Years." In S. Marks and S. Trapido, eds., *The Politics of Race, Class and Nationalism in Twentieth Century South Africa*. London: Longmans, 1987, 71–94.

Elling, R. "Industrialization and Occupational Health in Underdeveloped Countries." *International Journal of Health Services*, 7 (1977): 209–235.

Etkin, N., and Ross, P. "Food as Medicine and Medicine as Food: An Adaptive Framework for the Interpretation of Plant Utilization among the Hausa of Northern Nigeria." *Social Science and Medicine*, 16 (1982): 1559–1573.

———. "Malaria, Medicine, and Meals: Plant Use and Its Impact on Disease." In L. Romanucci et al., *The Anthropology of Medicine*. New York: Praeger, 1983, 231–259.

Ford, J. *The Role of Trypanosomiasis in African Ecology*. Oxford: Clarendon Press, 1971.

Grigg, E. R. N. "The Arcana of Tuberculosis." *The American Review of Tuberculosis and Pulmonary Disease* 78, 2 (1958): 151–172; 78, 3 (1958): 426–446.

Guy, J. *The Destruction of the Zulu Kingdom*. London: Longmans, 1982.

Harries, P. "Kinship, Ideology and the Nature of Pre-colonial Labour Migration: Labour Migration from the Delagoa Bay Hinterland to South Africa up to 1895." In S. Marks and R. Rathbone, eds., *Industrialization and Social Change in South Africa*. London: Longmans, 1982.

Hunter, M. *Reaction to Conquest*. London: Oxford University Press, 1936.

Jeeves, A. *Migrant Labour in South African's Mining Economy*. Kingston: McGill-Queens University Press, 1985.

Johnstone, F. A. *Class, Race, and Gold*. London: Routledge and Kegan Paul, 1976.

Kark, S. L. "The Influence of Rural–Urban Migration on Bantu Health and Disease." *The Leech* 21 (1950): 23–37.

Katz, E. "White Workers' Grievances and the Industrial Color Bar." *South African Journal of Economics* 42 (1974): 127–156.

———. "Silicosis on the South African Gold Mines." In F. Wilson and W. Gill, Westcott, *Economics of Health in South Africa* Vol. 2. Johannesburg: Ravan Press, 1980.

Keegan, T. "The Sharecropping Economy: African Class Formation and the 1913 Land Act in the Highveld Maize Belt." In S. Marks and R. Rothbone, *Industrialization and Social Change in South Africa*, London: Longmans, 1982, 195–211.

Kjekshus, H. *Ecology Control and Economic Development in East Africa*. Berkeley, Los Angeles, London: University of California Press, 1977.

Koch, E. " 'Without Visible Means of Subsistence': Slumyard Culture in Johannesburg, 1918–1940." In B. Bozzoli, ed., *Town and Countryside in the Transvaal*. Johannesburg, Ravan Press, 1983, 151–175.

Kuhn, T. *The Structure of Scientific Revolutions*. Chicago: University of Chicago Press, 1970.

Kuper, H. *Uniform of Colour*. Johannesburg: University of Witwatersrand Press, 1947.

Laidler, P. W., and Gelfand, M. *South Africa: Its Medical History, 1652–1898*. Cape Town: C. Struik, 1971.

Marks, S., and Andersson, N. "The State, Class and the Allocation of Health Resources." *Social Science and Medicine*, Special Issue on the Political Economy of Health in Africa and Latin America (1988), 28 (1989): 515–530.

———. "Industrialization, Rural Health and the 1944 Health Services Commission in South Africa." In S. Feierman and J. Janzen, *The Social Basis of Health and Healing in Africa*. Berkeley, Los Angeles, London: University of California Press, forthcoming.

———. "Epidemics and Social Control in Twentieth Century South Africa." *Bulletin of the Society of the Social History of Medicine* 34 (1984).

Marks, S., and Trapido, S. "Lord Milner and the South African State." *History Workshop* 8 (1979): 50–80.

Martiny, O. "Attitudes to TB in the Mining Industry." In University of Cape Town, Medical Students Council, *Consumption in the Land of Plenty—TB in South Africa*. Conference Papers. Cape Town, 1982, 94–95.

McKeown, T. *The Modern Rise of Population*. London: Edward Arnold, 1976.

———, and Lowe, C. R. *An Introduction to Social Medicine*. Oxford: Blackwell, 1974.

McNeill, W. H. *Plagues and Peoples*. New York: Doubleday, 1976.

Mayer, P., and Mayer, I. *Townsmen or Tribemen*. Cape Town: Oxford University Press, 1974.

Murray, C. *Families Divided*. Cambridge: Cambridge University Press, 1981.

Navarro, V. *Medicine Under Capitalism*. New York: Prodist, 1976.

O'Meara, D. *Volkskapitalisme*. Johannesburg: Ravan Press, 1983.

Packard, R. M. "Industrial Production, Health and Disease in Sub-Saharan Africa." *Social Science and Medicine*. Special Issue on the Political Economy of Health in Africa and Latin America (1988), 28 (1989): 475–496.

———. "Tuberculosis and the Development of Industrial Health Policy on the Witwatersrand, 1902–1932." *JSAS* 13, 2 (1987): 187–209.

———. "Agricultural Development, Migrant Labor and the Resurgence of Malaria in Swaziland." *Social Science and Medicine* 22, 8 (1986): 861–867.

———. "Maize, Cattle, and Mosquitoes: The Political Economy of Malaria Epidemics in Colonial Swaziland." *Journal of African History* 25 (1984): 189–212.

Phimister, I. R. "African Labour Conditions and Health in the Southern Rhodesian Mining Industry, 1898–1953." *Central African Medical Journal* 21, 10 (1975): 214–219; 22, 4 (1976): 63–67; 22, 9 (1976): 173–181; 22, 12 (1976): 244–249.

Platzky, L., and Walker, C. *The Surplus People: Forced Removals in South Africa*. Johannesburg: Ravan Press, 1985.

Proctor, A. "Class Struggle, Segregation and the City: A History of Sophiatown, 1905–1940." In B. Bozzoli, ed., *Labour, Townships and Protest*. Johannesburg: Ravan Press, 1979, 49–89.

Richardson, P., and Van-Helten, J. J. "Labour in the South African Gold Mining Industry." In S. Marks and R. Rathbone, eds., *Industrialization and Social Change in South Africa*. London: Longmans, 1982, 77–98.

Rosenberg, C. *The Cholera Years*. Chicago: University of Chicago Press, 1962.
———. "The Bitter Fruit: Heredity, Disease, and Social Thought in Nineteenth Century America." *Perspective in American History* 8 (1974): 189–235.
Sanders, D. *The Struggle for Health*. London: Macmillan, 1985.
Saul, J., and Gelb, S. *The Crisis in South Africa*. New York: The Monthly Review Press, 1981.
Schapera, I. *Migrant Labour and Tribal Life*. New York: Oxford University Press, 1947.
Segall, M. "The Politics of Primary Health Care." *IDS Bulletin* 14 (1983): 27–37.
Simkins, C. "Agricultural Production in the African Reserves." *JSAS* 7 (1981): 256–283.
———. *The Demographic Demand for Labour and Institutional Context of African Unemployment in South Africa, 1960–1980*. Cape Town: SALDRU, 1981.
Slater, H. "The Changing Pattern of Economic Relationships in Rural Natal, 1838–1914." In S. Marks and A. Atmore, eds., *Economy and Society in Industrial South Africa*. London: Longmans, 1980, 148–170.
Southall, R. J. *South Africa's Transkei*. New York: Monthly Review Press, 1983.
Stadler, A. W. "Birds in the Cornfields: Squatters Movements in Johannesburg, 1944–1947." In B. Bozzoli, ed., *Labour, Townships and Protest*. Johannesburg: Ravan Press, 1979, 19–48.
Steadman Jones, G. *Languages of Class*. Cambridge: Cambridge University Press, 1983.
Swanson, M. " 'The Sanitation Syndrome': Bubonic Plague and Urban Native Policy in the Cape Colony, 1900–1909." *JAH* 18 (1977): 387–410.
Torchia, M. "Tuberculosis among American Negroes: Medical Research on a Racial Disease, 1830–1950." *Journal of the History of Medicine and Allied Sciences* 32 (1977): 261–262.
Turrell, R. "Kimberley Model Compounds." *JAH* 25, 1 (1984): 59–76.
———. "Kimberly, Labour and Compounds, 1877–1888." In S. Marks and R. Rathbone, eds., *Industrialization and Social Change in South Africa*. London: Longmans, 1982, 45–76.
Turshen, M. *The Political Ecology of Disease in Tanzania*. New Brunswick: Rutgers University Press, 1984.
University of Cape Town, Medical School. *Consumption in the Land of Plenty—TB in South Africa*. Conference Papers, Cape Town, 1982.
Unterhalter, B. "Inequalities in Health and Disease: The Case of Mortality Rates for the City of Johannesburg, South Africa, 1910–1979." *International Journal of Health Services* 12, 4 (1982): 617–636.
Vail, L. "Ecology and History: The Example of Eastern Zambia." *JSAS* 3, 2 (1977): 129–155.
Van Onselen, C. *Studies in the Social and Economic History of the Witwatersrand, 1886–1914*, vol. 1, *New Babylon*. London: Longmans, 1982.
———. *Chibaro: African Mine Labour in Southern Rhodesia*. Johannesburg, Ravan Press, 1980.

Webster, D. "Capital, Class and Consumption: A Social History of Tuberculo-
    sis in South Africa." In University of Cape Town, Medical Students Council,
    Consumption in the Land of Plenty—TB in South Africa. Cape Town, 1982.
———. "The Political Economy of Food Production and Nutrition in Southern
    Africa in Historical Perspective." *Critical Health* (Nov. 1981): 8–11.
Western, J. *Outcast Cape Town.* Minneapolis: University of Minnesota Press,
    1981.
Wilcocks, C. *Aspects of Medical Investigation in Africa.* London: Oxford Uni-
    versity Press, 1962.
Wilkinson, P. "Providing 'Adequate Shelter': The South African State and the
    Resolution of the African Urban Crisis, 1948–1954." In D. C. Hindson, ed.,
    Working Papers in Southern African Studies. Vol. 3. Johannesburg: Ravan
    Press, 1983, 65–90.
Wilson, F. *Labour in the South African Gold Mines.* Cambridge: Cambridge
    University Press, 1972.
———, and Perrot, D., eds. *Outlook on a Century: South Africa 1870–1970.*
    Lovedale, S.A.: Lovedale Press, 1973.
Wohl, A. *Endangered Lives.* London: Methuen, 1983.
World Health Organization. *Apartheid and Health.* Geneva, WHO, 1982.
Yach, D. "Tuberculosis Deaths in South Africa, 1980." *SAMJ,* in press.
———. "Tuberculosis in the Western Cape Health Region of South Africa."
    Social Science and Medicine, in press.
Yudelman, D., and Jeeves, A. "New Labour Frontiers for Old: Black Mi-
    grants to the South African Gold Mines, 1920–1985." *JSAS* 13, 1 (1986):
    107–124.

UNPUBLISHED PAPERS

Buch, E., et al., "Can Good Tuberculosis Care Be Provided in the Face of Pov-
    erty?" Carnegie Conference Paper No. 198, University of Cape Town, 1984.
Denny, J. "Epidemiology of Tuberculous Meningitis in the Western Cape,
    1979–1981." Carnegie Conference Paper No. 175, Cape Town, 1984.
Elias, C. "A Housing Study: Legislation and the Control of Urban African
    Accommodation." Carnegie Conference Paper No. 157, Cape Town, 1984.
Fisher, S. "Measles and Poverty in Port Elizabeth." Carnegie Conference Paper
    No. 172, Cape Town, 1984.
McCord, C. "Persistent and Increasing High Risk of Tuberculosis after Work in
    the South African Gold Mines." Unpublished paper, 1988.
Morris, M., and Padayachee, V. "State Reform Policy in South Africa." Paper
    presented for the Canadian Studies Association Meeting, Kingston, Ontario,
    May 11–14, 1988.
Olver, C. "Poverty, Health and Health Care in South Africa." Carnegie Confer-
    ence Paper No. 166, Cape Town, 1984.
Saunders, L. D., et al. "An Evaluation of the Management of TB patients in
    Soweto." Paper presented to Conference on Tuberculosis in the 1980s, Preto-
    ria, 1982.
Savage, M. "Pass Laws and the Disorganization and Reorganization of the

African Population in South Africa." Carnegie Conference Paper No. 281, Cape Town, 1984.

Shennan, D. H. "Changes in Problems of Tuberculosis Control in Africa Between the Sixties and Eighties." Paper presented to Conference on Tuberculosis in the 1980s, Pretoria, 1982.

Simkins, C. "Household Structure and Poverty among Black People." Carnegie Conference Paper No. 7, Cape Town, 1984.

Webster, D. "The Reproduction of Labor Power and the Struggle for Survival in Soweto." Carnegie Conference Paper No. 20, Cape Town, 1984.

White, C. "Poverty in Port Elizabeth." Carnegie Conference Paper No. 21, Cape Town, 1984.

Wilkinson, P. "The Sale of the Century: A Critical Review of Recent Developments in African Housing Policy in South Africa." Carnegie Conference Paper No. 160, Cape Town, 1984.

COMPARATIVE STUDIES OF HEALTH SYSTEMS AND MEDICAL CARE

Index

Designer:	U.C. Press Staff
Compositor:	Huron Valley Graphics
Text:	10/13 Sabon
Display:	Sabon
Printer:	Maple-Vail
Binder:	Maple-Vail